In general terms, one way of describing the world we live in is to say that it is made up of nature and society, and that human beings belong to both.

A distinguished international team aims to contribute – through selective, interdisciplinary studies – to a much-needed but currently scant debate over the reciprocal links between perceptions of nature and perceptions of society from the ancient Greek *kosmos* to late twentieth-century 'ecology'. Individual essays and the general conclusions of the volume are important not only for our understanding of the evolution of knowledge of nature and of society but also for an awareness of the types of truth and perception produced in the process.

NATURE AND SOCIETY IN HISTORICAL CONTEXT

Volumes edited by Roy Porter and Mikuláš Teich

The Enlightenment in national context
Revolution in history
Romanticism in national context
Fin de siècle and its legacy
The Renaissance in national context
The Scientific Revolution in national context
The national question in Europe in historical context
The Reformation in national context (with R. W. Scribner)
Sexual knowledge, sexual science: the history of attitudes to sexuality
Drugs and narcotics in history
The Industrial Revolution in national context: Europe and the USA
Nature and society in historical context (with Bo Gustafsson)

NATURE AND SOCIETY IN HISTORICAL CONTEXT

EDITED BY

MIKULÁŠ TEICH

Robinson College, Cambridge

ROY PORTER

The Wellcome Institute for the History of Medicine, London

AND

BO GUSTAFSSON

The Swedish Collegium for Advanced Study in the Social Sciences (SCASSS), Uppsala

Published by the Press Syndicate of the University of Cambridge
The Pitt Building, Trumpington Street, Cambridge CB2 1RP
40 West 20th Street, New York, NY 10011-4211, USA
10 Stamford Road, Oakleigh, Melbourne 3166, Australia

First published 1997

Printed in Great Britain at the University Press, Cambridge

A catalogue record for this book is available from the British Library

Library of Congress cataloguing in publication data

Nature and society in historical context / edited by Mikuláš Teich,
Roy Porter, and Bo Gustafsson.
p. cm.
Outgrowth of a round-table discussion held Mar. 1, 1991, at Robinson College and a symposium held Sept. 8–11, 1993 at Friiberghs Herrgärd near Uppsala, Sweden.
Includes index.
ISBN 0 521 49530 X (hbk.) – ISBN 0 521 49881 3 (pbk)
1. Human ecology – History – Congresses.
2. Human ecology – Philosophy – Congresses.
I. Teich, Mikuláš. II. Porter, Roy, 1946– . III. Gustafsson, Bo, 1931– .
GF13.N37 1997 96–14063 CIP

ISBN 0 521 49530 X hardback
ISBN 0 521 49881 3 paperback

CE

CONTENTS

FIGURES

NOTES ON CONTRIBUTORS

KURT BAYERTZ is Professor of Philosophy at the University of Münster. His main interests lie in ethics, political philosophy and philosophy of science. Recent publications include articles on evolutionary ethics, on the concept of responsibility, and his book *GenEthics. Technological Intervention in Human Reproduction as a Philosophical Problem* (Cambridge, 1994).

BENGT-ERIK BORGSTRÖM is Lecturer in the Department of Social Anthropology, Stockholm University. He has done fieldwork in Nepal and Northern Sweden. His publications include books and articles on Nepalese development ideology, the relationship between culture and technology in Nepal and Northern Sweden as well as studies of local perceptions of the past in a parish in Northern Sweden.

PETER BURKE studied at Oxford and taught in the School of European Studies, University of Sussex before coming to Cambridge, where he is currently Reader in Cultural History and Fellow of Emmanuel College. His books include *Popular Culture in Early Modern Europe* (2nd edn, 1994), *The Italian Renaissance* (3rd edn, 1987) and *History and Social Theory* (1992).

DIETRICH VON ENGELHARDT studied philosophy, history, and Slavic languages in Tübingen, Munich, and Heidelberg. He was Assistant in the Institute for the History of Medicine (Heidelberg) from 1971 to 1976; Professor for History of Medicine and Natural Sciences from 1976 (Heidelberg); Director of the Institute for History of Medicine and Natural Sciences at the Medical University of Lübeck from 1983. Among his numerous publications are *Hegel und die Chemie* (Wiesbaden, 1976); *Historisches Bewusstsein in der Naturwissenschaft von der Aufklärung bis zum Positivismus* (Freiburg and Munich, 1979); *Mit der Krankheit leben* (Heidelberg, 1986); *Wissenschaftsgeschichte auf den Versammlungen der GDNÄ 1822–1972* (Stuttgart,

1987); and (edited with F. Hartmann) *Klassiker der Medizin*, 2 vols. (Munich, 1991).

PAUL LAWRENCE FARBER is OSU Distinguished Professor of the History of Science at Oregon State University, Corvallis, Oregon. He has recently published *The Temptations of Evolutionary Ethics* and is currently working on a history of natural history.

*ERNEST GELLNER was educated in Prague and England. He received a PhD in Social Anthropology from the London School of Economics where he taught from 1949 to 1984. He was William Wyse Professor of Anthropology, Cambridge University, and Professorial Fellow of King's College 1984–1993. From 1993 he held the post of Director for the Centre for the Study of Nationalism at the Central European University, Prague. His numerous published works have addressed: Western philosophy, Soviet ideology, Muslim tribal structure, general social theory, and nationalism. He was also a Fellow of the British Academy, and a Member of both Academiea Europaea, and the American Academy of Arts and Sciences.

RICHARD GROVE is a Senior Fellow of the Institute of Advanced Studies at the Australian National University. He is also a Senior Research Associate of the History of Science Department at the University of Cambridge and Founder-Editor of the Journal *Environment and History*. His books include *The Cambridgeshire Coprolite Mining Rush* (1976), *The Future for Forestry* (1983), *The SSSI Handbook* (1985), *Conservation in Africa: People, Policies and Practice* (1987) and *Green Imperialism* (1995). He has published articles in *Nature*, *Scientific American* and many other journals.

BO GUSTAFSSON is Professor of Economic History at Uppsala University and a Director of the Swedish Collegium for Advanced Study in Social Sciences (SCASSS), Uppsala. He has published monographs and papers on the industrial revolution, public sector growth, the history of economic theories and historical modes of production. His publications include: *The Saw-Mill Workers of Northern Sweden 1890–1913* (Uppsala 1965, in Swedish); *Marxismus und Revisionismus* (Frankfurt-on-Main, 1972); *The Silent Revolution. The Rise and Growth of a Local Welfare Community* (Stockholm 1988, in Swedish); *Power and Economic Institutions. Reinterpretations in Economic History* (Aldershot, 1991).

* As this volume went to press, we were deeply saddened by the sudden death (5 November 1995) of Ernest Gellner at the age of 69. He will be greatly missed. [Eds.]

LARS HERLITZ is Emeritus Professor in Economic History, University of Göteborg. He has written about agrarian development in eighteenth-century Sweden and the history of economic ideas, mainly mercantilism and physiocracy. Among his works are *Ideas of Capital and Development in Pre-classical Economic Thought* (1989) and a paper on the *Tableau économique* in *The European Journal of the History of Economic Thought* (1995).

JAN JANKO studied biology at Charles University in Prague where he graduated in 1965. He has specialized in the history of science and is author of several books and numerous articles, mainly on topics in the history of biology. From 1988 to 1993 he headed the Department of the History of Science and Technology within the framework of the Czechoslovak (later Czech) Academy and Sciences. He lectures currently at Charles University's Institute of the Foundations of Education.

ADAM KUPER is a social anthropologist, author of a number of books on African ethnography and on the history of anthropological theory. Among his recent books are: *The Invention of Primitive Society* (1988) and *The Chosen Primate: Human Nature and Cultural Diversity* (1994). He teaches at Brunel University.

GERHARD JARITZ works at the Institute for Research into Daily Life of the Middle Ages, Krems, Austria. He is Professor of Medieval Studies at the Central European University Budapest (Hungary) and Lecturer at the Universities of Vienna and Graz (Austria). His main research interest is the history of everyday life and material culture of the Middle Ages. He is the author of numerous publications.

LENOS MAVROMMATIS read history at the Athens National University (Department of History and Archaeology), and holds a doctorate from the Université de Paris I (Sorbonne-Panthéon) in History (Medieval History). He worked as a researcher at the Centre National de la Recherche Scientifique (CNRS) in Paris and taught at the École des Hautes Études en Sciences Sociales in Paris and other European Universities. Since 1985 he has worked at the Institute of Byzantine Studies of the National (Hellenic) Research Foundation in Athens where he is Research Professor. He is currently directing a research team and programme on 'Byzantium and the Slav World'. He is the author of two monographs and a number of articles on the Byzantine and Balkan society, polity and economy.

CHRIS PHILO is Professor in the Department of Geography, University of Glasgow. He is the co-author of *Approaching Human Geography* (1991) and the co-editor of *Selling Places* (1993). His primary research interest is the changing geography of 'madness' in England and Wales, exploring aspects of the spatial distributions exhibited by madhouses, lunatic asylums and other mental health facilities.

ROY PORTER is Professor in the Social History of Medicine at the Wellcome Institute for the History of Medicine. He is currently working on the history of hysteria. Recent books include *Mind Forg'd Manacles. Madness in England from the Restoration to the Regency* (London, 1987); *A Social History of Madness* (London, 1987); *In Sickness and in Health. The British Experience, 1650–1850* (London, 1988); *Patient's Progress* (Oxford, 1989) – these last two co-authored with Dorothy Porter; *Health for Sale. Quackery in England 1660–1850* (Manchester, 1989); *Doctor of Society: Thomas Beddoes and the Sick Trade in Late Enlightenment England* (London, 1991) and *London: A Social History* (London, 1994).

JOACHIM RADKAU studied at the Universities of Münster, Hamburg and Berlin (Free University). Since 1980 he has been Professor of Modern History at the University of Bielefeld. His main works include *Die deutsche Emigration in den USA* (1971), *Aufstieg und Krise der deutschen Atomwirtschaft* (1983), *Technik in Deutschland* (1989).

SIMON SCHAFFER is Reader in History and Philosophy of Science in the University of Cambridge. His recent publications on eighteenth-century natural philosophy include papers on demonstration devices in mechanics in (in *Osiris*), on perpetual motion machines in court society (in *British Journal for the History of Science*) and on the *Florilegium* of Joseph Banks (in *Visions of Empire*, ed. Peter Reill and David Philip Miller).

MART A. STEWART is an Associate Professor at Western Washington University in Bellingham, Washington and the author of *'What Nature Suffers to Groe'; Life, Labor, and Landscape on the Georgia Coast, 1680–1910*, to be published by the University of Georgia Press in 1996.

GERHARD STROHMEIER is a sociologist who graduated at the University of Vienna with a PhD. His research is in urban sociology, public administration, work organization, regional development. He is Director of the Department 'Space and Economy' of the Institute for Interdisciplinary Research and Continuing Education at the Universities of Vienna, Klagenfurt and Innsbruck.

MIKULÁŠ TEICH is Emeritus Fellow of Robinson College, Cambridge, and Honorary Professor of the Technical University, Vienna. His publications cover topics in the history of chemistry and biomedical sciences, social and philosophical aspects of the development of science, technology and the economy, and in the history of scientific organizations, and include *A Documentary History of Biochemistry, 1770–1940* (with the late Dorothy Needham), published in 1992.

VERENA WINIWARTER studied history and communication sciences in Vienna and has a background in technical chemistry. She is working in the field of environmental history of the Middle Ages and Early Modern times. Currently with Gerhard Jaritz, she is engaged in setting up an 'Environmental History Database – Austria'.

NINA WITOSZEK is a research fellow at the Centre for Development and the Environment at Oslo University and a lecturer in the semiotics of culture at University College Galway, Ireland. Her studies include *The Theatre of Recollection* (Stockholm, 1988) and *Talking to the Dead* (Oxford, 1995). She also writes fiction under the pen-name Nina FitzPatrick.

ACKNOWLEDGEMENTS

THIS volume grew out of two gatherings: an informal, small-scale, round-table discussion held at Robinson College (1 March 1991) and a large-scale symposium under the auspices of SCASSS (The Swedish Collegium for Advanced Study in the Social Sciences) held at Friiberghs Herrgård near Uppsala (8–11 September 1993).

We have incurred various debts to these institutions, to the Academic Unit of the Wellcome Institute for the History of Medicine, and particularly to the staff of SCASSS, for which we record our grateful thanks. Here we wish to pay tribute to the memory of Dr Getacho Woldemeskel, who bore the brunt of organizing the symposium, and whose unexpected death shocked us deeply.

We owe a debt of gratitude to the Swedish Council of Planning and Coordinating of Research, the Swedish Council for Research in the Humanities and Social Sciences, and the Bank of Sweden Tercentary Foundation, which made the holding of the symposium possible. Nor can we omit thanks to William Davies of Cambridge University Press for his constant interest in the completion of the volume.

INTRODUCTION

IN general terms, one way of encompassing the world we live in is to say that it is made up of society and nature with human beings belonging to both. This collection of essays attempts to contribute through selective, interdisciplinary studies to a much needed but scant debate over reciprocal links between perceptions of nature and perceptions of society from Antiquity to the present.[1] This is most important not only for the understanding of evolution of knowledge of nature as well as knowledge of society but also of type of truth produced in the process. This takes us to the heart of the issue provocatively highlighted by Ernest Gellner when he begins his introductory essay as follows: 'The basic characteristics of our age can be defined simply: effective knowledge of nature does exist, but there is *no* effective knowledge of man and society.'

It is reasonable to connect the beginnings of human cognition of inanimate and animate nature (stones, animals, plants) with the ability of systematic making of tools/arms within a framework of a hunting-and-gathering way of life, presently traceable to about $2\frac{1}{2}$–2 million years ago. It is also reasonable to perceive in the intentional Neanderthal burial, about 100,000 years ago, the earliest known expression of overlapping social and individual awareness of a natural phenomenon: death.[2]

Indeed, the theme of interpenetration of the social, human and natural has a long history. It makes itself felt, as Jan Janko argues, in cosmogonical texts of Greek and Roman authors, exercised by opposing linear and circular visions of the development of the universe. In the case of the former, deterioration and in the case of the latter, stability were the resulting conditions of the world.

Moving on to the Middle Ages, the theme of the volume is explored valuably in two approaches to madness from the social perspective, in the Byzantine and English–Welsh contexts respectively, which inevitably invite comparison. At the heart of Lenos Mavrommatis' approach lies the contention that in Byzantine society madness was associated not so much with illness (impairment of natural physiological processes) as with the devil's perversive activities. Persons thought to be mentally deranged were not excluded but incorporated into Byzantine society and could be instrumentalized purposefully as channels of communication by authorities in the political and religious spheres. Mavrommatis' claim that, in contrast to Byzantine practice, Western Christendom pursued policies of rejecting mad people as social outcasts, is relativized by Chris Philo who finds the involvement of 'thoroughly *intermingled* exclusionary and inclusionary elements'.

What emerges from the inquiry into perceptions of nature during the Renaissance by Gerhard Jaritz and Verena Winiwarter is how much their variability was entangled with social relationships and economic interests, including spatial and temporal circumstances, religious faiths, supranatural beliefs. By consulting Lower Austrian village laws as well as pictorial representations, they point out that the different social groups perceived and sought to utilize for their own ends such economically highly valued constituents of nature as fish and woods: 'The landlord's nature is another nature from the peasant community's nature.'

The next five essays deal, largely in the British and French contexts, with developments more or less between the Renaissance and the Enlightenment, and a few general points may be made.

For Peter Burke, before the Scientific Revolution there is no sharp boundary between populating society with notions of natural order and populating nature with notions of social order. To view the king as the sun of the social world was as current as it was to think of the lion as the king of the beasts. In fact, interpenetrating images of nature and society embodied in terms, such as the mineral kingdom, vegetable kingdom and animal kingdom, persisted long into the nineteenth century.

Simon Schaffer documents the interaction between the natural and social in his discussion of the early modern debate on the earth's fertility in Britain. He holds that different approaches to it, including agricultural theorizing, depended on different models of society, and notes:

> As nature's capacities were transmuted into market values, so the laws of political economy were naturalised ... Both nature and society were redefined and remoralised. In the agricultural crises of the period after 1815, natural laws of supply and demand were ingeniously combined with moral principles of the fallen nature of humanity. The implications were global. British landlords and agrarian scientists applied their doctrines to colonial land management and in contests with indigenous social ecologies.

The latter topic is specifically treated by Richard Grove in his review of the origins of what he calls 'from hindsight' British colonial environmentalism. It concerns the Kings Hill Forest Act passed on St Vincent in 1791 which, reflecting as it did 'a novel climatic theory, that deforestation might cause rainfall decline', Grove links to French conservationism indebted to physiocratic thinking as practised on Mauritius.

A more extended discussion of physiocracy and its place in the history of economic thought, from about 1620 to 1770, is to be found in the contribution by Lars Herlitz who suggests that 'the economics of this time were explicitly ideas about society and nature'. This leads him, among others, to ponder on works/issues also considered by Burke (Mandeville's *The Fable of the Bees*) and Schaffer (morality and agriculture). Neatly pointing out that 'physiocracy means literally rule of nature', one of Herlitz's main concerns is to explain the physiocratic notion of nature, identified with the land, as an order governed by laws 'which were physical and moral, the physical laws regulating the course of physical events, and the moral laws guiding human actions in conformity with the physical order'.

One way of looking at physiocracy and its place in the history of economic and social thought is to see it as concerned with the role of landed property in the development of agrarian capitalism within French feudal society before the revolutionary events of 1789. By then, in England, capitalism was well entrenched not only in commerce but also in the agricultural sector – hence the virtual disinterest of the aristocratic owners of landed property in the ideas of the physiocrats. Instead, they developed effectively a feudal rural perspective on the quality of urban life – *rus in urbe* – which Roy Porter exposes as an artifice:

> It is easy to say why the great aristocratic developers of the Georgian age basked in the ideology of *rus in urbe*, for it reinforced *domini in urbe* or *equites in urbe*: in a nation where dominion was rooted in the shires, and the country house was still the power house, bringing the country into the city meant imposing upon the townscape the stamp of grandee glamour and authority – no difficult task, since the peerage owned the freeholds to the great estates around the old Cities of London and Westminster. Indeed, many forces in the Georgian age were drawing the leaders of the landowning nation to town as never before: Parliament and politics, shops and entertainments, the marriage market, money and mortgages, the pleasures of fashionable society and the Season. The metropolis was the site for the parade of superiority and the elegant expense of time and money.

This volume, in contrast to some in the sequence of collections of which it is a part, is not explicitly concerned with distinct national aspects. Nevertheless, as we have seen and shall see, such aspects make themselves felt. The next three essays discuss attitudes to and meanings of nature in the nineteenth and twentieth centuries in German and Scandinavian contexts.

German *Naturphilosophie* (nature philosophy) and Romantic *Naturforschung* (nature study), which flourished at the turn of the eighteenth and nineteenth centuries, continue to be controversial subjects in the history of science and philosophy. This is not surprising, given the boldly speculative claims their protagonists made about principles governing reality, such as unity and polarity in nature, society and history. Romantic *Naturforschung* receives in this volume an understanding, albeit not uncritical, treatment by Dietrich von Engelhardt who has long urged the need to gain a broader perspective on it. He attributes the fateful divorce between natural and human sciences to the victory of positivistically minded natural sciences over Romantic *Naturforschung* in the nineteenth century.

A significant feature of German Romanticism was its celebration of imagined Norwegian/Nordic attitudes to nature and society. Pristine, Norway, writes Nina Witoszek, was 'an epitome over land where "nature man" lived for centuries in a "natural state"'. Witoszek also makes it abundantly clear that such a romantic reading of the North was seriously flawed. It failed to take on board a major strand in Norwegian social thought cross-bred, as it were, from a union of naturalism and humanism, which she labels provisionally 'ecohumanism'. Witoszek's concern

> is not merely to de-romanticise a tradition which still employs Nature as an emblem of identity; it is to suggest that the dominant system of values which in the last 200 years empowered social change in Norway has been based on a pragmatic, ecohumanist code of action. Although there is no doubt that this code was not shared equally by all classes, it has nevertheless constituted a crucial axiological reference system. Nobody who has aspired to political or cultural leadership could afford to ignore it in the past century.

Joachim Radkau writing as an environmental historian approaches nature through the 'forest' and demands a more rigorous treatment of the history of German forestry which 'has too often been written as a mere history of the forest regulations'. Radkau argues that the historian should also allow for the ecologically notable influence of their being disregarded. Radkau raises altogether a variety of topics which the history of German forestry should address. Among others, he points to the tradition persisting from the Romantics through the Nazi period up to the present time, which extols the forest as the embodiment of unspoilt nature. This position collides with the economic attitude toward the forest as an exploitable and manageable resource.

Relationships between perceptions of the natural and social, within the framework of nineteenth-century North American history, are considered by Mart Stewart and Gerhard Strohmeier respectively. Stewart's contribution centres on climate which, since the Enlightenment, was thought to determine racial differences. Indeed, Stewart emphasizes, that the climate–race nexus constituted the 'objective' core of the argument put forward in support of slavery before the Civil War. Strohmeier is interested in nature represented by images of the West American landscape, recorded in literary sources and paintings. He finds that they can largely be understood as metaphors for visions of religious mission as well as political and economic expansion, which were pushing the American trek to the West.

In a volume, such as this one, a discussion of historical approaches to the issue of human nature is virtually obligatory. It is variously contained in the contributions by Adam Kuper, Paul Farber and Mikuláš Teich.

Because of Darwin's surpassing influence of buttressing the idea that man is part of nature, his views on the evolution of human nature, including morality, are of more than passing interest. Kuper, whose essay is focused on this matter, points out that here Darwin was affected by contributions from socially oriented British anthropology, which was in the process of becoming a scholarly discipline during the last three decades of the nineteenth century. Kuper argues that, in this area in the end, Darwin owed more to the social anthropologists than they to him:

> Most strikingly, he was prepared to compromise his materialism, shifting the emphasis from the growth of the brain (which was, he came to believe, the most significant single factor in the emergence of the human species) to the development of the forms of knowledge and moral principles (which explained the subsequent progress of humanity); and knowledge and morality, he argued, were learnt rather than inherited.

Charles Darwin heads and Edward O. Wilson concludes the list of Anglo-American scientists and philosophers, referred to in Farber's critical examination of the century-old debate about the theory of evolution providing insight into and, indeed, serving as a foundation for norms of ethical behaviour which he contests unequivocally:

> The history of evolutionary ethics also underscores the danger of accepting facile links between nature and society. Gleaning social lessons

> from nature should make anyone familiar with history uncomfortable. This, of course, does not mean that we can naively separate nature and society. Superficial judgments, however, about what is 'natural', or abstract intellectualizations of the 'natural state' of humans (or forests) for that matter – are not likely to be particularly productive. Such facile links, more likely, will destruct us from exploring potentially fruitful avenues rather than providing keys for answers.

The beginnings of human genetics as a recognized biomedical scientific discipline go back to the turn of the century. Ever since then, its theoreticians and practitioners have been inclined to favour primacy of heredity over environment with respect to human nature/behaviour and this attitude underlies, despite disclaimers, the Human Genome Project's perspective on human nature. This concerns Mikuláš Teich who examines critically historical aspects of the Human Genome Project, which belongs both to nature and society.

We have seen that in several contributions topics emerged which intertwine with the ecological agenda. Ecology is prominently present in the essay by Bengt-Erik Borgström who points to rhetorics used in the approach to underdevelopment and development through notions of nature and society. That is, the underdeveloped South is being equated to nature and the developed North to society. Ecology also enters into Bo Gustafsson's assessment of the circumscribed role of the market mechanism in coping with the nature–economy interconnection in general, and the environmental management in particular.

Is there a philosophical dimension to ecology? This is the problem addressed in the last essay by Kurt Bayertz, who draws attention to the dilemma of seeking to link philosophy and ecology through the category of rationality believed 'to be capable of nothing and everything at the same time'. That is, while rationality does not guide rapacious mankind for whom nature is merely a matter for exploitation, it underlies calls for establishing ecological norms to protect it as an inherently valuable entity.

Nature is infinitely faceted; in this book it is approached through facets from the ancient Greek 'kosmos' to the end-of-twentieth-century 'ecology'. One has not to be Mertonian or, *horribile dictu*, Marxist to profess that there is more to acquiring knowledge of nature and producing ideas on it than 'curiosity'. Not a built-in human disposition, curiosity manifests itself as such only within human society whose various forces it is exposed to and shaped by. It is due to them, as several of the contributors show, 'when, why and for whom [natural] science is done – also in what kind of [natural] science gets done and what is left undone'.[3]

THE

TEMPLE OF NATURE;

OR, THE

ORIGIN OF SOCIETY:

A POEM.

WITH PHILOSOPHICAL NOTES.

BY

ERASMUS DARWIN, M.D. F.R.S.

AUTHOR OF THE BOTANIC GARDEN, OF ZOONOMIA, AND OF PHYTOLOGIA.

Unde hominum peeudumque genus, vitæque volantum,
Et quæ marmoreo fert monstra sub æquore pontus?
Igneus est illis vigor, & cælestis origo. Virg. Æn. VI. 728.

LONDON:

PRINTED FOR J. JOHNSON, ST. PAUL'S CHURCHYARD,

BY T. BENSLEY, BOLT COURT, FLEET STREET.

1803.

Figure 1 Title page of E. Darwin, *Temple of Nature; or, The Origin of Society: A Poem with Philosophical Notes* (1803)

This collection of essays is distinctly exploratory and inevitably there are gaps: for example, the virtual absence of reference regarding historical relations between human law and the laws of nature.[4] Because of and despite it, we believe that a convincing case has been made for the need to investigate the still insufficiently comprehended ways perceptions of nature and society interlink in different historical contexts. The theme inspired the eighteenth-century polymath Erasmus Darwin to compose his last, posthumously, published poetical work *The Temple of Nature; or, The Origin of Society: A Poem with Philosophical Notes*, (1803).[5] May its beginnings serve as the ending of the Introduction:

> By firm immutable immortal laws
> Impress'd on Nature by the GREAT FIRST CAUSE.
> Say, MUSE! how rose from elemental strife
> Organic forms, and kindled into life;
> How Love and Sympathy with potent charm
> Warm the cold heart, the lifted hand disarm;
> Allure with pleasures, and alarm with pains,
> And bind Society in golden chains.

Mikuláš Teich
Roy Porter
Bo Gustafsson

NOTES

1 During the preparation of this book *Natural Images in Economic Thought* appeared (1994) edited by Ph. Mirowski and published by Cambridge University Press. The collection, which investigates 'how images in the history of the natural and physical sciences have been used to shape the history of economic thought' may be viewed as a contribution to the debate.

2 R. L. Leakey summarizes 'the present state of play in the complex field of human evolution' in *The Origin of Humankind* (London, 1994); see also S. J. Gould, 'So near and yet so far', *The New York Review*, 20 October 1994.

3 R. N. Proctor, 'The author responds', *Social Anthropology*, 7 (1993), 322–6 (p. 322).

4 For a stimulating overview, see J. Needham, *Science and Civilization in China* (Cambridge, 1956), II, ch. 18; see also W. Krohn, 'Zur Geschichte des Gesetzesbegriffs in Naturphilosophie und Naturwissenschaft', in M. Hahn and J. Sandkühler (eds.), *Gesellschaftliche Bewegung und Naturprozess* (Cologne, 1981), pp. 61–70.

5 'The poem was published in 1803, a year after his death, at a time when his evolutionary views were unacceptable in either literary or scientific circles. The poem was generally condemned for its irreligious tendencies . . .'. See D. King-Hele, 'Introductory note' to the Scolar Press Facsimile, *The Temple of Nature* (London, 1973).

ONE

KNOWLEDGE OF NATURE AND OF SOCIETY

(†) ERNEST GELLNER

THE basic characteristics of our age can be defined simply: effective knowledge of nature does exist, but there is *no* effective knowledge of man and society. Each of these propositions has profound implications for our general condition. They also have important consequences jointly. Liberal social order is possible largely because *both* are true. If either of them did not hold, or ceased to be valid, free society would become very much more problematic.

Agrarian society, such as prevailed during the period between the Neolithic and the Scientific/Industrial revolutions, is defined by certain general traits. It is based on food production and storage, and on a fairly stable technology and no genuine, accumulative science. The consequence of this technological stability or stagnation is that it is also Malthusian: resources are limited and cannot be expanded indefinitely, so that any population increase is liable eventually to press upon the limits of supplies. Hunger is never too far away: 'give us this day our daily bread' is no trivial request. People starve in accordance with rank: the social hierarchy is a kind of queue to the storehouse. The place in the queue is determined by power, or it *is* power. The place is enforced, but occupancy of a place in time confers power.

The correct strategy for any group or individual is to be concerned with its or his position in the queue, rather than to be concerned with the augmentation of overall output. The latter idea is indeed largely absent, partly because it is unrealistic, partly because its absence in turn creates a situation in which it is *made* unrealistic. If everyone believes that power not work engenders well-being, no one creates institutions which would protect wealth from power. A kind of vicious or self-perpetuating circle operates: the fact that what matters is one's position in the queue rather than the improvement of output, means that the dominant values are those which elevate aggressiveness and strength and domination, and spurn work or innovation. But in a society dominated by such values, those foolish enough to work and innovate will be despoiled by the strong and dominant. This will further reinforce the values in question, and so undermine any tendency towards concern with economic improvement, and by confirming the system, strengthen the values which perpetuate it.

Both the social *and* the conceptual organization of such an order militate against economic growth and against the cognitive penetration of nature. The preoccupation with status, aggressiveness and honour does not encourage efforts at productive innovation, which are not rewarded (power holders take all), or actually punished, in as far as novelty of technique is liable to violate the rules which are made rigid as part of the sacralization of status. To do something new is to go against custom, which is to undermine the hierarchy. Something similar operates in the sphere of ideas. Inquiry requires doubt: status and faith exclude it. Descartes commended the solecism of doubt in the hope of finding a firmer base for conviction, but in fact opened an age of Perpetual Doubt. There does of course even in such a society have to be some reference to external, natural fact: it is no use sowing and hoping to reap, unless the natural conditions of the growth of plants are respected. But the ideas-markers guiding the ploughman to respect the natural conditions are overlaid by a much heavier set of markers impelling him to maintain the social order. The maintenance of the social order is even more important for the perpetuation of an agrarian society than the production of sustenance: or rather, the latter cannot be achieved without the former.

In these circumstances, there is no serious knowledge of either nature or society. There is of course a certain sensitivity to some natural facts: the farmer cannot produce, nor the craftsman turn materials into tools, unless the realities of the relevant aspects of the environment are respected. But these sensitivities to bits of the environment are not connected to each other to form general theories of nature; they are disconnected from each other by being embedded in the socially local idiom of individual specialized craft guilds. Knowledge, such as it is, is tied to the social order and dominated by it: there is little if any trans-social knowledge. Some aspects of the life of agrarian society encouraged the notion of trans-social truth: the discovery of *proof*, which is independent of status; the use of *writing*, which liberates assertions from the status of the speaker; and the conspicuously ordered behaviour of some parts of nature (astronomy).

How did mankind escape from this condition of socially inhibited production of cognition?

Two independent but inter-acting processes were involved.

From time to time, there occurs a transition from coercive to productive values, from honour to interest. In Marxist terms, this appears as a transition from a feudal to a bourgeois order. This transition occurred more than once: trading cities acquire not merely wealth but also power, and learn how to use their wealth to protect themselves from those who would despoil them. Generally speaking, however, the condition which results from this process is very unstable. The Marxist thesis that class conflict is a universal feature of human societies (except perhaps for the first and the last of them), and is never far from the surface, is probably inspired to a large extent by societies of this kind. Plato already proposed something of this kind, when, in *The Republic*, he attributed instability to the coming of men of honour and of wealth, replacing the rule of the wise. Anyway: a shift from aggressiveness to productivity, from honour to wealth, does happen under favourable conditions, but it does not seem to last. Inner conflict, and the need for stability, causes societies to revert to the old order. Commercial city states are not unduly long-lived.

But there is one crucial exception. The shift from martial to commercial values in NW Europe in modern times, though it did lead to class conflict and political turbulence, did *not* in the end lead to a reversal and a return to the status quo. On the contrary, it led to permanent and, it would seem, irreversible change in the social order, in the general rules of the human game. Change not stability becomes the norm; perpetual improvement, under the name of Progress, becomes the key notion of a new vision, and the basis of a new morality; and, in the more concrete form of economic growth, it also becomes the principal agent and legitimator of social peace. Riches are worth seeking when they are protected, and constitute the path to power, rather than the other way around.

Why was this particular transformation more fortunate than its predecessors? There are various reasons perhaps, but one crucial and necessary condition was the emergence of science, of effective cognition. The new science did not cause the temporary victory of the commercial/productive spirit over its rival, but it baled out, made it permanently viable, ensured its final victory, by granting it, through the technology which it engendered, the means of bribing itself out of its difficulties and hence permanently – or so it now seems – converting humanity to the new ethos.

The entrepreneurial and the scientific spirit were similar in style and, perhaps, in origin. In each case, there was a marked individualism and atomism. It was necessary to go it alone, to pursue one's own aims in one's own individually chosen way, and in the choice of means, to break up the problem into its constituent parts, without respect for those constraining package-deals known as customs and traditions. Descartes, who codified and preached this style of thought in science, sounds as if he were training entrepreneurs for a free market society: you need only replace the pursuit of truth by the pursuit of wealth, and he might well be addressing a Business School. A plausible but much contested sociological theory also credits the two forms of the new spirit with the same source – Protestantism, or even more specifically, Calvinism. A predestinarian deity persuaded a class of men to become disinterested and orderly in the pursuit of wealth, by denying them the possibility of influencing their salvation through bribing the supernatural, or its representatives on earth, and so deviously including them to try to prove their own salvation to themselves by prospering on earth (fruits of such disinterested acquisitiveness were then ploughed back, not blown on display or salvation). An orderly deity not given to magical displays or privileged disclosure, led investigators to seek Its laws by orderly investigation, unaided by short-cuts.

In the case of production, this spirit notoriously took economic activity out of the rest of social life, 'alienated' it from it, subjecting it exclusively to cost-benefit calculations in terms of single-minded, clearly specified ends. It worked: the economy detached itself from society, and in the end, conquered it. The market is not simply a place where people behave in a certain way, where they trade their products for those of others to their own maximal advantage: what is really important is the negative trait – they do it all in abstraction from, in ignorance of, and indifference to, the rest of their social life. A man selling or buying a share on the Stock Exchange knows nothing of the personal character, marital status, kin links, religious affiliation, political commitments, or aesthetic preferences of his partner in the operation. They are irrelevant. All this was not so under the old dispensation, when these characteristics influenced the commercial operation, if indeed they did not wholly determine its terms. The new spirit worked: it led to great new wealth, great new tensions, and the discontents engendered by the tensions were bought off, or altogether quietened, by the great new resources.

The new spirit also worked within science – though not quite so soon or so quickly. But the technology made possible by the new science came to save the new social order at the very time when many of its commentators were predicting its doom . . .

At this point, it is necessary to relate this overall development to the two main events of our century, 1945 and 1991. The former of these two years witnessed the defeat of a major attempt to re-organize industrial society in terms of the values of agrarian society – aggressiveness, hierarchy, authority, territoriality. This attempt was a curious sequel to the Enlightenment, inverting its values but perpetuating its major premise, the incorporation of man in nature. The Enlightenment affirmed the unity of nature, against religious dualism, but on that basis commended a humanitarian ethic. The new romantic Right preached an ethic of ruthlessness on a naturalistic basis. In effect they said that they could and would run industrial society in terms of *Blut and Boden*, blood and soil. They were defeated by the very criterion they had commended – trial by combat. But ironically, their vision was refuted not so much by the rather close-run war, as by its sequel: they, or rather their successors, found that industrial-commercial activity (contrary to the medieval adage) was a quicker way to wealth and power, and now also more honoured, than warfare. Not *Boden* but growth makes you rich, powerful and respected. The *Bundesbank* may conquer where the *Bundeswehr* would fail. The lesson has since been widely assimilated.

1991 eliminated another rival, the supposition that industrial, growth-oriented society could be run, not so much on the red-military, but the black-clerical values of agrarian society, that it could be the basis, at long last, of the reign of virtue and righteousness on earth. Marxism claimed to possess knowledge of society, continuous with knowledge of nature, and of both kinds – both explanatory and moral-prescriptive. In fact, as in the old religious style, the path to salvation was a corollary of the revelation of the nature of things. Marxism satisfied the craving of Russia's Westernizers for science and that of the Russian populist mystics for righteousness, by promising the latter in terms of, and as fruit of, the former.

The idea that Marxism leads to totalitarianism is by now old and banal, and has been eloquently formulated by Hayek and others. The converse – industrial totalitarianism must be Marxist – is far less obvious or well diffused, but is probably also true. I do not mean, of course, that any totalitarian system in an industrial society must uphold that particular cocktail of ideas which Marx and Engels assembled between the 1840s and the 1890s from current available science, from Hegel to Morgan so to speak: *that* particular amalgam is no doubt an historical accident. What is not accidental but inescapable is that any attempt to impose the Rule of Righteousness on earth, in an industrial setting, must fuse the ideological, political and economic hierarchies in one single homogeneous pyramid with a single dominant apex – this being the main and central feature of 'real Socialism'. In a social system in which the economic activities are and must be carried on separately from others, if they are also given full autonomy, inevitably create a powerful and eventually independent sphere. Either/or: as Lenin would put it, *kto kovo*. The Idea must dominate the economy or the economy will corrode the Idea. You cannot have an ideocracy without a cowed economy. The economy is so powerful in a technological age, that if you give it an inch it will take a yard. This was not so in the past when the economy was feeble. In traditional society, economy is controlled because it is weak, and in industrial society, because it is strong.

For various reasons, the attempt failed. Central direction seems far less efficient than uncoordinated or loosely coordinated individual trial-and-error, and growth based on technology based on science must not throttle science in the name of a Final Creed, even one articulated in the idiom of the science of some particular date. It can only grow by being free. Progress philosophies such as Marxism wanted to have a Faith in Growth, a Faith vindicated *by* Growth. They thought they could have both Growth and Faith, because the law of growth had been revealed unto them; but in the end, the two elements are incompatible. If you really have growth you can have surmises, but not a stable Faith, as a moral and social Foundation.

So a society has emerged – ours – which owes almost everything to a successful knowledge of nature, which by making growth possible, by making production a far-more-than-zero-sum-game, thereby also makes possible the escape from a stagnant, violence-based, dogmatically validated social order. Science did not actually engender the shift to commercialism, but made possible its final triumph. But at the same time, this society is also only possible on the basis of the failure of the attempt to extend really effective cognition to society itself. Had Marxist societies really possessed the secret of man and the social order, they would unquestionably have used it fortifying themselves through effective control, and would not have collapsed in the bizarre and astonishing manner in which in fact they did. Even if the knowledge in question had not sprung from within Marxism, but had somehow been available, they would still have made use of it. But it simply wasn't there to be used.

Why does it not exist? We do not know the answer, at least so far. We know not why there is no symmetry between nature and society, why nature is intelligible and manipulable, and society is not. So far, it is simply a fact. There are of course various well known candidates and explanations. They are plausible, and in part, they overlap with each other. They are: 1) the complexity of the human-social material, 2) the fact that meaning enters into human conduct in the way in which it is absent in nature – what men *do* is defined, partly governed, by their own ideas and interpretations, and 3) the feedback character of social processes, 4) the fact that in culture, unlike nature, acquired characteristics *are* transmitted, and 5) the Joker card of free will and, if it obtains, inherent unpredictability.

We do not know which of these explanations (or which combination) is the correct one: we do not even know that what they purport to explain, will continue to be the case. That which they claim to explain may turn out to be a temporary failure, rather than a permanent datum; or it may be forever valid, or be explained in some other manner.

The pattern of the relationship between common-sense knowledge – socially embedded, unspecialized, unsystematized – and proper, abstract, socially liberated science, can best be characterized by two curves. Ordinary knowledge starts at a certain point and then grows a little, not very much, and not very tidily. Technological advances occur from time to time, are sometimes retained and sometimes lost. But the curve – it is hardly a *curve* in any proper sense – is messy, jerky, like an un-made-up road, and never, never becomes exponential. It does not rise to heaven. The curve of abstract knowledge is quite different. Initially, it actually *dips* far below common-sense, 'practical' knowledge. Schoolmen, scholastics, actually know *less* about nature than practising craftsmen. It is this which enables romantic conservatives to vaunt the unspoken wisdom of a guild or a political class, inherently superior to the mere book learning of the doctors. Once upon a time, this was also true of the knowledge of nature. There was more empirical information about nature in the fingertips of craftsmen than in scholastic compendia. But this did not last forever: the time came when the curve of abstract knowledge took an ever steeper upward turn, overtaking common-sense and in the end dominating it. Those who nowadays seek fundamental innovation in modern technology, turn to professors, not to craftsmen.

So it was with nature. When it comes to social-human knowledge, we are still at the point at which the curve of abstract knowledge is below that of practitioners. Sometimes the abstract theoreticians are also successful practitioners. (Keynes made a fortune on the stock exchange, though he also lost on occasion, as well as temporarily transforming an abstract discipline.) But on the whole this is rare. It certainly is not the case often enough to enable us to say that the curves have as yet crossed.

We simply do not know whether, in the sphere of social knowledge, the same crossing-of-the-curves, which took place in natural science, will or will not also occur. In general it would be absurd to argue that something which happens in one sphere, *must* also happen in another. As against this justified critique of a naive argument from analogy, it could also be said – this is one world, the same principles of intelligibility must apply to all of it, to man as well as non-human nature.

Must they? All we know so far is that there are parts of social science which are rigorous, and others that relate to reality, but in the main, those which are rigorous do not relate to reality, and those which relate to reality are not rigorous. (There are also some which are *neither* rigorous *nor* in any way related to reality, such as the recent vogue for indulgent subjectivism, justified by 'hermeneutics', which says that because we only see things through our ideas, we can or need only look at our own ideas, and that because all men are equal, therefore all ideas must also be equal – otherwise carriers of true ideas would be superior to carriers of false ideas, which is anathema – and therefore everything is allowed, and the denial of all this is Politically Incorrect.) *One* man may perhaps be in error, but *all* men together are a culture, and to credit a culture with error is a form of imperialism. The obscurity which this also sanctions or requires, also enables status-seeking gurus to claim putative depths through real unintelligibility. This is simply the conceptual equivalent of the permissive society, but without the hedonic benefits conferred by permissiveness in conduct.

To return to our main theme: we simply do not know whether the social sciences will have their 17th century, whether the breakthrough and the subsequent fall-out will occur. What we do know is that *if* it did occur, it would, once again, completely change the rules of the game, as radically – perhaps more so – than was the case when technologically based natural science made possible Perpetual Growth and the vision of World-as-Progress.

The Rules under Agrarian Society were: we cannot escape hunger for all of us, but we can mitigate it and improve the chances for some of us by maintaining order and our position. Therefore status and aggression trump production, and we have an Honour ethic, not a Work or Ideas ethic.

Growing Industrial society, our own: growth is possible, and not even all that difficult, and in principle, no one need go short, at any rate if we succeed in beating the population problem. An ethic of work, pluralism, consumerism trumps both a return to Honour and a secular Messianism. Excessive control is counter-productive, especially as we lack the levers for social control. A variant to this ethic may need to be invented when affluence-saturation sets in and a new kind of inducement (other than anticipation of growth) is required for pluralist tolerance – or, if too many of the late but successful entrants into industrialism lack that certain taste for tolerance which the earlier participants, either possessed from the very start, or acquired through the defeat of their alternative in 1945 or 1991.

A society which really possesses both natural and social knowledge would be quite different: control over men and their aims having become possible, policy will face an embarrassingly excessive freedom, rather like that of a deity before an Act of Creation. Being able to choose *anything*, but facing no possible constraints – nothing yet being created – nothing impels it to choose *this* rather than *that*. Nothing yet exists, as everything is a manipulable variable, and so there is nothing to lead us to any preference. We, or rather our successor, can face this problem when it comes, if it comes. The fact that we do not need to face it, however, underscores the absence of real social knowledge. When we have it, we'll have a new problem.

FURTHER READING

E. Gellner, *Plough, Sword and Book: The Structure of Human History* (London, 1988).

E. Gellner, 'Origins of society' in A. C. Fabian (ed.), *Origins. The Darwin College Lectures* (Cambridge, 1988), 128–40.

TWO

TWO CONCEPTS OF THE WORLD IN GREEK AND ROMAN THOUGHT: CYCLICITY AND DEGENERATION

JAN JANKO

INTRODUCTION

CLASSICAL Greek society has attracted and initiated a great many attempts to throw light on the relations between nature and society and on the place of each within philosophical, scientific or religious thought. This endeavour has been greatly helped by the extensiveness and accessibility of diverse sources as well as by the tradition of Western scholarship.

At the same time, though, the very richness of sources and the difficulty in their interpretation present many problems. The history of philosophy, for example, has for a long time had to cope with the possibility of serious distortions arising from the use of doxographical sources. In mythography, on the other hand, records are multi-layered and relatively recent apologetics distort every attempt at interpretation.

This study addresses some problems in the interaction between ideas of society and nature by comparing various notions of time in natural, historical and human contexts which emerged in particular periods of ancient society. These cosmogonical ideas express the degree of optimism or pessimism in the hopes and fears of their creators, thus characterizing the historical situation in which they came into being. They also present in a condensed form important ontological and epistemological foundations of consciousness of ancient society, as well as certain philosophical, religious or especially political 'recipes' for solving contemporary pressing problems.

The focus here is on those passages in Classical texts that anticipate the influence of certain social experiences upon the genesis of natural scientific concepts or alternatively, the influence of already full-fledged scientific (physical, biological) ideas upon concepts of state and society. In a number of cases, however, the origin of these concepts is obscured by residual, indeterminate, mythical elements in which the natural and social are not yet sufficiently differentiated, and express themselves only as two poles or opposing tendencies. Particular attention is paid to an issue Plato raises in the *Statesman* concerning the directional change in the development of the universe. This concept represents an original contribution to the evolution of Western thought, and up to now in philosophy or natural sciences has not received the attention it deserves. By introducing a novel factor, resembling a vector, Plato overcame the hitherto existing problems in natural and historical time which ranged from the belief in cyclicity of cosmic time to time's linearity.

The study is based on the analysis of original sources. Secondary literature is invoked mainly where its findings are utilized or where it is necessary to refer the more detailed questions to standard works. For reasons of space, it has been necessary to omit discussion of interpretations and opinions of other writers. The same reasons limit the number of quotations from sources; Latin sources are given in the original, and Greek in English translation. Important Greek terms are transcribed by capital letters in the Latin alphabet.

COSMIC CYCLE AND LINEAR DEVELOPMENT

According to one common view, ancient thought subscribed to time's cyclicity while Judaeo-Christian thought subscribed to time's linearity. The antagonism between the two concepts is stressed by many Christian thinkers. Thus according to C. Tresmontant the Greek cosmos represents an enclosed constant entity which does not permit any evolution in the linear sense. This is obviously meant to emphasize the uniqueness of historical change which came with the acceptance of the Holy Scripture in Western civilization. Tresmontant himself admits, however, that antiquity's cyclic concept of the cosmic course existed alongside degenerative concepts which emphasized universal deterioration that affected both nature and society.[1] Such concepts can be encapsulated by the traditional term KATAGENESIS.

As we shall see, it is not really possible to exhaust Greek and non-Greek ideas on the course of the universe by one single model. The cyclicity of world processes, both natural and social, was generally accepted not only by early Greek thinkers, but also by thinkers in early China, Mesopotamia, Egypt and so on. The common source of such a concept is the knowledge of the periodicity of the natural phenomena which influence human life: the alternation of the annual seasons, the daily movement of the heavens, the moon cycle, the motions of planets (the heavenly cycles were foregrounded in cases, such as in old Babylonia, where seasonable alternation was not especially striking). By integrating their activities into the agricultural or pastoral cycle, people repeated or imitated, as it were, the cosmic cycle. Mankind created rituals to ensure the return of the individual phases of the cycle – often, as ancient mythologies disclose, through drastic means. In this sense the cosmic event (the cycle of events as well as its origin, mythologically elucidated) represented a model for any human activity.[2]

According to Mircea Eliade, archaic societies such as the Greek society when it was creating its rich mythology, were built on the imitation of mythic archetypes. Such a repetition was supposed, on one side, to prevent the 'spoiling' of human activity and surrounding nature by the invasion of non-anticipated events, or by succumbing to the profane or banal, deprived of all that is sacred, i.e. uplifting and cosmically effective.[3] But mankind condemned itself to being exiled from the 'paradise of archetypes': its own activity brought about events which could not be anticipated on the basis of knowledge of natural cycles and rhythms, nor dealt with by the rituals sanctified by the examples of cosmic deities, gods of vegetation, and heroes. The intrusion of the historical process, connected with a certain state of the old society, was undoubtedly more significant than irregular natural catastrophes. After all, a typical and strikingly specific feature of Greek religion was – in contrast to other religions – its anthropomorphism.[4] It is within the context of this anthropomorphism that we can discover one of the roots of relatively early and highly sophisticated reflections on history by Greek thinkers.

The fact that human acts bring about consequences which defy the original intentions, or that they lead to completely unexpected catastrophes, marked not only mythology (remember the fates of the heroes of Homer's *Iliad*) but also the art of the early Greeks, above all, tragedy. It does not matter if we connect the concept of fate with the ethical order of an archaic society and its practical application in the form of unatonable revenge for breaking it;[5] or with the chaos of unpredictable historical events. It is certain that Greek tragedy reflects not only the old traditional mythology of the first shocks to the 'paradise of archetypes' but also new critical moments in the development of contemporary society. However, the remarkable ability of the old mythologies to absorb new problems and new meanings produces numerous stumbling blocks to reinterpretation. Interestingly, the intermingling of the old and new layers of mythologies in tragedy occurs at around the time of the opposite process of differentiation and of 'clearing up' of Greek thought in another area which leads to the differentiation between LOGOS and MYTHOS, NOMOS and PHYSIS; hence to the birth of philosophy and rationalization of the world – nature and society. It seems that the contradiction between the two processes is among the factors which influenced the parallel development of differing concepts of the universe in Greek and later Roman thought.

Undoubtedly decisive was the dichotomy between the cyclic and the linear course of the world which we have presented here in the sense of Eliade's expositions. In the course of further development of Greek thought an interesting shift occurs. The concept of cyclicity is gradually moved to the periphery of social consciousness and interest; it becomes rather more relevant to more abstract speculations on nature. In contrast, 'the terror of history' (M. Eliade) had such an effect that the anxiety over the gradual heaping up of unhappiness on mankind, fear of most varied disasters and evils, became a constantly fascinating theme, above all in social thought. From here unfolds the distinct sway of KATAGENESIS as a picture of the course of the world which stagnates more and more, and deteriorates so that it needs divine (or at least violent) intervention to save it, if such salvation is at all possible.[6] Quietist doctrines of salvation as well as activist programmes of revolutionary remedies for evils in society (and also in nature) obviously originate in this fear of the historical process. To overcome it intellectually became a matter for only a few thinkers in ancient society.

CYCLIC CONCEPTS

In ancient society, even at the time of its decay and termination, we find many remains of the cyclic concept of the course of the world, primarily in various local cults of vegetation gods and in legends connected with them; further, in mystery cults such as the one at Eleusis; and possibly also in newly imported cults from the East. But it is obvious that these are relics of earlier forms of thought rather than part of development of more exacting ones. They were remains from the period of an archaic society accommodating the desires of broad social strata to achieve salvation and participation in the sacred – desires which were endangered by new doctrines of salvation connected with a completely different concept of time. Also in these relics we can still see the original stage when the social and natural were not sharply separated by an abyss but, on the contrary, deeply linked. Here archaic thought, adhering to ideas connected with rituals from previous periods, completely turned away from history, and eventually history sharply turned away from archaic thinking. The advent of a new concept of time, connected with the Jewish and Christian religions, brought a sudden end to ideas which in the main could not accommodate a longer period of time than one year.

By contrast, cyclic concepts caught on in the process of differentiation in Greek thought in inquiries dealing with nature. In the Ionian philosophy of nature, they already occupied a rather important place but we have to be careful regarding their interpretation, in view of the state of the preserved sources. It is quite possible that an attempt to deduce new systems of the Elements from the original cyclic concepts connected with vegetational and astronomical periodicity would confirm the generally recognized link between the beginnings of Greek philosophical thought and the extant mythological legacy of Hesiod and Pherecydes. The elements or certain qualities which play a significant role in the Aristotelian and Hippocratic systems of Four Elements (Earth, Air, Fire, Water) may be related, without great difficulty, to the rotation of the four seasons of the year. Nevertheless, it remains difficult to prove whether the systems are relics of archaic cycles or the result of completely novel concepts grown out of already wholly new intellectual assumptions. But the comparison between Orphic and Anaximandrian cosmogony made by Guthrie points to gradual development from mythic roots.[7] At the same time, the preserved sources hardly permit a more exact notion of the Anaximandrian cyclic concept and the idea of development must remain hypothetical.[8]

Before the emergence of the natural science of the Four Elements the cyclic concept is usually traced to Heraclitus. It concerns the transformation of fire into other primary substances 'by the way up and down':[9]

> Change he called a pathway up and down, and this determines the birth of the world.
>
> For fire by contracting turns into moisture, and this condensing turns into water; water again when congealed turns into earth. This process he calls the downward path. Then again earth is liquefied, and thus gives rise to water, and from water the rest of the series is derived. He reduces nearly everything to exhalation from the sea. This process is the upward path.

In spite of the fact that Heraclitus' concept was expressly interpreted as cyclical,[10] it can be much more easily (and more in line with other fragments) be represented by a wavy curve with peaks and troughs created by the up-and-down paths which, as a whole, stand for continuous flow of things on a par with a river.

In Anaximander where he speaks about the 'punishment of things' which commit injustice upon each other,[11] it is still possible to trace the original social inspiration of his 'physics'. But the model of the world of Heraclitus is already more distinctly built on natural scientific foundations though the social context is not absent: 'Fire will come, and judge and convict all things'.[12] Numerous biologico-anthropological similes of

Heraclitus show his main source of inspiration: the life of man as a natural being. The same source is also valid for Empedocles' teaching on the Four Elements ('roots'). In it we find unquestionably an example of the cyclic concept of the world based on natural scientific speculation. This appears to secure for the author maximum recognition by his fellow citizens:[13]

> An immortal god, mortal no more, I go about honoured by all, as is fitting, crowned with ribbons and fresh garlands; and by all whom I come upon as I enter their prospering towns, by men and women, I am revered.

According to Empedocles, all things arise from the combination of Four Elements and in proportions determined by one of the dominating tendencies in the world process – Love and Strife respectively. In the period of absolute domination by Love, the hitherto separated elements combine into matter and order of unified quality and sphericity, indicated by the name of this state, SFAIROS. In contrast, the domination by Strife leads to AKOSMIA, the state when the elements are completely separated. They are not able to mix so that things, which otherwise originate from mixture, can neither arise nor exist.[14] This scheme also includes 'zoogony', a kind of pre-Darwinian theory of the origin of animals on the basis of the selection of functional organs and the exclusion of non-functional ones. As in the Darwinian theory of evolution, a significant role here is played by chance (it is active throughout the whole Empedoclean cosmogony). We are interested in zoogony because in Greek thought it provides one of the few examples of ANAGENESIS, the notion of ascending evolution. There can be no doubt about the generation of animal life progressing from less developed beings to more perfect and improved creatures. But if we understand zoogony as part of the whole Empedoclean cosmogony, we must allow only a limited period of duration for it. Logically, in that part of the world cycle where Strife dominates, 'evolution' has to move in the *opposite* direction, to primordial chimeras and monsters. This conclusion is, however, hypothetical – it is impossible to substantiate with Empedoclean fragments. There also remains the possibility that zoogony was conceived separately without a more obvious link with general cosmogony.[15]

The possible contradiction between zoogony and cosmogony need not surprise us. With Empedocles, the idea of a process of differentiation and fragmentation had considerably strengthened. In effect, his theories belong to the sphere of natural science – we do not find any attempt to apply the forces he terms Love and Strife to the evolution of mankind as a whole, even though from the present point of view such a temptation can hardly be resisted. The development of thought was already divided and only rarely was there a fruitful interaction between the investigation of nature and the investigation of society. Interestingly evidence to this effect is represented by the work of Aristotle where the doctrine of the Four Elements in natural science attains highest perfection. There are very few thinkers who could compare with Aristotle in his universal mastery of both the science of nature and the science of society. But basically he does not mix them: *Physics*, *Ethics* and *Politics* already represent distinct disciplines with specific methodologies and concepts.[16]

This development is also documented through the first treatise in the Hippocratic Corpus, *De diaeta*, which is remarkable for its Heraclitean inspiration.[17] Here we obviously witness the first explicit differentiation between *physis*, the domain of natural processes and regularities, and *nomos*, the sphere of human activities and competency. Passages reminiscent of Heraclitus suggest that such a division – of extraordinary importance for a physician – was theoretically already being prepared by that pre-Socratic philosopher. The sphere of nature is understood as something 'divine', independent of human manipulation. But notice is given of a 'modern' understanding of natural science according to which it is objective and thus superior to the humanities. The repetition of events – archaic man's support against the 'terror of history' – acquires here a novel form and significance. But even in the form of objective natural science it betrays traces of nostalgia for a paradise of unchanging archetypes and permanently returning rituals.[18]

THE GOLDEN AGE – DEGENERATION

Catagenic concepts expressing catastrophism in Greek thought may be traced to Hesiod's *Works and Days*. Here we meet already – even though mythically veiled – a certain historical reflection upon the evolution of mankind. The cycle of constant return to the same condition, the certainty of the vegetational and cosmic year, becomes an unattainable ideal which the poet embodies in the idea of the Golden Age:[19]

> The gods, who live on Mount Olympus, first
> Fashioned a golden race of mortal men;
> These lived in the reign of Kronos, king of heaven,
> And like the gods they lived with happy hearts
> Untouched by work or sorrow. Vile old age
> Never appeared, but always lively-limbed,
> Far from all ills, they feasted happily.
> Death came to them as sleep, and all good things
> Were theirs; ungrudgingly, the fertile land

Gave up her fruits unasked. Happy to be
At peace, they lived with every want supplied.
(Rich in their flocks, dear to the blessed gods.)

The next generation of the Silver Age already has two serious defects: first a biological one, based on prolonged growth and on a brief adulthood; and second an ethical one: it does not honour the gods and for that reason is extinguished by Zeus. The third generation of the Bronze Age or Ashen Age is characterized by employing the same criteria. It is endowed with immense strength and manifests itself as arrogant, with a great liking for wars. It perishes when its members kill each other. Then Zeus creates the fourth generation of the Heroic Age which is better than the previous generation. It is the generation of the heroes of Homeric compositions and the heroes, upon their death and for their merits, are transported to the Land of Bliss.[20] But the contemporary fifth generation is again characterized biologically, by a high rate of early death and, ethically, by complete lack of shame and justice. Besides a real characterization of the historical situation appears.[21]

Now, by day,
Men work and grieve unceasingly, by night
They waste away and die. The gods will give
Harsh burdens, but will mingle in some good.

This chronological sequence eventually permits Hesiod to forecast further developments: Shame and Justice will depart for Olympus, and abandoned mankind will be left at the mercy of evil.

The successive arrangement of the five ages in Hesiod's presentation, where with one exception a worse age always follows, turned into a permanent source of inspiration in Greek and Roman thought. Its Latin version, presented by Ovid in the introduction to his *Metamorphoses* became the best known. It is, however, more consistent than the original. Ovid removed Hesiod's positive deviation in the shape of the heroic generation, and thus he preserved only four periods, the Golden, Silver, Bronze and Iron Ages. According to Ovid, the Iron Age came to its end: the Goddess of Justice did depart.[22] Also worthy of notice is the cosmogonical introduction which, compared with Hesiod's *Theogony*, abandons the genealogical scheme and, though it explains the origin of the world as the work of god, bases itself on contemporary natural scientific knowledge.[23] These reflections, influenced by natural science, in a way balance the crushing impression created by the destruction of society (in Hesiod such balance is missing and that is why the sense of his work is more straightforward and its effect is rawer). The purposeful and elaborate arrangement of the world constitutes a counterpoint to destruction resulting from deteriorating human generations. We must therefore understand the introduction to *Metamorphoses* as a promise of hope that manifests itself most distinctly in its reflection upon the creation of man.[24]

At the philosophical level the catagenetic concept of the world is expressed distinctly in Plato's *Timaeus*. Its reference is to the degenerative descent of women and animals from originally perfect men. Women were descended from men who yielded to cowardliness; birds from men of volatile mind; quadrupeds from men uninterested in philosophy and knowledge of the heavens; fishes and other aquatic animals from the most ignorant and sinful of men.[25] Here the loss of reason is the cause of degeneration. But before concluding the treatise, Plato also admits the possibility of a change that upgrades living beings through gain of reason, that is, ANAGENESIS. It should be remembered that Plato regarded the cosmos as animate; 'most great and good and fair and perfect',[26] it occupied the highest place on the scale of living beings.

The suggestiveness of the degeneration thesis of societal development – close not only to poets and philosophers, but also to visionaries such as the Orphics[27] – forces the question: what made it possible for Hesiod and Ovid, half a millennium apart, to express similar ideas? The existing explanations are not too persuasive. The Marxist viewpoint referring to the longing for the state of primitive communism can hardly be upheld if opponents to egalitarianism, such as Pindar or Theognis of Megara, are rightly placed among the followers of the degeneration thesis.[28] Hardly more satisfying is the link with Greek tragedy and, connected with it, socio-psychological explanations, such as we find in Rohde and Nietzsche.[29] The question of cause remains open; the most suggestive view is Eliade's concept of the archaic society and its time, which can obviously contribute most to the understanding of the initial historical situation of ancient man.

THE RETURN OF THE GOLDEN AGE AS THE WORK OF GODS, RULERS AND VIRTUES

The ambivalence between KATAGENESIS and ANAGENESIS in the *Timaeus*, when Plato is explaining the creation of the world and man, indicates the general notion advanced in the excerpt from *Metamorphoses* in the previous section. The world is created perfect on the basis of rational-thinking gods but man (and human society) is more prone to destruction, that is he degenerates. The divine construction of the world, however, provides hope for salvation. The return of the Golden Age, as the consequence of godly intervention and acts of Caesar and Augustus, became a favourable theme for poets in Rome at the turn of the millennium. Poets, such as Virgil, put this return into parallel with the renewal of Roman rule and the strengthening of the empire.[30] Obviously, this *renovatio imperii* is connected with the growth of central governmental power and territorial expansion. It may seem, in fact, that the whole concept of the *Aeneid* conforms with the idea justifying the rule of Augustus, and that to this end are paradigmatically directed the eventful adventures of Aeneas and his companions, wandering after the destruction of Troy. But the comparison with the well-known Fourth Eclogue leads to another conclusion. Here Virgil expresses longings of people suffering from wars and other evils in contemporary society as well as his own utopian optimism, foreseeing a sort of end to history: the First Age links with the Last Age, the new effectively regenerates the old.[31]

Virgil's ANAGENESIS, as indicated in the *Aeneid*, constitutes in fact a return to the starting point in the general cyclical movement of nature and society. The age of Augustus is the restoration of the Golden Age, the Kingdom of Saturn. Deterioration of society is now replaced by its improvement. From this angle both KATAGENESIS and ANAGENESIS appear as approximative components of a giant circle, demarcating the path of the completed natural as well as social cycle.[32]

Ovid had a more difficult position when forced to reconcile in some way his pessimistic vision of the Four Ages with the reality of Augustus' principate and his active 'cultural politics'. Ovid found a way out by emphasizing the naturalistic foundations of society – cosmic phenomena change continuously but their essence remains.[33]

In this manner, based on naturalistic ontology, Ovid succeeded in avoiding the dangerous contradiction between the pessimistic evaluation of the course of human society and the political pressure in Augustus' time. That was what undoubtedly also gave rise to Ovid's leaning towards ANAGENESIS in the conclusion of the *Metamorphoses*. As Atreus steps aside to pave the way for fame for his son Agamemnon, as Aegeus does for Theseus and Peleus for Achilles, so Caesar takes pleasure in the acts of 'son' Augustus, according to the mythical example 'sic et Saturnus minor est Iove'.[34] The orientation towards nature obviously inspired Ovid to choose another approach than Virgil: it is not a merging of the 'golden' beginning of the ages with the also 'golden' end, but a constant coming into being, a continuous renovation.[35]

It is impossible not to notice that in Ovid's presentation we find considerable contradictions regarding time. On the one hand, time brings about degenerative development; on the other, it generates constant renovation, involving the 'improvement' of Saturn's empire thanks to the advent of Jove. If there is persistence of the essence of things, there is also constant change. These contradictions may be explained in various ways, but for us it is decisive that it supplies a time-tested way for a poet to evade the labyrinth of topical political pressures and save face – that is, to explore themes concerning nature which do not constitute an immediate threat to those in power at the top of society.

With Virgil and Ovid, cooperation between divine intention and intervention of concrete rulers was helping to correct the degenerative course of human society. But ancient thinking also knew another, individualist approach (and one independent of big cosmic epochs) whereby to ameliorate one's own destiny, and thus indirectly also the destiny of society. In the *Republic* dealing with the myth of Er's death and resurrection Plato's stress is on moral qualities and merits.[36] According to whether they lived virtuously or sinfully, souls (judged or from personal choice) enter bodies of higher and lower living beings respectively. As with Orphics, the ethical starting point is decisive – rational argumentation, typical for the *Timaeus*, is here suppressed. The doctrine of transfiguration of souls forms the common anthropological background to both modes. Thus Plato puts considerable means for salvation into the hands of the individual even in unfavourable times and circumstances, and extricates him, or at least his soul, from the chain of inexorable causes and consequences. We shall see that this hero of Plato will really need it because, after all, certain epochs do exist when destinies of human beings are determined by their individual nature.[37]

TWO DIRECTIONS OF MOTION OF THE WORLD

If we compare Plato's concepts of 'deterioration' and 'improvement' in the fate of individuals (in the *Timaeus* and *Republic*) we can see clearly that they are put into differing contexts. Whereas a biological framework dominates in the *Timaeus*, a sociological one prevails in the *Republic*. This is confirmed by Plato's simultaneous interest in both nature and society. But the biological and sociological parallels and analogies are not sufficient to explain Plato's ideas. It is necessary to take into account the special features of Plato's ontology and epistemology. H. Morin showed that the diversity of concepts of life that we meet in Plato's case exclude unambiguous holistic, reductionist or teleological explanations.[38]

The myths concerning the two directions of motion of the world which occurs in the *Statesman* is Plato's most striking expression of the influence of the natural and social upon each other. But it is a hard nut to crack. Plato, the philosopher of archaic society *par excellence*,[39] presents it by referring to the reversal of the course of stars in the myth of Atreus and Thyestes, and in the myth of earthborn mankind.[40] This is followed by cosmological considerations:[41]

> Absolute and perpetual immutability is a property of only the most divine things of all, and body does not belong to this class. Now that which we call heaven and the universe has received from its creator many blessed qualities, but then, too, it partakes also of a bodily nature; therefore it is impossible for it to be entirely free from change; it moves, however, so far as it is able to do so, with a single motion in the same place and the same manner, and therefore it has acquired the reverse motion in a circle, because that involves the least deviation from its own motion. But to turn itself forever is hardly possible except for the power that guides all moving things; and that this should turn now in one direction and now in the opposite direction is contrary to divine law ... The only remaining alternative is that the universe is guided at one time by an extrinsic divine cause, acquiring the power of living again and receiving renewed immortality from the Creator, and at another time it is left to itself and then moves by its own motion, being left to itself at such a moment that it moves backwards through countless ages, because it is immensely large and most evenly balanced, and turns upon the smallest pivot.

The consequences of the reversal in the motion of the world are discussed, in the first place, in biological terms: ageing reverts to its opposite, rejuvenation; the old become young; the young become infants; the infants become newborn who simply disappear. The biological illustration is followed by a socio-historico-mythological one. Plato assigns the reversal to the time when the reign of Cronus was coming to an end. Then there were neither states or families, nor was there agriculture. The earth was fertile of its own accord and capable of nourishing the population. People had all the time for leisure and even communicated with animals. Thus they acquired immense wisdom and 'were immeasurably happier than those of our epoch', said to be under the rule of Zeus.[42]

In the fullness of time coinciding with the end of Cronus' rule, the course of the world reverses without 'higher assistance', under its own steam so to speak:[43]

> For when the time of all those conditions was accomplished and the change was to take place and all the earth-born race had at length been used up, since every soul had fulfilled all its births by falling into the earth as seed its prescribed number of times, then the helmsman of the universe

> dropped the tiller and withdrew to his place of outlook, and fate and innate desire made the earth turn backwards.

After initial derangement caused by sudden natural changes such as earthquakes, which accompanied the reversal, the situation calmed down and the world continued to move in an orderly manner, as was its wont. But, after an interval of time, due to the corrupting influence of the material component of the world, disorder returned to the world threatening to ruin it.[44] Therefore

> at that moment God, who made the order of the universe, perceived that it was in dire trouble, and fearing that it might founder in the tempest of confusion and sink in the boundless sea of diversity, he took again his place as its helmsman, reversed whatever had become unsound and unsettled in the previous period when the world was left to itself, set the world in order, restored it and made it immortal and ageless.[45]

It is generally known that Plato was constructing his myths *ad hoc* for apodictical solutions of difficult problems where he did not trust the persuasive power of the LOGOS and rational proofs, or for ceremonial announcements of lofty and significant results of his philosophizing. In the *Statesman* Plato is concerned with defining the essential attributes and duties of a statesman. This is undertaken not without regard to nature – it springs from cosmological premises. Plato's notion of the cosmos' dual motion represents a unique theme in ancient thought. Cyclicity in the history of society as well as nature is linked here with both catagenetical and anagenetical linearity. The concept of regeneration, degeneration or constant repetition in cycles is replaced by reversibility – pivoted on cataclysmic points of reversal – enclosing both natural and social phenomena.

Possible sources of Plato's concept are hard to find. The reversal of the world's motion, regarded as circular, faintly echoes the up-and-down paths of Heraclitus. In this context it is also possible to refer to the statement, ascribed to Anaximenes, about the world revolving in the manner of a millstone.[46] Otherwise we hardly find a suitable analogy in ancient thought. But even in Plato's philosophy this theme does not play a more significant role and the author does not return to it. Cosmologically, it is closest to themes dealt with in the *Timaeus* but there the basic premises are presented in a completely different manner. However, this fact does not eliminate the possibility of making use of the *Timaeus* and other works of Plato for the elucidation of the uncommon myth in the *Statesman*. In this we completely abstain from trying to deduce axiological hierarchies between the individual dialogues in Plato from their relatively uncertain chronological relations.

For the specific context of Plato's thinking, the reference in the *Statesman* is of particular importance. He observes how men, deprived of protective control by *daimones*, were imitating the work of gods and acquiring their knowledge to be able to make a living and later even (relatively) to emancipate themselves:[47]

> On all these accounts they were in great straits; and that is the reason why the gifts of the gods that are told of in the old traditions were given us with the need for information and instruction, – fire by Prometheus, the arts by Hephaestus and the goddess who is his fellow-artisan, seeds and plants by other deities. [The fellow-artisan of Hephaestus is Athena; seeds and plants are the gifts of Demeter and Dionysus. *Note by translator.*] And from these has arisen all that constitutes human life, since ... the care of the gods had failed men and they had to direct their own lives and take care of themselves, like the whole universe, which we imitate and follow through all time, being born and living now in our present manner and in that other epoch in the other manner.

The bio-sociological viewpoint in the *Statesman* has its ontological roots elucidated in the *Timaeus*. The irrational, mechanical nature of necessity is a source of evil and degeneration – necessity in the *Timaeus* corresponds to fate in the *Statesman*.[48] But it is a mystery as to which of the ten motions listed by Plato in the *Laws* belongs the changing course of the world that fascinates us so much. Plato deals most extensively with motion in the *Laws*.[49] The changing course of the world corresponds most probably to two motions identified in the *Laws*. One relates to motion caused by another (and not by itself), that is by God, the Steersman of the world; the other pertains to change (ALLOIOSIS).

But with this we have chosen two kinds of motion that are otherwise compatible only with difficulty in Plato's thinking: one concerns the sphere of heavenly motions, the other the sphere of earthly motions. Theoretically, the one should exclude the other but we must not forget that the world of the ten kinds of motion in the *Laws* is the world of the *logos*, whereas the course of the world in the *Statesman* is presented through a myth. What is not possible for the *logos* is possible in myth.

According to Plato in the *Statesman*, the course of the world itself is determined by fate and inborn instincts.[50] From the *Timaeus* we know that circular motion is perfect and controlled by reason. Inasmuch as objects in the cosmos move rectilinearly, it is a case of motions against reason – irrational motions ('wandering motions').[51] In addition, it is necessary to take into consideration Plato's thinking on whether living beings possess eternal naturalness (here it is necessary to refer to Plato's doctrine of the soul in the *Timaeus*) which, however, does not apply to the entire cosmos – a notion hardly to be expected. Fate (and necessity) are therefore factors which lower the value of the cosmos, in comparison with the value of a living being. Here we are getting into an area of considerable contradiction which nevertheless, helps to comprehend Plato's intention in the *Statesman* (insofar as it is at all possible) resting on ontological assumptions that differ from those conveyed in the *Timaeus*.

We can amplify the bio-sociological viewpoint in the *Statesman*, including its ontological roots illumined by the *Timaeus*, by the epistemological context. By emphasizing how partial faculties or qualities (DYNAMEIS) lead to corresponding (i.e. different) results concerning diverse objects of cognitive faculties, Plato anticipated the later, more detailed reasoning of Aristotle devoted to this topic. Plato's epistemological viewpoint corresponds to his concept of the primacy of function and production (ERGON).[52] With respect to the myth in the *Statesman*, the causes and conditions of the knowledge of function and product are considered as the consequences of antagonistic events in two completely different world epochs. The result is a political doctrine supported by biology, more generally by cosmogony, and set into a special epistemological field.

Plato's myth in the *Statesman* shows how its author was searching in the cosmological domain for explanations of political and social events. He was connecting causes of events in society with potential natural events and biological peculiarities. But it is uncertain whether in Plato's scheme society and nature obey the same laws. We have seen that what applies to the cosmos does not have to apply to living beings (as long as the cosmos was not construed as a living being). The parallelism of natural and social events is caused more by divine intervention than by their inner nature. Here Plato indicated a possible path to the 'naturalization' of society which began in the seventeenth century, but he obviously was not in a position to develop completely rational foundations for such a turnabout. The link between society and nature in Plato rested on myth, on divine intervention with consequences (ERGAI) which applied to both spheres.

In comparison with other concepts of the course of the world already mentioned, Plato's notion of the reversibility of development of nature and human history is unique. It differs radically from cyclicity with its inevitable return to the original state by the same route. With Plato, the world returns to one of the original states but only through forced divine intervention, at the price of reversing existing naturalness and thereby also at the price of cataclysmic upheavals. Plato raises an issue suggestive of a 'vector' which, however, is not taken account of subsequently in the classification of motions in the *Laws*.

What may somewhat modify the significance of Plato's original contribution is its context in his work as a whole. Plato's logical reasoning and his myth often contradict each other greatly. Even as regards the nature of the course of the world, he produces positions which can be interpreted in terms of degenerative and evolutionary development, and to this has to be added the original approach in the *Statesman.* The reasons for Plato's equivocation are difficult to specify and, probably, to establish exactly. We have encountered similar inconsistencies in other authors, but in those cases it was rather easier to understand why – in Hesiod with his positive deviation, in Ovid, Virgil and others. The fact that the ideas of ancient writers baffle later classifiers is certainly not a disaster.

CONCLUSION

The diverse and contradictory notions of society and nature in ancient society often reflect the dependence of their creators upon the historical conditions of a given epoch. Archaic man's awe of history provoked discrepancies between the security of cyclic development and the peril of evolutionary linearity. The typical positions may be characterized as follows:

1 degenerative conceptions connected with progressive deterioration following the end of the Golden Age (Hesiod);
2 compensating conceptions generated by political situations which do not deny the decline of society but, thanks to intervention by gods, rulers and others, signal change for the better and regeneration respectively (Virgil, Ovid);
3 cyclic conceptions which lost their original connotation and became more relevant for explanation in the context of nature than in the context of society (Heraclitus, Empedocles);
4 Plato's original conception of two motions of the world comprising both cataclysmic changes in nature and society, and their remedy.

Of these conceptions the first and third became dominant and, through reception and interpretation by scholars, overshadowed approaches such as the one suggested by Plato in the *Statesman.* The fourth conception explains the world process as degeneration modified by political considerations.

An important concomitant feature of the foregoing conceptions was that the study of nature appeared to be a possible way of avoiding concrete political pressures. But this did not materialize within the framework of decaying ancient society and had to wait its chance for another millennium.

NOTES

The author expresses his thanks to the Swedish Collegium for Advanced Study in the Social Sciences for their generous support which enabled him to present his contribution to the symposium at Friiberghs Herrgård near Uppsala. He is also grateful to Professor Mikuláš Teich and Dr Nina Witoszek (Oslo) for their friendly and stimulating criticism.

1 See C. Tresmontant, *Bible a antická tradice* [Essai sur la pensée hebraique, transl. J. Sokol] (Prague, 1970), p. 27.

2 See 'The fruitful repetition of divine models has a twofold result: (1) by imitating the gods, man remains in the sacred, hence in reality; (2) by the continuous reactualization of paradigmatic divine gestures, the world is sacrificed', in M. Eliade, *The Sacred and the Profane* (New York, 1959), p. 49.

3 *Ibid.*, 111. See also M. Eliade, *Kosmos und Geschichte. Der Mythos der ewigen Wiederkehr* (Reinbek, 1966), p. 93.

4 M. P. Nilsson, *A History of Greek Religion* (Oxford, 1925), p. 144. Cf. also Th. Gomperz, *Griechische Denker*, 4th edn (Berlin, 1922), I, p. 29, who in this context speaks of the humanization of nature.

5 See U.v. Willamowitz-Moellendorf, *Der Glaube der Hellenen* (Berlin, 1955), II, pp. 114f.

6 See Eliade, *Kosmos*, p. 131.

7 W. K. C. Guthrie, *Orpheus and Greek Religion: A Study of the Orphic Movement* (London, 1935), p. 222.

8 See W. K. C. Guthrie, *History of Greek Philosophy*, repr. (Cambridge, 1967), I, p. 101.

9 H. Diels and W. Kranz, *Die Fragmente der Vorsokratiker*, 6th edn (Berlin, 1974), I, 'Herakleitos' Fragment A 1; see Diogenes Laertius, IX, pp. 8–9. Trans. R. D. Hicks in The Loeb Classical Library (Cambridge MA: 1970).

10 See M. Bartling, *Der Logosbegriff bei Heraklit und seine Beziehung zur Kosmologie* (Göppingen, 1985), p. 145 (based on the interpretation of fragment B 31). On the other hand G. S. Kirk, *Heraclitus: The Cosmic Fragments* (Cambridge, 1954), pp. 330f. explains this rather as two separate ways. The problem common to various interpretations is the term *prester* which can be rendered as 'firewind'; the open question remains whether Heraclitus put the accent on the fiery or the aerial nature of this Element.

11 Diels and Kranz, 'Anaximandros', Fragment B1.

12 *Ibid.*, 'Herakleitos', Fragment B66. Translation follows Guthrie, I, p. 473. K. Reinhardt points out the possible influence of late doxographical tradition (Christian or Stoic); see his 'Herakleitos' Lehre vom Feuer', *Hermes*, 77 (1942), 1–27.

13 Diels and Kranz, 'Empedokles', Fragment B112, vv. 4f. Translation follows G. S. Kirk, J. E. Raven and M. Schofield, *The Presocratic Philosophers*, 2nd edn (Cambridge, 1983), p. 313.

14 This interpretation has been questioned by U. Hölscher, 'Weltzeiten und Lebenszyklus. Eine Nachprüfung der Empedokles-Doxographie', *Hermes*, 93 (1965), pp. 2–33. See also M. R. Wright, *Empedocles. The Extant Fragments* (New Haven, 1981), p. 54.

15 See Kirk *et al.*, *Presocratic Philosophers*, p. 294.

16 On the other hand, Aristotle in *Politics*, 1254b compares the relation between the

soul and the body, man and animal, male and female to the relation between the ruler and the slave.

17 See H. Diller, 'Weltbild und Sprache im Heraklitismus', in H. Berve (ed.), *Das neue Bild der Antike* (Leipzig, 1942), pp. 302–16.

18 Eliade, *Kosmos*, 132 and *The Sacred*, p. 80.

19 Hesiod, *Works and Days*, vv. 108–22. Translation by D. Wender in *Penguin Classics* (Harmondsworth, 1973). See W. J. Verdenius, *A Commentary on Hesiod Works and Days* (Leiden, 1965), p. 79.

20 The ruler is Cronus, see Hesiod, v. 166f. According to P. Reitzenstein, *Studien zum antiken Synkretismus* (Leipzig-Berlin, 1926), p. 62, the supposed happiness is due to the influence of Greek nobility *in illo tempore* that regarded the Homeric heroes as its progenitors.

21 Hesiod, vv. 180–3.

22 Ovid, *Metamorphoses*, I, vv. 89f., especially vv. 149–50.

23 L. P. Wilkinson, *Ovid Recalled* (Cambridge, 1955), 213, derives Ovid's cosmology from Poseidonian Stoicism.

24 *Metamorphoses*, I, vv. 76–88.

> Sanctius his animal mentisque capacius altae
> deerat adhuc et quod dominari in cetera posset:
> natus homo est, sive hunc divino semine fecit
> ille opifex rerum, mundi melioris origo,
> sive recens tellus seductaque nuper ab alto
> aethere cognati retinebat semina caeli.
> quam satus Iapeto, mixtam pluvialibus undis,
> finxit in effigiem moderantum cuncta deorum,
> pronaque cum spectent animalia cetera terram,
> os homini sublime dedit caelumque videre
> iussit et erectos ad sidera tollere vultus:
> sic, modo quae fuerat rudis et sine imagine, tellus
> induit ignotas hominum conversa figuras.

25 Plato, *Timaeus*, 90e–f. Translation by R. G. Bury in The Loeb Classical Library (1975).

26 Ibid., 92c.

27 See Gomperz, *Griechische Denker*, p. 70.

28 See the eloquent verses of Theognis, *Elegies*, vv. 161–64; on Pindar's pessimism, see E. Rohde, *Psyche* (Leipzig, n.d.), p. 201f. For a Marxist approach, see G. Thomson, *The First Philosophers* (London, 1955), ch. 11.

29 F. Nietzsche, *Philosophie im tragischem Zeitalter der Griechen*, in *Werke* (Leipzig, 1906), I, p. 501, connects pessimistic Greek thinking with the rise of pre-Socratic philosophy but he considers Socratean optimism as a sign of the decline.

30 Virgil, *Aeneid*, VI, vv. 792–5:

> Augustus Caesar, Divi genus, aurea condet
> saecula qui rursus Latio regnata per arva
> Saturno quondam, super et Garamantas et Indos
> proferet imperium ...

31 Virgil, *Eclogues*, IV, pp. 4–7:

Ultima Cumaei venit iam carminis aetas;
magnus ab integro saeclorum nascitur ordo.
iam redit et virgo, redeunt Saturnia regna;
iam nova progenies caelo demittitur alto.

32 An interesting point of view is that of M. W. Schiebe, *Das ideale Dasein bei Tibull und die Goldzeitkonzeption Vergils* (Uppsala, 1981), 43, who distinguishes between the emphasis on nature in the Golden Age in the *Eclogues* and on history in the *Aeneid.*

33 Ovid, *Metamorphoses*, XV, vv. 252–55:

'Nec species sua cuique manet, rerumque novatrix
ex aliis alias reparat natura figuras:
nec perit in toto quicquam, mihi credite, mundo,
sed variat faciemque novat . . .'

34 Ibid., v. 858.

35 Ibid., v. 184–85:

'nam quod fuit ante, relictum est,
fitque, quod haut fuerat, momentaque cuncta novantur.'

A detailed comparison of Ovid's and Virgil's concepts of history is made by G. K. Galinsky, *Ovid's Metamorphoses: An Introduction to the Basic Aspects* (Oxford, 1975), pp. 230f.

36 Plato, *Republic*, 614b. Translated by P. Shorey in The Loeb Classical Library (1956).

37 Plato, *Timaeus*, 90.

38 H. Morin, *Der Begriff des Lebens im 'Timaios' Platons unter Berücksichtigung seiner früheren Philosophie*, (Uppsala, 1965), pp. 132, 137.

39 Eliade, *Kosmos*, p. 34.

40 Plato, *The Statesman*, 268e, 271a. Translated by H. N. Fowler and W. R. M. Lamb in The Loeb Classical Library (1975).

41 Ibid., 269d, f.

42 Ibid., 272c.

43 Ibid., 272d:e.

44 Ibid., 273d:a, b.

45 Ibid., 273e.

46 Diels and Kranz, 'Anaximenes', Fragment A12. Cf. W. Capelle, *Die Vorsokratiker* (Berlin, 1958), p. 93.

47 Plato, *Statesman*, 274c:d.

48 F. C. Cornford, *Plato's Cosmology* (London, 1971), p. 208.

49 Plato, *Laws*, 893c. Translation by R. G. Bury in The Loeb Classical Library (1961). The explanation given follows J. Patočka, *Aristoteles, jeho předchůdci a dědicové* (Aristotle, His Forerunners and Heirs) (Prague, 1964), pp. 37f.

50 Plato, *Statesman*, 272e.

51 See Cornford's commentary to *Timaeus*, 43a.

52 See H. Hintikka 'Knowledge and its Objects in Plato', in J. M. E. Moravcsik (ed.), *Patterns in Plato's Thought* (Dordrecht, 1973), pp. 1–30.

THREE

BYZANTINE FOOLS: THE LINK BETWEEN NATURE AND SOCIETY

LENOS MAVROMMATIS

INTRODUCTION

FOR the Byzantines and for a period of over ten centuries, nature, whether in the form of a forest, or as a river or as the sea, or as any sort of animal, in reality was an enemy with which man daily came into contact, if not in conflict. This was no different from what was happening in the West during the medieval period. Survival depended directly on how well nature could be tamed and how well largely unpredictable natural phenomena such as floods, droughts, earthquakes and so on could be predicted and controlled. On the other hand, famine and epidemics such as the plague, smallpox or leprosy and infantile mortality combined with the birth of handicapped children exacerbated a deep fear of nature and its unpredictability.

In contrast, with the advent of Christianity, an ideal perception of the world was counterposed to this hostile reality of nature. Man who was expelled from a harmonious universe created in the image of God, was called to imitate it, to draw examples and principles from it and to consider it as the direct expression either of Providence or of Judgement. Anything that was out of the ordinary in human behaviour could not be placed outside the confines of this ensemble of real nature and ideal universe and was therefore interpreted as a godly message.

This was the result of the radical difference introduced with the choice and imposition of Christianity as the sole religion of the Roman state. The moral value which was introduced and adopted, and which achieved predominance, was that of *agape* – Christian love – which could be expressed through welfare.[1] The emperor of Constantinople, the mimesis (imitation)[2] and viceroy[3] of God, is by definition philanthropic and beneficent. This new notion of a charitable God, as formulated by St Paul, was developed, given a theoretical framework and put into practice by the Church Fathers and above all by John Chrysostomos, Basil of Caesarea and Gregory of Nazianzus.

In the following pages we shall explore whether known cases of madness during the Middle Ages in Byzantium were part of this welfare notion, what treatment they received, and whether they were considered part of nature or of the society. Were they imbued with negativity, wildness or animality or were they, even in their most extreme expression, cases of eccentric but candid, even 'holy', behaviour.

Before we proceed any further, a few comments are in order about the state of welfare, medicine and treatment in the Byzantine world.

WELFARE (PHILANTHROPY) AND MEDICINE

Evidence for the existence and functioning of welfare foundations, as well as for the kind and quality of care or nursing they provided, is scattered and frequently uneven.[4] Most of it – and this probably is not coincidence – comes from areas where the Hellenistic city had flourished: Asia Minor, the Near East, Egypt, and of course Constantinople. The names of the various foundations – ξενον, ξενοδοχεῖον, πανδοχεῖον, καταγώγιον and so on – give the impression that they were places with varying functions, something which should make the historian wary of identifying them with the modern notion of a clinic, or more generally, with the modern understanding of illness. The human body was an object that did not as yet interest the intellectuals of the day, and medicine could not yet be characterized as a science. It is true that the antique tradition of providing medical services was still practised, but the focusing of Christianity on the internal world, that is, on the world of the soul, contributed to a reluctant toleration of the medical treatment of corruptible flesh without, however, contributing to the development and cultivation of scientific medical curiosity. Medicine as a branch of knowledge was passed on from one generation to the next, and frequently from father to son, as an art rather than a science. Nevertheless, a general look at the occupants of these 'hospitals', or indeed at the unfortunate in general throughout the whole of medieval Christendom, allows us to conclude that these patients were chiefly incurables (the blind, invalids with physical malformations and lepers), orphans and widows.[5]

Here we have not mentioned epidemic diseases or, in particular, the plague. All societies faced this problem in much the same way seeing as it was not until the very end of the nineteenth century that the bacterium responsible for the plague (*yersinia pestis*) was discovered. The appearance of this disease was held to be an act of God which went beyond the bounds of organized or spontaneous philanthropy since it posed the requirement that it not be allowed to spread further, and that those not yet afflicted protect themselves from possible infection: divine salvation for those who survived and divine justice for the victims. Everything was inscribed in God's ordering of human affairs. It should be noted, however, that there is a need for a wider investigation of the phenomenon in the Balkans although very little relevant evidence is available for the region in the medieval period.

We shall not refer in detail to the presence or the geographical distribution of philanthropical institutions in Byzantium, nor to the principles they observed and the aims which they were supposed to fulfil.[6] Byzantine 'hospitals', whether they were run by the church or members of the laity, followed the spirit and the orders of the central power which, by means of various acts and decrees, as well as by defining the internal ordering or regulation of affairs (such as with the *typika*) in the more important foundations, determined their organization and their mode of operation.[7] From the surviving texts we are thus able to form a picture of the attitudes of state and society towards sickness and how to confront or treat it, the relationship between physician and patient and their status as mutually dependent members of a special group within society, and the philosophy that lay behind the web of relationships that developed out of the phenomenon of illness.

The Asclepian tradition, the Hippocratic approach and the methodology of Galen gradually merged with Christian philosophy and the system of values which it imposed. One could argue that this fusion took place relatively smoothly, and that ancient tradition did not clash irreconcilably with Christian morality, its code of values, and the way of life of its members, irrespective of social class, throughout the Oecumene.

Doctors, their 'clients', and the places where diagnosis and treatment could be carried out (whether at the doctor's house, the agora, or, of course, places of worship dedicated to Asclepius) had been a common feature of life in the urban centres of the Roman and Hellenistic East. There was also – and this was of prime importance – the tradition of the medical profession and the passing on of medical knowledge, even if confined to family circles or small associations. Roman aristocrats and men of learning may have shunned the ancient Greek approach to medical knowledge and may have viewed the 'Asclepiads' with suspicion or even contempt (a view which they were to pass on to Byzantine intellectual life and education: the trivium and quadrivium systematically ignored this branch of learning), yet they did not obstruct the provision or acceptance of the services of the disciples of Hippocrates and Galen, even if they classed them on the same level with astrologers and diviners. Nevertheless, the East had the theoretical and material infrastructure ready and waiting, and the whole mentality would allow the continuation of the tradition. One important step, however, had still to be taken: to reconcile Asclepius and Christ within the triumphant ideology of the church. The threshold was crossed with ease by Basil of Caesarea and John Chrysostom: a basis was provided and very soon (though not of course without objections and protest) the Asclepiads and the Anargyrol were to be identified with one another and medical practice would continue unhindered right up to the end of the Byzantine period. A vast number of saints throughout the Christian world acquire healing properties, thus giving a framework to the activity and efficiency of their mortal colleagues.

Furthermore, the sophisticated Church machinery (the patriarchate, dioceses and monasteries) allowed the creation and development of various kinds of foundations that were based on the ideals of philanthropy and the provision of health care. As a result, such centres providing medical services (as well as religious and ecclesiastical doctrine and propaganda) increased markedly in number. The profession of physician achieved recognition, both moral and material, and it was accessible to all the social classes. Christianity, however, gave a strict definition of the field of medical knowledge: it should concern itself with the body and nothing more. For the more learned, medical discourse was conducted on the basis of the fairly widespread manuals of the Galen school, and it was accompanied by techniques that were significantly limited in the methods they could use. If the surviving descriptions of symptoms are frequently surprising in their clarity, and often written by learned scholars rather than doctors, the practice which corresponds to the phenomenon described is fixed and repeated unchanged throughout the centuries. An example is the serious illness that led to the death of the emperor Alexios Komnenos as described by his daughter Anna Komnene in her history of his life, the *Alexiad*. A highly learned woman, the writer followed closely the progress of the illness and even took part in the decisions concerning the treatment that was to be applied, surrounded as she was by the doctors of whom the most prominent were also members of the imperial court. Although the illness was serious the doctors proposed purgatives, blood-letting, herbal compresses to be applied to the head and various spiced potages to be administered from time to time.

Anna remarks that her father had always been a healthy man and abstemious in his way of life, but he had been afflicted by continual stress and overwork. The emperor was not left solely in the hands of his illustrious doctors. From the moment the severity of his illness had been realized he also looked to God for succour, distributing lavish amounts of money to the poor but also to those in prison and to the sick so that they might pray for him. Finally, money was also given to those monks who practised their life of devotion to God in the mountains and caves. All these people were to offer prayers for the salvation of their emperor. Here we see a reversed flow of charity: the less fortunate in general (the sick, those in prison) and monks who had retreated from society are called upon to return the alms or charity they have received by buying, in turn, atonement from God for the sins of the emperor.

The emperor Alexios' illness is not the only medical case to be found in our sources. But it does serve to demonstrate that still in the eleventh and twelfth centuries medicine was based on knowledge that had remained unchanged since ancient times, and that diagnosis and therapy were no different from what ancient medicine prescribed, regardless of the nature of the illness in each patient, regardless of the social class, and regardless of whether the illness was treated within the confines of the family environment or in a place specialising in the treatment of sickness, and whether free of charge or not. All this leads to the conclusion that such specialized places were generally designed for long-term illness or for surgery (such as amputations and cauterizations).

MADNESS: WAS IT AN ILLNESS?

Madness, as we have already mentioned was not included in the family of illnesses dealt with by Byzantine as well as Serbian, Bulgarian and, later, Russian society. Madness had no place in medical discourse and by extension was allotted little importance as an illness for the individual, society and the state: it was not in fact an illness. It is not included in any medical manual or treatise, it was never defined by legislation and no foundation was established to treat patients suffering from it. In particular legislation concerning madness was unequivocal and confined to the following exclusion: if an individual was held to have lost his senses his right to act as a member of society was denied him, he was placed under the guardianship of others, and henceforth ceased to exist in the state's eyes.

On the eve of the modern era, in 1402, Patriarch Matthaios of Constantinople and the Holy Synod confirmed that a wealthy woman, Tzourakina had become possessed (δαίμονι κάτοχος γεγονυῖα) and was in danger of falling victim to exploitation and losing all her property. It was decided that she be confined to the monastery of Andrew of the Judgement and her property be put up for auction. The money was then deposited with the monastery to pay for her maintenance there. One should not jump to the conclusion that the Patriarch acted thus from charitable motives. He was laying a claim to the woman's property, and the ruling of the Patriarch, as is clearly stated, aimed chiefly at legalizing the acquisition of the property by the buyer and only secondary importance was attached to the concern that she be taken care of and not end up impoverished and in misery.[8]

The document makes one thing clear: Tzourakina has been possessed by the devil, she has lost her senses and she is in danger of being exploited or ending up penniless and so she will spend the rest of her days confined to the monastery. Leaving aside the procedure which was followed and the fact that she was placed under the special guardianship of the patriarch, we can look more closely at the causes to which the lady's behaviour was attributed. The cause was that of 'demons', or in other words the devil. For the Byzantines, following the spread of Christianity and the establishment of a moral code based on the opposition of good and evil, the prime cause of madness was the devil. The devil and his accomplices, they believed, were attempting to intervene in the affairs of men with the intention of diverting them from a series of fundamental codes of behaviour within society. When this deviation from the accepted code of behaviour was significant, it meant that the subject (man) had been changed into an object (instrument) of the devil, who was out to achieve two things: to destroy his victim both mentally and physically, and to shake the faith of the other members of society whose conduct was otherwise dictated by the teaching of Christ. Of course, this was accompanied by a second cause that was accepted by both eastern and western Christendom: this activity of the devil was inscribed in the divine order. The possessed person was punished for sins committed both by himself and by others (eg. other members of his family) and at the same time he served as an example to others around him. Thus we have the Manichaean conception of the struggle between good and evil, and a second that attributed the madness to the higher workings of divine providence and divine justice. They were conceptions that complemented one another, and which defined madness for the entire medieval period, placing its diagnosis and treatment beyond the reach of human science. Right up to the sixteenth century, as Foucault remarks, Lady Macbeth's doctor declared that this disease was beyond his practice.[9]

Indeed, in none of the descriptions of hospitals that the historian has at his disposal for the Byzantine period will he meet either a direct or indirect reference to the provision of care for fools. This care was undertaken by the family or by the church, though of course they did not recognize the character of the illness and consequently the possibility of treatment as with other illnesses using a specialized approach or institutions designed for the purpose. Rather they undertook the spiritual purification and salvation of the 'patient'. There was only one method by which this could be achieved: exorcism, the treatment *par excellence* of sick souls. The view was formed that certain charitable foundations (such as the Hospice of the Pantokrator in Constantinople), churches and monasteries (for example, the Church of Saint Anastasia in Constantinople) undertook the 'care' of such cases. We suspect, however, that here the sources have been misinterpreted.[10] The so-called *hiera nosos* or holy illness that is stated to have been treated at the Hospice of the Pantokrator was surely leprosy. At the church of Saint Anastasia (who had the power to cure and heal by means of appearing in dreams and visions) we are not dealing with systematic treatment of patients. On the contrary, these were cases of temporary confinement.

'HOLY FOOLS'

The sources, along with indications about the functions of such institutions, also give us information about a particular type of fool found in the Byzantine World. Such was the case of St Andrew the Fool whom we shall discuss in more detail below. He was most probably an imaginary figure whose 'life and career' are placed in fifth-century Constantinople by the author of his Life who was writing in the tenth century. St Andrew the Fool was a young, intelligent and charming Scythian slave. His master, a prominent member of the imperial entourage, took the trouble to have him taught the *hiera grammata* or primary course of education and thus he learned Greek. Andrew proved to be an exceptional pupil and eventually rose to become his master's private secretary. This idyllic life, however, was interrupted abruptly when the God-fearing slave and secretary began to be disturbed by dreams in which he saw Althiopes (blacks) fighting with *most reverent men* (whites), and in which he himself was challenged to a duel by the leader of the Althiopes. He was encouraged to accept the challenge by a handsome young man who was holding garlands in his hands. The leader of the blacks was a general of Satan's forces. The young man had been sent by God. The hero of this tale was persuaded and promptly went out and defeated the Althiopes. The Althiop forces were defeated and the whites were jubilant. The young man gave Andrew the garlands and so enrolled him in the ranks of his *friends* and *brothers*; then he commanded him to fight the good fight, to become a *salos*, or fool, for Him (Christ), and finally he told Andrew that when the Day came he would find a place in His kingdom.

Andrew related what he had seen in his dream to the writer of his Life and they decided together that he should pretend to be possessed and insane. Indeed, from that very night Andrew started to behave like a lunatic: he slashed his clothes with a knife and began raving and ranting. His master took him to the church of St Anastasia and, having paid a large sum of money to the intendant of the church, he ordered that the slave be put in irons. At night Andrew beseeched St Anastasia to come to his aid. St Anastasia appeared surrounded by her attendants and she declared to them that she was unable to do anything because God had already judged the matter: Andrew would be a Fool (*salos*) – this was his cure, and consequently he had no need of a doctor. He would remain this way, practising his *techne*, or 'craft', until the day he died, all for the sake of God. After being confined for four months in the church, it was observed that his situation was worsening. Andrew's master was informed that his slave was mad (*exechos*) and possessed. His master decided therefore that Andrew be released from his chains and left to go free in Constantinople.

Another famous version on the same cliché refers to Syria-Palestine. St Symeon the Fool, of Syrian origins, was not a fictitious character. He lived in the sixth century and his Life was written in the seventh century. He lived with his old mother. His friend, John, had just been married (they both knew excellent Greek). Along the river Jordan they met angels who, pointing to the river, indicated to them that this was the real way. With the help of a priest, they interpreted this sign as an invitation to choose the monastic way. Symeon was very close to his mother with whom he shared a bed at night, while John had a passion for his beautiful young wife. They eventually convinced one another to leave both women and they found refuge in a monastery where they were welcomed by St Nicon who in the face of Symeon he already recognized a holy fool. After a long test period they were eventually ordained. They dreamed, heard messages, had visions in which either God or Satan tempted them (especially Symeon) using the mother of the one and the wife of the other as instruments of lust. When, after twenty-nine years of tests Symeon reached perfection in the desert, he decided to go back to the world and make a fool of it with the help of Christ, and went to the town of Emessa. From the moment the two fools entered the 'world' their lives went parallel to each other.

However, there were differences in their madness. The life of Symeon followed, at least initially, a milder and more familiar transition to madness (choosing the monastic life and the test in the desert). The author introduced and insisted upon a new element: in contrast to Andrew who right from the beginning was supposed to speak to himself and to suffer fits of mania, in the case of Symeon, sensual temptation and lust in two forms – implicit for the mother and explicit for the wife – were present. This new topic is worth noting because it constituted one of the main characteristics of this kind of literature and was of equal, if not greater, importance than mania itself. Nevertheless, it would be wrong to analyse this element of erotism psychoanalytically;[11] such an analysis would in any way concern the authors of these two Lives, who, in their turn, followed patterns used by other authors and ultimately referred, among others, to a major theme of the whole Christianity and the Church, i.e. the control and regulation of the sexual life of the citizens/subjects. Suffice it to look at the canons of the Fathers of the Church and at the legislation of the Byzantine emperors to see how systematically the state and the Church imposed control on individual sexual behaviour.[12]

For the holy saints coming from the desert, the main scope of their test was to achieve apathy, or that stage of self control whereby no temptation, real or imaginary, could destroy the shell that protected the body and the soul. This was what Symeon meant, when he stated that he was going to fool the world or in other words, to pretend that he was similar (or worse) than men in order to prove his sanctity (and to bring them back to the virtuous way) by means of madness. Symeon entered Emessa pulling behind him a dead dog, tied with his belt. Children ran after him, made fun of and beat him. On the following Sunday, he went to the church and threw nuts at the candles and at the women present. When he was thrown out, he began to turn over the tables of peddlers who consequently almost beat him to death.

Apathy was not central to the case of Andrew. He barged into a tavern in a mad state, the customers gave him wine in abundance, made fun of him, beat him and led him to the town's brothels where he stayed until well into the night. Brothels were one of the areas where holy fools settled. The others were public spaces, streets and squares, public baths – for men and women; taverns where they could eat beans and drink wine, and which were frequented from morning to night by all sorts of idle people, by clowns/mimes and dice gamblers; brothels where visitors and clients constituted a special public. Our holy fools took active part in this life. They got blind drunk, played dice even in 'secret' places, were accused of adultery or of rape. When having one of their fits, they stripped naked, relieved themselves publicly, anointed themselves with excrement, slept at the gates of the town, together with dogs in order to keep warm. Even the poor had only contempt for them, and jeered and beat them.

Yet their innocence and sanctity in one way or another was made obvious to some of their confidants to whom they related their deeds, their dreams and their visions: Andrew related to the author of his Life that during a very cold winter he slept with the dogs and the angels led him to Heaven (Paradeisos) where he saw Christ himself in his full imperial grandeur. Christ welcomed him and blessed his madness before sending him back to worldly life.

Temptations were not absent either when they were awake or asleep and they saw the devil masqueraded into an old witch or a female poisoner, a Jewish pederast or an Ethiopian man. In contrast, when in a normal state, these holy men were candid and wonderful discussants and interpreters of the holy scriptures, peaceful, generous and merciful. They had the gift of propheing the near future and in their own way made that known to those interested in it.

The narration however mainly focused in detail on the resistance against temptations of the flesh. The aim was double. On the one hand sexual abstinence was portrayed as the most obvious demonstration of sanctity and human perfection and on the other, the public's interest was maintained by giving them titillating details. Two facets of sensualism can be discerned: on the one hand, exhibitionism, that is, moving in the streets naked and frequenting women's public baths where the 'heroes' demonstrated their apathy by stating that they were made of wood: on the other hand, their behaviour in the brothels where the prostitutes invited them and challenged them either verbally or with daring gestures, fondling their genitals, to enjoy pleasure. Both Andrew and Symeon successfully resisted, although, as becomes apparent from the narration, Symeon risked being stimulated. He found refuge near a holy man in the river Jordan who made the sign of the cross on the particular spot of his body and the fool was released from evil. His extraordinary resistance to sexual desire caused spectators to wonder and be amazed. Most of them attributed it to hardship but some realized that something else was happening.

This spectacular aspect of everyday life provoked various comments and reactions. The narration however, clearly suggests that neither the state nor the church reacted to forms of behaviour that lay outside the established moral code or the norms they were trying to impose and maintain. Our two heroes never got in conflict with the authorities. When their behaviour became excessive, the public itself punished them by beating them and temporarily chasing them away. They lived always intra-muros unperturbed and often loved by the people either for their madness or their innocence.

This acceptance of the fools was in stark contrast to the Western Christendom, where madness was often the object of ecclesiastical, administrative and police repression. An example of this was the 'Ship of Fools' and the compulsory ban from the towns. The two cases just mentioned should not be considered isolated examples. The proliferation in urban centres of such itinerant holy fools was such that both the state and the church became concerned and the issue was discussed at the Oecumenical Council of Trullo (Constantinople, AD 692). The Council tried to establish barriers between the authentic possessed and those pretending to be possessed and stipulated that the way to obtain the truth was to apply 'hardship and pain' i.e. torture. If somebody was authentically possessed then exorcism would be used as catharsis. However, as is indicated by the comments of Byzantine jurists, it was difficult to discern between authenticity and fraud and the probability of error deterred them from applying such harsh measures. Thus, despite the strict regulation dictated by the Oecumenical Council, our sources do not confirm any spectacular repression. According to interpreters of the spirit of the Council, such as Balsamon, the issue lay rather within the jurisdiction of the Church, i.e. the Oecumenical Patriarch, and any suspects were remanded in custody as a result of an ecclesiastical and not a state order. We can tentatively hypothesize that the church of St Anastasia in Constantinople had a sort of prison where Andrew's master put his slave in the hope that hardship would cure him. This hypothesis seems reinforced by an eleventh-century text.[13] Kekaumenos, in his Strategy for Politicians and Military men, looking at fools from the side of institutionalized society, advised his readers not to interfere with fools, even if they pretended to be holy (*saloi*), lest they ridiculed themselves. Better, they should give them charity rather than offend them and in any case listen carefully to what they (the fools) have to say.

Madness was not restricted to male fools. Mad women are scarce in the sources but they existed, though they were never seen as holy fools. They were usually interned in monasteries; they lived in excrement, talked to themselves and often drank wine all day; they hoped to reach that stage of apathy which would have enabled them to go into the town like their male counterparts, who in contrast, could more easily afford to exhibit their madness/sanctity to the town folk.

CONCLUSION

The incidence of holy fools gradually diminished in the Mediterranean areas of Byzantium but it increased and survived in the orthodox Slav world, especially in Russia, where the particular mysticism characterizing Russian Christendom allowed the possessed to be assimilated by society. In the Balkans, mad men and women continued to move around and were considered either sent by God (*theopropoi*) or possessed by the devil (*daimonoplectoi*). In urban centres, their presence was so familiar that they were often manipulated by politicians in their propaganda. Two examples will help illustrate this point. In 1185 the leaders of the Bulgarian ruling class, Peter and Asen were preparing their rebellion against the Byzantine Empire. They built a church in Tarnovo and dedicated it to St Demetrius. They then gathered all those who were possessed and persuaded them that, as messengers of God, they should disseminate to the whole of Bulgaria the message that the Lord had consented that Bulgarians should overthrow the old Roman yoke and gain their freedom. The fools began to spread the word that St Demetrius had abandoned his old town of Thessaloniki so that not only could he help the revolution but he could also ensure the very destruction of the Romans.

In 1186, in Constantinople, the Emperor Isaakios Angelos ordered all itinerant, barefoot and homeless monks, including 'stylites' (hermits living in rudimentary huts on top of columns), to pray to bring about the failure of the rebellion led by General Alexios Branas and an impending civil war.

The above examples suggest that, on the one hand, incumbents of central power communicated with their subjects through these personalities and obviously expected and achieved greater and more important results than if they had appealed directly to the principal intermediary which was the church and organized monasticism; on the other, that fools enjoyed the respect of all social strata, especially of the common people as seen in the lives of Symeon and Andrew.

In view of the preceding remarks, it is clear that fools in Byzantium were not 'marginal' in the same way that they had been considered by western medieval Christendom.[14] Their sometimes wild behaviour was only temporarily seen as negative. Nor were they mental patients either. Rather, they were fully integrated in society, they served various purposes, including political, and seem to have constituted the direct link with nature/God.

NOTES

1 J. Ph. Thomas, *Private religious foundations in the Byzantine Empire* (Washington, 1987); E. Kislinger, 'Taverne, alberghi e filantropia ecclesiastica a Bizancio', *Atti della Academia de Scienze di Torino*, 120 (1986), 83–96; T. S. Miller, *The Birth of the Hospital in the Byzantine Empire* (Baltimore, London, 1985); R. Volk, *Gesundheitswesen und Wohltätigkeit im Spiegel der byzantinischen Klostertypika* (Munich, 1983); Konstantina Mentzou-Meïmari, 'Ἐπαρχιακα εὐαγῆ ζορύματα μέχρι τοῦ τέλους τῆς Εἰκονομαχίας' (*Provincial philanthropical foundations up to the end of the Iconoclast period*), *Vizantina*, 11 (1982) 243–308; P. Lemerle, *Cinq études sur le XIe siècle Byzantin* (Paris, 1977), pp. 67–191; P. Gautier, 'Le Typikon du Christ Sauveur Pantocrator', *Revue des Etudes Byzantines*, 32 (1974) 1–145; D. J. Konstantelos, *Byzantine Philanthropy and Social Welfare* (New Brunswick, New Jersey, 1969). An

older discussion of the subject can be found in E. Jeanselme and L. Oekonomos, 'Les oeuvres d'assistance et les hôpitaux byzantins', *Actes du 1er Congrès Historique de l'acte de guérir* (1920) (Anvers, 1921), pp. 239–256; L. Mavrommatis, 'Facets of Philanthropy in Byzantium', in Centre of Byzantine Studies, *Everyday Life in Byzantium* (Athens, 1989), pp. 147–152 (in Greek).

2 See Z. V. Oudaltsova and K. A. Ossipova, 'Traits distinctifs des rapports féodaux de Byzance', *Vizantiaka*, 7 (1987), 11–54.

3 *Ibid.*, pp. 11–54.

4 Mavrommatis 'Facets of Philanthropy'.

5 It is worth remembering that the meaning of mental illness, as we understand it today, is not to be found in the sources – in contrast to western Europe. The mentally ill in eastern Christendom, perhaps under the influence of other more eastern cultures, were regarded both by the members of the community in which the patient lived, as well as by the state (or the Church), as prophetic (θεοπρόπος) or possessed by demons (δαιμονόληπτος) (see, for example, N. Choniates, 'Historia', *CFHB*, pp. 11, 1, 371). Konstantelos (*Byzantine Philanthropy*), considers wrongly that the philanthropical foundation of the Pantokrator included a mental clinic. The typikon of the foundation refers to patients who are afflicted by the 'holy sickness' (*hiera nosos*): by this, however, is meant leprosy and not epilepsy or some mental illness. Cf. Gautier, 'Le Typikon', pp. 111–13.

6 For details, see Anne Comnene, *Alexiade*, ed. B. Leib (Paris, 1937–45), II, pp. 108–218 and note 1 above.

7 Lemerle, *Cinq études*.

8 In this account madness should not necessarily be linked to the old practice, which originated in the Roman law code, of referring in various legal acts, such as wills, to the fact that the author at the time of drawing up the document was of sound mind and senses.

9 Foucault, *Folie*, p. 46.

10 Christina Angelidi, 'The *saloi* in Byzantine Society', in Goulandris Foundation, *The Marginals in Byzantium* (Athens, 1993) pp. 85–102 (in Greek); Also, A. J. Festugière (ed.), 'Leontios de Neapolis', *Vie de Symeon le Fou et Vie de Jean de Chypre* (Paris, 1974); J. P. Migne (ed.), *Patrologia Graeca*, vol. 111, col. 622–888; Despite any disagreement about some of the author's arguments, a very interesting contribution is by J. Grosdidier de Matons, 'Les thèmes d'edification dans la vie d'Andre Salos', in *Travaux et Memoires* (Paris, 1970), IV, pp. 277–328; On the life of Andrew and Symeon the Fools, P. Cesaretti and L. Ryden, *Santi Foli di Bisanzio* (Milan, 1990).

11 P. A. Sigal, 'La possession demoniaque dans la Région de Florence au XIV siècle d'après les miracles de St. Jean Gualbert', *Melanges offerts par G. Duby* (Aix en Provence, 1992), III, pp. 101–9. Sigal in his article suggests a psychoanalytic approach which does not seem well founded.

12 On sexual repression and regulation, see S. Troianos, 'Magic in Byzantine Legal Texts', in Centre of Byzantine Research, *Everyday Life in Byzantium* (Athens, 1989), pp. 549–72 (in Greek); E. Laiou Angeliki, *Marriage, Amour et Parenté à Byzance au XIe–XIIIe s.* (Paris, 1992), and same author, *Consent and Coercion to Sex and Marriage in Ancient and Medieval Societies* (Washington, 1993).

13 *Strategikon Kekaumenou*, ed. V. Karalis & D. Tsoungarakis (Athens, 1993), pp. 207–9.

14 J. Le Goff, 'Les marginaux dans l'Occident Médiéval', in Legoff, *Les Marginaux et les exclus dans l'Histoire* (Paris, 1979), pp. 19–28; L. Mavrommatis 'The Concept of Marginals in the Balkans during the late Middle Ages', in Goulandris Foundation, *The Marginals in Byzantium* (Athens, 1993), pp. 15–23 (in Greek).

FOUR

THE 'CHAOTIC SPACES' OF MEDIEVAL MADNESS: THOUGHTS ON THE ENGLISH AND WELSH EXPERIENCE

CHRIS PHILO

GEOGRAPHIES OF DARKNESS AND LIGHT

THE span of years usually designated as the medieval period – stretching from the sixth century through to the fifteenth – has not been treated kindly by historians of madness, and negative portrayals of how medieval European society responded to the 'natural' phenomenon of mental distress are commonplace.[1] Here is H. C. Burdett, writing in 1891:

> [D]uring many centuries, the lot of the insane was not only one of mental but of bodily torment. Those who were not burnt or brutally done to death in some other way, were either permitted to roam at large – usually in the most miserable plight – or, being violent, were placed in dungeons and cruelly ill-treated and starved, to the lasting disgrace of those who were responsible for their incarceration.[2]

For Burdett, this was hence a 'period of demoniacal possession, witch-craft and *auto da fe*', and he underlines his negative portrayal by stressing how much worse medieval practices looked in comparison to the humanitarian treatment of mad people that was common throughout the Ancient world. He condemns the medieval period as the 'Dark Ages' of his study, and this play on nomenclature is one that surfaces again in an influential essay by Gregory Zilboorg describing 'the Dark Ages of psychiatric history'.[3] The emblem of *darkness* actually recurs many times in accounts of medieval madness, with various authors casting their subject against an historical context that was supposedly 'dark and troublous',[4] 'dark and deadening'[5] or 'dark and disturbed'.[6]

This 'Dark Ages' stereotype keys into a depiction of medieval mad people being excluded from the normal everyday spaces of human interaction, and in the process either banished to the dark forest or incarcerated in the dark dungeon. Threatened by the Inquisition's fires, shunned by those fearful of either demons or God's wrath, abandoned by the physician and unprotected by the lawyer, mad people could surely have expected nothing better than to be chased into the wilderness or chained and neglected in cells. And it is this miserable picture of an exclusionary geography that is conveyed in a passage such as this:

> Only now and then a community or a religious organisation made some special provision for the mentally sick, and it is not at all improbable that these unfortunate persons fared better when left to their own resources. Those who were shunned by their fellow beings wandered about in lonely places at night and remained in hiding during the day. Some of the more excited and violent were flogged and confined with chains, occasionally without human contact except at such times as food might be thrown to them.[7]

The difficulty of this claim is that it gives the impression of being grounded in detailed empirical knowledge, when it can be little more than casual speculation buttressed by limited historical evidence. The facts usually paraded on such occasions are those documenting the enforced exclusion of lunatics from late-medieval German towns,[8] as well as those hinting at lunatics being entrusted to boat-owners whose 'ships of fools' (such as Brant's *Narrenschiff*) would voyage up and down the major rivers of Western Europe,[9] but such scraps hardly constitute compelling proof that the geography of the medieval 'mad-business'[10] was an exclusionary one.

Some little-questioned *a priori* assumptions and historical materials have been stitched together to produce the stereotype of an exclusionary psychiatric 'Dark Ages', then, but some historians of madness now caution that it may not be enough to 'content ourselves with the reaffirmation that the Dark Ages were indeed dark'.[11] Some are beginning to show how the darkness of this era was relieved by at least a few chinks of *light*, and J. S. P. Tatlock goes so far as to claim that a whole 'system' of enlightened understandings and practices may yet emerge from the confusion of difficult and scattered medieval records.[12] Perhaps the boldest if somewhat polemical statement to appear in this connection, however, is that offered by Michael Foucault in *Madness and Civilization* when declaring the need

> to return, in history, to that zero point in the course of madness at which madness is an undifferentiated experience, a not yet divided experience of division itself. We must describe, from the start of its trajectory, that 'other form' which relegates Reason and Madness to one side or the other of its action as things henceforth external, and as though dead to one another.[13]

The brilliance and the drawbacks of Foucault's thesis about the birth and subsequent entrenchment of a schism between 'Reason and

Madness' are well-known,[14] but the relevant suggestion here is that the medieval period encompassed the 'zero point' when madness was still an 'undifferentiated experience': to have been a time when the not-mad and the mad entered daily into shared activities, conducting a 'dialogue' that was later to be silenced as the Middle Ages moved into the Early Modern. To quote from the jacket commentary on the British edition of *Madness and Civilization*, for much of the medieval period 'insanity was considered part of everyday life' and as a result 'fools and mad people walked on the streets', and the clear suggestion here is of medieval mad people being greeted either with indifference – which would have permitted them to come and go as they pleased – or even with occasional attempts to include them at centres of charity and hospitality. In this latter respect Foucault describes various medieval 'gathering places' where mad people from many countries collected in numbers, and in particular he references the Flemish village of Gheel to which the insane were sometimes 'taken as pilgrims'.[15] Moreover, it is not the mad person but the *leper* who Foucault identifies as the victim in medieval Europe, which leads him to propose that European society would have to wait until the Early Modern period before the 'structures' left behind by the disappearance of leprosy – the 'formulae of exclusion'; the ceremonial expulsion to 'low places'; even the buildings themselves – could be inherited by populations which included the idle, the wicked and the mad.[16] As far as the medieval mad-business is concerned, it is possible to arrive here at an impression of a much more inclusionary, as opposed to exclusionary, geography.

The account that Foucault gives of medieval madness is more complex than this, though, particularly when he discusses the above-mentioned evidence about the treatment of mad people in late-medieval Germany:

> The madman's [river] voyage is at once a rigorous division and an absolute Passage. In one sense, it simply develops, across a half-real, half-imaginary geography, the madman's *liminal* position on the horizon of Medieval concern – a position symbolized and made real at the same time by the madman's privilege of being *confined* within the city *gates*: his exclusion must enclose him; if he cannot and must not have another *prison* than the *threshold* itself, he is kept at the point of passage. He is put in the interior of the exterior, and inversely.[17]

To the initial glance this statement may appear conformable with the exclusionary geography envisaged by Burdett and others, but a closer reading reveals that Foucault is not so much describing a blanket exclusion of mad people as a situation in which the medieval lunatic was suspended in a delicate balance *between* exclusion and inclusion: as either being marooned inside boats ploughing the rivers and seas of the great 'outdoors' (in the interior of the exterior) or as being confined inside cells set above a city's gates to the outside world (in the exterior of the interior). It must also be realized that Foucault supposes this balance between exclusion and inclusion to have been peculiarly bound up with the *closing* years of the medieval period, and as such signals a crucial transition from an earlier and inclusionary treatment of mad people (identified above) to a *later* and on occasion more exclusionary treatment.[18] In short, Foucault might draw upon the same scraps of evidence as do other historians of madness, but the 'half-real, half-imaginary geography' of which he writes is less one of exclusion and more one of inclusion or – when dealing specifically with late-medieval matters – of a delicate balance between exclusion and inclusion.

The purpose of this essay is to probe more deeply into these issues, and to do so principally through an engagement with a range of materials concerning the circumstances of madness in medieval England and Wales. To some extent it will simply reiterate the message of Basil Clarke's *Mental Disorder in Earlier Britain*, notably his insistence that the 'one generalization' approach is hopelessly inadequate for capturing the messy realities of madness prior to the Early Modern period,[19] but what it hopes to add is a heightened sensitivity to the complex 'social-cultural geography'[20] – the co-existence of exclusionary and inclusionary sites, buildings and institutions, spread across a diversity of localities and regions – through which the 'natural' phenomenon of mental distress entered into the thought and action of medieval people. What follows is extracted from a longer study, one where an attempt is made to trace in detail the discourses and practices surrounding madness in medieval England and Wales, and one which seeks continually to relate these discourses and practices back to the precise 'places' where they were formulated, nurtured, diffused, enforced and even contested.[21] A flavour of the study will be given in the third section of the essay, but in order to link from the broader concerns of the introductory comments above to this more empirical section it is proposed first to consider the contents of a medieval poem where madness is heavily featured, the *Vita Merlini.*

THE WILD AND THE WISE IN THE MADNESS OF MERLIN

This poetic work was almost certainly written by Geoffrey of Monmouth, who spent most of his days teaching and writing in the vicinity of Oxford, and expert opinion suggests it to have been drafted (initially at least) for a 'limited audience of friends' some time between 1148 and 1155.[22] The character of Merlin is best known to modern readers as the wily magician of King Arthur's court, but the 'theme of Merlin' actually surfaces in different guises throughout the 'vast mass of material' described by A. O. H. Jarman as the 'major contribution of Welsh and Celtic traditions to the European culture of the Middle Ages'.[23] The Merlin of the *Vita* is hence not so much an 'Arthurian' Merlin – even though in an earlier work Geoffrey had spoken of a Merlinus Ambrosius contemporary with Arthur, the great knight and monarch[24] – as a condensation of several shadowy figures whose outlines can be discerned in a series of older and undoubtedly cross-fertilized Welsh, Scottish and Irish legends.[25] This Merlin is hence a mixture of Myrddin, Lailoken, Suibhne Geilt, Elladhan and maybe even an eastern hero or two, and it is from these roots rather than from the better-known 'Arthurian' tradition that the complex images of mental distress so central to the *Vita* have been derived.[26]

Perhaps the most striking image of mental distress that arises here consists of the unreasoning animality displayed by Merlin as the 'wild thing' or the furtive 'Man of the Woods'. According to the story Merlin was overtaken by madness during the crash and death of a fierce battle in which he was involved as the leader of the Welsh Demetae, the men of Dyfed in south-west Wales, who were fighting alongside the men of Cumberland against a powerful Scottish force. Despairing at the death of three brothers to whom he was greatly attached, and also recoiling from the 'loud complainings' of armed conflict, Merlin fell into a mental confusion that caused him to flee for refuge in the forest of Calidon[27] and there to begin living with the beasts:

> Then, when the air was full with these loud complainings, a strange madness came upon him ... Into the forest he went, glad to lie hidden beneath the ash trees. He watched the wild creatures grazing on the pasture of the glades. Sometimes he would follow them, sometimes pass them in his course. He made use of the roots of plants and grasses, of fruit from trees and of blackberries in the thicket. He became a Man of the Woods, as if dedicated to the woods. So for a whole summer he stayed hidden in the woods, discovered by none, forgetful of himself and of his own, lurking like a wild thing.[28]

Over the months that followed King Rodarch of the Cumbri sought to have Merlin brought back to the settled world, and he implored the Welsh leader to be 'reasonable' and once more to 'wield a royal sceptre and rule a nation of warriors', but when Merlin did re-enter Rodarch's city – his sanity apparently regained – the crowds of people disturbed him so much that once more his derangement filled him with a desire to escape to the forest. Rodarch ordered him to be 'held under guard' and placed in chains if necessary, but it was not long before Merlin was able to secure his release and hence a passage back to the shelter of the ash trees. This cycle of events – of escape, capture and re-escape – was twice more re-enacted, but ultimately even the long-term restoration of his reason could not persuade Merlin to leave his beloved Calidon, and it was here that he chose to live out the remainder of his days with his wife and two other companions.

The composite image of madness trawled here from the *Vita* is in many ways a negative one, for it depicts an individual who had cast aside all reason and was unprepared to bear the vital responsibilities of kingship and statecraft. This would have made him a failure by many medieval standards, as too would his desire to live like a forest animal impervious to 'existing on frozen moss in the snow, in the rain, in the angry blast'. The appeal in this latter case is clearly to the mythology of the *wild man* – the 'hairy man curiously compounded of human and animal traits' – which pervaded medieval art and literature,[29] and which represented a 'darker' side of medieval civilization: an emblem of untamed brute 'Nature' lurking beneath the veneer of an ordered and cultured society.[30] Thus, as R. Bernheimer explains:

> The picture drawn by Medieval authors of the appearance and life of the wild man is . . . very largely a negative one, dominated by the loss or absence of faculties which make of human beings what they are. The wild man may be without the faculty of human speech, the power to recognise or conceive of the Divinity, or the usual meaningful processes of mind. What remains, after losses of this kind and magnitude, is a creature human only in overall physical appearance, but so degenerate that to call him a beast were more than an empty metaphor.[31]

Given that the wild man was portrayed as lacking the 'usual meaningful processes of mind', it is not hard to see that the negativities of madness and wildness were perceived by medieval people to be complementary (if not entirely interchangeable) and hence could be roped together in the shape of a fictional character such as Merlin.[32] As a result Merlin's madness carried with it not only a reprehensible dereliction of both reason and duty, but also an association with wildness – and hence with a darker side; with the forces of disorder – that the *Vita*'s early readers may well have found disturbing as well as stimulating.[33]

There is a second image of mental distress to be found in the *Vita*, however, and this entails the compelling equation of madness, wisdom and prophecy. As already indicated, Merlin's madness was at first a wood-abiding wildness, but over the months this wildness was supplemented by a wiseness which enabled him to foretell the future when captive in Rodarch's city and which eventually led him to utter long and detailed prophecies on matters such as the fate of Britain. Furthermore, when he escaped to the forest for the last time he abandoned the ash trees and took instead to living in a 'forest house' that his sister had built for him, and by this time his condition had improved sufficiently for him to be 'still disturbed but more rational and no longer wood-wild (living like an animal)'. It was while he was staying in the forest house that he met Taliesin, with whom he talked at length on the subjects of philosophy, science, geography and politics, and the scholarly and refined cast of these conversations contrasted with the unthinking brutishness of his earlier madness. Following these debates the two men visited a forest spring that had just been discovered, and it was here that Merlin was cured of his mental affliction as he drank from the stream, his 'reason' swiftly returning as the waters 'settled the humours of his system'. Merlin thanked God for this miracle, and then launched straight into his speech about how madness and deeper knowledge had mingled together in his head, both distressing him and giving him an advantage over those who could only boast the ordinary mental capacities of a human being:

> I was taken out of my true self, I was as a spirit and knew the history of people long past and could foretell the future. I knew then the secrets of nature, bird flight, star wanderings and the way fish glide. This distressed me and, by a hard law, deprived me of the rest that is natural to the human mind.[34]

This composite image of madness drawn from the *Vita* has some positive elements, for it depicts an individual who had acquired the powers of wisdom as allied to prophecy which allowed him to transcend the banality of everyday existence. And, just as it is possible to find an artistic and literary counterpart to Merlin's initial madness (the wild man), so it is possible to find a literary and even anthropological counterpart to Merlin's later madness in the shape of the *shaman* who supposedly acts as an intermediary between a people and their gods. This association is not so clear-cut, but a forceful case is argued by Nikolai Tolstoy, who proposes that the 'real world' referent for the Merlin of the *Vita* must have been a late-sixth-century figure – perhaps a Druid – who was perceived by pagan society in the vicinity of Calidon to be in communication with the 'bright culture-god' known as Lug.[35] Tolstoy outlines the characteristics and role of the shaman as follows:

> Whether chosen hereditarily or at random, the neophyte becomes suddenly subject to aberrant behaviour, usually taken as akin to some

> neurotic ailment – madness ... Eventually he [*sic*] retreats to the wilderness where he lives alone like a wild animal, surviving on roots, berries and what wild creatures he may catch, until after some time he returns to his people. His behaviour marks him as a shaman, and he begins to shamanise ... As the mantic fit comes upon him he ascends the World-Tree which links this and the Otherworld, symbolised by a real tree, a specially prepared wooden pillar or the central post of a tent. Through an increasingly frantic babble of semi-coherent chanting, he provides a commentary explanatory of the long and arduous journey his soul (usually conceived in the form of a bird) undergoes.[36]

Tolstoy admits that in no single narrative (whether in the *Vita* or its predecessors) does the Merlin-figure internalize all of these shamanistic attributes, but it is still intriguing to speculate that 'descriptions of Merlin's madness and flight to the wilds represent a misunderstood description of his mantic "call"'.[37] Moreover, although Tolstoy's own interpretations become increasingly unbelievable as his book progresses,[38] his simplest claims – equating Merlin's madness with the wisdom and prophetic powers of the shaman, and conjecturing that settled society relied heavily upon his ability to keep open channels of communication with the 'Otherworld' – do seem plausible. Furthermore, it was the desire to tap Merlin's special powers which excited Rodarch's attempts to capture the fugitive, and which also prompted a later episode in the story when the 'leaders of Merlin's country come to ask him to return'.

This latter episode is significant for another reason, since it indicates the respect that Merlin commanded despite – or perhaps even because of – his madness, and it thereby hints at medieval madness being treated better than other passages in the *Vita* might suggest. Indeed, Tatlock does not so much see here a document riddled with harsh treatments for the lunatic, as one which presents a 'lifelike picture of the light and the humane attitude to the insane'.[39] In defence of this assertion he emphasizes that

> There is nothing of any Christian explanation of insanity, such as demoniacal possession, or of cure by exorcism or relics. No exact theory lies behind. Rather, Geoffrey shows some insights into the actual facts, the provocation of insanity by shock, grief, crowds and ordinary life, and its alleviation by solitude, rest, music and affection ... [I]n Geoffrey's picture we should see a victory of humaneness and common-sense over theory.[40]

Tatlock counterposes literary depictions of enlightened medieval practices to the common supposition that religious intolerance was all that the medieval lunatic would experience,[41] and the *Vita* serves his purpose admirably, for – and notwithstanding the claims of Penelope Doob[42] –

there is little in the text to suggest either wholesale religious condemnation of madness or even localized instances of Church servants ill-treating lunatics. Even the mockery of both frenzied mad people and court fools can be given a charitable gloss in Tatlock's account, and this only leaves the occasional harshness directed at 'wild men of the woods' as a practice in the poem which involves discrimination.

The conclusion to be reached is hence that the *Vita* bears witness to two rather different images of madness: one which implies wildness and the attendant deficiencies of total unreason, animality and dereliction of responsibility; and the other which implies wiseness and the more unusual attributes of prophesying and shamanising. The first of these is essentially a negative image while the second is somewhat more positive, and running alongside these two images – although not interlocking with them in any simple fashion – are remarks suggesting both the harsh treatment of medieval madness and the outlines of a more respectful and enlightened treatment. The point is not to deny the existence of these differing images and remarks in the poem, and neither is it to dragoon them into representing some unitary but fictitious medieval nexus of thought and action. Rather, it is to see in the medieval period a complex fusion of the negative and the positive; of the vicious and the kindly; of the Christian and the Pagan; of the 'global' system with the 'local' empiricism. Yet few historians of madness have spoken of anything but the negative and the vicious – and in effect have never looked beyond the *Vita*'s equation of madness, wildness and harshness – and this orientation has to date produced a one-sided and impoverished account of medieval responses to madness (as already indicated).

Society, space and madness in the legend of merlin

Just as it is possible to find both negative and positive images of madness in the legend of Merlin, so it is possible to find both negative and positive images of how *space* was implicated in the dealings of medieval society with madness. For instance, a casual reading of the *Vita* and its predecessors could lead to the impression that madness was deliberately *excluded* from settled society, and that strenuous efforts were made to chase mad people into marginal spaces such as the forest and the mountains. Indeed, in one of the ancient Welsh poems, the *Afallenau*, Myrddin complained that:

> For ten and forty years, in the wretchedness
> of outlawry,
> I have been wandering with madness and
> madmen,[43]

and the reference here to 'outlawry' implies that he had been banished from the normal 'lawful' places of living and working in early Wales. And this negative impression can be reinforced by recalling the passage where Rodarch excluded Merlin, not by hounding him to the hills but by having him chained and then removed to a guarded space in the city precincts. The literary creation of Merlin hence experienced the two sets of exclusionary spatial practices commonly emphasized by historical notes on medieval madness: banishment to the forest or to other remote places, and incarceration in municipal gaols, towers and dungeons.

But a closer examination suggests that the emphasis here on *enforced* exclusion furnishes only a partial account of Merlin's 'spatial relations', and in particular it reveals that outlawry is not the only optic through which the wood-abiding character of his madness can be assessed. To begin with, it must be remembered that the representation of Merlin's madness was influenced by the mythology of the wild man, and as such the medieval poets would have followed artistic and literary convention in choosing an appropriate location for his descent into insanity and animality. It is well known that the medieval wild man was 'associated with the idea of wilderness – with the desert, forest, jungle and mountains; those parts of the physical world that had not yet been domesticated',[44] and the ubiquity and power of this geographical symbolism (which comforted the medieval imagination in locating its darkest fears somewhere 'out there') would have suggested that the poets situate Merlin's predicament in wild spaces away from settled society. In addition, to the medieval mind there was possibly an even more direct equation of madness and wildness, which curiously enough may have inspired the wild men myths in the first place. As Bernheimer explains:

> We may suspect that the category of wildness had its corollary in contemporary reality, even though the writers may have forced the facts into a pattern of their own. It was a habit in the Middle Ages to let many lunatics go free unless they were believed to be obsessed and subject to the exorcism appropriate to their case. Such insane persons were thus at liberty to follow their irrational urges and desires. If we are to believe the romances, they commonly chose to retire into the woods, thus laying a barrier of distance between themselves and their fellow men.[45]

Indeed, the 'Romances' portray virtually every medieval forest as packed to the treetops with lunatics, and the ubiquity of this notion would surely have influenced, and in its turn have been influenced by, the originators and the transcribers of the Merlin story.

What should also be noted here is that the mad people referenced by Bernheimer supposedly 'chose to retire into the woods', and in so doing sought quite deliberately to place a 'barrier of distance' between themselves and a world that they did not like nor understand. The issue was therefore far from being one of enforced exclusion, and in the text of the *Vita* and its predecessors the maddened Merlin, fleeing from the calamities of battle, actively *chooses* to take his madness into the shelter of Calidon. This is not to imply that his lot in the forest was always a happy one, but there can be no doubt that his life in the wilderness 'satisfied him more than administering the law in cities and ruling over a warrior people'. The more general possibility of specific wilderness places becoming popular haunts for run-away lunatics is raised in relation to the 'ever-delightful' Glen Bolcain visited by Suibhne Geilt:

> It is there that the madmen of Ireland used to go when their year in madness was complete, that glen being ever a place of great delight for madmen. For it is thus Glen Bolcain is: it has four gaps to the wind, likewise a wood very beautiful, very pleasant, and clean-banked wells and cool springs, and sandy, clear-water streams, and green-topped watercress and brooklime bent and long on their surface ... The madmen moreover used to smite each other for the pick of watercress of that glen and for the choice of its couches.[46]

It can only be speculated how many more 'Glen Bolcains' would be revealed to the historian had all of the Merlin stories displayed the same 'extraordinary love of place' as the Suibhne Geilt text,[47] and yet the precise reasons for this particular valley's association with madness remain frustratingly obscure. The presence of 'cool springs' and streams is perhaps a clue, given that both superstition and elementary humoural theories pointed to the efficacy of fresh water in curing madness, and it should be remembered that Merlin's own madness was cured by a spring and that Taliesin provided a detailed discourse on the healing properties of 'springs, rivers and lakes'.

Merlin did not choose only to frequent wilderness places, however, and there are hints in the *Vita* and its predecessors that he was also prepared on occasion to enter places such as towns, castles and monasteries where he could momentarily reacquaint himself with the ways of normal living. The Irish composition is again useful here, for it tells of Suibhne Geilt spending time with the King of the Britons at the latter's royal fortress and later in the community of St Moling at Tech Moling. Similarly, in the Scottish legend where Lailoken – or Lalocen, as he is referred to in this particular context – is cast as a court fool whose professional foolishness became entwined with true madness and 'extreme grief' following the death of St Kentigern, the impression is that he continued to perform at court in the royal town of Pertnech (possibly Partick). In these cases the Merlin-figure sought inclusion in settled society – he *chose* it – and in the process he sidestepped attempts at chasing him into the wilderness. But Merlin's inclusion in settled society could also be *enforced* against his wishes, and such enforcement occurred when the secular authorities strove to capture him, in part to benefit from his prophesying and in part to convince him of the need to reclaim the leadership of the Demetae.

A final point worth making is that Rodarch's attempts to include Merlin quickly shaded into the overtly exclusionary tactic of having him chained up in a guarded space, ostensibly to prevent him from absconding again but perhaps also in recognition of the violent acts to which this particular madman was prone. Once again this is not necessarily the whole story, for when Merlin was confined Rodarch ordered 'music to be played on the guitar to calm his madness', and in so doing an appeal was made to an ancient tradition of using vocal and instrumental music to soothe and maybe even to cure the mentally distressed individual. George Rosen traces this tradition to biblical times, and in particular to a psalm that David supposedly composed and sang to Saul in order to drive away an evil spirit,[48] and it is well known that both the Greeks and the Romans recommended musical therapies for the insane. The Roman physician Soranus might be mentioned in this respect, for he claimed that discretion was needed in using musical therapies, but that these 'may have good results when properly applied'.[49] Moreover, Soranus proposed that the employment of music and other therapeutic devices – which were to be both somatic and psychological – should be accompanied by a careful regulation of the mad person's immediate environment:

> Maniacs ought to be placed in a moderately light room with regulated temperature, the quiet of which no [unwanted] noise can disturb. No paintings shall ornament the walls of their dwelling-place; the air shall penetrate into them through raised windows. They shall be placed on the ground-floor rather than in the upper stories, for most of them are inclined in their fury to throw themselves on the ground.[50]

It cannot be denied that a measure of exclusion was achieved by these spatial arrangements, but it is also obvious that Soranus viewed the placing of lunatics in a special room as vital to the pursuit of a whole therapeutic regime. He was evidently not in the business of exclusion for its own sake, and his proposals did not entail leaving lunatics to rot in dingy cells.[51] Rodarch's incarceration of Merlin may also be given a favourable inflection, then, since it throws off references to medieval mad people being placed (perhaps even voluntarily) in locations where they could receive specialist ministrations; and it may even be that in this connection the legend of Merlin hints at exclusionary spatial practices with humanitarian dimensions.

This 'geographical reading' of the *Vita* and its predecessors demonstrates that the interweaving of society, space and madness in the legend of Merlin is rather more complex than at first might have been expected. This complexity arises in part because both negative and positive 'uses' of space can be detected in accounts of Merlin's madness, and it is amplified because no neat mapping can be made from these negative and positive aspects to the respective spatial practices of exclusion and inclusion.[52] Thus, insofar as Merlin can be said to open a window on medieval places of madness, then it must be concluded that many different sorts of places were involved: some were places of enforced exclusion to which mad people were outlawed or in which they were imprisoned; some were places of exclusion to which they retired voluntarily; some were places of enforced inclusion where they were compelled to live as members of settled society; and some were places of inclusion which they visited and utilized through their own choice. In the third section of the essay this many-paned window on medieval places of madness – complete with its glimpses of forests, glens, springs, fortresses, monasteries and cells – will be employed to frame a brief *resumé* of the actual sites that figured in the mad-business of medieval England and Wales.

THE PLACES OF MADNESS IN MEDIEVAL ENGLAND AND WALES

Madness in medieval England and Wales was caught up in a complex network of discourses and practices – certainly not just the condemnatory-exclusionary ones stressed by many historians – and, whether the assumptions and actions that were involved derived from the realms of medicine, religion or law, there appears to be no single 'master-key' awaiting discovery by the researcher (no all-encompassing 'darkness' or 'lightness' of thinking, no all-pervading will to eject or to embrace). Precisely *who* would have been producing discourses and practices directed at mad people must have been of relevance in this respect, of course, and questions about the status, power, resources and even 'class' of the people responsible for making decisions about the fate of mad people – even if merely writing poetry in which madness was represented – should always be kept in mind (however impossible it is to extract definite sociological conclusions from the evidence available).[53] At the same time these discourses and practices were unavoidably knotted up with a maze of material places, a chaos of real sites, buildings and institutions, through which a variety of possibilities – exclusionary of mad people or inclusionary of them, enforced on mad people or chosen by them – were apparently worked out 'on the ground'.

Places of confinement

Some historians consider gaols, dungeons and other prison-like structures as the most likely places to which troublesome and unwanted mad people would have been consigned. J. Sibbald speaks of just such a carceral experience when describing that the 'kinds of structures' colonized by medieval mad people,[54] and a similar vision is conjured up by the oft-cited evidence of late-medieval German towns imprisoning lunatics (see above). A few fragments of evidence bear witness to such incarceration in medieval England and Wales, a well-known example arising in the *Book of Margery Kempe* when Margery encounters a woman who went 'out of her mind' after childbirth:

> She roareth and crieth so that she maketh folk evil afeared. She will both smite and bite, and therefore is she manacled on her wrists . . . Then was she taken to the furthest end of the town [presumably Lynn], *into a chamber* [my emphasis], so that people should not hear her crying, and there was she bound, hand and foot with chains of iron, so that she should smite nobody.[55]

Similarly, in the records of the miracles worked posthumously by Henry VI it is said that William Barker of Luton was 'confined' during his madness and that Agnes Greene of Sutton Courtenay was shut away when she descended into a violent mania, and in this second case 'it may not have been entirely to secure her from crowds and noise (as the chronicler suggests) that she was locked up in a small cell'.[56] Instances of mad people being imprisoned following their involvement in violent crimes can be gleaned from the *Calendar of Inquisitions Miscellaneous*, and particularly notable is the gruesome case of Richard de Cheddeston, who had murdered his wife and two children when in a state of 'frenzy' and who had ended up being 'imprisoned at Norwich'. The jurors who inspected Cheddeston to establish 'whether he may now safely be released' were hesitant to give a positive verdict, and thereby concluded that 'it cannot be said he is so far restored to sanity as to be set free without danger, especially in the heat of the summer'.[57]

References to frenzied people being locked up in churches are an essential component of Nigel Walker's broader thesis regarding the incarceration of medieval mad people, and it is helpful to consult Clarke's concise summary of this thesis:

> In a Saxon community where most homes would be timber buildings with infilling, they would be relatively flimsy as places of confinement for an aggressive or wandering patient, and an open-plan layout would add to the inconvenience for the rest of the household; since the occurrence of a case would be rare, however, the risk would have no effect on architectural development. When more churches were [made] of stone, they might be available in an emergency ... Walker saw a progression from the use of houses and churches to the use of prisons (in castles and bishops' seats).[58]

Such a progression would have had important consequences for the geography of the medieval mad-business, since it would have concentrated criminal lunatics in specific sorts of buildings with their own specific spatial distributions, but the 'evidence seems thin' for claiming that the confining of even dangerous lunatics in churches, castles and bishops' seats had become a 'regular custom' by late-medieval times.[59]

Places of shelter

Some dangerous mad people may have been locked away in places of confinement, but it is crucial to consider the possibility that some mad people – and not necessarily just those who were a public nuisance – would have ended up in built-institutional settings serving more or less straightforwardly as places of shelter. It is often assumed that the monasteries acted as 'centres of relief' offering alms to the poor and practical ministrations to the sick, lame and elderly, and that they would therefore have sheltered mad people, and it does seem likely that many people who today 'succumb physically or mentally' to the problems of life were then able to find 'maintenance and a retreat' behind monastery walls.[60] This being said, tracking down examples of people with mental afflictions entering medieval monasteries for treatment is not easy, and it is necessary to rely on more indirect evidence regarding the office of 'soul-friend' or 'guest-master' which was so important in Celtic monasteries:

> The arrangement which has special relevance to mental health is the office of the 'soul-friend' (*anam-chara*), a personal guide. This office was held by a monk who served both fellow monks and the public ... [It is] claimed that much attention was paid at the reception centre of Celtic monasteries to those in personal need as well as to travellers ... Cuthbert is said to have once been in charge of the reception centre of a north of

> England Celtic monastery, and he was later certainly involved with what we should now call psychiatric cases.[61]

The monastery at which St Cuthbert (see below) held the office of 'soul-friend' was located near the Yorkshire settlement of Ripon,[62] and it might be added that such an office could have been instituted at his own Lindisfarne monastery to cope with the many lay people who journeyed there with their physical, mental and other problems. It is highly unlikely that St Guthlac (Cuthbert's near-contemporary) was a 'soul-friend' receiving mad people into a monastic environment, but there is one tantilizing indication that the monastery eventually founded at his hermit retreat of Crowland[63] became an important place of resort for late-medieval mad people. An entry in the *Calendar of Inquisitions Miscellaneous* for the 1340s reads as follows:

> Inquisition as to the trespass of Simon son of William le Vineter of Drauton with dogs, bows and arrows in the park at Northampton ... *He is a lunatic and has often been taken to Crowland on that account* [my emphasis]. He went to the park when he was out of his senses, and not in malice. He took [stole] nothing there, and was not sent there by anybody's procurement.[64]

The tone of this passage implies that there was nothing unusual or deserving of special comment in taking a lunatic to the abbey at Crowland, but it can only be speculated whether or not this practice owed anything to a tradition of treating madness at Crowland that Guthlac had set in train some 600 years earlier (see below).

A further point of salience is that in one sense if in no other the monasteries were medieval places of madness, in that many of their inhabitants themselves became mentally distressed. In the *Observances* of a Cambridgeshire monastery it was specified that one of the tasks of the monastery's infirmarian was to look after those brethren who

> sometimes fall into a state of weak health from the irksomeness of life in the cloister, or from long continuance of silence; sometimes from fatigue in the Quire or extension of fasting; sometimes from sleeplessness or overwork ... Some, on the other hand, if severely punished for their excesses, or if leave be refused them, or if they hear evil reports about their friends, are so much disturbed in spirit that they move about among their fellows as though they were half-dead.[65]

Interestingly enough, it was supposed that these distressed brothers required not medicine but 'only repose and comfort', and in consequence it was proposed that they should leave the infirmary and 'walk in the vineyard, the garden and along the riverside' or even 'go beyond the precincts into the fields, meadows, woods or any other place'.[66] The

Barnwell priory was not alone in adopting such a policy towards its resident mad monks, for an even more dramatic spatial-environmental policy was pursued by the authorities of Westminster Abbey:

> Mentally sick monks who suffered from the irksomeness of the cloistered life, or who found the silence of the monastery and the fasting and long services too much for them, and who suffered from the work, sleeplessness, heaviness in the head or pains in the stomach were sent to dependent houses in the country, usually to Battersea, Wandsworth or Hendon.[67]

The chief reason for this relocation was that unwell monks could be placed in a more salubrious rural atmosphere than was afforded by the urban surroundings of late-medieval London, and it is possible to find records of brothers such as Nicholas de Litlington and William Pelham being sent to Hendon 'to take the air' or 'for a change of air'.[68]

It is now necessary to consider the contribution made by those curious institutions known as the medieval hospitals, and to acknowledge at once that these hospitals were undoubtedly perceived by contemporaries as likely to deal with mad people. It is sometimes assumed that there was little difference between the hospitals and the smaller monastic houses (the priories), and it is true to say that most of the hospitals followed a 'Rule' – which was usually the unspecific and hence flexible 'Rule' of Augustine – and that the appearance of both the buildings and their occupants would have differed little from that of a typical monastery with its brethren or sisters.[69] These circumstances lead Rotha Clay to describe their function as rather more ecclesiastical than medical,[70] but it might be objected that this characterization undervalues the extent to which their officers did involve themselves with the problems of the sickly and the needy. George Gask and John Todd trace the origins of a hospital tradition to the Ancient Greek temples of Aesculapius, which were seemingly 'pleasant places' furnishing 'welcome refreshment to mind and body',[71] and the association with treatments of 'mind' appears to have continued into the reputation of at least some of these establishments in medieval England and Wales for taking in mad people.[72] The most persuasive piece of evidence in this connection comes from the wording of a statute from the Leicester Parliament of 1414, which includes the following lines about the 'many hospitals within the realm of England':

> to the which hospitals ... the founders have given a great part of their moveable goods for the buildings of the same, and a great part of their lands and tenements, therewith to sustain impotent men and women, lazars, *men and women out of their wits and mind* [my emphasis] and poor women with child, and to nourish, relieve and refresh the same ...[73]

This reference in a national statute to hospitals taking *hommes et femmes hors de lour sennes et memoire*[74] is extremely suggestive, and so too is the fact that the rules of several hospitals explicitly stated that such people should *not* be received through their doors.[75] Miri Rubin speculates that mad people were deliberately barred from hospitals due to the 'hopelessness of cure, basic incapability of self-help and moral turpitude reflected in this illness',[76] and she supposes this bar to have operated generally throughout the hospital system of medieval England and Wales,[77] but this is both to ignore the above-mentioned clause from the 1414 statute and to overlook the possibility that the explicit banning of mad people from some hospitals may have been fuelled by the fact that – whether deliberately or not, whether happily or not – a few of their counterparts were already taking in such people as a matter of course.

This conclusion can be supported with more direct evidence of mad people being treated in hospitals, a good example of which is a reference in the mid-fourteenth century foundation deed for the hospital of Holy Trinity in Salisbury to 'the mad [being] kept safe until they are restored to reason'.[78] It is also possible that the hospital incorporated into the institutional complex of St Bartholomew's in London would have received some of the 'psychiatric-social' cases which (as discussed below) were serviced in the church, and this possibility prompts H. A. Wilmer and R. E. Scammon to assume that many of the people presenting at the church would have been treated in the hospital.[79] Neither of the hospitals discussed here could properly be described as a specialist facility for mad people, but the historical record does contain glimpses of three and maybe four such early 'lunatic asylums' from medieval England and Wales. Only one of these was located outside of the capital, and this was – to use J. M. Hobson's label – the 'little hospital of St Mary Magdalene for lunatics' which was sited at Holloway near Bath and which was 'probably appropriated to the use of lunatics by Prior Cartlow, who rebuilt the chapel in about 1489'.[80] The first ever suggestion of a specialist asylum dates to over a century earlier, though, and the important document here is an entry in the *Calendar of Patent Rolls* for July 1370 which records:

> Licence, for 40s., paid to the King by Robert de Denton, chaplain, for him to found a hospital or house within his messuage in the parish of Berkyngchirche [Barking Church] in the City of London for the habitation of poor priests and other men and women who have suddenly lapsed into madness (*frenesim*) and lost their memory, until they shall have recovered from their infirmity and regained sound memory . . .[81]

In his exhaustive survey of 1598 John Stow described this hospital as if it had actually existed,[82] but it seems clear that Denton shelved his plan and that the mantle of the first English and Welsh asylum ever to make it into bricks and mortar must go to the so-called 'Stone House' located in the London parish of St Martins-in-the-Fields on the site of what is now Trafalgar Square. Stow is the key source here:

> Then had ye one house, wherein sometime were distraught and lunatic people, of what antiquity founded or by whom I have not read, neither of the suppression; but it was said that sometime a King of England, not liking such a kind of people to remain so near his palace, caused them to be removed further off, to Bethlem without Bishopsgate of London, and to that hospital the said house by Charing Cross doth yet remain.[83]

Sadly, little additional light can be shed on this house for 'lunatic people' other than to note that the 'receiving' establishment – the hospital of 'Bethlem without Bishopsgate' – continued to own a property in Charing Cross until well into the nineteenth century.

The 'Stone House' was closely bound up with this other institution, which was of course St Mary of Bethlehem: a hospital that stood during medieval times in the London parish of St Botolph just beyond Bishopsgate (a gate in the city walls) and an asylum that – particularly through its corrupted names of 'Bethlem' and 'Bedlam' – has since become such a potent icon in debates surrounding the history and the politics of psychiatry. The house was founded in 1247 by Godfrey, the Bishop of the 'Church of the Glorious Virgin Mary of Bethlehem', as a priory whose prime function would be to receive the Bishop and his officers whenever they travelled to England from their base in the Holy Land.[84] The location of the house was determined by the location of landholdings presented to Godfrey by one Simon FitzMary, and it is interesting that in Blome's addition to Stow's survey the institution is noted as standing in an 'obscure and close place' inappropriate to the task which it had then acquired of caring for large numbers of mad people.[85] By at least 1292 the foundation was known as a 'hospital' treating 'poor and infirm' persons,[86] and must have first acquired a specialist reputation as a lunatic asylum with the transfer of lunatcs from the 'Stone House' which is assumed to have occurred *c.* 1377, but the first unambiguous references to the reception of mad people occur in the proceedings of a 'Visitation' conducted during March 1402.[87] This investigation by a Royal Commission was ordered by the king when he learned of 'divers defects' in the hospital's running, and it rapidly became apparent that the main culprit was one Peter Taverner – the hospital's janitor or porter – whose impressive catalogue of misdeeds included appropriating funds, over-charging patients, stealing hospital property, admitting dubious strangers, encouraging gambling and even selling ale from the hospital gate. In the course of the many indictments against Peter there were numerous remarks about the sick inmates of the establishment, and in one testimony it was complained that he 'takes no pains to keep week by week any men or women, *insane* [my emphasis] or sick, within the hospital aforesaid'.[88] Furthermore, it was claimed that amongst the items which had gone missing there were 'six chains with the locks and keys belonging to them', 'four pairs of iron manacles', 'five other chains of iron' and 'two pairs of stocks', and this claim must be viewed as convincing evidence both that Bethlem housed mad people *c.* 1400 and that its treatment of these unfortunates may have left much to be desired (and been as much about enforced confinement as about chosen shelter). Finally, when Peter was himself questioned he revealed that 'there are therein (in the hospital) six of the insane and three other people who are sick'.[89] Peter was duly removed from his position and instructed to return all of the funds and the goods that he had appropriated, but Bethlem itself stayed open and continued to receive mentally distressed patients into its wards, as can be seen from evidence such as a record of how in 1436 a London tailor named William Mawere was discharged from serving on juries 'owing to his constant attention to the poor mad inmates of the hospital of St Mary de Bedlem without Bishopesgate'.[90] The implication is that by the close of the medieval period in England and Wales this particular institution was indeed well-known as a special place of shelter – if not necessarily of enlightened treatment – for at least a few of the kingdom's mad people.

Places of resort

It is appropriate now to consider the more informal pseudo-religious sites such as 'holy waters' to which mad people both retired voluntarily and were on occasion forced to visit by their kith and kin. There can be little doubt that these holy pieces of water would have served the inhabitants of early Britain in a variety of ways – as 'wishing wells'; as sources of prophecy; as fertility-inducers; as sites of veneration, ceremony and festival – but the archaeological and iconographic evidence points beyond these specific services to a more general association between holy waters and the healing of physical and maybe even mental complaints.[91] It is not possible to surmise much about the treatment of mental complaints at these wet locations, of course, but Clarke is prepared to conclude that

> in the Gaelic areas [and] despite the broken evidence ... some of the usages which were not strongly Christian, if at all, did concern the handling of mental distress. Where treatment was by shock or cathartic frightening, spring cults can be taken as paralleling Christian exorcism but not derived from it.[92]

As the medieval period progressed a host of popular legends began to attach themselves to these sites, and it is in the legends surrounding one particular set of places – the holy wells – that mad people occasionally come to light. Some years ago an antiquarian called Robert Hope compiled a comprehensive county-by-county listing of England's holy wells and their attendant 'legendary lores', and in the process he uncovered a highly uneven geographical distribution which seemed to correlate high frequencies of wells with regions where Celtic traditions had suffered only minimal interference from Roman and other alien influences.[93] He hence found a large number of wells in Cornwall, four of which had at some point acquired a reputation for healing mental distress,[94] and if an earlier work on such matters is consulted the following observation can be encountered:

> In our forefathers' days, when devotion as much exceeded knowledge as knowledge now cometh short of devotion, there were many *bowssening* [my emphasis] places for curing of madmen, and amongst the rest, one at Altarnun in this hundred [Lewnewth Hundred, including Tintagel] called St. Nunn's Pool ...[95]

It is the practice of 'bowssening' that Clarke alludes to when writing of 'shock or cathartic frightening', for the object of the exercise was to knock the unsuspecting lunatic backwards into the water of a 'small square enclosure' which was fed from the well, and once in the water to 'tumble' this unfortunate individual around 'in a most unmerciful manner until fatigue had subdued the rage which unmerited violence had occasioned'. The cessation of rage was apparently taken as a sign of 'returning sanity', and the treatment was completed by conveying the lunatic 'with much solemnity' to a nearby church 'where certain masses were said for him'.[96] As the above quotation indicates, the best-known bowssening well was St Nunn's Well in the parish of Altarnun – and here the cure of mad people was attributed to the special healing powers bestowed upon the local waters by St Nunn – but Hope also identifies similar wells near the settlements of St Agnes (St Agnes' Well) and of Liskeard (St Cleer's Well).[97] The fourth Cornish well that he identifies as boasting a connection with madness was not really a well at all, but a large body of water called Gwavas Lake whose contents had curative qualities when administered by a saint who lived in a hermitage on its banks:

> The saint of the lake was celebrated far and near for his holiness, and his small oratory was constantly resorted to by the distressed in body and the *afflicted in mind* [my emphasis]. None ever came in the true spirit who failed to find relief. The prayers of the saint and the waters of the lake removed the pains from the limbs and the deepest sorrows from the minds.[98]

This passage is doubly interesting for highlighting not only the role of the holy waters but also the role of a hermit-saint (see below). Hope only considered English wells, it should be noted, and it would be wrong to leave this topic without referencing a study of Welsh holy wells in which no less than eight sites are identified as having an association with madness. As the author remarks: '[m]ental distress received attention [at] wells in Anglesey, Caernarvonshire and Pembrokeshire, and nervous debility was cured by a Flintshire well',[99] and it is intriguing to speculate whether these Cornish and Welsh examples of wells associated with madness together reflect specifically Celtic notions about the sorts of places likely to cure this condition.

The role of the Gwavas Lake saint in helping people 'afflicted in mind' has just been mentioned, and there is some evidence to suggest that this link between a hermit-saint and the treatment of madness was not uncommon in medieval England and Wales. The so-called 'solitary' tradition was far from unimportant to the medieval world, and Clay traces its roots in England to the wandering Celtic saints for whom asceticism – severe abstinence from normal habits and pleasures - was a way of life which supposedly preserved their special closeness to God.[100] This tradition encompassed two rather different classes of recluse: the anchorite or ancress, who spent his or her days enclosed (literally 'bricked in') between the four walls of a cell attached to a church or some other religious house; and the hermit, who tended to live alone in remote places but who might sometimes be found in more frequented places such as next to highways, under bridges and even in town centres. In both cases the recluse would occupy his or her waking hours deep in prayer, writing works of devotion and occasionally speaking with visitors, and it is this latter activity that Clarke supposes may have led many recluses to gain a 'local reputation' for a kind of therapeutic counselling:

> The various kinds of recluses who gave counselling services throughout the Medieval period were by definition individual and diverse people, and the intentions of most were not in the first place to be advisers, still

> less mental healers, but there is a great deal to be discovered about their actual impact in these roles. No hint of a common system ... can be expected; and Julian of Norwich's sensible, sincere but slightly rambling style, as suggested by her own work and by the account of her in interview, is very likely to be one of the better examples of these exchanges.[101]

It might not even be too far-fetched to claim that medieval England and Wales possessed in the anchorites, ancresses and town hermits a fairly widespread and accessible geography of 'psychiatric counsellors', but it must be admitted that the relevant evidence is circumstantial and that the few explicit references to recluses treating madness actually occur in relation to the activities and places of distinctly *in*accessible 'practitioners'.

It is instructive to mention two such individuals, and also to stress that in both cases the basis for their specific lifestyles was to be found far more in the depths of Celtic antiquity than in the 'rational' practices of the Romano-British Church centred on Canterbury.[102] The slightly earlier figure was St Cuthbert, who was born in about 634, passed through various monasteries, and finally ended up overseeing a religious colony on the island of Lindisfarne, just off the coast of north-east England.[103] It was during his days as a hermit-saint that Cuthbert's standing as both a holy man and a healer began to grow, although there is some indication that even as a youth he had performed 'abundant works' and already acquired a reputation for being especially able in the case of mental complaints. Indeed, near the beginning of his *Anonymous Life* it is stated that the author will 'refrain from telling how wonderfully the young Cuthbert put demons to flight and healed the insane by his prayers', and towards the close of the same work a similar note is included as an apology for failing to detail the saint's many later cures of demoniacs.[104] Cuthbert cured numerous mad people at places other than either Lindisfarne or Farne, whether by journeying to their own homes or through the power of prayer, but it may be that the rocky north-eastern islands where he dwelt for much of the time can still be interpreted as significant places of madness in medieval England and Wales. An interpretation along these lines seems even more appropriate in relation to St Guthlac, whose life as a saint was intimately wrapped up with the 'dismal' landscape of the medieval Fenland in eastern England, and who deliberately sought out a forbidding 'wild place' in this 'vast desert' to be his home.[105] It was here that Guthlac built his hermit's cell and began his life of extreme austerity and holiness, and it was to here that all manner of visitors – from warriors and aspirant kings seeking fortune-telling to 'simple folk' seeking cures for physical and mental infirmities – made their way. As with Cuthbert, there are various reports of Guthlac treating mad people (sometimes identified here as 'demoniacs'), and one of the cases involved a young man of noble stock called Hwaetred who became 'affected with so great a madness that he tore his own limbs with wood and iron and with his nails and his teeth', and who was taken by his parents to the 'holy places of the saints' in the hope of attaining a cure. After many unsuccessful travels Hwaetred and his parents arrived at the remote island of Crowland, where Guthlac duly dispelled the evil spirit through a combination of prayer, washing in holy water and breathing into the madman's face the 'breath of healing'.[106] In this and other cases the mad person had to be transported to Crowland, which was obviously not a journey to be undertaken lightly in medieval times, and there is also the suggestion that an association between this particular wild place and the treatment of lunacy continued even after Guthlac's death in 715 (see above).

It is apparent that some saints continued to work 'miracles' even after they had died, and a good example of this was provided by the case of a demoniac boy who was brought 'shouting and weeping and tearing his body' to Lindisfarne, and who was there cured by drinking holy waters containing earth taken from the trench in which the body of Cuthbert had been washed prior to burial.[107] In the *Ecclesiastical History* Bede recalls a couple of cases in which the remains of a holy individual were allegedly implicated in a lunatic's recovery of sanity,[108] and an exhaustive academic study of medieval pilgrimages stresses that many visits to the resting places or shrines of holy figures were made by mad people in search of a cure (sometimes voluntarily but often under compulsion):

> the violent ones were ... bound hand and foot and carried to shrines, where they lay with blood-shot eyes, foaming mouths, dishevelled hair, torn clothes – one man ripped off his clothes and ran naked and screaming through the church – and twisted features, their 'gnashing teeth' were a standard attribute. When he was a young boy the twelfth-century historian William of Malmesbury was terrified by a demoniac at a shrine who glared and spat at him.[109]

There are at least three places connected with deceased holy men which surviving records show to have received (or to have been involved in the cure of) medieval mad people, and it may be of some significance – given Clarke's observation that faith in saints and their shrines 'cannot be assumed universal in England Medievally, still less in the Celtic areas'[110] – that these three places were all located in the south and the east. The oldest of these was actually not a true shrine at all, but a church which was sited just beyond the walls of the City of London as part of a church and hospital complex dedicated to St Bartholomew,[111] and the other two sites were the shrines of St Thomas à 'Becket in Canterbury[112] and Henry VI in Windsor.[113]

Places of wandering

What must also be mentioned here (particularly given the contents of the *Vita*) are the wandering lunatics who inspired the mythology of the wild man and who supposedly littered the highways, fields and forests of medieval England and Wales. Bernheimer suggests that many mad people must have disappeared off into the 'vast stretches of forest between medieval settlements', and that they would have been joined there by numerous 'other forlorn souls' such as eccentrics, criminals and victims of religious persecution.[114] This raises the possibility that medieval mad people should be viewed through the lens of J. J. Jusserand, who long ago speculated that the many marginal and 'wayfaring' peoples of medieval England 'served as a link between the human groups of various districts' and thereby brought at least a measure of socio-spatial coherence to the emerging kingdom.[115] Furthermore, Jusserand also mentioned the professional 'fools' and 'buffoons' who travelled from place to place – and often from one noble's castle to the next – earning their keep by amusing audiences rich and poor alike,[116] and there must have been some interplay in the popular imagination between these wanderers and their wood-abiding 'madfolk' cousins.[117] Having said this, it should be acknowledged that perilously little documentary evidence has survived to cast light on the lives of actual wandering mad people, although it *was* recorded in 1309 that one Thomas de la Corderye 'became a lunatic and went wandering through Somerset and elsewhere'.[118]

In the well-known fourteenth-century allegory *Piers Plowman* written by William Langland of Malvern there is a remarkable passage which indicates both the reality of wandering mad people and the possibility of their receiving inclusionary treatment from the inhabitants of settled society.[119] Three versions of this work were prepared by Langland between 1370 and 1399, and it is described as 'written from below' and as voicing a 'whole nation's way of thinking and feeling'.[120] A measure of disagreement exists over the extent to which Langland condemns social outsiders, and hence over his views regarding the legitimate scope of Christian charity,[121] but what cannot be denied is his compassionate attitude towards wandering mad people. He introduces these individuals thus:

> But there are other beggars, healthy in appearance,
> Who want their wits – men and women also.
> They are the lunatic lollers and leapers about the country,
> And are mad as the moons grow more or less.
> They are careless of winter and careless of summer,
> They move with the moon, and are moneyless travellers,
> With a good will, but witless, through many wide countries.[122]

The poet decides that these 'lunatic lollers' are not really beggars at all, since they actually 'beg of no man' despite being 'silverless' and also 'barefoot and breadless', and he then offers the even more startling revelation that these curious travellers – although being neither preachers nor miracle-doers – should be interpreted as God's 'apostles' or 'privy disciples'; as his 'servants' or his 'jesters'; as his very own 'minstrels of heaven':

> . . . you rich men, should you receive truly,
> Welcome and honour and help with your presents,
> God's minstrels and his messengers and his merry jesters,
> Who are lunatic lollers and leapers about the country;
> For under God's secret seal their sins are covered.[123]

Elsewhere Langland urges 'Holy Church' to look after 'all fools and frantik folk who are in default of judgment' and over whom the Devil can exert 'no mastery', and towards the end of the poem he calls the 'fools' who reject the Devil's ministrations to stay with 'Holy Church' as she faces the evil hoards mustering under the banner of 'Anti-Christ'. The inspiration for these tracts was almost certainly contemporary notions of divine enthusiasm and of being 'fools for Christ's sake',[124] and the implication is that for Langland these notions signalled the virtue of treating worldly mad people with both respect and kindness on account of their special closeness to God. It has been hypothesized on at least one occasion that Langland himself must have been a disturbed mystic experiencing life as a vagrant 'lunatic loller',[125] but whatever the truth of the matter there can be no doubt that *Piers* casts a light on the itinerant insane which departs radically from the whippings and expulsions revealed by the records of late-medieval German towns.[126]

It might even be conjectured that the message conveyed in a text such as *Piers* would have made it easier for people in late-medieval England and Wales to accept the eccentricities of an individual such as Margery Kempe, who lived most of her life in an 'ordinary house' in an 'ordinary street' – in Fyncham Street, Kings Lynn[127] – but who also imposed her madness upon the inhabitants of the many different places that she visited or passed through. She certainly travelled widely, undertaking a lengthy pilgrimage to Rome and the Holy Land, and in subsequent years she went on minor pilgrimages to holy places in England and to shrines in northern Germany, travelled to have audiences with various prominent Churchmen, and at one point ended up on trial for heresy in Leicester.[128] It was this geographical mobility that rendered her autobiography so valuable 'in the light which it throws upon the life of the fifteenth century in one of the more important English towns and on the roads from shrine to shrine and from town to town',[129] and it was this mobility that also allowed her text to be peppered with 'poetic descriptions of landscapes'.[130] However, R. W. Chambers does consider whether or not

> Things might have been easier for Margery if she had been a recluse. At large in the world people found her a nuisance. In a cell, where people could come and speak to her when they wished and depart when they liked, Margery would have fitted better into medieval life.[131]

Herbert Thurston wonders something similar, and in the process contrasts the life of a cell-bound ancress with Margery's insistence 'on going everywhere',[132] but the salient finding is that for all her undoubted nuisance value this particular wandering mad person was neither shunned nor committed to a cell, and was for the most part left in peace to drift in and out of settled society as she pleased.

CONCLUDING COMMENTS: TOTALITY AND DIFFERENCE, NATURE AND SOCIETY

There is a very real danger that interpretations of the medieval mad-business – particularly when stressing 'darkness' and exclusionary spatial practices, but the danger also arises in claiming too much about 'light' and inclusionary spatial practices – can become *totalizing* exercises where the desire to provide all-encompassing statements obliterates all of the many *differences* (some extremely subtle, some blindingly obvious) that existed in medieval thought and action surrounding the object of madness. Furthermore, such totalizing exercises are inevitably insensitive to geographical variations in the mad-business, since they commonly proceed as if everywhere in the medieval world witnessed the kinds of dealings with mad people that seemingly occurred in fourteenth- and fifteenth-century Germany. It is precisely this realization that permeates S. E. Jeliffe's self-confessed 'rambling' discussion of medieval psychiatry, since he acknowledges that this animal varied greatly between 'geographical situations' and then challenges the 'Dark Ages' stereotype with reference to the relatively enlightened practices of medieval Arabia.[133] And it is much the same realization that shapes Clarke's text, where his inquiry into an incredible range of spirit beliefs, religious interventions and medical technologies is itself underlain by a feeling for the complex political, cultural and social geographies of medieval Britain (including both grander regional patterns and subtle local variations). If there are here 'missing links' in the story of how nature and society come together, then they are – perhaps even more for the medieval world than for the more interconnected post-medieval world – resolutely geographical ones: the barely explicable but none the less real specificities of the different regions, localities and places in which the 'natural' phenomenon of mental distress was culturally conceived and then socially practised upon.

As demonstrated in the essay, simply describing the many places of the mad-business in medieval England and Wales does indeed reveal myriad differences that speak at one and the same time of both the impossibility of a 'one generalization' approach and the importance of a geographical sensitivity (and they hence illustrate the more theoretical claim that critiquing totalization is almost inevitably also a retrieval of geography). In effect this essay has attempted to 'map' the geography of the medieval mad-business, although it must be admitted immediately that the result is highly sketchy and that many of the places identified never coexisted as sites, buildings or institutions associated with madness. But it may still be the case that this 'map' exposes the tip of an iceberg comprising a real but now largely unrecoverable geography, one which contained a regional patterning (perhaps with a south east-north west or a centre-margins dimension) overlain by rural and urban contrasts (perhaps with a specific London effect in operation) and pockmarked by much more locally-specific variations between individual places of madness. Could there be any significance, for instance, in the exclusively western distribution of holy wells associated with the cure of madness? Or could there be any significance in the apparent difference between a Celtic 'periphery' where mad people were taken to holy wells or to hermit-saints, and more southerly and easterly parts where greater emphasis was given to concrete provisions in the shape of monasteries, hospitals and prisons? And what can be said about the implied emergence of institutional arrangements in specific parts of the country such as in South Yorkshire, in Norfolk and in the vicinity of London? Can it be concluded that in the latter locality the seeds of specialist provision were sown in response to a perceived metropolitan demand of the late-fourteenth century – a suggestion which Carole Rawcliffe describes as 'obviously a growing need at this time for the establishment of a house devoted, in part at least, to the care of lunatics'[134] – and can it also be concluded that a 'knock-on' effect led to the opening of more than one London asylum, or was it that the conversion of Bethlem into an asylum discouraged more extensive London-based experiments in this direction?[135] Alternatively, might not Bethlem's example have inspired developments elsewhere, perhaps at the hospitals in Bath, Chichester and Salisbury, and might it not also have influenced the practices of southern monasteries with respect to their treatment of mentally distressed monks and nuns? These questions are clearly built around little more than imaginative speculation, but what may be concluded from this excursion into the untidy geography of the medieval mad-business – complete with its thoroughly *intermingled* exclusionary and inclusionary elements – is that it can best be described using the terms that Michel Serres employs when examining Foucault's thoughts on medieval madness: '[t]he pre-Classical [pre-1600] period ... can be imagined as the original chaotic space in which madness had many points of contact with the world'.[136]

NOTES

1 My underlying understanding in this essay runs somewhat against the 'constructionist' claim – as set in train by the 'anti-psychiatrists' – that there is no reality other than normal human complexities and sufferings behind the labels of 'mental illness', 'madness', 'lunacy', 'insanity' or whatever terminology is being employed. In this respect I sympathize with a view that incorporates an element of 'essentialism' in assuming that, notwithstanding the power and the potential oppression of 'labelling', there *is* still an inner reality (a 'state of being') to the kinds of experiences, interpretations, despairs, frustrations and angers lived through by many people who might receive the sorts of labels mentioned above. In this respect I have been influenced by the arguments in P. Hirst and P. Woolley, *Social Relations and Human Attributes* (London, 1982).

2 H. C. Burdett, *Hospitals and Asylums of the World, Vol. I: Asylums – History and Administration* (London, 1891), p. 40.

3 G. Zilboorg, 'The dark ages of psychiatric history', *Journal of Mental & Nervous Disorders*, 74 (1931), 610–35, reprinted in G. Zilboorg and G. W. Henry, *A History of Medical Psychology* (New York, 1941).

4 J. Sibbald, 'Insanity in the Middle Ages', *Journal of Mental Science*, 23 (1877), 337.

5 J. R. Whitwell, *Historical Notes on Psychiatry (Early Times – End of Sixteenth Century)* (London, 1936), p. 142.

6 L. E. Martin, *Mental Health/Mental Illness: Revolution in Progress* (New York, 1970), p. 9.

7 G. W. Henry, 1941, 'Mental Hospitals', being chapter 14 in Zilboorg and Henry, *Medical Psychology*, pp. 560–1.

8 M. Foucault, *Madness and Civilization: A History of Insanity in the Age of Reason* (London, 1967), p. 8; G. Rosen, *Madness in Society: Chapters in the Historical Sociology of Mental Illness* (Chicago, 1968), pp. 139–43.

9 Foucault, *Madness and Civilization*, pp. 7–8, 10–13. Foucault's account is chiefly concerned with the powerful symbolism whereby 'water and madness have long been linked in the dreams of European [peoples]' (p. 12); but he does seek to explain why in the late-medieval period the 'figure of the ship of fools and its insane crew [should] all at once invade the most familiar landscapes' (p. 13), and he does insist that this dream vessel 'had a real existence – for they did exist, these boats that conveyed their insane cargo from town to town' (p. 8). A scathing attack on claims regarding the reality of 'madships' is launched in W. B. Maher and B. Maher, 'The Ship of Fools: *Stultifera Navis* or *Ignis Fatuus*', *American Psychologist*, 37 (1982), 756–61, and echoed in K. Jones and A. J. Fowles, *Ideas on Institutions: Analysing the Literature on Long-Term Care and Custody* (London, 1984), pp. 30–1, who accuse Foucault of 'inventing' history. A more sophisticated critique – which questions Foucault's extrapolations from his sources, but which also appreciates the insights generated by his 'rhapsody on the power of water' – is provided in H. C. E. Midelfort, 'Madness and Civilization in Early Modern Europe: A Reappraisal of Michel Foucault', in B. Malament (ed.), *After the Reformation: Essays in Honour of J. H. Hexter* (Philadelphia, 1980), pp. 247–65.

10 The term 'mad-business' is used to identify the great variety of places, particularly institutional ones, that have acquired an association with mental distress over the centuries. In so doing the example of I. Macalpine and R. A. Hunter, *George III and the Mad-Business* (London, 1969) is followed.

11 I. Galdston, 'Psyche and Soul: Psychiatry in the Middle Ages', in I. Galdston (ed.), *Historic Derivations of Modern Psychiatry* (New York, 1967), p. 21.

12 J. S. P. Tatlock, 'Geoffrey of Monmouth's *Vita Merlini*', Speculum, XVIII (1943) 265–87.

13 Foucault, *Madness and Civilization*, p. ix. It should be acknowledged that the 'phenomenological' overtones of these prefatory comments – with their allusion to a true language of madness now silenced by centuries of speaking in the language of 'Reason' (or 'Non-Madness') – earned Foucault much criticism, and in later editions of the work he suppressed the original preface. However, it could be argued that his chapter 1 – which deals with both medieval 'openness' to madness and the beginnings of exclusion – makes less sense in the absence of the original preface.

14 The most famous critique of Foucault's text, and one which takes issue with his positing of two great oppositional entities ('Reason' and 'Madness') marching down the ages, is J. Derrida, 'Cogito and the history of madness', in Derrida, *Writing and Difference* (London, 1981), pp. 31–63. See also R. Boyne, *Foucault and Derrida: The Other Side of Reason* (London, 1990).

15 Foucault, *Madness and Civilization*, pp. 9–10, and note that Foucault claims Gheel to have been a 'shrine that became a ward, a holy land where madness hoped for deliverance' (p. 10). Moreover, he refers to the late-medieval towns where lunatics were sometimes confined as 'places of counterpilgrimage' (p. 10).

16 *Ibid.*, pp. 3–7.

17 *Ibid.*, p. 11. See also Midelfort, 'Madness and Civilization', p. 249.

18 Foucault suggests that madness became a 'major figure' of European culture towards the end of the Middle Ages, 'symbolising a great disquiet ... a menace and mockery, the dizzying unreason of the world' (Foucault, *Madness and*

Civilization, p. 13), and he obviously supposes this perceptual development to have been paralleled by the gradual emergence of exclusionary spatial practices. See also Rosen, *Madness in Society*, p. 150.

19 B. Clarke, *Mental Disorder in Earlier Britain: Exploratory Essays* (Cardiff, 1975).

20 It is important to recognize that this essay has been written by someone with an academic background in the discipline of geography, and that he strongly supports the claims currently being made by geographers and others about the value of conceptualising 'society' as always being at once a *spatial* phenomena (something 'accomplished' in and 'constituted' through geographical space). See J. Bird *et al.* (eds.), *Mapping the Futures: Local Cultures, Global Change* (London, 1993); D. Gregory, *Geographical Imaginations* (Oxford, 1994); E. Soja, *Postmodern Geographies: The Reassertion of Space in Social Thought* (London, 1989).

21 C. Philo, 'The Space Reserved for Insanity: Studies in the Historical Geography of the Mad-Business in England and Wales', Unpublished PhD thesis (Cambridge, 1992, ch. 2).

22 The poem, in translation from the original Latin, can be found in B. Clarke (ed.), *Life of Merlin: Geoffrey of Monmouth's* Vita Merlini (Cardiff, 1973). Unattributed quotations and phrases in this section of the essay are from this source. For details about the poem, its dating, its manuscript survivals and its author, see *ibid.*, 'Introduction' and chs. 1–6; J. J. Parry and R. A. Caldwell, 'Geoffrey of Monmouth', in R. S. Loomis (ed.), *Arthurian Literature in the Middle Ages: A Collaborative History* (Oxford, 1959), pp. 72–93; N. Tolstoy, *The Quest for Merlin* (London, 1985), chs. 1–2.

23 A. O. H. Jarman, *The Legend of Merlin (An Inaugural Lecture)* (Cardiff, 1960), p. 6. Jarman distinguishes between the 'continental tradition' which tells of Merlin's early life up to and including his involvement with Arthur, and the Welsh, Scottish and Irish traditions which coalesce to give the rather older Merlin depicted in Geoffrey's *Vita*. See also Tolstoy, *Quest*, p. 23, who suggests that the 'Arthurian' Merlin stories are set in the first part of the fifth century, whereas the *Vita* stories are set in the late-sixth century.

24 Some time in the 1130s Geoffrey wrote his *Historia Regum Britanniae*, a pseudo-history based upon an earlier text by a Welsh priest called Nennius, and this culminates with the exploits of Arthur alongside a figure called Merlinus Ambrosius: see Jarman, *Legend*, pp. 9–11; Parry and Caldwell, 'Geoffrey of Monmouth', pp. 81–5.

25 These shadowy origins are discussed in the secondary texts already referenced, but see in particular Jarman, *Legend*, pp. 3–23. For the Welsh material, see A. O. H. Jarman, 'The Welsh Myrddin Poems', in Loomis (ed.), *Arthurian Literature*, pp. 20–30: for the Scottish material see A. P. Forbes (ed.), *Lives of St. Ninian and St. Kentigern* (Edinburgh, 1874); H. D. L. Ward, 'Lailoken (or Merlin Silvester)', *Romania*, XXII (1893), 504–26: for the Irish material see J. G. O'Keeffe (ed.), *Buile Suibhne (The Frenzy of Suibhne), Being the Adventures of Suibhne Geilt* (London, 1913).

26 One commentator – M. Gaster, 'The Legend of Merlin', *Folk-Lore*, XVI (1905), 407–26 – claims that the legend originated from within a broadly Christian tradition, and so denies its Celtic roots, but in a response – J. L. Weston, 'Response', *Folk-Lore*, XVI (1905), 427 – it is objected that Gaster only considers the early Merlin (and in particular the birth-story) and that his conclusion

'affects nothing in Merlin's later life and offers no parallel to the shape-shifting which was so marked a feature of his career; nor for his wood-abiding madness and his prophecies'.

27 According to B. Clarke, 'Calidon and the Caledonian Forest', *Bulletin of the Board of Celtic Studies*, XXIII (1969), 191–201, Calidon can be traced to a series of wooded tracts 'east of Dumfries, in Annandale, Liddesdale and the valleys and fells east of Carlisle' (198). An even more precise site identification is attempted in Tolstoy, *Legend*, ch. 5 and map, p. 61.

28 Clarke, *Life of Merlin*, p. 57.

29 R. Bernheimer, *Wild Men in the Middle Ages: A Study in Art, Sentiment and Demonology* (Cambridge, MA, 1952), pp. 1–2. See also C. McIntosh, 'The Eternal Wild Man', *Country Life Annual*, 72 (1972), 72–3.

30 Bernheimer, *Wild Men*, pp. 2–3. See also E. Dudley and M. E. Novak, 'Introduction', in E. Dudley and M. E. Novak (eds.), *The Wild Man Within: An Image in Western Thought from the Renaissance to Romanticism* (Pittsburgh, 1972), pp. ix–xi, who develop the same theme with respect to the seventeenth and eighteenth centuries.

31 Bernheimer, *Wild Men*, p. 9.

32 Bernheimer directly addresses the association of wildness with the negativity or the 'deficiency' of madness, and he also discusses Merlin as an excellent literary example of where the two conditions fuse together (Bernheimer, *Wild Men*, pp. 12–14).

33 It is important to realize – particularly given the overall direction in which my argument is heading – that Bernheimer supposes the medieval wild man to have possessed some positive qualities alongside the negative ones already listed: indeed, he stresses the interpretative tension that existed in artistic and literary portrayals between ('on the side of life') the wild man as both a guardian of animals and a source of 'advice' for ordinary humans, and ('on the side of death') the wild man as an ugly, bad-tempered cannibal skulking in his 'wilderness habitat' (Bernheimer, *Wild Men*, p. 44).

34 Clarke, *Life of Merlin*, p. 113.

35 Tolstoy, *Legend*, pp. xv–xvi. In the ms. versions of the stories involving Merlin, Myrrdin and the other figures, most of which were transcriptions prepared by clerics during the later-Medieval period, the deity with whom Merlin communes almost inevitably acquires the gloss of the Christian 'God'.

36 *Ibid.*, pp. 142–3. See also N. Drury, *The Shaman and the Magician: Journeys Between the Worlds* (London, 1982), p. 3, who describes the shaman as an 'intermediary between the sacred and profane worlds, between (hu)mankind and the realm of gods and spirits'.

37 *Ibid.*, p. 144.

38 A plausible claim is that Merlin (and shamans more generally) should be interpreted in the context of the 'Trickster' archetype familiar to anthropologists: see *ibid.*, ch. 12; P. Radin, *The Trickster: A Study in American Indian Mythology* (London, 1956), pp. 168–9, who describes this figure as a crucial symbol in which 'opposite psychological entities' collide, and in which he or she can be 'god, animal, human being, hero, buffoon', as well as 'good and evil, denier, affirmer, destroyer and creator'.

39 Tatlock, 'Geoffrey', p. 282. Tatlock interprets the whole work as a 'light, entertaining poem on Merlin and his madness' (p. 278), although this description should not obscure the seriousness of the more general points that he is making about Medieval reactions to madness.

40 *Ibid.*, p. 284.

41 *Ibid.*, pp. 280–1, and see the vigorous critique of existing historical works pursued in his note 1, p. 281. See also E. A. Wright, 'Medieval Attitudes towards Mental Illness', *Bulletin of the History of Medicine*, 7 (1939), 352–6.

42 P. B. R. Doob, *Nebuchadnezzar's Children: Conventions of Madness in Middle English Literature* (New Haven, 1974), esp. pp. 153–8. Doob's basic thesis is that medieval society perceived madness as a sin in itself or as a punishment for past sins, and this means that she places a religious and decidedly Christian template over the medieval response to madness. She describes Merlin as an 'Unholy Wild Man' – an individual 'driven mad by God's grace so that he may suffer and eventually be saved' (p. 139) – and adds that 'throughout the poem madness and moral depravity are equated' (p. 157). If she is correct, and if her criticisms of Tatlock are valid (p. 153), then the *Vita* emblematizes a highly condemnatory medieval stance towards madness which in no way stands as a 'victory for humaneness and common sense'. But the rigidness with which Doob connects up her argument to medieval Christianity is surely her undoing, for the origins of the Merlin legend (and particularly of its madness theme) can be traced to Welsh, Scottish and Irish communities whose pagan and Celtic character had little in common with the teachings of the Church based in Rome. A similar regret at the rigidity of Doob's thesis is expressed in L. Feder, *Madness in Literature* (Princeton, 1980), note 7, p. 299.

43 Jarman, 'Myrddin Poems', p. 21, and this translation of the *Afallenau* is reproduced in Clarke, *Life of Merlin*, app. II. Jarman suggests that this poem may have been committed to written verse form as early as 850 (Jarman, 'Myrddin Poems', pp. 20–1).

44 H. White, 'The Forms of Wildness: Archaeology of an Idea', in Dudley and Novak (eds.), *Wild Man*, pp. 6–7. See also Tolstoy, *Legend*, p. 192, who stresses that the wild man has never been conceived of as totally 'remote in time and space', but has rather been thought of as 'just out of sight, over the horizon, in the nearby forest'.

45 Bernheimer, *Wild Men*, p. 12. This quote indicates just how difficult it is to sort out the various components – fictitious, symbolic and even real – that became entangled in the wild man mythology *and* in the stories surrounding Merlin. The depiction of Merlin's madness evidently owed much to the wild man mythology, whereas here Bernheimer is suggesting that this mythology was itself inspired by the reality of lunatics running away into the woods: the conclusion must be that the lines of influence leading between the respective images and realities of both madness and wildness operated in every direction possible.

46 O'Keeffe, *Buile Suibhne*, p. 23, who suggests that the actual location of Glen Bolcain is probably in northern Antrim. See also N. Fitzpatrick, 'Prologue', in N. Fitzpatrick (ed.), *Tales of the Irish Intelligentsia* (London, 1991), pp. 1–2.

47 O'Keeffe, *Buile Suibhne*, p. xxxvii.

48 Rosen, *Madness in Society*, pp. 25 and 31–4.

49 H. C. Burdett, *Hospitals and Asylums of the World, Vol. I: Asylums – History and Administration* (London, 1891), pp. 30–6. Soranus probably lived and worked in the first or second centuries, and in retrospect he is considered to be one of the most enlightened 'mad-doctors' of Ancient times: see F. G. Alexander and S. T. Selesnick, *The History of Psychiatry: An Evaluation of Psychiatric Thought and Practice from Prehistoric Times to the Present* (London, 1966), pp. 47–8.

50 Quoted in Burdett, *Hospitals and Asylums*, p. 31. See also Alexander and Selesnick, *History of Psychiatry*, pp. 47–8.

51 Soranus called for the utmost care and discretion in restraining individuals using ligatures: see Burdett, *Hospitals and Asylums*, p. 32. His proposals differed greatly from those of an earlier Roman physician called Celsus, 'who believed that rough treatment would frighten a patient out of mental illness' and who 'chained patients, starved them, isolated them in total darkness, and administered cathartics in his efforts to frighten them into health': see Alexander and Selesnick, *History of Psychiatry*, p. 48.

52 On *a priori* grounds it might be expected that exclusion would have negative connotations for a mad person, whilst inclusion would have positive connotations, but these correspondences do not seem to be born out in the case of Merlin.

53 Remarks about social status and access to differing kinds of medical response to madness – as well as a few notes on social status and the differing religious and legal discourses 'on offer' to people – are provided in Philo, 'Space Reserved for Insanity', ch. 2.

54 Sibbald, 'Insanity', p. 333.

55 W. Butler-Bowdon (ed.), *The Book of Margery Kempe, 1436: A Modern Version* (London, 1936), pp. 262–3.

56 R. Knox and S. Leslie (eds.), *The Miracles of King Henry VI* (Cambridge, 1923), pp. 170–1.

57 *Calendar of Miscellaneous Inquisitions (1219–1307)* (London, 1916), entry 2202, pp. 589–90.

58 Clarke, *Mental Disorder*, p. 56, drawing upon N. Walker, *Crime and Insanity in England, Vol. I: The Historical Perspective* (Edinburgh, 1968), esp. p. 30.

59 Clarke, *Mental Disorder*, pp. 56–7. But see also P. Allderidge, 'Hospitals, Madhouses and Asylums: Cycles in the Care of the Insane', *British Journal of Psychiatry*, 134 (1979), esp. pp. 325–6, who finds a hint that some years prior to 1482 a precedent had been established in English Common Law rendering it lawful for citizens to imprison people who were obviously mad and likely to commit a public mischief.

60 C. S. Loch, *Charity and Social Life: A Short Study of Religious and Social Thought in Relation to Charitable Methods and Institutions* (London, 1910), p. 277.

61 Clarke, *Mental Disorder*, pp. 29–30.

62 This fact can be discerned from B. Colgrave (ed.), *Two Lives of Saint Cuthbert: A Life by an Anonymous Monk of Lindisfarne and Bede's Prose Life* (Cambridge, 1940), *Anonymous Life*, p. 77, and *Bede's Prose Life*, p. 177.

63 See D. Knowles and R. N. Hadcock, *Medieval Religious Houses: England and Wales* (London, 1971), p. 63, who mention the possibility that a monastery had existed at Crowland during the eighth and ninth centuries, but are obviously on firmer

ground when stating that an abbey (a large monastery) was founded on this site during the reign of Edred (946–955).

64 *Calendar of Inquisitions Miscellaneous (1307–1349)* (London, 1916), entry 2093, p. 526. The village referenced here is presumably Drayton, which is located in Lincolnshire several miles to the north of Crowland, and it is interesting that Simon should have ended up trespassing on a park in Northamptonshire. To the best of my knowledge, this highly suggestive piece of evidence has never before been utilized in a history of madness.

65 J. W. Clark (ed.), *The Observances in Use at the Augustinian Priory of Barnwell, Cambridgeshire* (Cambridge, 1897), pp. 205–7, and note that Clark has translated the 'Observances' into Modern English.

66 Ibid., p. 207.

67 Lord Amulree, 'Monastic Infirmaries', in F. N. L. Poynter (ed.), *The Evolution of Hospitals in Britain* (London, 1964), p. 19.

68 E. H. Pearce (ed.), *The Monks of Westminster, Being a Register of the Brethren of the Convent from the Time of the Confessor to the Dissolution* (Cambridge, 1916), pp. 84 and 88, and note that both of these cases date to 1334–1335.

69 Knowles and Hadcock, *Medieval Religious Houses*, p. 41; M. A. Seymour, 'The Organisation, Personnel and Function of the Medieval Hospital in the Later Middle Ages', unpublished PhD thesis, London, 1946, pp. 30–1, who notes that the Augustinian 'Rule' was 'sufficiently elastic to enable it to be adapted to the needs of hospitals founded for the sick, leprous or impotent'.

70 R. M. Clay, *The Medieval Hospitals of England* (London, 1909), esp. pp. vii–xviii.

71 G. E. Gask and J. Todd, 'The Origins of Hospitals', in E. A. Underwood (ed.), *Science, Medicine and History: Essays on the Evolution of Scientific Thought and Medical Practice, Vol. I* (London, 1953), p. 122.

72 In Clay, *Medieval Hospitals*, ch. III, explicit attention is paid to mental distress being treated in these establishments of Medieval England. See also C. H. Talbot, *Medicine in Medieval England* (London, 1967), pp. 182–5, who provides an account of the role played by medieval hospitals in treating mad people.

73 *Statutes of the Realm*, Vol. II (London, 1963), p. 175b (English version).

74 Ibid., p. 175a (French version).

75 For evidence of such bans, see H. C. Maxwell-Lyte and M. C. B. Dawes (eds.), *The Register of Thomas Bekynton, Bishop of Bath and Wells, 1443–1465* (Somerset, 1934), p. 289; M. E. Rubin(-Ungar), 'Charitable Activity in the Middle Ages: The Case of Cambridge', unpublished PhD thesis, Cambridge, 1984, p. 163; H. E. Salter (ed.), *A Cartulary of the Hospital of St. John the Baptist, Vol. III* (Oxford, 1917), p. xxiv (for Salter's summary) and p. 4 (for a transcription of the original Latin reference to not admitting *defectum membrorum patientes*).

76 Rubin(-Ungar), 'Charitable Activity', p. 64.

77 *Ibid.*, pp. 163–4, who supposes that 'few facilities for these tormented people existed in the Middle Ages'. Seymour argues slightly differently in claiming that the exclusion of both lunatics and other undesirables was one manifestation of a growing specialization on the part of hospitals during the late-medieval period, and that it should be seen in the context of a trend towards taking the impotent rather than the sick in order to reduce the drain on increasingly limited resources (Seymour, 'Organisation, Personnel and Function', pp. 60–84).

78 The translation from the Latin – which includes the phrase *furiosi custodiantur donec sensum adipiscantur* – is given in Clay, *Medieval Hospitals*, p. 90, and see also her commentary on pp. 33–4.

79 H. A. Wilmer and R. E. Scammon, 'Neuropsychiatric Patients Reported Cured at St Bartholomew's Hospital in the Twelfth Century', *Journal of Nervous and Mental Disease*, 119 (1954), 1–22. See also G. Mora, 'From Demonology to the *Narrenturm*', in Galdston (ed.), *Historic Derivations*, fig. 3.1, p. 43.

80 Clay, *Medieval Hospitals*, p. 34; J. M. Hobson, *Some Early and Later Houses of Pity* (London, 1926), pp. 40–1.

81 *Calendar of Patent Rolls (1367–1370)* (London, 1913), p. 449.

82 H. B. Wheatley (ed.), *The Survey of London by John Stow (Citizen of London)* (London, 1912), p. 125, which includes this passage: 'I read in the 44th. of Edward III, that a hospital in the parish of Barking Church was founded by Robert Denton, chaplain, for the sustentation of poor priests, and other both men and women, that were sick of the frenzy, there to remain till they were perfectly whole, and restored to good memory'.

83 *Ibid.*, p. 399.

84 For the history of Bethlem, see F. O. Martin, 'Bridewell and Bethlem Hospitals', in *Thirty-Second Report of the Commissioners for Inquiring Concerning Charities, dated June 30, 1837* (PP, 1840, vol. XIX, pt. 1), p. 487; E. G. O'Donoghue, 'Bethlem Hospital in History and Literature', *Under the Dome*, 20 (1911), 92–6; E. G. O'Donoghue, *The Story of Bethlem Hospital from its Foundation in 1247* (London, 1914); J. G. White, *A Short History of the Royal Hospitals of Bridewell and Bethlem* (London, 1899).

85 Quoted in A. J. Copeland, 'Bethlem Royal Hospital, Part II', *Under the Dome*, 2 (1892), 5–6.

86 For example, see *Calendar of Patent Rolls* (1281–1292) (London, 1893), p. 484, which records a protection given to the 'envoys of the Bishop and brethren of the Church of St. Mary's, Bethleem, collecting alms for the poor and inform in their hospitals there'. See also *Calendar of Patent Rolls* (1327–1330) (London, 1891), p. 446, which records a protection given to the 'Master and Brethren of the hospital of St. Mary, Bethleem'.

87 As translated from the Latin and commented upon in E. G. O'Donoghue (ed.), 'The *Visitation* of Bethlem (Four Parts)', *Under the Dome*, 10 (1901), 101–7 and 141–7, and *Under the Dome*, 11 (1902), 1–8 and 39–50.

88 *Ibid.*, 'The *Visitation* (Second Part)', *Under the Dome*, 10 (1901), 143.

89 *Ibid.*, 'The *Visitation* (Third Part)', *Under the Dome*, 11 (1902), 4.

90 *Calendar of Letter Books of the City of London, Book K* (London, 1911), p. 194.

91 J. P. Alcock, 'Celtic Water Cults in Roman Britain', *Archaeological Journal*, CXII (1965), 1–2.

92 Clarke, *Mental Disorder*, p. 141.

93 R. C. Hope, *The Legendary Lore of the Holy Wells of England* (London, 1893), esp. p. xxi.

94 Curiously, no such association between holy wells and madness seems to have grown up in the neighbouring county of Devon: see T. Brown, 'Holy and Notable Wells of Devon', *Transactions of the Devonshire Association for the Advancement of Science, Literature and Art*, 89 (1957), 205–15.

95 F. E. Halliday (ed.), *Richard Carew of Antony: The Survey of Cornwall* (London, 1953), p. 193. Carew first published his survey in 1602, and it has since provided material for a number of other compendia such as R. Hunt, *Popular Romances of the West of England (or the Drolls, Traditions and Superstitions of Old Cornwall), First and Second Series* (London, 1865).

96 Halliday, *Richard Carew*, pp. 193–4.

97 Hope, *Legendary Lore*, pp. 20 and 26. Hunt, on the other hand, declares that St Nunn's Well 'is the only one (in Cornwall), as far as I can learn, which possessed the virtue of curing the insane': see Hunt, *Popular Romances, Second Series*, p. 50.

98 Hope, *Legendary Lore*, p. 23. This lake was supposed to have been situated in a forest of beech trees that lined a tract of land occupying what is now part of Mount's Bay between the fishing towns of Newlyn and Mousehole, and (so the legend goes) the whole lot was inundated by the great flood which separated the Scilly Isles from England. See also Hunt, *Popular Romances, First Series*, pp. 218–19.

99 F. Jones, *The Holy Wells of Wales* (Cardiff, 1954). In this minutely researched study, Jones breaks down the Welsh wells both by 'type' and by 'county', and in this latter respect he says much about the geography of the wells (and see his maps 1–6, pp. 219–21), and it might be added that he regards his wells as boasting an intimate association with pre-Christian beliefs (pp. vii and 11). To the best of my knowledge, Jones's findings have never before been drawn upon in a history of madness.

100 R. M. Clay, *The Hermits and Anchorites of England* (London, 1914), p. xviii. Note that this ascetic behaviour squared with medieval conceptions of being a 'fool' for God, and it is also the case that many of these recluses were described as 'mad' or 'demented' by their contemporaries: see Clay's reference to such descriptions in the case of Richard of Hampole, the 'hermit-preacher' (p. 161, and see more generally her commentary in chs. 11 and 12).

101 Clarke, *Mental Disorder*, p. 142, and see also pp. 133–6.

102 The two cases date from the seventh and eighth centuries, by which time something of a religious struggle was occurring in England and Wales between a Celtic vision of Christianity associated with the wandering saints and centred on Lindisfarne (the 'heart of the English Christian mission') and a Roman vision of Christianity (a 'new kind of Roman colonisation'). This struggle was sparked off by Augustine's landing in Kent circa 597 and subsequent success at converting powerful Anglo-Saxon rulers to Roman Christianity: see D. L. Edwards, *Christian England: Its Story to the Reformation* (London, 1981), pp. 45–56.

103 Colgrave, *Two Lives*, pp. 1–5. This volume contains both some introductory comments on the *Lives* and translations into Modern English of the original Latin texts, and in the following notes some page references apply to Colgrave's commentary and some apply to the translated texts.

104 *Ibid.*, *Anonymous Life*, pp. 73 and 139. Note the equation here of madness with demonic possession, but note too the portrayal of the condition as something that can be cured and not as something requiring beatings or burnings. The complex issue of whether 'demonic' explanations for madness were indeed predominant in medieval England and Wales, including a detailed critique of overly simple reasoning in this respect by some historians of madness, is addressed in Philo, 'Space Reserved for Insanity', pp. 35–41.

105 B. Colgrave (ed.), *Felix's Life of Saint Guthlac* (Cambridge, 1956), p. 87.
106 *Ibid.*, pp. 127–31.
107 Colgrave, *Two Lives*, *Anonymous Life*, pp. 133–5, and *Bede's Prose Life*, pp. 289–91.
108 J. E. King (ed.), *Baedae Opera Historica (Ecclesiastical History of the English Nation), Vol. I* (London, 1930), pp. 379–83; *ibid.*, *Vol. II*, p. 29.
109 R. C. Finucane, *Miracles and Pilgrims: Popular Beliefs in Medieval England* (London, 1977), p. 108. For his more detailed analysis of mad people at shrines, see pp. 107–9. He also offers a description of the dramatic incidents surrounding the healing of demoniacs (pp. 91–2), and it is revealing that he introduces his study by imagining the 'astonishment' that a modern visitor to Becket's tomb would feel if surrounded by medieval pilgrims such as 'fettered madmen struggling at their bonds' (p. 9).
110 Clarke, *Mental Disorder*, p. 122.
111 For records of and commentaries on this establishment, including various indications of mentally distressed people visiting both the shrine in the church and the associated hospital, see Clarke, *Mental Disorder*, pp. 140–8; Clay, *Medieval Hospitals*, p. 253; T. Foster (ed.), *The Book of the Foundation of St. Bartholomew's Church and Hospital Rendered into Modern English* (London, 1980); N. Moore (ed.), *The Book of the Foundation of St. Bartholomew's Church in London* (London, 1923); Wilmer and Scammon, 'Neuropsychiatric Patients'.
112 See E. A. Abbott (ed.), *St. Thomas of Canterbury: His Death and his Miracles, Vol. I* (London, 1898), p. 244, where is quoted the report of a medieval French clerk called Garnier who told of how Thomas's earthly remains helped '[the] mad to return to their senses'. See also various cases described in *ibid.*, *Vols. I* and *II*, and assessed in Clarke, *Mental Disorder*, pp. 127 and 149–51.
113 See B. Wolffe, *Henry VI* (London, 1981), p. 354, where madness is noted as one of the most important medieval complaints which a visit to the late King's grave (or even simply praying to him) could often cure. See also various cases described in Knox and Leslie, *Miracles*, and assessed in Clarke, *Mental Disorder*, pp. 154–75.
114 Bernheimer, *Wild Men*, p. 16.
115 J. J. Jusserand, *English Wayfaring Life in the Middle Ages* (Bath, 1970), esp. pp. 11–12. This work was first published in 1889 and doubtless more recent scholars would quarrel with some of Jusserand's conclusions, although his argument about 'wayfarers' being the 'microbes' of medieval history is still subscribed to in G. M. Trevelyan, *English Social History: A Survey of Six Centuries* (London, 1944), pp. 44–5.
116 Jusserand, *Wayfaring*, pp. 118–19.
117 R. Porter, *A Social History of Madness: Stories of the Insane* (London, 1987), ch. 7.
118 *Calendar of Inquisitions Miscellaneous (1307–1349)* (London, 1916), entry 47, p. 13, which suggests that Thomas's mental condition was worsened by an argument over a piece of property.
119 A recent transcription which preserves the original Middle English text is D. Pearsall (ed.), *Piers Plowman by William Langland: An Edition of the C-Text* (London, 1978), but the passages reproduced here are taken from H. W. Wells (ed.); *William Langland: The Vision of* Piers Plowman (London, 1935), which contains a Modern English rendering based principally upon the B-Text. Note that

controversy continues as to whether Langland was indeed the author of the three surviving versions the so-called A-, B- and C-Texts.

120 Coghill, 'Introduction', in Wells, *William Langland*, p. vii.

121 Langland criticizes professional beggars and all other able-bodied but idle people, reserving some particularly biting comments for the mendicant and itinerant clergy, and it is clear that he did not regard such individuals as deserving of society's charity: see N. Coghill, 'Langland, the Naket, the Naugty and the Dole', *Review of English Studies*, 8 (1932), 303–9; M. Day, '*Piers Plowman* and Poor Relief', *Review of English Studies* 8 (1932), 445–6. However, it is also argued that Langland recognized a category or 'worthy poor' (society's many 'unfortunates') who warranted ' local acts of kindness', and that the theme of 'questing' for charity thereby remains central to the poem: see G. Sheppard, 'Poverty in *Piers Plowman*', in T. H. Aston *et al.* (eds.), *Social Relations and Ideas: Essays in Honour of R. H. Hilton* (Cambridge, 1983), pp. 169–89; B. H. Smith, *Traditional Images of Charity in Piers Plowman* (The Hague, 1966).

122 Wells, *William Langland*, p. 93 (from Passus VII). Note here that reference to madness being influenced by the phases of the moon, and hence to the original but obscure derivation of the term 'lunatic'.

123 *Ibid.*, p. 94.

124 Pearsall, *Piers Plowman*, notes, pp. 165–7, and note that he describes the fools in the scenario of 'Holy Church against Antichrist' as representing 'faithful Christians' (note, p. 364).

125 S. B. James, 'The Mad Poet of Malvern: William Langland', *The Month*, 159 (1932), 221–7, who finds evidence to support his thesis from both the poem's content and its writing style. See also J. Margin, 'Wil as fool and wanderer in *Piers Plowman*', *Texas Studies in Literature and Language*, III (1962), 535–48, who claims that the whole poem is written in the 'mode of the fool' (in the words of a witless individual blessed with 'divinely inspired visions') but goes on to argue that Langland's faith in a 'foolish' life of inner spiritual 'wandering' sits uneasily with his satirical attack on all earthly wanderers. This contradiction perhaps disappears, however, if it is remembered that Langland *does* champion the cause of one particular set of earthly wanderers – namely, the 'lunatic lollers' – in whom true 'foolishness' is clearly manifested.

126 One or two commentators have noted Langland's benevolent attitude towards mentally distressed people: see D. Chadwick, *Social Life in the Days of Piers Plowman* (Cambridge, 1922), p. 77. See also the specialist history of madness, J.Neaman, *Suggestion of the Devil: The Origins of Madness* (London, 1975), esp. pp. 131–3, who emphasizes the 'God-struck' nature of Langland's 'lunatic lollers'.

127 This house is identified by N. Marzac-Holland, *Three Norfolk Mystics* (Burnham Market, 1983), p. 43, who uses some *Account Rolls* and a *Rentale* to locate the house where John Kempe (Margery's husband) lived between 1391 and 1425.

128 For information on her trips to north German shrines and to Julian of Norwich see Porter, *Social History*, pp. 107–9.

129 R. W. Chambers, 'Introduction', in Butler-Bowden, *Margery Kempe*, p. 13.

130 Marzac-Holland, *Norfolk Mystics*, pp. 24–5.

131 Chambers, 'Introduction', p. 7.

132 H. Thurston, 'Review of *The Book of Margery Kempe*', *The Tablet*, 168 (October, 1936), 570.

133 S. E. Jeliffe, 'Some Random Notes on the History of Psychiatry of the Middle Ages', *American Journal of Insanity*, 10 n.s. (1930), 278–83.

134 C. Rawcliffe, 'The Hospitals of Later Medieval London', *Medical History*, 28 (1984), 11.

135 *Ibid.*, where it is suggested that Denton's decision to scrap his project for establishing an asylum 'may have been influenced by the sudden development of Bethlehem, a comparatively well-established institution, as an alternative centre for the custody of the mentally ill'.

136 P. Major-Poetzl, *Michel Foucault's Archaeology of Western Culture: Towards a New Science of History* (Brighton, 1983), p. 120, drawing upon M. Serres, *Hermes I: La Communication* (Paris, 1968).

FIVE

ON THE PERCEPTION OF NATURE IN A RENAISSANCE SOCIETY

GERHARD JARITZ AND VERENA WINIWARTER

For the 'report' told less of the Mozambican soldiers than of the culture that had conjured them up as its inverted self-image[1]

INTRODUCTION AND PRE-CONDITIONS

A topic such as the *Perception of Nature* for such a period as the *Renaissance* and with regard to *Society* cannot be dealt with in general, particularly not within a relatively short contribution as this one. Research into the relation between man and nature has so far mainly concentrated on a level of perception found in philosophy, theology and the sciences.[2] Dealing with sources from *c.* 1400 to *c.* 1800 this paper investigates levels of perception of Nature which might have influenced a far larger number of people than did the statements of philosophers, theologians, scientists, humanists, etc. The question of how humanity perceived Nature cannot and must not be concentrated on the thoughts of Nicolaus Cusanus, Marsilio Ficino, Giovanni Pico della Mirandola, Agrippa v. Nettesheim, Paracelsus, Giordano Bruno, Jakob Böhme or Galileo Galilei.[3]

Perception of nature cannot be seen as one, more or less uniform phenomenon – as well as culture, popular culture or everyday life must not be taken as something which can be defined, described or analysed as a homogeneous whole.[4] Perceiving nature necessarily has to mean something very different for a peasant, whose existence is daily influenced and determined by the confrontation with nature, for a theologian dealing with the subject theoretically and for didactic purposes, for the owner of land trying to maximize his revenue by exploiting nature, for somebody – whoever it might have been – being interested in her or his *own* surrounding nature or somebody dealing with *the other's* nature, for somebody to dominate nature or for somebody seeing nature in the broadest sense as a phenomenon dominating man.

In Renaissance society, dealing with nature often follows patterns similar to the treatment of various other phenomena being important enough to find their way into written or visually depicted statements:

a. It is dominated by a clear systematization and methodization of interest, by schematizing and collecting. This fact can be traced in a rich number of fields: in the prodigy collections becoming relevant at the beginning of the sixteenth century,[5] for travel descriptions,[6] for systematic reports on natural catastrophes,[7] for the creation of collections of cabinet pieces filled with 'real' objects from a nature far away,[8] for the creation and development of zoological gardens as a means of upper-class prestige and joy, etc. Those and many other developments amount to a clear change compared to medieval methods of reception and publication.

b. This does not necessarily mean, though, that all the conceptual approaches towards phenomena of nature changed in the same way.

c. On the other hand, this fact is connected with a general rise of 'interest' in the broadest sense of the word, at least being proved by the increase of various 'new' (written) information being produced and becoming available. The development and spread of printed media certainly plays its decisive role in this connection.[9] Such 'new' information, though, had to be and was included into a tradition of specific argumentation, a tradition that came from medieval times and belonged to the accepted pool of knowledge.

ASPECTS OF 'INTEREST' INTO NATURE

Closeness vs. distance

Closeness and distance represent two components of perception which can act as an indispensable pair of argumentation. They are used to motivate, to explain, or to teach. In particular, various kinds of 'distance' of nature constitute a field which was systematically brought closer to Renaissance man. Those patterns of 'closeness' and 'distance' might, on the one hand, really be understood geographically; on the other hand, though, they might be understood much more generally and with regard to the criteria of 'one's own' and/vs. 'the other's'. People working in distant and remote environment could serve as authority to testify the existence of wild and evil creatures in such remote places as, for example, the Pilatus-mountain in Switzerland. Truth could be represented not only by Classical writers or by generally accepted well-known authorities, or by secular rulers and the church, but also by the authority of 'very distant' people like Alpine cowherds giving testimony of the existence of again distant but real, strange and evil-minded beings living in the heights of the mountains and ruled by the devil.[10] Such and similar attempts to raise interest and to bring aspects of distance closer to various members of the society is one of the major components of Renaissance argumentation. It can be traced on a number of other, more general levels of a direct relation between man and nature, with which we would like to deal.

Closeness vs. distance and the level of continuous concern

Nature is an omnipresent phenomenon. This omnipresence is especially reflected in sources concerning the regulation of the economic prosperity of a rural society or a society respectively, which is dependent on and can survive only through the success of its agriculture. This is, of course, albeit to a varied degree, true for any society, anywhere and anytime.

This economic aspect also played a decisive role during the Renaissance. If perception was determined by such a material point of view, nature was in general seen as a reservoir of resources (e.g. edible plants, construction materials, dyes, etc.). Attitudes towards nature in this case were determined by questions of utilization and regulation of resource allocation.

Analyzing, for example, village laws ('Weistümer') in these terms, a large number of comparable (mass-)sources is available, mainly from the end of the fourteenth to the eighteenth century. They are an indispensable source for dealing with the 'reality' of the norm, if based on a comparative approach. This reality of the norm need not have anything to do with a reality of life. It can show a certain kind of actual approach towards problems, however, which occurred when dealing directly and economically with nature. Moreover, the village laws give regular information with regard to the management of such problems.

For one region of Austria, Lower Austria, systematic research was done with regard to the contents of village laws[11] concerning nature and environment.[12] Additionally, territorial laws were integrated into the research project.[13] Certainly, more or less nothing of a so-called ecological factor can be traced in either type of sources[14] but nearly everything is based on socio-economic components. Breaking the rules when dealing with nature as an economic resource is certainly an act to be mentioned and regulated in the village laws as well as in all kinds of other legislative sources.

Patterns of the relevance of problems and of problem solving are generally dominated by the explicit closeness of the phenomena to be

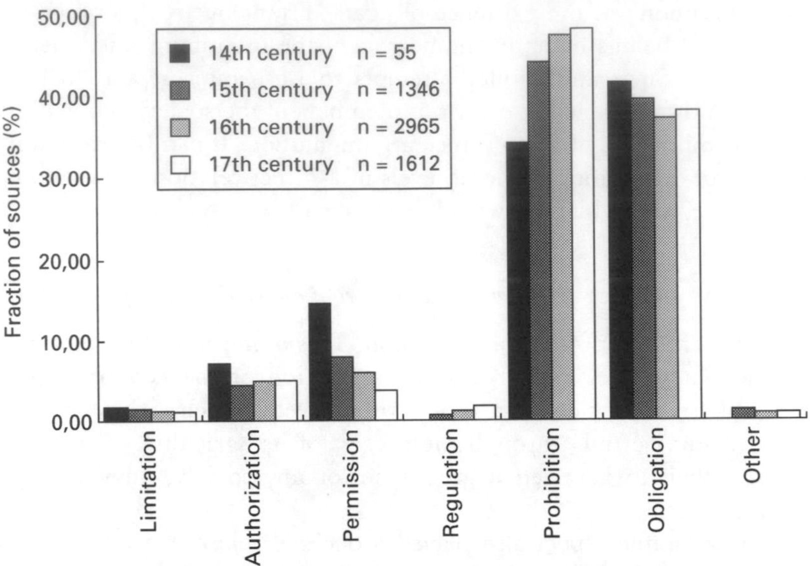

Figure 2 Patterns of environmental management by means of village laws from the fourteenth century to the seventeenth.

regulated towards 'everyday needs' of those who gave the laws and/or those who received them. They are influenced by the social hierarchy and the economic necessities within a community. They are connected with general aspects of 'development' in a given society.

For several reasons, village laws are particularly interesting sources for our questions. On the one hand, they have survived in large numbers, allowing quantitative approaches. On the other hand, they generally in most of the cases seem to be very slow in their reactions to occurring changes.

In a way highly abstracted from the sources, it is possible to follow the general development of environmental management through the centuries. Prohibitions and obligations always play the decisive role in the laws. Nevertheless, there is a slow development in their even more overwhelming relevance. All other sorts of management further decrease, to the advantage of restrictions as prohibitions and obligations. This could be attributed to the needs of more rigidly governed regions. A general overview is given in figure 2.

If obviously relevant changes touching the community life took place, there was a reaction in the laws.[15] Village laws, therefore, can be used to check the extent to which a changed image of nature really became relevant for a number of aspects of everyday confrontation with nature, in the case of peasants as well as agricultural workers or the landlords.

In the normative sources, in village laws[16] as well as in territorial laws,[17] a broad or direct approach is taken towards (in fact: against) somebody not belonging to one's own status in the broadest sense, or something not being one's own.

a. At the lowest level it concerns the general protection of fields, vineyards, etc. 'Do not throw stones into the field or the vineyard which is not yours' or similar are the typical norms on this level. The rights of the owner or user of an object have to be protected against anybody else.
b. A second level is dealing with people not being members of the community: strangers, who are excluded from community rights or only should receive them, if there was danger or an emergency. Typical examples are the protection of community forests and meadows from the collection of wood or grass respectively by strangers, prohibition on the selling of fish to strangers, before offering them to the members of the community, the protection of pastures from cattle not belonging to the community. In some cases – particularly when it concerned penalties – a remarkable distinction was made in dealing with strangers. One characteristic example of sixteenth-century village laws comes from Krummbach in Lower Austria.[18] The fine for the stranger was to be five times as high as the one for a member of the community, accompanied by very severe corporal punishment.
c. The third level is the one dealing with objects or people from abroad or from outside the territory respectively and the protection from them. This level was often very generalized and took no particular account of natural resources being endangered.

In general all these norms are certainly based on economic needs. Checking the different aspects in connection with the above-mentioned three levels, the following situation appears to reflect a general pattern: Level I represents a phenomenon being relevant during the whole period from the fourteenth century onwards until the eighteenth century; level II got its major importance particularly from the sixteenth century onwards, while level III received its main emphasis as a typical pattern of the seventeenth century, with special emphasis on the reduction of the rights of foreigners whether they were beggars or craftsmen. Some matters, obviously economically relevant at the highest level, play their role during the whole period. For example, we find paragraphs concerning laws against the import of Hungarian wine to

Austria, already dating from the fifteenth century and continuing through the sixteenth and seventeenth centuries.

'Distance' and 'closeness' play a decisive role. One's own nature was to be protected from the influence of others. This attempt to cope with the influence of others, though, became increasingly important and must have been seen under new perspectives. A decisive development took place during the Renaissance, in particular. On the one hand, one's own nature obviously had to be better protected from harm and influences from the outside. On the other hand, the protection no longer concentrated on rather small communities or ended at their borders but focused more and more at the level of territory. Again, even if one's own nature did not change factually, the attitude towards it became modified. Closeness and distance received other meanings.

The question of change in the period under consideration may be applied to two areas of exemplary interest: (1) the problem of dealing with woods and (2) the problem of dealing with fish in the laws. One way of approaching these areas is through changes in penalties for forbidden acts.[19]

Woods and man's relation to them play a decisive role in environmental history research in particular.[20] In the case of uncontrolled cutting and deforestation, the main emphasis in normative sources was put on the question of forest protection. Analysis of the penalties mentioned in the village laws suggests a change in the relevance of the factor 'woods' in society, certainly based mainly on its economic importance.

If all relevant material concerning forests is analysed, we find that the issue of fines is dominant. The differences in amount, however, are remarkable. The variation in the case of the *same* offence may be shown in one example. In the village law of Araburg at the beginning of the sixteenth century, violations in the landlord's forests incurred a fine of 32 Pfund, as against 6 Schilling 2 Pfennig for the same offence in the community woods.[21]

To systematize this approach, it is necessary to take account of the clear distinction between woods of the community and woods of the landlords. Village laws represent the landlords' interests as well as the interests of the peasant communities. Although a clear distinction between the two sets of interest is difficult to maintain, the following development can be shown. The offences with regard to both kinds of forest might often be the same, but one sees quite clearly the much higher concern of the landlords to protect their interests in woods, than it is evident for the community woods. Irrespective of the actual damage, breaking of the law with regard to the landlords' interests incurred much higher penalties.

The example of fishing regulations proves that different strategies were applied to different parts of the environment, albeit with comparable aims. With woods regulations, the decisive change took place from the fifteenth to the sixteenth century; in the example of fishing regulations a striking increase in high fines emerges in the seventeenth century. For both phenomena a decrease of the amount of fines can be traced through the eighteenth century. The strongest articulation of fishing rights is therefore to be found in the seventeenth century, whereas this already took place 100 years earlier for the woods.

But fishing regulations also involve a distinction between different interests. The economically relevant 'nature of the landlord' is even more explicitly separated from the 'nature of the community'. Landlord's rights are much more important than community's rights. Again parts of the landlord's interests in economically relevant nature are much more protected than the community's. This is particularly true with regard to the fines mentioned in the village laws.

The 'same' nature, therefore, can obviously be another nature. Closeness concerning the situation, the objects and the region may at the same time mean distance with regard to their value or their valuation respectively. The landlord's nature is of another nature than the peasant community's nature.

This increase of the gap between the ruling class and the ruled class is quite generally typical for an economic development in the sixteenth and seventeenth centuries. If an obvious danger concerning the economic situation was occurring early, as certainly could be proved for the resource of forests and woods in the sixteenth century, the reaction and the development of a greater gap also took place earlier. Nevertheless, there was certainly no really radical change but a continuous development influenced by different factors.

One last example is intended to show the large difference between the valuation of economically relevant natural resources and the value of a clean environment, reaching from clean wells to clean brooks, riversides and roads. Again most of the penalties are fines, although reparations do play a bigger role as compared to fish penalties, at least in the eighteenth century. Remarkable, though, is the decrease of direct economic relevance of a clean environment, even if dirty water could heavily threaten the health of a community. The modest fines which make for 92 per cent of all the penalties also obviously meant a radical decrease of protection.

Besides analysing those (to a certain degree) remarkable differences and changes concerning the penalties, it must also be asked whether other changes are traceable in this rather static group of sources. Could they show particularities of society in the period of the Renaissance? Did these coincide with developments in other areas of life? One rather interesting answer to these questions is that, concerning explicit problems or offences being dealt with in the norms, no significant change can be found. This means more or less that in an economic relation of man and nature, which can be considered as an indispensable pre-condition of life and lifestyle, the remarkable changes to be found in humanist thought, in art, and literature did not initiate a special reaction.

On a lower level, though, some new characteristics deserve to be emphasized. This touches, for example, the above mentioned systematization and classification concerning particular aspects of dealing with nature. With regard to penalties, woods regulation obviously acquired an earlier relevance concerning a distinction between the nature of the landlord and the nature of the community; in another respect, fish regulation shows some general changes.

It is often the case that analysis of legislative sources leads from rather general norms to ones which go into close detail, thus creating new distinctions and shades of differentiation. This is also the case with attempts to classify nature in the sixteenth century.[22] With fishing, for example the regulations covered catching fish at certain times, by certain persons, and with certain tools – a remarkable emphasis on details sometimes dealing with every thinkable possibility. To a certain degree we might talk of a 'scientification' of the norm. Therefore, when concerning the obvious danger to forests and woods it is penalties which play the decisive role, while with regard to fish it requires a more elaborate classification system, which is supposed to protect the amount of available fish – a situation replaced by a clear distinction concerning fines only in the seventeenth century.

For other evidence we know about similar or comparable 'protectionist' tendencies in the period of territorialization from the end of the fifteenth century onwards. Only soap produced in the country should, for example, be sold and used in Austria, and restrictions were given concerning the import of Venetian soap,[23] etc. Sumptuary laws in Germany went through a comparable general development.[24] The normative sources dealing with natural resources, with the access to them and with their protection fit well into this trend, though perhaps somewhat delayed. A general and particular emphasis on all the three mentioned levels of relevance simultaneously can be found only in the seventeenth century. Through this, the distant became closer and the close became part of a more general pattern.

Among the parts of nature regulated in the mentioned normative sources, one which is multifunctional but rather rarely dealt with (about fifty paragraphs from the fifteenth to the eighteenth century) is the riverside, providing the landlord or community with grass, woods and fruit and serving as pasture, garbage deposit or fishing ground. It is to a high degree non-cultivated land being used for a larger number of purposes. Once again, the wide variety of possible uses and abuses of the riverside became significant in the sixteenth century. Remarkable from the economic point of view are the conflicts possible in perceptions of its function. We find not only as above mentioned, a polarity between community's and landlord's interests, or a restriction of the rights of strangers. The riverside can also be used as a deposit[25] as well as a resource.[26] Moreover, it could prove relevant to protect the riverside woods, but also to remove it,[27] when other economical interests became more important. Concerning the riverside of the Danube from about 1530 onwards we find the often repeated law to keep it clear of woodland to make it possible to pull the boats upstream.[28] In this case, the other's nature had developed a function contrary to one's own nature and vice versa.[29]

Closeness vs. distance and the level of exceptional concern

Natural phenomena have always been important regarding their description, their interpretation and their meaning. This is particularly so during the period of the Renaissance when interest in them accelerated.[30] But it is in no way just a kind of descriptive interest which confronts us. On the one hand, we can observe the already-known systematizations and classifications and, on the other, a declared and consequent interest to deal with the meaning and the moral of those phenomena. The systematic extraction of their moral could even be called a paradigmatic act of the Renaissance.

Blood rain is a good example. Its appearance in the sources shows clearly a combination of closeness and distance, of nature and 'supernature', again without any actual contradictions or borderlines between them.[31]

The occurrence of blood rain is dependent on certain meteorological pre-conditions. It is rare, but also more or less regular – about one instance per year, or at least biennial blood rains seem to be typical. A powerful wind from the Sahara is needed to produce it. In such cases sand from the Sahara, the cause of most blood rains, is transported in larger amounts to the North either directly via the Alps or across part of the Atlantic Ocean, drifting above Europe from the west. Such events can be continental in dimension, possibly reaching the Alps, Germany and Scandinavia, in some places clearly recognized when connected with rain or snow, in other places untraceable.

Blood rain, though, is also a matter of perception, thus its importance for our topic. Analysis of the sources makes it clear that the perception and treatment of the blood rain phenomena is very much dependent on the mentality or patterns of thought in a given society at a certain time.

In Antiquity, blood rain and other natural phenomena already had a role as *prodigia*,[32] and the phenomenon never completely lost its relevance. In the Renaissance, however, it began to flourish supported by the new medium of print. A real wave of literary products (books, pamphlets and broadsheets) issued forth in the sixteenth century containing collections of exceptional natural phenomena from Antiquity to present times and dealing with their role as *prodigia*, usually dealing not with specific future events but general religious and moral warnings and admonitions.[33] Starting from Italy (Gaspar Torella, 1507), this type of literature spread throughout Europe. Classical collections of them (Julius Obsequens, fourth century) were printed in a number of different editions. In Germany the print medium became particularly popular in Protestantism in dealing with the natural phenomena as a sign either of the fury (Gnesiolutheran) or of the mercy (Philippines) of God.[34] The normally rather distant phenomenon of blood rain was made more familiar for a general audience.

It might be seen as typical evidence that the field of Catholic miraculous belief of the Middle Ages was replaced by the systematization of the miraculous signs of nature. Catholicism itself clung to the miracles of saints. Only belatedly, at the very end of the wave of *prodigia* literature, did Catholicism incorporate those means systematically, and the most universal collection of *prodigia* was published by the Jesuit Caspar Schott in 1662. In France, though, *prodigia* literature was from the very beginning a domain of the Catholics.

The mentioned situation led to the obvious fact that nature, or certain phenomena of nature, must have been perceived differently in different regions at different times and by the members of different religious bodies. Blood rain makes the case in an exemplary way. Only to a limited extent did the perception of the exceptional natural phenomenon possess a natural background.

Firstly, we analysed the number of occurrences in a certain period. The difference in the number of cases (being based on European examples) through the centuries certainly cannot have been caused only by the different rate of sources having survived. The thirteenth, fourteenth and fifteenth centuries each contain less than 10 reported cases, whereas in the sixteenth century we find 90 cases, and 100 in the seventeenth century. The number goes down to 43 in the eighteenth century to finally rise to 146 in the nineteenth, which is comparable with the 50 cases reported in our century until 1950, accounting for the given natural variability of blood rain.

The Reformation and post-Reformation period obviously shows a striking rise of blood rain events in comparison to the periods before and after. Only with the onset of scientific treatment of natural phenomena in the nineteenth century are the high numbers of the sixteenth and seventeenth centuries reached again.

Secondly, we compared religious bodies and area. In doing so for different regions of Germany we find a high density of data in the Protestant areas with the peaks in Saxony and in Wurttemberg, with 27 and 16 cases respectively in the sixteenth and seventeenth centuries. This shows the overwhelming relevance of the phenomenon in mainly Protestant regions (128 of 190 cases of the sixteenth and seventeenth century = 67 per cent).

Again, it can clearly be shown that the exceptional natural phenomenon (in our example, the blood rain) must have been perceived very differently in various European regions. A large number of reported cases may be seen as a proof that the phenomena were brought much closer to the population than in areas with low quantities of occurrences. A description of the distant or at least only rarely visible could become part of the personal experience of people, although they perhaps never were confronted in their life with a situation like it. The supernatural certainly stayed supernatural or a matter of God's will, respectively but became very well known and could thereby be used as a source for means of didactic teaching on God's fury or mercy.

Distance vs. closeness: the visual representation

As the previous examples have shown, the perception of nature is significant for the Renaissance on different levels and to differing degrees of concern. This situation can be demonstrated by a number of further examples, concentrating in particular on the polarity between one's own nature and the nature of the other. To an extent, this has already been demonstrated through the 'landlord's nature' and the 'community's nature' in the village laws.

Once again, the phenomenon of closeness can disclose the same trends in source materials which are very different from the materials dealt with above.

One level of perception which seems very different at first sight also appears to possess characteristics very similar to the components dealt with above. It is the visual depiction of nature. A large number of books and articles about nature in the pictorial arts has been published, and there is no space here for rehearsing the facts and interpretations already made. One aspect, though, should be discussed: the importance of the phenomenon of closeness of nature in the images, which show the same trends as the written sources.

Distance and closeness are of the utmost importance in those pictorial sources of the Renaissance period which are devoted to the depiction of nature in the broadest sense. Book and broadsheet-illustrations, paintings, woodcuts and copperplate engravings, etc. are in many ways illustrating a written or spoken word, to an extent which was certainly unknown before. All the well-known new interests do not only create new topics to be written or talked about, but also to be painted or drawn.

Phenomena and creatures from a near and distant world are systematically collected, at least in their depicted form. Various and numerous images support the information given by writing. More or less 'everything' can be visualized, independent of the actual knowledge about its original appearance. There is certainly no general difference to be made between objects which – from our knowledge of today – really did exist and those which were a product of imagination. They may possess the same level of reality, in description and in depiction.

In the Renaissance, it is still possible to depict the same towns, houses, people and nature as part of different areas, be they in Poland, Lithuania or Italy.[35] Motives are copied and are used for different aspects and reasons. The portrait of nature is to a high degree still a 'typical' portrait and not an 'authentic' one, containing components which may be used for portraits of other and very different natures.[36]

On the other hand the trends towards and the use of the authentic are increasing. The well-known, so-called first landscape of Konrad Witz from 1444 gives a particular authenticity to the background of the 'Miraculous Draught of Fishes'.[37] The 'real' lakeside and landscape of Lake of Geneva is seen as a part of a 'portrait' of Buon Governo', using the authentic as well as the typical to give the impression of a land being in perfect order. Part of this perfect order is nature, particularly authentic and cultivated nature. Nature functions as an explicit symbol and sign.

Authentic portraits of nature are getting more relevant. Nevertheless, different levels of portraits of nature certainly are existing side by side, intermingling the typical and the authentic. From a general point of perception there is no strict difference between them. The authentic portrait represents a certain type to be visualized, and the typical portrait gets through its specificity also its authenticity. No actual borderline can be drawn.

In both variants the role of the cultivated nature seems to receive major importance. Already in Late Gothic religious images[38] from the end of the fifteenth century, the depicted background nature increasingly is containing particularly one additional feature: its cultivation or domination with obviously special emphasis put on one's own nature (figure 3).

Images showing the patron saints of miners or mining communities may represent a direct connection between religious message and the prosperity and success of the community by visualizing (the right order of) mining work in the background (figure 4).[39] All those background mining scenes certainly show cultivation or let us better say, domination of nature. Such typical background portraits of exploited nature are to be seen not only as a means of creating a general identity by raising connections between the recipients of an image and its message. At the same time they might also be understood as a means of raising the relevance of one's 'own' nature and of the success gained through cultivation and/or exploitation of it. The depiction of one's 'own' nature is to show the (symbolic) value of one's own work. It is enough to be put into direct context with the religious contents of the image, be it a patron saint directly connected to the background depiction or another scene. It still might not be an authentic portrait, but may contain several components clearly visualizing objects and signs of one's own successful cultivation. In this way, the treatment of nature in the background can be seen in terms of a symbol of the good and correct life in the area where the image is offered to and 'used' by its recipients.

Therefore, particularly from the second half of the fifteenth century onwards, depictions of living in and cultivating one's own nature are not only published in media dealing directly with a specific topic connected with the image but can also be found as a relevant addition to the 'old media' of religious images.

Representing one's own nature in this way is to be distinguished from the depictions of the other's nature – another area which received attention in this period. But it is another form of interest. Both natures are drawn closer to their recipients, the difference not only to be found in the degree of their authenticity but also in the explicit aspect of integrating the factor of cultivation into one's own nature. This initiates a possibility for a kind of positive self-identification, whereas the image of the other's nature might have a number of other functions, be they connected with the prestige of making the unknown known, with

Figure 3 Cultivating nature by cutting trees and taking them to town. Mural, *The Labours of the Months: December*. Early fifteenth century, Castello di Buonconsiglio, Trento.

Figure 4 Mining in the background of St Anne, the Virgin and the Christ child. Panel painting, Rožňava, Slovakia, 1513.

'scientific' interest, with didactics, etc. It might also contain a number of negative connotations.[40]

The background of a (religious) image showing cultivated nature may, therefore, be seen as a broadening and a generalization of the 'Buon Governo' theme which is based on one's own nature. Windmills, cut willow trees, cultivated orchards (figure 5) mining work, etc. symbolize the success of the community for which the (religious) image was painted. This development co-exists with all the other nuances of authentically or typically portraying nature, one's own nature and others' nature. But it may be seen as one of the developments which best fits into the paradigm of closeness and/vs. distance with regard to nature in the Renaissance. Not only did the distant become better known (independently of its truth, reality or imaginative character), but also the close, the well-known got another range.

A FIELD OF MULTIPLE CONJUNCTIONS

Only a few of the many possible ways of perceiving nature in the Renaissance could be discussed in this chapter.[41] Particular emphasis was put on elements which obviously had touched a large number of people. The paradigm of closeness and distance seems to fit well into our attempts to follow a 'popular approach' leaving the great developments of Renaissance thought more or less in the background.

Talking about the past certainly always means also to talk about one's own culture. The distant therefore comes very close to oneself. In this respect, there is no general difference between dealing with the 'perception of nature in Renaissance society' and with the 'Mozambican soldiers' of our motto. Nevertheless, particularly concerning a period of the Renaissance filled with the developments often characterized as 'revolutionary' or 'sensational', we are convinced that besides the 'Mystic Warriors'[42] another approach, being on one hand very narrow, on the other hand, though, very general, has been necessary.

None of the fields mentioned can be analysed by itself but must be seen in the context of others. Changes had taken place in the relation of man and nature. All actions, undertaken on various scales and for divergent reasons had a general effect not only on nature and environment themselves but also and particularly on the way people used to deal with them. Many other elements of humankind's direct confrontation with nature and its perception of nature stayed stable or developed only very slowly and calmly.

Figure 5 Cultivated nature in the background of *The Visitation* (figure of St Elizabeth). Panel painting from the south Tyrol, 1460/70.

NOTES

1 John and Jean Comaroff, *Ethnography and the Historical Imagination* (Oxford, 1992), p. 4, with regard to an article of the *Chicago Tribune* (9 December 1990) entitled 'Mystic Warriors Gaining Ground in Mozambique War'.

2 See generally, e.g., Jörg Zimmermann (ed.), *Das Naturbild des Menschen* (Munich, 1982); Edward William Tayler, *Nature and Art in Renaissance Literature* (New York and London, 1964); and, particularly, Keith Thomas, *Man and the Natural World. Changing Attitudes in England 1500–1800* (London, 1987); Allen G. Debus, *Man and Nature in the Renaissance* (Cambridge, 1978); John Torrance (ed.), *The Concept of Nature* (Oxford, 1992) (The Herbert Spencer Lectures).

3 See Peter Cornelius Mayer-Tasch (ed.), *Natur Denken. Eine Genealogie der ökologischen Idee*, vol. 2 (Frankfurt-o-M., 1991), pp. 27–78.

4 See *Mensch und Objekt im Mittelalter. Leben-Alltag-Kultur* (Vienna, 1990) (Veröffentlichungen des Instituts für Realienkunde des Mittelalters und der frühen Neuzeit 13 = Sb. Ak. Wien, phil-hist. Klasse 568).

5 See Rudolf Schenda, 'Die deutschen Prodigiensammlungen des 16. und 17. Jahrhunderts', *Börsenblatt für den deutschen Buchhandel*, 17 (1961), 637–710; and, *Die französische Prodigienliteratur in der 2. Hälfte des 16. Jahrhunderts* (Munich, 1961). See also below.

6 See Justin Stagl, 'Die Methodisierung des Reisens im 16. Jahrhundert', in Peter J. Brenner, *Der Reisebericht. Die Entwicklung einer Gattung in der deutschen Literatur* (Frankfurt-o-M., 1989), pp. 140–77.

7 See Lorenzo Huertas Vallejos (ed.), *Ecologia e Historia. Probanzas de Indios y Españoles referentes a las catastroficas lluvias de 1578, en los corregimientos de Trujillo y Saña* (Chiclayo (Peru), 1987).

8 See, e.g., Julius von Schlosser, *Kunst- und Wunderkammern der Spätrenaissance* (Leipzig, 1908).

9 See, e.g., Elizabeth Eisenstein, *The Printing Press as an Agent of Change: Communication and Cultural Transformation in Early Modern Europe*, 2 vols. (New York, 1979).

10 'was eine wyse Oberkeit, geistlich und welltlich, schaffet, das sol billich guot geheissen vnd für wolgeschafft erkennt werden, allein wöllen wir hie nit ungemeldet lassen, das gar nitt zuo verlougnen, sondern dem ganzen Land kundtbar gnuog ist, sonderlich aber den Sennen – wie ich dann selbst vff dem Berg von Alphütten vnd andern allten gloubwürdigen Menner, die umb Jagens und Pirsens willen vff diesem Berg Handel, Wandel und Wonung gehept, wann jch bi innen benachtet, by ernstigem Bethüwren vernommen habe, wie das diss Gebirg Pilatj, und am meisten vff der Höhe vnd da es ruch vnd wild ist, mit bösem tüfflischen Gespenst- vnd Geisterwerck ebenwol besetzt und erfüllt ist' quoted from Leopold Zehnder, *Volkskundliches aus der älteren Schweizer Chronistik* (Basel, 1976), p. 30 (= *Schriften der Schweizerischen Gesellschaft für Volkskunde*, 60) after the Luzern chronist Reynward Cysad, second half of the sixteenth century. Concerning the 'Pilatus' having become famous from Petrarca's description onwards, cf. Beat Wyss, 'Der Pilatus. Entzauberungsgeschichte eines Naturdenkmals', in Wolfgang Kos (ed.), *Die Eroberung der Landschaft* (Vienna, 1992), pp. 71–81 (= *Katalog des Niederösterreichischen Landesmuseums*, NS 295).

11 Gustav Winter (ed.), *Niederösterreichische Weistümer* 4 vols. (Vienna, 1886–1913).

12 Gerhard Jaritz and Verna Winiwarter (ed.), *Historische Umweltdatenbank Österreichs, public domain database* (Krems and Vienna, 1992). Cf. Gerhard Jaritz, Werner Schwarz and Verena Winiwarter, 'Umweltbewältigung, Historische Muster des Umgangs mit der Krise', *Medium Aevum Quotidianum*, 24 (1991), 7–19; Verena Winiwarter, 'Historische Umweltbewältigung', *Historicum*, 32 (1993), 36–40.

13 For the analysis of territorial laws the relevant normative sources of the *Codex Austriacus*, 2 vols. Vienna, 1704, were chosen. They also became part of Jaritz and Winiwarter, *Historische Umweltdatenbank*.

14 For a discussion on the history of ecology see recently Ludwig Trepl, *Geschichte der Ökologie. Vom 17. Jahrhundert bis zur Gegenwart* (Frankfurt-o-M., 1987); Jean-Paul Deléage, *Histoire de l'écologie, une science de l'homme et de la nature* (Paris, 1992).

15 See, e.g., the introduction of tobacco, which is, from the second half of the seventeenth century onwards, reflected in the laws by paragraphs against smoking in stables, etc. to prevent fire.

16 Again the Lower Austrian village laws were used as a sample.

17 The analysis again was based on the *Codex Austriacus*.

18 'Item, welcher in meines gnedigen herren panwalt an urlaub geet deß anwalt und daruber begriffen wiert, ist verfallen ain pfunt pfening der herschaft. Item, ain fremdter der aines andern herrn hold ist und geet in den walt, ist verfallen 5 tal.d und die rechte hant sol man im auf ainem stock abschlagen' (Winter (ed.), *Niederösterreichische Weistümer*, I, p. 14).

19 The analysis is based on Jaritz and Winiwarter, *Historische Umweltdatenbank*. For the following, see Werner Michael Schwarz, 'Umweltstrafen. Fragen nach den historischen Bewertungskriterien von Umweltdelikten', in Gerhard Jaritz and Verena Winiwarter (ed.), *Umweltbewältigung. Die historische Perspektive* (Bielefeld, 1994), pp. 77–98. In this contribution the facts discussed hereafter are given in detail in tables.

20 See, e.g., Margrit Irniger, *Die Sihlwald und sein Umland. Waldnutzung, Viehzucht und Ackerbau im Albisgebiet von 1400–1600* (Zurich, 1991).

21 Winter (ed.), *Niederösterreichische Weistümer*, III, p. 327.

22 Such a development, e.g., can be clearly found for sumptuary laws, especially concerning dress. See, e.g., Liselotte Constanze Eisenbart, *Kleiderordnungen der deutschen Städte zwischen 1350 und 1700. Ein Beitrag zur Kulturgeschichte des deutschen Bürgertums* (Göttingen, Berlin and Frankfurt-o-M., 1962), esp. pp. 68–71 (*Göttinger Bausteine zur Geschichtswissenschaft*, 32).

23 See Harry Kühnel, '"Mit Seife mißt man die Kultur ...". Mentalität und Alltagshygiene', *Archiv für Kulturgeschichte*, 73, 1 (1991), 72.

24 See Neithard Bulst, 'Zum Problem städtischer und territorialer Kleider-, Aufwands- und Luxusgesetzgebung in Deutschland (13.–Mitte 16. Jahrhundert), in André Gourdon and Albert Rigaudière (ed.), *Renaissance du pouvoir legislatif et genèse de l'état* (Montpellier, 1988), pp. 36–7 (Publications de la Société d'histoire du droit et des institutions des anciens pays de droit écrit III).

25 E.g., law from Herzogenburg, 1566: 'Wir wöllen und ordnen auch das kainer kain aschen oder andern unlust auf die gassen noch für das Khremser thor schüt sonder in die aw bei der Traisen tragen lasse ....' (Winter, *Niederösterreichische Weistümer*, III, p. 261).

26 E.g., law from Stockerau, 1590:

Nachdem durch ettliche personen alhie ain fürkauf in dem gehackten holz in der aw beschiecht, und das di dasselb holz hinwegk füren and an andere orth verkaufen und derhalben die armen zu ihrer hausnotturft alhie umb das gelt nit zuwegen bringen künden, das ain grosse beschwär ist, hierauf ist allen so thail in der aw haben verbotten das si kain holz nit hingeben sonder zuvor dem richter anzaigen, darauf solle der richter durch den diener beruefen lassen, und welcher burger alhie holz bedürftig, solle demselben umb ainen zimblichen pfenning gegeben und vergunt werden.

(Winter, *Niederösterreichische Weistümer*, II, p. 454).

27 See note 40.

28 E.g., territorial law of 1531, 1539, 1540, 1541, 1549, etc.: 'daß ihr in euren Auen das Holtz auch grosse Stöck, Stämmen, rauhe Bäume an den Gestätten berührtes WasserStroms abmaissen, hindan ziehen, oder schleiffen und außhacken lassen, und ohn all fernere Weigerung daran nicht säumig erscheinen sollet' (*Codex Austriacus*, I, p. 282).

29 See also Gerhard Jaritz and Verena Winiwarter, 'Wasser. Zu den historischen Mustern eines Problembewußtseins (Annäherungen anhand der "Historischen Umweltdatenbank Österreichs")', *Wissenschaftliche Mitteilungen aus dem Niederösterreichischen Landesmuseum*, 8 (1994), 163–74.

30 See, e.g. Ulgard Folkmann, 'Natur und Wundererscheinung in der Berichterstattung des sechzehnten Jahrhunderts', diss., Vienna, 1967.

31 The analysis is based on a specific part of Jaritz and Winiwarter, *Historische Umweltdatenbank*; cf. Alexander Sperl, 'Blutregen', in Jaritz and Winiwarter (ed.), *Umweltbewältigung. Die historische Perspektive*, pp. 56–76.

32 Particular reason for this fact is certainly the special 'supernaturality' of bloodrain. The Bible itself provided proof: One of the seven plagues to come upon Egypt is the miraculous change of water into blood, which then becomes undrinkable and makes all the fish die (*Exodus*, 7, 19–21). In *The Revelation of John*, 11,6 the two witnesses have the power to shut up the sky, so that no rain may fall ... and ... to turn water into blood; etc. Moreover, the change of water into blood contains the deepest mystery of the Christian religion.

33 '... aus sonderlich rat, schickung oder ja zulassung und verhängnis Gottes.' Schenda, *Die deutschen Prodigiensammlungen*, p. 660f.

34 See Sperl, 'Blutregen'.

35 See Gerhard Jaritz, *Zwischen Augenblick und Ewigkeit. Einführung in die Alltagsgeschichte des Mittelalters* (Vienna and Cologne, 1989), p. 60f.; Elisabeth Rückert, *Die Schedelsche Weltchronik* (Munich, 1973), esp. pp. 73–135 (*Bibliothek des Germanischen Nationalmuseums Nürnberg zur deutschen Kunst- und Kulturgeschichte*, 33).

36 See Enrico Castelnuovo, *Das künstlerische Portrait in der Gesellschaft. Das Bildnis und seine Geschichte in Italien von 1300 bis heute* (Frankfurt-o-M., 1993), p. 13f.

37 See Florens Deuchler, 'Warum malte Konrad Witz die "erste" Landschaft? Hic et nunc im Genfer Altar von 1444', in *Medium Aevum Quotidianum Newsletter*, 3 (1984), 39–49.

38 All the examples are taken from German or Austrian medieval or Renaissance images.

39 This certainly is not to say that all reactions to mining during these times were

positive. There are enough examples of critical or negative statements concerning various problems caused by mining.

40 The polarity between positive and negative with regard to the perception of nature by man also plays an important role in many argumentations. In our contribution we could deal with that phenomenon only marginally and not in a detailed way. As an example, see Horst Bredekamp, 'Wasserangst und Wasserfreude in der Renaissance und im Manierismus', in Hartmut Böhme (ed.), *Kulturgeschichte des Wassers* (Frankfurt-o-M., 1988), pp. 145–88.

41 As a short contribution on the topic dealing with other aspects, cf. Hubertus Fischer, 'Naturwahrnehmung in Mittelalter und Neuzeit', *Stadt und Landschaft*, 17 (1985), 97–110.

42 See note 1.

SIX

FABLES OF THE BEES: A CASE-STUDY IN VIEWS OF NATURE AND SOCIETY

PETER BURKE

THE changing relation between views of nature and views of society in Europe, especially though not exclusively in the Early Modern period, is a subject which has attracted many scholars in the last sixty years or so, from Hans Kelsen to Hans Blumenberg, from Arthur Lovejoy to Ernst Kantorowicz and from Michel Foucault to Serge Moscovici.[1] Their main conclusions may be summarized in the following seven propositions.

1. Early Modern social arrangements and conventions were generally viewed and presented as if they were natural; the king, for example, was frequently described as the sun of the social cosmos, the head of the body politic, and so on.[2] This 'construction of society' (as we might call it) was explicitly articulated in treatises on political theory, but it seems to have operated most effectively at the level of 'mentalities', in other words of what is implicit or taken for granted.

2. Conversely, social arrangements, notably the social hierarchy, was projected on to the universe, the lion being perceived or presented as the king of beasts, the eagle as the king of birds, nature (whether or not a goddess), being viewed as passive and feminine, and so on.[3] Thus Ulisse Aldrovandi of Bologna, the famous naturalist (or late Renaissance universal man), organized his ornithology according to 'the order of nobility' of the birds described.[4] The contents of the universe were described as being linked in a 'great chain of being'.[5]

3. These analogies or metaphors (as we think of them) were generally believed to be more than analogies or metaphors; they were seen as objective 'correspondences', part of what is variously known as the 'moralized universe', the prose of the world, and so on.[6]

That this was indeed the case can be seen from the way in which people appealed to these analogies in the course of political debates. In the English parliament in 1625, for example, William Laud justified the king's request for funds on the grounds that 'The King is the sun. He draws up some vapours, some support, some supply from us. For if the sun draw up no vapours, it can pour down no rain'.[7] Similarly, writers of political treatises assumed the validity of these analogies. To choose examples almost at random, Edward Forset's *Comparative Discourse* (1606) and Caspar Dornavius's *Menenius Agrippa* (1615) both made an elaborate formal comparison between a commonwealth and a human body, while Sir Robert Filmer's *Patriarcha*, written a little later, and published posthumously in 1680, is based on the analogy between kings and fathers.[8]

4. The master-metaphor to describe this moralized universe was that of an organism, or, to keep closer to early modern phrasing, an 'animal'. As Campanella put it in one of his sonnets, 'Il mondo è un animale grande e perfetto'.[9]

5. This system of correspondences went back a long way in Western thought. The 'Elizabethan world picture', as an English literary historian once – somewhat ethnocentrically – described it, followed the classical tradition and might be better described as the 'Aristotelian-Ptolemaic' world picture, though cosmic kingship (for example) is a complex of ideas with a still longer history.[10]

6. This intellectual system is part of a family of systems which have been identified in traditional China, Africa, and so on, varying in detail (five elements in China, for example) but sharing the treatment of what we call the inanimate in terms of the animate, as well as the absence of awareness of alternatives to the system.[11] As Mary Douglas has observed, 'The whole universe is harnessed to men's attempts to force one another into good citizenship'.[12] A historian might want to add that this harnessing, although recurrent, is not a constant, but subject to change over time.

7. In the course of the seventeenth century, as a part of the complex of changes often described as the 'scientific revolution', a substantial proportion of European elites abandoned this intellectual system, or at least modified it in two ways, both concerned with the place of images, analogies and metaphors in the study of nature and society. Metaphor is of course impossible to banish from human discourse altogether, but dominant metaphors and attitudes to metaphor are subject to change over the long term.

In the first place, there was a change in the content of metaphor, that is, in the kind of metaphor used to describe the cosmos. There was a 'mechanization of the world picture', in other words a replacement of the previously dominant metaphor of the world as an 'animal' with the metaphor of the world as a machine (though the organic metaphor would of course make a come-back, in a modified form, in the nineteenth century).[13] Another major change, studied by historians only relatively recently, was the shift from a view of nature as active (*natura naturans*) to the idea of a passive female nature, a body on which male scientists could operate.[14]

In the second place, there was a change in attitudes to metaphor or analogy. Some investigators of nature called metaphor into question, like rhetoric and imagination more generally. They would have liked to reject metaphor altogether in favour of a plain, unambiguous language on the model of mathematics. Others did not go so far as to reject metaphor, but they viewed it less respectfully than their predecessors, treating figures of speech as merely human devices rather than as the language of God or the universe itself.[15] One might refer to this change in attitudes as a 'crisis of representations'.[16]

All the foregoing is well known in the sense that it has been much discussed while arousing relatively little controversy – and when there has been controversy, it has been concerned with the reasons for the double intellectual shift or with its exact dating than about the question whether such a shift occurred at all. However iconoclastic Foucault may have been in other respects, the introductory section of his *Order of Things*, discussing 'the prose of the world', is not very different in its argument – intellectual sophistication apart – from that of the Cambridge literary historian E. M. W. Tillyard some twenty years before.

Why these particular changes should have taken place at this particular time is a more difficult question to answer. Foucault, of course, avoided (and perhaps evaded) the question altogether. In the *Order of Things* (in contrast to the author's later work, in which the relation between power and knowledge was often discussed), intellectual discontinuities simply happen, without explanation. Generally speaking, however, historians are concerned to explain the Scientific Revolution in one of two different ways. The dominant approach is essentially an 'internalist' one, following the model – or should one say the paradigm? – of Thomas Kuhn, in which the discovery of new information leads to awareness of 'anomalies'; then to a 'crisis' of accepted views of the universe; and finally to the formulation of a new orthodoxy or paradigm. On the other side, we find attempts to offer an 'externalist' or social explanation for what happened, as in the case of Franz Borkenau's famous description of the change from the organic to the mechanical model of the universe as 'the transition from the feudal to the bourgeois world view'.[17]

We seem to be faced with a choice between an interpretation of history which assumes the active role of the study of nature in transforming society, and a view which takes for granted the active role of society in transforming the study of nature. In fact, however, we do not have to make such a stark choice. It is surely possible to go beyond this sterile debate between internalists and externalists and view the relation between science and society as one of reciprocal interaction. However, a general formula of this kind is no more than a point of departure for more precise investigations. What I shall try to do in this chapter, therefore, is first to illustrate the great intellectual shift of the seventeenth century with an extended concrete example, and then to reflect on a few of its implications.

The example to be discussed may seem on first acquaintance to be more than a little bizarre, or even frivolous. It concerns the place of bees in Early Modern political thought. These obedient and hard-working creatures have been pressed into the service of a number of arguments in the history of the west. For Francis Bacon, for example, they exemplified the right method of intellectual inquiry, collecting their material and then transforming it, thus avoiding the mistakes of both the ants (empiricists who only collected material) and spiders (who spun their webs like scholastic philosophers from material within themselves).[18] Combining the Baconian intellectual tradition with radical politics, John Webster urged the reform of universities, sweeping away the webs of scholasticism and encouraging 'laborious bees, that seek to gather into their hives the sweet honey of learning and knowledge'.[19]

More commonly, the different kinds of bee have been employed as symbols of peace, plenty, commerce and above all, industry and idleness. The term 'drone', for example was sometimes used by sixteenth-century writers to refer to what one of them called 'idle loiterers', useless to the commonwealth.[20] The comparison was extended and adapted by a Calvinist writer, Philips van Marnix, in his *Byencorf* (1569), a satire on the Church of Rome as a bee-hive in which the work-shy mendicant friars play the role of drones, while the inquisitors are compared to wasps.[21] This analogy between nature and society appealed to writers on the economy, notably Bernard Mandeville, whose *Grumbling Hive* (1705), later expanded into *The Fable of the Bees*, is a moral fable in the style of Aesop and Lafontaine. Based on the idea that 'These Insects lived like Men, and all / Our Actions they perform'd in small', the poem and its commentary discuss – among other economic themes – that of laziness and industry.[22] The editors of *The Beehive*, a weekly paper for members of trade unions, cooperatives and friendly societies published in the 1860s, doubtless chose the name for its associations with industry and cooperation.

However, the bees were invoked even more often in the course of political debates. Their example suggests that whatever may be the case for philosophy, a good deal of the history of political thought may be written in the form of footnotes to Aristotle. In his treatise *On the Generation of Animals*, Aristotle describes three kinds of bee, the ordinary bees, the drones, and the ones he calls the 'leaders' or 'kings'. In the *History of Animals*, he refers to the 'so-called kings' of the bees.[23] On the basis of this laconic comparison, later writers erected a remarkable intellectual edifice.

Virgil, for example, in his *Georgics*, describes the ordinary bees as paying homage to their ruler ('the guardian of the work', *operum custos*) and crowding round him: 'illum admirantur et omnes / Circumstant fremitu denso stipantque frequentes'.[24] One might have thought that Virgil was using poetic licence, but the generally prosaic treatise on agriculture by another Roman writer, Columella, uses the example of the bees to make the point that animals and insects, like humans, allow 'no sharing of royal power' (*nulla regni societas*).[25] This point was amplified by Seneca in his treatise on clemency, in which he takes the social order of the bees as a demonstration that 'Nature herself conceived the idea of king' (*Natura enim commenta est regem*) and the fact that the king has no sting as an illustration of the need for rulers to exercise clemency.[26]

The question whether or not the king bee had a sting was in fact controversial. It was discussed by Pliny, for example, in his *Natural History*, which also declares that the bees 'are unable to do without a king' and that the ruler has a 'bodyguard' around him (*circa eum satellites quidam lictores*).[27] It was also discussed by the historian Ammianus Marcellinus, who explains that the Egyptians compared kings to bees because they exercised power in two complementary ways, by sweetness and by the sting (or as we might say, by the carrot and by the stick).[28]

Perhaps the most instructive comparison with Aristotle, however, is that of the late ancient writer Aelian in his treatise *On the Characteristics of Animals*. Like Aristotle, his aim is descriptive, but he takes the analogies between the insect world and the human world more seriously and develops them in more detail. The bees have a 'king' (*Basileus*), not a 'so-called' king. The king has a 'palace' and a 'bodyguard'. The king rules the hive and gives the workers their various tasks.[29] One is left with the impression that the structure of belief was changing in late antiquity, even if the content often remained the same. Early Christian writers such as Basil, Ambrose and Augustine reconstructed the classical tradition in order to make more room for God, the creator of the natural world. What had once been a metaphor or analogy was turning into an objective 'correspondence'.

In the Middle Ages, these late classical ideas were revived with the study of the texts in which they were expressed. For example, the thirteenth-century treatise *On the Rule of Princes*, attributed to Thomas Aquinas (and either written, or finished, by Ptolemy of Lucca), begins where Aelian rather than Aristotle leaves off. Chapter 2 declares monarchy to be the best form of government on the grounds that rule by one is 'natural'. The heart rules the body, and the bees have a single king (*est etiam apibus unus rex*).[30]

This kind of analogy between the cosmos and the political world appears to have been even more appealing in the Renaissance than it was in earlier centuries. At any rate, the example of the bee, like that of the sun or the heart (so prominent in the writings of William Harvey), was frequently discussed and elaborated still further at this time.

Girolamo Savonarola's treatise on the Florentine constitution, for example, written at the end of the fifteenth century, quotes this example.[31] So do commentators on Virgil's *Georgics*, such as those by Jodocus Badius (1501) and Guillaume Michel (1520). Sir Thomas Elyot's *The Book named the Governor* (1531) uses the bee as the most telling example of the case for 'one sovereign governor' in 'a public weal': 'in a little beast, which of all other is most to be marvelled at, I mean the bee, is left to man by nature, as it seemeth, a perpetual figure of a just governance or rule: who hath among them one principal bee for their governor, who excelleth all other in greatness, yet hath he no prick or sting, but in him is more knowledge than in the residue.'[32]

These analogies were put forward not only in texts but also in one of the fashionable mixed genres of the Renaissance, the emblem-book, in which an apparently enigmatic image was combined with a motto and verses which pointed a moral, often showing that the little world of humans, animals, birds, insects or plants epitomized fundamental truths about the working of the universe. In the first and most famous of these compilations, the *Emblemata* of Andrea Alciati (1531), an image of the beehive illustrated the theme of royal clemency. Bees continued to be invoked to make political points in emblem-books until the decline of the genre at the beginning of the eighteenth century.[33] It is tempting to speculate whether the decline of the emblem-book is not related to the major intellectual shift already discussed. At the height of their popularity, emblems were taken to reveal true if hidden connections made by God between different parts of the cosmos. When they were seen as no more than vivid illustrations of human analogies, the genre went into decline.

The irony of this particular example, a time-bomb ticking away inside the emblem-book, was of course that masculine writers, who generally accepted common male assumptions about the inferiority of women, took the bees as a paradigm of good government without realizing that their 'king' was a queen. John Knox, who published a treatise in 1558 against what he called the 'monstrous' rule of women such as Queen Elizabeth, used the argument that such rule was 'repugnant to nature'. 'Nature hath in all beasts printed a certain mark of dominion in the male, and a certain subjection in the female'. What would Knox have said if he had known the sex of the ruler-bee?[34]

In the seventeenth century, appeal continued to be made to the example of the hive. On the political side, Giovanni Bonifacio published his *Republica delle api* (1627). On the side of natural philosophy, Aldrovandi began his study with the bee because it was the most noble of insects, quoted a wide range of ancient writers and like them held up the 'polity' of the bees as an example for humans.[35] So did his Spanish colleague Cortés, who declared that of all 'animals', the bees are the ones most concerned 'to choose a king and leader' (*elegir Rey y caudillo*), to obey him, and to surround him, thus teaching vassals how to behave towards their king.[36] For a vivid example of the analogy inverted, we may turn to the Italian nobleman Primi Visconti, who visited Versailles and observed Louis XIV leaving the palace, surrounded by a confusion of courtiers and servants. 'It reminds me', he wrote, consciously or unconsciously echoing Virgil, 'of the queen of the bees, when she leaves the hive with her swarm'.[37]

It will be noted that Visconti describes the bee's leader as a female. It was in the seventeenth century that doubts about the sex of the 'king' began to be raised. Charles Butler, for instance, a Buckinghamshire vicar and bee-keeper, called his book on bees, first published in 1609, the 'feminine monarchy'. He claimed that 'The bees abhor as well Polyarchy as Anarchy, God having showed in them unto men the most natural and absolute form of government'. However, Butler did not draw political conclusions from the gender of the ruler.[38] Nor did the Jesuit Pierre Le Moyne, whose emblem-book of 1647 featured a Queen Bee with the motto 'a king in spirit but not in gender' (*rex animo non sexu*), allowing the exception but refraining from reformulating the rule that kings should be male.[39] As Jeffrey Merrick has remarked, 'Instead of supporting the case against the subordination of women during the *querelle des femmes*, gynaecocratic bees ended up reinforcing the patriarchal attitudes which natural history had endorsed ever since classical times'.[40]

Charles Butler seems to have guessed rather than proved that the bees had a queen. For a demonstration of the fact, it was necessary to wait another sixty years, till 1669, when Jan Swammerdam published the results of his dissections and observations, some of them made with the aid of a new scientific instrument, the microscope. An internalist approach to the history of science would emphasize the use of this instrument, which certainly facilitated the discovery of the queen's true gender.

On the other hand, it might reasonably be argued that it was no accident that this achievement was the work of a citizen of a republic, a man without emotional investment in monarchy, and consequently someone who was able to look through his microscope with eyes unclouded by prejudice in favour of the traditional assumption that bees are ruled by a king. Swammerdam does in fact hint at his own social attitudes at this point in his work, since he considers traditional descriptions of the constitution of the hive to be not only inaccurate but ridiculous as well. He finds it quite absurd to credit bees with 'fancied ceremonies of honour, and a numerous retinue of old and venerable bees ranged in order, accompanied with the harmonious sound of trumpeters, hautboys and musicians, or in the tremendous presence of executioners standing around, as authors have feigned, ingeniously indeed, but derogatory to nature'.[41]

Ironically enough, Swammerdam's demonstration, however important in the history of zoology, came just too late to be of much relevance to political theorists. Rather more fundamental assumptions of theirs were in the process of being shattered in the course of what it remains convenient to call the 'intellectual revolution' of the seventeenth century, described in the opening paragraphs of this paper.[42] There was at this time a gradual but decisive repudiation of the argument from analogy or correspondence of the kind taken for granted in Aelian, Aquinas, etc. and made explicit in the treatises by Dornau, Filmer, and Forset mentioned above. To be precise, Forset had warned his readers against 'straining' similitudes and ignoring dissimilitudes, while continuing to accept the principle of 'good correspondence', as he called it.[43] However, the principle was increasingly called into question in the course of the seventeenth century.

It has been argued that it was Calvinism which snapped the great chain of being.[44] At any rate, Calvinists or Puritans were among the first to reject correspondences. The Englishman George Hakewill, for example, criticized the analogy between the microcosm, the little world of man, and the macrocosm, on the grounds that man and the universe 'subsist not of the same principles, nor are in all things alike'.[45] After 1650 or so, this kind of criticism becomes almost commonplace. It was of course employed to deadly effect by John Locke in his critique of Filmer's *Patriarcha*.[46] It was this turn against analogy, even more than the changing views of nature and society, which justifies the use of the phrase 'the intellectual revolution'. *The Fable of the Bees* does not provide evidence against this view of the period, for unlike his sixteenth- and seventeenth-century predecessors, Mandeville does not breathe a word about correspondences. His bees are humans in insects' clothing, designed simply to illustrate his argument more vividly.

All the same, we should not exaggerate the speed of the changes just described, especially among thinkers of the second or third rank. For example, the apothecary Moses Rusden wrote about bees in 1679 as if the traditional view of 'the royal race of king-bees' had not been undermined (he mentions Butler in passing, but does not appear to think his book worth refuting). In a prefatory letter to the king, the author expresses the hope that the subjects of Charles II will be as loyal to him 'as these little people are to their Sovereign'. The treatise refers to politics on more than one occasion. Rusden claims to show nature 'naked and unadorned with metaphors', but he also asserts that Nature is 'the favourer and founder of monarchy', describes the king as 'stately', 'majestic' and 'absolute', and the other bees as obedient subjects who 'naturally abhor rebellion and treason'.[47]

Two eighteenth-century writers, Warder and Thorley, accepted the results of Swammerdam's research, but they also show how new wine could be poured into old bottles, and new scientific information combined with political attitudes much like those of Rusden. Joseph Warder's *The True Amazons* (1712) declares that 'no Monarch in the World is so absolute as the Queen of the Bees'. Writing in the reign of Queen Anne, he praises bees for their 'innate loyalty' which leads them to fight 'in Defence of their beloved Queen'. Republishing his book under George I, he utters the wish 'that all the thousands of this Britannic Israel were but so loyal to our most gracious King George' as the bees to their ruler.[48] In similar fashion John Thorley's *Female Monarchy* (1744) emphasised the 'great affection, love and loyalty' of the bees to 'their lawful sovereign', an implicit condemnation of the behaviour of Britons in 1641 and 1715.[49]

To sum up. In the Renaissance, the link between nature and society was not 'missing'. It was established by an argument from 'correspondence' which we now see to have been essentially circular. Social arrangements were projected on to nature, and this socialized or domesticated nature was in turn invoked to legitimate society by 'naturalizing' it. In the seventeenth century, however, the link snapped, in the sense that some observers became suspicious of particular correspondences, while others challenged the whole system and 'demoralized' the universe. What Mary Douglas calls 'natural symbols' may well persist in our thinking at a more or less unconscious level, but it has ceased to be possible to appeal to them in the course of a reasonably sophisticated political argument, in the way in which this was generally the case before 1650 or so. The ways in which arguments were justified or beliefs legitimated – at least in print – changed in a decisive fashion in the course of the seventeenth century.[50]

What is more difficult to determine is when, where, among whom and to what extent this style of thought was replaced. The case-study presented here should be taken as a warning against dating these developments too early, even in the case of Western European elites.

NOTES

1 See: Hans Kelsen, *Society and Nature* (Chicago, 1943); Hans Blumenberg, *Paradigmen zu einer Metaphorologie* (Frankfurt, 1960); Arthur O. Lovejoy, *The Great Chain of Being* (Cambridge, MA; 1936); Ernst H. Kantorowicz, *The King's Two Bodies* (Princeton, 1957); Serge Moscovici, *Essai sur L'histoire humaine de la nature* (Paris, 1968).

2 Christopher Hill, 'William Harvey and the Idea of Monarchy', in Charles Webster (ed.), *The Intellectual Revolution of the Seventeenth Century* (London, 1974); P. Archambault, 'The Analogy of the Body in Renaissance Political Literature', *Bulletin d'Humanisme et Renaissance* (1967), 21–53; James Daly, *Cosmic Harmony and Political Thinking in Early Stuart England* (Philadelphia, 1979).

3 Brian Easlea, *Witch-Hunting, Magic and the New Philosophy* (Brighton, 1980); Carolyn Merchant, *The Death of Nature* (New York, 1980); Keith V. Thomas, *Man and the Natural World* (London, 1983).

4 Ulisse Aldrovandi, *Ornithologiae*, 3 vols. (Bologna, 1599–1603); and *De animalibus insectis* (Bologna, 1602).

5 Lovejoy, *Great Chain.*

6 Marjorie Nicolson, *Science and Imagination* (Ithaca, 1956). On metaphor, see Blumenberg, *Paradigmen*; Paul Ricoeur, *La métaphore vive* (1975), Eng. trans. *The Rule of Metaphor* (London, 1986); O. Petersson, *Metaforernas Makt* (Stockholm, 1987).

7 William Laud, *Works*, 7 vols. (Oxford, 1847–60), I.

8 Edward Forset, *Comparative Discourse of the Bodies Natural and Political* (1606), Caspar Dornavius, *Menenius Agrippa, hoc est, corporis humani cum republica perpetua comparatio* (Hanau, 1615); Robert Filmer, *Patriarcha* (London, 1680).

9 Tommaso Campanella, *Opere*, ed. A. Guzzo and R. Amerio (Milan and Naples, 1956), p. 789.

10 E. M. W. Tillyard, *The Elizabethan World Picture* (London, 1943); H. P. L'Orange, *Studies on the Iconography of Cosmic Kingship in the Ancient World* (Oslo, 1953).

11 Marcel Granet, *La pensée chinoise* (Paris, 1934); Robin Horton, 'Religion', *Journal of the Royal Anthropological Institute*, 90 (1960), 201–26; Ernest Gellner, *Legitimation of Belief* (Cambridge, 1974).

12 Mary Douglas, *Purity and Danger*, 2nd edn (Harmondsworth, 1970), p. 13; cf. Mary Douglas, *Natural Symbols* (London, 1970).

13 Anneliese Maier, *Die Mechanisierung des Weltbildes*, 2nd edn (Rome, 1968); E. J. Dijksterhuis, *Het mechanisiering van het wereldbild*, English trans., *The Mechanization of the World Picture* (Oxford, 1950); Paolo Casini, *L'universo-macchine* (Bari, 1969);

A. Meyer, 'Mechanische und organische Metaphorik Politischer Philosophie, *Archiv für Begriffsgeschichte*, 13 (1969), 128–99.

14 Merchant, *Death of Nature*; Easlea, *Witch-Hunting*; Lorida Schiebinger, *Nature's Body: Gender in the Making of Modern Science* (Boston, 1993).

15 Paul Hazard, *La crise de la conscience européenne* (1935), English trans., *The European Mind 1680–1720* (New Haven, 1952); Basil Willey, *The Seventeenth-Century Background* (London, 1934).

16 Peter Burke, *The Fabrication of Louis XIV* (New Haven, 1992), ch. 9; cf. Peter Burke, 'The Demise of Royal Mythologies', in A. Ellenius (ed.), *Iconography, Propaganda and Legitimation* (Cambridge, 1997).

17 Franz Borkenau, *Der Übergang vom feudalen zum bürgerlichen Weltbild* (Paris, 1934).

18 Francis Bacon, *The New Organon* (1620), ed. Fulton Anderson (Indianapolis, 1960), no. xcv. References to Classical and Early Modern texts are, where possible, by book, chapter and section, not by page.

19 John Webster, *Academiarum Examen* (London, 1654), pp. 15, 33, 84, 92.

20 Nicholas Udall, *Erasmus's Apopthegmes* (1542), reprinted (Amsterdam, 1969).

21 Philips van Marnix, *Den Byencorf der H. Roomsche Kerke* (1569), English trans., *The Beehive of the Romish Church* (London, 1579).

22 Bernard Mandeville, *The Fable of the Bees* (1714), ed. P. Harth (Harmondsworth, 1970).

23 Aristotle, *On the Generation of Animals*, in *Works*, 10 vols. (Oxford, 1910), v, 3.10, cf. Geoffrey Lloyd, *Aristotle: The Growth and Structure of his Thought* (Cambridge, 1968), pp. 76–8; Aristotle, *History of Animals*, bilingual edn, 3 vols. (Cambridge, MA, and London, 1965–91), 5.21.

24 Virgil, *Georgics*, bilingual edn (Cambridge, MA, and London, 1935), IV, 212–18.

25 Columella, *De agricultura*, bilingual edn, 3 vols. (Cambridge, MA, and London, 1960–8), 9.9, my translation.

26 Seneca, 'De clementia', in *Moral Essays*, bilingual edn, 3 vols. (Cambridge, MA, and London, 1970), 1.19.2.

27 Pliny, *Natural History*, bilingual edn, 10 vols. (Cambridge, MA, and London, 1938), 11.16–18.

28 Ammianus Marcellinus, bilingual edn, 3 vols. (Cambridge, MA, and London, 1963–4), 17.4.11.

29 Aelianus, *On the Characteristics of Animals*, bilingual edn, 3 vols (Cambridge, MA, and London, 1958–9), 1.59–60, 5.10–11.

30 Thomas Aquinas (attrib.), *De regimine principum*, ed. A. P. D'Entrèves (Oxford, 1959), p. 12.

31 Girolamo Savonarola, *Trattato* (Rome, 1965), p. 442.

32 Thomas Elyot, *The Book of the Governor*, ed. S. E. Lehmberg (London, 1962), 1.2.

33 Jeffrey Merrick, 'Royal Bees: The Gender Politics of the Beehive in Early Modern Europe', *Studies in Eighteenth-Century Culture*, 18 (1988), figs. 3, 5.6. Cf. note 38 below. On the genre, see Robert Klein, 'The Theory of Figurative Expression in Renaissance Treatises on the Impresa', trans. in Klein, *Form and Meaning* (New York, 1957), pp. 3–24.

34 John Knox, *First Blast of the Trumpet against the Monstrous Regiment of Women* (1558), reprinted (Amsterdam, 1972), 30a. Cf. Merrick, 'Royal Bees', p. 15.

35 Aldrovandi, *De animalibus insectis*, 1.1.

36 G. Cortes, *Libro de los animales* (Valencia, 1613), 2.130.
37 Primi Visconti, *Mémoires*, ed. Lemoine (Paris, 1909), pp. 35–6.
38 Charles Butler, *The Feminine Monarchy* (London, 1609); cf. George Sarton, 'The Feminine Monarchy of Charles Butler', *Isis*, 34 (1942–3), 469–71.
39 Ian Maclean, *Woman Triumphant* (Oxford, 1977), p. 217 and plate 8.
40 Merrick, 'Royal Bees', p. 17.
41 Jan Swammerdam, *Historia insectorum* (1669), English trans., *The Book of Nature* (London, 1758), pp. 159, 188; cf. Louis S. Miall, *The Early Naturalists* (London, 1912), pp. 184–5.
42 Webster, *Academiarum Examen*.
43 Forset, *Comparative Discourse*, 'to the reader'.
44 Michael Walzer, *The Revolution of the Saints: A Study in the Origins of Radical Politics* (London, 1965), pp. 160ff, 176ff.
45 Quoted in Walter H. Greenleaf, *Order and Empiricism in Politics* (Oxford, 1964), pp. 150–1.
46 John Locke, *Two Treatises of Government* (London, 1690), 1.65.
47 Moses Rusden, *A Further Discovery of Bees* (London, 1679), preface, dedication, pp. 2–3, 21, 23, 28.
48 Joseph Warder, *The True Amazons* (1712), 3rd edn (London, 1716), pp. vii, 31, 44.
49 John Thorley, *Melisselogia or, the Female Monarchy* (London, 1744), p. 11.
50 Douglas, *Natural Symbols*; Gellner, *Legitimation of Belief*.

SEVEN

THE EARTH'S FERTILITY AS A SOCIAL FACT IN EARLY MODERN BRITAIN

SIMON SCHAFFER

> The Fruits of the Earth were at first spontaneous, and the Ground, without being torn and tormented, satisfied the Wants or Desires of Man. But now she must be prest and squeez'd, and her productions taste more of the Earth and of Bitterness.
>
> (Thomas Burnet, *Sacred Theory of the Earth*, 1684)

THE natural and the social are hard to tease apart. Social relations are naturalized and nature appropriated by the social order. In the early modern as in the postmodern world, challenges to cultural order were often seen as threats to nature itself. Consider, for example, the revival in capitalist societies of historicist values which deny an Enlightenment faith in progress and the growth of social movements aimed at preserving a carefully defined national (and natural) heritage.[1] At the start of his exploration of the relation between humanity and the natural world in early modern England, Keith Thomas points out a salient aspect of this conservative memory of the harmonies of Augustan society. In an age sometimes seen as a moment of rare equipoise, it was a commonplace that humanity must master the threats which uncultivated nature represented. 'Nostalgia, it can be said, is universal and persistent: only other men's nostalgias offend': wrote Raymond Williams on the 'change of social relationships and essential morality' involved in changing British stereotypes of the pastoral. To ask about the proper contents of nature and the right ordering of society is always to ask questions of those representatives in our culture in whom trust should be vested and to ask about the constitution of knowledge and its bearers. Williams was right to emphasize the social and moral challenges involved in this issue.[2]

Especially important in the morality and culture of early modern Britain were differing accounts of the natural place of agricultural labour. Farming might return humanity to Eden or else mark the difference between current toil and the glorious leisure of a past and future paradise. In 1659, for example, the significantly named farming text *Adam out of Eden* announced that cultivation was divine, 'for which cause the actions of body or mind are called Recreations, as carrying on the grand design of God himself'. A potent political combination of nostalgia and urgent struggle had major effects. The late E. P. Thompson and his colleagues described contests around a moral economy which celebrated use rights and custom in the name of a profoundly theological account of the sacred bounty of the soil. Food riots were not 'rebellions of the belly', but appealed against profiteers to a principled understanding of the proper means of price formation and the transfer of the earth's produce to the market, often matched by state regulation of the corn trade. Crop failures would be seen as acts of God and attempts to profit from high prices as blasphemy.[3]

The tenets of this moral order were used against, and were increasingly challenged by, a political economy which transmuted such customs into cash-values and denied the godly origin of soil's fertility. Roy Porter has argued that 'from the 1690s the natural world had been stabilized': the 'world garden' was there to be developed and the chance of revolutionary change in nature or society was minimized.[4] Enclosure and capitalization of the national food markets prompted fierce legal attacks on customs of harvest and labour in the field. Such contests were especially visible after the failure of Scottish rebellions against the Hanoverian regime, when the government established Commissioners to run confiscated Highland estates. In 1773 the commissioner Lord Kames, an eminent improver and jurist, threatened to expel any tenant who rioted 'upon pretense of scarcity and want of victualls or any other pretense whatsoever'. Three years later he published *The Gentleman Farmer*: landlords, not tenants, should profit from soil fertility because 'fertility is a quality of land; and a subject belongs to the proprietor with all its qualities'. Fertility was secularized and rendered a legally controlled economic good: 'where a tenant by superior skill or extreme diligence raises on an acre a bushel more than usual, the profit is owing to himself, not to the fertility of the soil'.[5] Kames' intellectual and political ally Adam Smith reckoned that laws to regulate the corn market were just like laws against witchcraft – absurd attempts to manipulate fantasies. By 1800 some economic journalists, in awe of Smith's claim that all famines were due to government intervention in the natural process of price formation, chorused that 'the notion of agriculture yielding a produce, and a rent in consequence, because nature concurs with human industry in the process of cultivation, is a mere fancy.' As nature's capacities were transmuted into market values, so the laws of political economy were naturalized. Smith's editor David

Buchanan reckoned in 1814 that the price of grain 'is got, not because nature assists in the production, but because it is the price which suits the consumption to the supply'.[6] Both nature and society were redefined and remoralized. In the agricultural crises of the period after 1815, natural laws of supply and demand were ingeniously combined with moral principles of the fallen nature of humanity. The implications were global. British landlords and agrarian scientists applied their doctrines to colonial land management and in contests with indigenous social ecologies.[7]

This chapter indicates that these different models of society involved different accounts of the fertility of the soil and the role of the agricultural theorist. Shifts in earth history in early modern Britain tracked concerns with social order and the divine warrant for human knowledge of the Earth itself. Scriptural narratives and accounts of a primitive state of nature were used to ground immediate claims for political legitimacy. Agricultural production was central to national wealth, and political order was chronically unstable. So analyses of the source of agricultural surplus were couched in political and scriptural terms.[8] The three decades before the Civil War witnessed some of the worst crises of subsistence the nation ever suffered. In the 1590s and in 1623 famine affected large parts of England. But from the mid-century, in the midst of major political turmoil, stable population growth and increase in food supply through agricultural technique and a more reliable national market secured Britain against a relapse into widespread disaster. These changes marked the emergence of a self-conscious cadre of spokesmen for improvement increasingly differentiated from the labouring poor, recognizing in traditional custom a set of obstacles to the self-evident rationalities of new systems of agricultural production. Protests were most common where wage-earners reckoned the norms of good conduct had been violated in grain pricing or in the implementation of vaunted improvement. Writers on agricultural reform reworked the divinely sanctioned moral code to make their specific proposals plausible.[9]

The earth's fertility was divine because it provided the basis of morality and an unworked surplus. Farmwork could easily be represented as sacred – a Quaker ploughman in Yorkshire in the 1690s recalled that 'being expert' in 'the Knowledge of ordering my Plow' gave him occasion 'to contemplate the ways and works of God'. Yet fully to realize the soil's surplus and to improve the land might involve the violation of moral obligation and thus the subversion of social virtue. In a closely connected set of mid-seventeenth-century pamphlet debates, aided by the lifting of press control in the 1640s, propagandists used conventional moral categories of nature to show how their account of society could be furthered and how their identification of the principle of earth's fertility would promote growth. Texts proliferated on the spiritual and economic significance of gardens and orchards, of drainage and the reclamation of waste. The virtuoso John Evelyn, a promoter of remarkable new garden schemes, argued in 1657 for 'a society of *paradisi cultores*, persons of ancient simplicity, Paradisean and Hortulan saints'.[10] Authors close to the Commonwealth newsmonger Samuel Hartlib told their audience how to return Britain's farmland to its prelapsarian state of grace. Hartlibian technique was based on the claim that God had placed active principles deep in the soil. The earth was a 'treasure-house' whose wealth lay temporarily locked up and whose key was in the hands of chemically informed gentlemen. Paracelsian and Helmontian accounts of the spirits and agents which made matter productive were used to describe how divinity made farming moral. Hartlib canvassed a range of candidates for these fertile agents, including the possibility that 'the Earth, by reason of the divine Benefaction hath an Infinite multiplicative vertue, as fire and the seeds of all things have'. Older Aristotelian theories that plant food came from earth were displaced by accounts of vegetable salts carried in water. Helmont's trials on the growth of willow and ash from water were often cited to justify the search for some master chemical. This was the theme of markedly utopian and chemically theorized texts such as Gabriel Plattes' *Macaria* (1641) and Cressy Dymock's *Reformed Husband-Man* (1651), directed at Parliament and its Council of Trade. 'This very Nation might be made the paradise of the World, if we can but bring ingenuity into fashion', exclaimed Hartlib's friend, the midlands landowner and parliamentary officer Walter Blith, in 1652. Agricultural doctrine was made into the central natural philosophical concern of the Commonwealth. The changes had obvious economic motives: abolition of feudal tenures, the expropriation of crown and church lands, schemes for fen drainage or for new crops, were proposed in the name of a universal advance in the republic's welfare.[11]

These appeals were scarcely innocent. There was an obvious contrast between the everyday management of soil fertility in British husbandry and these projectors' search for a single source of fertility in some chemically vital salt. Large areas damned as 'unfertile' or 'waste' – fens, commons, uplands, forests – were in fact major sources of support for the rural population. In arable lands soil fertility, customarily identified with 'fatness', would traditionally be identified by rubbing clods between the fingers to test for clamminess, by digging and refilling pits on the land, or by looking for the places where elms or crab-apples grew.[12] This was field lore sanctioned by custom and pursued independently from programmes for chemical analysis. Republican radicals such as the Digger Gerrard Winstanley turned this lore into a wholesale programme for the defence of use rights and the resistance to unrestrained enclosure: 'true religion, and undefiled, is to let everyone quietly have earth to manure'. In James Harrington's 1656 utopian project for a new commonwealth, *Oceana*, ownership of fertile land was to become the basis of a republic of arms-bearing virtuous citizens. Both Winstanley and Harrington used the language of Scripture and of self-perpetuating circulation of vitality to back their proposals for a new society. Natural philosophers were not isolated from these issues: on estates such as those of the Boyle clan in southwestern England, improvements were countered with widespread riots in the mid-1650s. 'The use of the Earth', as Winstanley put it, depended on the uses of social power.[13] In the conflicting discourses of the morality of improvement, writers worked out ways in which the moral economy could be captured for social stability and elite management. Traditional custom was deliberately redescribed as a source of social disorder, superstition and unreason. Dymock explained to Hartlib in 1649 that 'a great error in husbandmen why they grow not richer is because they are only content with so much as gives them a livelihood whereas if they would manage more acres, they might come to great riches'. The depiction of soil as a godly and chemical treasury whose profits could be made available through the work of reasoned natural philosophy accompanied the ideology of individualist enterprise and the establishment of bulwarks against disorder.[14]

The new Royal Society established in the wake of the Restoration swiftly endorsed and then exploited these concerns with enterprise, improvement and the source of fertility. Robert Boyle had already begun to circulate his own views of the role of an aerial nitre in fertility and growth. His kinsman Kenelm Digby lectured the Society in 1661 on an alchemical 'Universal Spirit' which made plants grow. Clients of Boyle, such as the Hampshire clergyman Robert Sharrock, stressed the central role of vegetable salts in plant growth. The Somerset physician William Clarke, a close ally of the experimental philosophers, wrote a *Natural History of Nitre* (1670) which explained that 'the Earth from the beginning contained within itself not only the Seeds of Plants but their Alimentary Juices'.[15] After 1660 several Hartlibian texts, which had been dedicated to the Commonwealth and to the employment of the poor on the land, now switched their attention towards men like Boyle and to the profitability of crops. Some writers who had flourished under the Commonwealth, such as Walter Blith, were to be ignored. Amongst post-1660 republican writers, the place of Harrington's landed and virtuous society was shifted from the immediate future to a nostalgic and unfortunately corrupted past. Around the Society's new Georgical Committee clustered a series of projects whose intent was agricultural improvement in the name of moral duty and chemical expertise. In 1664–5 the Committee, chaired by the wealthy nobleman Charles Howard, investigated 'how waste lands, healthy grounds and boggs may be well employed and improuved'. John Beale, a west country priest and agricultural visionary, chaplain to the King, told the Royal Society that 'all our helps in agriculture' hinged on enclosure: 'how to devise this and to avoid insurrections is the main point'. These authors set out to forge a novel site from which their own expertise in managing the soil could be accepted.[16] The Royal Society's printed 'Enquiries concerning Agriculture' of summer 1665 explicitly stemmed from 'gentlemen' who encouraged 'those who are skilful in Husbandry' to witness 'their own Knowledge and Experience'. These were terms of some weight in the innovative discourse of the Royal Society. The fellows' social position was devised in conscious confrontation with the threats from rural disorder and possible subsistence crises to a generally moralized economy.[17]

Especially important was their conception of earth itself. Evelyn's *Sylva* (1666) and John Worlidge's *Systema agriculturae* (1668) both discussed the relation between the structure and composition of earth and its right use. Evelyn began with a lucid exposition of the proper social place for land management: 'the more Learning, the better Philosophers and the greater Abilities they possess, the more and the better are they qualified to Cultivate and Improve their Estates'. Worlidge, a gentleman farmer at Petersfield, rehearsed the most important points of the philosophy of earth. He asserted the basis of wealth in land and God: 'as the mother suckles the infant with her milk, so doth the Earth, the mother of us all, universally feed and nourish us at an easie, liberal and profitable rate'. Farm work taught divine knowledge, 'the secret and mystical things in nature'. While the earth was figured as bounteous and female, its active spirit was a distinctly masculine agent, an 'operator or workman that transmutes earth or water into those varieties of objects we daily behold or enjoy'. Right management of this 'operator' would generate productive improvement and social discipline. According to Worlidge, open land where the spirit's work was not encouraged was also the breeding ground of 'theft, pilfering, lechery and idleness and many other lewd actions, not so usual where every MAN hath his proper lands enclosed, where every tenant knows where to find his cattel, and every labourer knows where to have his days work'.[18]

Social order could be secured by mastering the principles of fertility.

This mastery was a programme for the expropriation of a wide range of potentially dangerous powers – those of the labouring or landless poor, of women, of spirits. There is evidence, for example, that grain riots were occasions where women took an active part in the assertion of rights to fertility's products and where imagery of gender reversal and of spirit possession was common. Royal Society fellows such as Evelyn and William Petty set out what has been called a 'managerial ecology' to maximize profit in the name of prudence and state power against what they saw as fallen nature.[19] Their philosophy of earth received important publicity through the work of journalists, such as Beale's erstwhile ally John Houghton, whose newsletters of the 1680s and after carried farm prices on one side and appropriate citations from *Genesis* and from experimental philosophy on the other.[20] In 1675 Evelyn read a 'Philosophical discourse of Earth' to the Royal Society, announcing that 'everybody has heard of van Helmont's ash-tree', that everyone could replicate this trial and that this indicated the key role of 'pregnant and subtle particles' which came from the air to earth to promote 'intestine fermentation'. Men such as Evelyn and Newton had personal experience of the problems of tenancy and landed wealth. At exactly the same period, Newton was working on problems of 'vegetation' and the subtle sources of earth's vitality: 'this Earth resembles a great animall or rather inanimate vegetable'. He told the Society's secretary that 'the frame of nature' was made of 'aetherial spirits' which were initially 'wrought into various forms ... by the immediate hand of the Creator and ever since by the power of nature'. In terms which matched those of Worlidge's agriculture texts, Newton reckoned that God's command 'to increase and multiply' turned these spirits condensed in earth and water 'into some kind of humid active matter for the continual uses of nature'.[21] In the next decades Newton and his closest allies forged an intimate link between the new mathematical cosmology of the *Principia* and this problem of the source of fertility. They claimed that comets, for example, were the source of a 'subtle spirit' which would 'in particular supply the diminution caused in the humid parts by vegetation and putrefaction'. The Newtonians chose the desiccation of fertile land as their best example of the decay of nature and the action of vegetative spirit as the obvious case of nature's restoration. Soil fertility would be restored by agents which men of the cloth and learning could predict.[22]

The philosophers of earth had to define the morality of farm labour. An economic journalist explained in 1669 that 'what wayes soever we take to pursue improvements, labour is almost the whole charge'. Stories about fertility, divinity and labour were turned into a full-blown scriptural history of nature, a new genre of 'sacred physics' which flourished in Britain between 1670 and 1720. The sacred theories of the Earth exemplified the morality of labour and of fertility by tracing their genealogy to God's creative act.[23] In an early example of the genre, backed by eminent fellows of the Royal Society, the Lord Chief Justice Matthew Hale argued in his *The Primitive Origination of Mankind* (1677) that 'the End of Man's Creation was that he should be [God's] steward, *villicus*, bayliff or farmer of this goodly Farm of the lower World and reserved to himself ... the greatest recognition or rent for the same'. These theories of the Earth scoured Scripture to locate the crucial moments – Creation, Fall, Deluge – when labour was instituted, the soil's fertility changed, and thus farm work given its natural role. The fallen earth made husbandry necessary (because fertility fell) and possible (because the Fall was blessed). Naturalists such as Robert Hooke and John Ray penned voluminous pages on the divine curse which had made soil less fruitful and drew the moral about role of God's activity and human labour.[24] The commonplaces that any apparent earthly imperfection was truly providential and that any success in agriculture was due to a universally active principle were turned to account. In the 1710s the landscape gardener Stephen Switzer described a process of circulation of activity in which the Sun, the prime mover, extracted vapour and dissolved salt from the earth, insinuated air into the vegetative earth, and drove fermentation. 'I mean those nitrous and prolific salts, being the *spiritus mundi* which by the cooperation of rain and water, sun and air, sets, or rather is by them set, to hasten forward the great work of vegetation, whilst the other part is only a lifeless, inanimate dead lump'.[25] Such phrases explicitly recall those of Newton's *Opticks*, printed a couple of years earlier, where without active principles, Newton now added, the Earth 'would grow cold and freeze and become inactive masses: and all putrefaction, generation, vegetation and life would cease'. To this extent, the cosmology of active principles stayed secure. In Newton's celebrated phrase, 'nature is a perpetual worker': surplus flowed from the alliance of natural and godly powers not from the exploitation of labour power.[26]

The credit of these universal histories of the earth hinged on the social status of those interpreting the moral meanings of its past. Sensible of the threats to their cultural authority, many Anglican clergymen perceived in this new genre a potentially subversive challenge to the rights of scriptural interpretation and moral discourse on nature. Wits mocked the pretensions of those who reckoned they could produce universal histories in which the contemporary landed social order was given its place. The notorious example, Thomas Burnet's *Sacred Theory of the Earth*, which appeared between 1681 and 1691, was viewed with enthusiasm by some fellow-philosophers. The curdling of cheese, Newton told him, was a good image of how the earth's fertile crust had originally been made. Burnet described a primitive earth 'mixt with a benign Juice ... what soil more proper for Vegetation than this warm moisture, which could have no fault, unless it was too fertile and luxuriant?' He reckoned that the antediluvian soil had bred 'fruit-trees and corn spontaneously' and that 'forests of trees' still did so – for the urbane Burnet, arboriculture obviously needed no-one's work. Where the toil of 'husbandry and humane arts' were now necessary, this was because of 'the decay of the Soil' and 'the diversity of the Seasons' which had only begun after the Flood. The details of Burnet's work were challenged, by such as Ray or the London physician John Woodward. But like many of its companion texts, the *Sacred Theory* found ways of explicating current political crises, such as the true meaning of the overthrow of the Catholic monarch James II and the Glorious Revolution of 1688, in terms of naturalized cosmology.[27]

In Woodward's counterblast, the *Natural History of the Earth* (1695), the issue of the origin and decay of the earth's fertility was explicitly connected with the urgent political problem of the historical origin of labour. Woodward's text emerged from the collections of works of nature and art energetically garnered by the curious. An eminent if risible naturalist and antiquarian, Woodward provided his audience with a means of interpreting the sense of these relics and of placing them in a history of the planet, vegetation and humankind. Woodward's claim that at the Deluge the Earth's crust had dissolved, farming began, ploughs were invented, and that fossils were relics of the antediluvian fertile world, was met with widespread incredulity. The severest criticism was mounted by the Calvinist divine John Edwards, who shared with Woodward the sense that Scriptural and natural interpretation must decide when the planet was sterilized, making agriculture necessary, and when thorns and thistles appeared, making labour necessary. This was a fight simultaneously directed at the rights of clerical interpreters of Scripture and at the moral meaning of husbandry. Woodward and Edwards agreed that the discourse of sacred physics must reinforce a transcendent principle in nature: the Flood could not 'have been done without the Assistance of a Supernatural Power'. They disagreed about the moral order which this Power warranted.[28]

Edwards reckoned that Woodward's story gave farming the wrong status. The Calvinist priest insisted that human sin had continued after the Flood, so the Deluge should not be seen as a great discontinuity in the moral history of humanity. Ploughing appeared at the Fall, not the

Flood, because it was then that morality lapsed. Farm tools 'became necessary for the subduing and managing of the Earth which was now deprived of its pristine fertility and easiness of production'. Woodward disagreed. The divine gift to man was moral labour not the infertile Earth. At the Flood, the Earth was given 'a make and constitution more agreeable to the laps'd state of mankind and retrenching and burying a great deal of that prolifique matter that rendered it so exhuberantly fruitfull'. He ransacked the records of ancient Greece and Egypt, and the reports of travellers to the Americas, for accounts of the plough's appearance and its divine significance.[29] He reckoned that Augustan landowners who followed the recipes set out in his own 'Thoughts and experiments concerning vegetation' by recovering this lost fertile matter were recapitulating the divine action of Fall and Deluge. The morality of this divine task was clear – labour was to be directed at the soil, 'the standing fund and promptuary out of which is derived the matter of all animal and vegetable bodies'. In these experiments on vegetation, Woodward told the Royal Society that Boyle and his allies were wrong to seek the secret of fertility in water: 'a certain peculiar terrestrial matter contained in large quantities in rain, spring and river water' was imbibed by growing plants. In his universal histories, Woodward matched these claims with the moral lesson drawn from his reading of nature's own medals: 'the Monuments I offer from the Earth give abundant Evidence of its pristine fecundity and of the retrenchment of it at the Deluge, which is all I was concerned directly for'. The Flood curbed the luxury and vices of humanity. God did this by dissolving the soil and by compelling husbandmen to restore its virtues with their own work on the recuperation of fertile matter. Ploughing could return society to the moral life.[30]

This moral life was to be sustained in the face of the contested extension of enclosure and improvement, the salient development in the British agricultural economy during the eighteenth century. Genteel imagery eschewed reference to labour on the land: the sacred physics of soil represented that labour solely as a part of God's purposes. John Barrell points out that a translator of Virgil's *Georgics* in 1753 apologized that such terms as 'plough, sow and wheat' would 'unconquerably disgust many a delicate reader'.[31] Because of new demands for the legitimation of improving interests, systems where active principles circulated within the Earth and where the Earth was an object of sacred history were displaced by systems where the product of general agriculture circulated in an economy and the planet itself became an object of analysis. The clearest example of the tensions of social authority and theological propriety was the controversy initiated by Jethro Tull's

New Horse Houghing Husbandry in 1731. Tull reported on his attempts at improvement in farms in Oxfordshire and Berkshire. His devotion to a 'philosophy of earth' has often been noted and his endorsement of the improved seed drill lauded. But Tull and his admirers, such as the Whig oligarch Robert Walpole, mark a much more important break in earth theory. Tull still sought a key active principle in the natural economy which would explain and validate farmwork. He explained that roots fed on earth particles, and that air, water and nitre broke up the soil to provide this food. Hoeing and ploughing made this system work well. When Tull decided to do battle with the aged John Woodward on the problem of soil fertility he still used the language of natural fertility: 'Nature may have provided a considerable overplus for maintaining the life of individual plants'. But Tull rejected each of Woodward's historical claims. Woodward said there was a fertile soil type for each plant type, while Tull reckoned all matter contained food for every plant. 'Nature has given to vegetables no such law of *meum* and *tuum*.' While Woodward's sacred physics suggested that after the Flood the 'sluggish and inactive' soil was to be revivified with some active solvent, Tull argued that earth structure was the key to fertility and that tillage, not solvency, would solve the problem.[32] Tull began his break with the entire discourse of which Woodward was the salient representative. He denied the possibility of legitimation through scriptural history and he accepted the possibility of speaking for an explicitly antagonistic social group – the improving landowner.

Tull attacked older authors, whom he damned as 'Virgilian', because they used the Bible to describe contemporary labour relations on the land. Tull shifted his readers' attention to actual labour practice. Attacking Woodward's 'Egyptian' history of the plough, Tull joked that 'swine had practised the art of turning the soil and so had men long before the fictitious deity of Ceres was invented'. He used the term 'mathematical' here to distinguish his work from that of the moral historians of the Earth and 'their Primitive theory, which gave no Mathematical Reason to shew wherein the true method of Tillage did consist'. The pastoral idyll sketched in mid-seventeenth-century agriculture books began to disappear here. So did the clerical and philosophical models which portrayed primitive nature as a site of virtue. It has been argued that 'the torch of science was passed on, but it never came into the hands of Tull': more accurately, Tull's work helped produce the imagery of science as a torch enlightening the darkness of primitive superstition.[33] Pictures of ancient harmony were replaced by the intense antagonism of Tull's social theory. He did not write of a patriarchal family-based husbandman but of an exploitative proprietor. Tull emphasized that his system would maximize labour discipline, correct inexpert technique and break the link between Scriptural morality and the product of social labour on the soil. It was characteristic that in damning Woodward's earth theory, Tull compared the London medical professor with an 'Old Woman' possessed of 'no good Eyes and as strong an Imagination'. Sacred physics was coupled with the rejected culture of traditional wisdom. An Oxford graduate and a London lawyer, Tull eventually took over Prosperous Farm in Berkshire, an estate he described as traditionally 'Virgilian'. His new system was backed by influential Whig patricians, including Walpole, and he was damned by sceptics who, as Tull put it, were 'abusing my vegetable principles and terming me an atheist'.[34] The charge of atheism was telling. Tull's autobiography spelt out how labour discipline prompted his abandonment of traditional scriptural morality. He began examining how to mechanize seeding because he inherited his farm 'about the time when plough servants first began to exalt their dominion over their masters, so that a gentleman farmer was allow'd to make but a little profit of his arable lands'. He set his servants to sow new seed more exactly and under greater supervision. But the following year 'I discover'd that those people had conspir'd to disappoint me for the future, and never to plant a row tolerably well again, perhaps jealous that if a great quantity of land should be taken from the plough, it might prove a diminution of their power.' Tull's search for a 'faithful Engine', his revolutionary seed drill, was here advertised for its role in social discipline. 'The wickedness of servants and labours in husbandry, of hedge-breakers, and of the takers away of corn at harvest' was crucial in the social transformation of the nature of husbandry and the introduction of Tull's combined system of the drill, the horse hoe and the four-blade plough.[35]

This transformation was most marked in the new regime of *field trials*. British agricultural writers had long advertised their claims that doctrines of fertility and husbandry had been based on practical experience of field technique. From the 1720s, however, the scene of such trials took on a specifically political quality. Customary tests for soil fertility were to be displaced by managed tests under the eye of the owner. In times of high corn prices, tenants would minimize their estimate of the owner's share. 'The thresher may throw one half out of the barn into the straw, to increase his wages if he threshes by the quarter, or to save much of his labour if he threshes by the day.' Labour indiscipline and the principles of the moral economy would make managers' estimates of productivity unreliable. To create a scene where the true nature of soil fertility would become visible, it was necessary to reorganize the social relations of husbandry. Tull suggested that assessments of his new technique be performed directly by the 'driller'.[36] Tull publicly reinterpreted customary rights, such as the tradition that ploughmen stir soil with comparatively shallow furrows, as cunning obstacles to labour discipline and to the accurate assessment of techniques' efficacy. These usages had been sanctioned by primordial nature: they were now to be seen as obstacles to the true understanding of nature's rational principles. Tull's project no longer involved the cursed Earth or fallen humanity, but the socially challenging 'treacherous ploughman'. The new husbandry declared its independence from the older understanding of nature: 'we do not even observe at what time of the Sun's course we till our land'. It did so in the name of an attack on superstition, a term which would henceforth be applied to the alleged idiocies of plebeian belief.[37]

Tull tried to make his projects seem original and singular. They should rather be taken as symptoms of a widespread transformation in the ideology and the management of agricultural improvement. By the 1720s Walpole's Norfolk estates, for example, had for more than half a century been subjected to the new regime of root crops, financial scrutiny of field trials and regulated discipline. The first botany professor at Cambridge, Richard Bradley, fiercely defended a model of aerial nitre as the source of fertility against Tull, but the trials Bradley ran were now couched in exclusively mathematical terms. He knew that the commercially minded readers of his writings of the 1720s on husbandry and gardening would accept the natural growth of money invested at interest as an *explanation* of the peculiar rate of increase of vegetable bulk.[38] There was nothing natural in the drive for quantitative surveillance. Ideologues of the moneyed interest and of the improving landlords strove to naturalize new social regimes of calculation. Raymond Williams reckoned that 'the open ideology of improvement is in fact most apparent in Defoe'. In 1719, Defoe told the story of Robinson Crusoe's encounter with an apparently miraculous crop of barley on his island. Crusoe's initial response was to treat this bounty as a direct intervention by God in his affairs: then as a rationally explicable event, since he recalled emptying a bag of chicken feed on the spot where the grains were now growing: finally, he accepted the event as an example of the rational providence through which the world system was governed. Thus Defoe made his hero recapitulate the history of early modern theories of fertility – from the age of primitive superstition, when all events in the soil were attributed to the direct hand of God, through sceptical atheism, when naturalists reckoned they could explain all such events by the action of natural causes alone, to the mature rationality of providential deism.[39]

The transformation in Crusoe's personal philosophy was matched by other changes in the attitude of the state to the bounty of the soil. In the opening decade of the eighteenth century local support for common rights prompted the passage of the first private enclosure bills and thence fierce contests over agrarian practice. In 1723 Defoe's erstwhile patron Robert Walpole engineered the passage of the Black Act, a penal code of unparalleled ferocity directed against a range of customary use rights to game and crops on newly enclosed estates and forests, especially those in Tull's county of Berkshire. And in Edinburgh, the capital of a North Britain whose economic and political union with England Defoe had strenuously supported, the same year saw the foundation of The Honourable the Society of Improvers in the Knowledge of Agriculture in Scotland. The Improvers' Secretary, Robert Maxwell, worked to make the new agriculture rational, damned custom as superstition and propagandized for Tull's system north of the border. 'The Truth is', Maxwell wrote in his reports of the Improvers' proceedings: 'the far greatest part of Land Labourers never trouble their Heads about Principles, but work more like Tools or Machines than men of Reason, going on blindly, as led by Custom in the often unaccountable Ways of their Forefathers'. In Maxwell's discourse plebeian resistance to mechanization was the result of 'mechanical' devotion to tradition, and the use rights of the rural poor were 'unaccountable' just because they challenged the accountancy which landlords deployed on the products of their soil.[40]

The new culture of accountancy and mechanization was realized in the programmes of the Scottish political economists and their intellectual allies. In an essay of the 1750s on 'the origin of philosophy', Adam Smith picked up the contrast between 'vulgar superstition' and prudent calculation and applied it to the epistemology of the moral economy. He satirized the moral economy in which 'every object of nature ... is supposed to act by the direction of some invisible and designing power. Does the earth pour forth an exuberant harvest? It is owing to the indulgence of Ceres'. Recall Tull's equally angry attack on 'the fictitious deity of Ceres'. This 'pusillanimous superstition', Smith reckoned, would disappear 'when law has established order and security and subsistence ceases to be precarious'. Rational philosophy, pursued 'by those of liberal fortunes', would construct a systematic account of the laws which governed both the social and the natural order and no longer attribute the harvest to 'the invisible hand' of the gods. These rational systems 'in many respects resemble machines', designed to connect together phenomena wrongly attributed to the individual will of independent spirits.[41] This essay, the first in which Smith used the phrase 'invisible hand', was published posthumously by his literary executors the chemist Joseph Black and the earth theorist James Hutton. These natural philosophers were close allies of the programme of improvement of which Smith was an eminent spokesman. The dislocations of the Scottish economy after the Union, the loss of political representation and the threats of recrudescent Jacobitism all led to the formation of a series of societies and committees committed to economic, especially agricultural, reform. University philosophers developed a new account of nature and society to found the work of the improvers.[42]

The network around Lord Kames was a dominant element of this programme. He helped a range of public agencies manage agrarian reform. In exchanges with Joseph Black, Kames discussed the role of lime and marl in soil fertility, challenging and rationalizing customary Scottish techniques of rendering 'good' land. Kames' patronage secured university posts for the brilliant chemist William Cullen in the 1750s. Kames encouraged him to experiment and lecture on soil fertility, especially when Cullen took over his own farm in 1752. Kames reckoned plants might grow on air alone, thus offering the chance of permanent fertility. Cullen argued that 'rent and labour' should be integrated into calculations of such trials' success. 'The lands of this country are mostly improvable and are really improving', Cullen wrote, while Kames urged that the obstacle to this improvement was 'the indolence of landholders, the obstinate docility of the peasantry and the stupid attachment of both classes to ancient habit and practices'. What Kames called 'the chains of custom' were to be broken with philosophical chemistry and economic management. The endogamous Highlands clan system, for example, must be destroyed 'for to exclude strangers is to shut the door against all improvements'.[43] Highland soil and society became an important concern for Kames and his allies. Legislation after 1745 gave the state huge estates, apprenticed young men to Lowland farmers, issued orders for growing clover and maintaining arable and applied the rents and profits 'for the better civilizing and improving the Highlands of Scotland and preventing disorders there for the future'. In 1764 Kames backed the Highland tour of the naturalist John Walker, who reported the scandalous idleness of the Highlanders, surrounded as they were by 'the most fertile lands I ever saw in my life without cultivation'. In the 1770s, the two resumed discussion of water as the source of plant growth, a theme Kames also developed in his exchanges with Joseph Black. In 1779 Walker became natural history professor in Edinburgh, lectured on agriculture to many audiences, including the new Highland Society, and in 1790 founded the Edinburgh Agricultural Society to integrate fertility theory and mineralogy into élite culture. Walker linked natural history with economic and social change. While botanists discovered new plants, Walker argued that naturalists should 'discover useful qualities in those that are already known'. In the queries he sent to the Highlands, Walker argued that 'Improvement' through enclosure, new seeds and soil analyses 'are introductory to every sort of polished culture and urge the Farmer to Inclose not only from Interest but through Necessity'.[44]

These campaigns for the necessity of self-interested agrarian change throughout Scotland depended on the social authority of the philosophers and reformers who peddled recipes for improvement. In changing the model of natural order on the land, Edinburgh intellectuals had to design a new model of the social order of knowledge. Fierce fights about interest and cultural property wracked the Scottish enlightened elites.[45] The vulnerable fragility of the alliance on which the theory of improvement depended provided the context for the most ambitious late eighteenth century account of fertility, earth history and the origin of society, that of James Hutton. After abandoning Edinburgh careers as lawyer and physician, Hutton toured the farms of Norfolk and the Low Countries in the 1750s before settling in a Berwickshire farm in 1754. His introduction of the Norfolk system drew visitors from surrounding estates. He ran field experiments on the source of soil fertility, judging that its virtue affected the quantity rather than the quality of his crops. Hutton used tests for phlogiston to assess the role of light on plant growth and adopted Black's tests for chalk content to assay his soils. Inspired by reading Tull's treatises, Hutton composed a vast agricultural essay of his own. In 1764 he travelled the Highlands for the Commissioners for Annexed Estates, studying the natural history and commenting harshly on the fertilizer schemes in use there: 'much labour thrown away'. In his agricultural programme, Hutton endorsed the virtues of the division of labour which his friend 'Mr Smith has so beautifully illustrated' and argued that the farm-owners, not their labourers, should be protected by state legislation.[46]

These concerns with the calculation of soil fertility and the secularization of the agrarian economy were absorbed into Hutton's earth history, inaugurated in the 1760s and published from the 1780s. Just as Smith argued in 1776 that the wise reason which governed the national economy was only to be made out by an impartial philosophical contemplation of the whole system, so Hutton reckoned that the systematic machine which governed earth history was visible to the philosophical historian, not to those absorbed by the startling events of apparently convulsive nature. Hutton explained that 'the *pabulum* of life' was prepared in 'living plants' and circulated throughout the natural economy. 'According to the theory, a soil adapted to the growth of plants is necessarily prepared, and carefully preserved, and in the necessary waste of land which is inhabited, the foundation is laid for future continents, in order to support the system of this living world.'[47] This 'system' had rather carefully defined social characteristics. It was 'peculiarly adapted to the purposes of man, who ... measures its extent and determines its productions at his pleasure'. The planet's history was uniquely apparent to the philosophic and measured gaze, 'those of liberal fortunes' whom Smith lauded in the essay Hutton published in the same year as his own *Theory of the Earth* (1795). Nature, 'considered as a machine', would always provide the agrarian basis for civil society, so rational philosophy's future was assured. And nature, this philosophy's topic, would never experience dramatic change, so its knowledge would be cumulative.[48]

Hutton made rational agriculture the mark of humanity's transition to civil society. Each landlord was 'like a God on earth' and such 'a philosophic view' was 'necessarily required in a person who shall, in acting deliberately or intentionally, controul the course of nature ... such a thing is agriculture'. This philosophy was institutionalized on a national scale. At the end of his *Gentleman Farmer* Kames set out plans for a Board of Agriculture to survey soils and husbandry. The Board was to be emblematic of the tenuous link between disinterested patriotism and self-interested economic advance which dominated Scottish debates on the position of the enlightened philosopher. Kames argued that 'computation is the touchstone of profit and loss' and computation of the agrarian economy would be the key to unlock the chains of custom: 'to break loose from slavery, a man must be blessed by nature with a superior degree of understanding and activity.' By 1793 the government had established an Agriculture Board with Kames' disciple John Sinclair as its president and Arthur Young as its secretary. Young's career represents the culmination of the assault on the moral economy and its displacement by a new programme of calculation, surveillance and soil chemistry. As Maureen McNeil and Sarah Wilmot have argued, his late eighteenth century account of profit and rent maximization depended on the identification of the real capital of scientific farming with the cultural capital of moral and social advance.[49] Young's farming tours of the 1770s and 1780s, and his journal, the *Annals of Agriculture*, acted as the focus of this class interest. His account of fertility derived from the materialist chemistry of the dissenter Joseph Priestley, which offered a new analysis of the *aerial economy* in which phlogiston fed plants through respiration and helped restore the balance of virtue in both nature and society.[50] This innovative pneumatics of vegetation, backed with the authority of Scottish philosophical chemistry, let Young and Priestley read soil fertility as a political question. They surveyed the aerial and agrarian virtue of different farms. Young thundered against 'the oppression of tythes', praised 'the progress of liberty' in France, and argued for a purely secular account of social order. Politics forced Young to trim the more radical implications of his agrarian politics in the anti-Jacobin scares of the 1790s. He swiftly turned on the English radicals and won himself the secretariship of the new Board of Agriculture in 1793. One conservative reviewer compared Young's chemical, political and agrarian tergiversations with 'alchemy', another complained that the Board's aim was 'to form a general code which was to regulate the agricultural operations of the whole kingdom.[51] Codification had immediate social meaning. Young railed against the moral economy and 'the glaring injustice in violently attempting to lower prices which are high from real scarcity by the hand of God'. He found allies on the bench. In 1788 judges in Young's county of Suffolk ruled that 'the Law of Moses is not obligatory on us' in matters of husbandry. Gleaning cut cornfields, though sanctioned by scripture and custom, could not tell against the economic rights of the landlord: 'the soil is his, the seed is his and in natural justice his also are the profits'.[52] This code was backed up with measured trials. Grain-market custom included definitions of extremely varying techniques and standards for the measure of grain. These variations included decisions whether the measure should be heaped or level, whether the grain should be shaken after pouring into the bushel, whether the same measure should be used in times of dearth or glut. Larger local standards for the bushel, for example, might help customers of grain but penalize those who paid tithes. Uncertain standards aided market manipulation, while central imposition of standards for the grain bushel, inaugurated from the later eighteenth century, helped centralize and regulate the market.[53]

The values of scientific management, and the commodification of corn, required standardization. Young and his allies, such as Jeremy Bentham, used these arguments to license the authority of precise trials. As Keith Tribe has pointed out, Young helped constitute the farm as a production unit by describing 'ideal farms' solely analysed in terms of capital flow. In 1786 Young explained to his readers that their 'talents, skill and industry' must be devoted to removing 'the intrusions of storms, thieves, crows, rabbits, hares, sportsmen or idlers'. Following Tull's precepts, Young argued that a natural setting for experimentation would only be achieved by the social reorganization of the land. The agricultural improver William Marshall reckoned that 'to make an Authentic Experiment, an identity of Place, Time, Element and Process must be strictly observed in every particular ... Nor can the Experiment be authentic, if the Process be in any instance left to an Agent; it must be performed by the immediate hand or under the immediate Eye of the Experimentalist'. Reliable knowledge of the soil's products required reliable social order on the farm and in the marketplace. The productivity of earth was no longer the basis of social order, but to be measured only as the residue left by social agents. Smith applied this doctrine to his analysis of rent, which he defined as 'the work of nature which remains after deducting or compensating every thing which can be regarded as the work of man'. The agricultural experimenters agreed that the authority of these measures depended on their disinterest, the withdrawal of the analyst from the corrupt distortions of society.[54]

The boom in grain prices and rents during the wars with republican France, the establishment of Young's Board and the culmination of parliamentary enclosure led directly to the establishment of the Royal Institution at the end of the 1790s. The new natural philosophers there, led by Humphry Davy, forged a combination of agricultural chemistry, patriarchal culture and heroic expertise. In his lectures for the Agriculture Board Davy urged that 'it is from the higher classes of society, from the proprietors of land ... that the principles of improvement must flow to the labouring classes of the community, and in all cases the benefit must be always likewise the interest of the proprietors of the soil'.[55] The tub-thumping discourses delivered at the Board of Agriculture and the Royal Institution during the Napoleonic Wars represented a series of displacements, towards the laboratory, the state and the wealthy landlord. Protagonists of improvement and capitalization needed a new history of natural philosophy, which made it obvious that chemists were the masters of the principles of soil fertility. They needed a new history of the planet, which denied the immediate role of God in its course. And they needed a new history of farming tradition, which made custom look like slavery and improvement look natural. These stories were never universally compelling. During the Napoleonic Wars, public authorities continued to intervene in grain markets to force down price or maintain supply. The Board of Agriculture looked more like one aspect of the Tory patronage system than an expert agency for agricultural planning, while the audience for Young and Davy remained sceptical of the efficacy of current agricultural chemistry to deliver the goods to untutored farmers or overambitious landlords. Sinclair campaigned for the establishment of 'experimental farms' which 'would remove every doubt on the subject'; Young complained that the Board hired men 'who scarcely knew the right end of a plough'. While Davy commended complex analytical techniques to any farmer who wished to test soil quality, he also used his public platform to stress the uniquely privileged powers which the specialist savant could command. These histories of science, the soil and society rarely found their warrant in existing practice, but instead promised visionary rewards to those classes who sustained them.[56]

Images of nature and of society are made up of visions like these. In the accounts of soil fertility, especially, we can see two salient features of our own contemporary version of natural and social history. Following Davy, Justus von Liebig, and other masters of early nineteenth century agricultural chemistry, modernity does not see the soil as a sempiternal treasure house. Davy argued that 'the vegetable kingdom' is not 'a secure and inalterable inheritance' but 'a doubtful and insecure possession, to be preserved only by labour and extended and perfected by ingenuity'. Liebig famously wrote that 'modern agriculture' was 'a system of exhaustion' and often cited Adam Smith's political economy to back his account of the farm cycle as an analogue of the circulation of industrial capital. The factory became the standard against which agricultural production was to be judged.[57] Modernity also inherited another important tenet from early modern debates on the basis of the social order in nature: the true picture of the world is supposedly attained by the removal of the observer from immediate social pressure. We have inherited both concerns. Nature's powers do not guarantee society's survival, nor do social powers guarantee knowledge of nature. British protagonists of Early Modern debates on the earth's fertility reckoned they could provide for the social order by managing nature and that they could escape from society's distortions by making their own social interests natural.

NOTES

My thanks to Mikuláš Teich, Chris Bertelli and Steven Shapin for very helpful discussions on the topic of this paper.

1 Patrick Wright, *On Living in an Old Country* (London, 1985).

2 Keith Thomas, *Man and the Natural World: Changing Attitudes in England 1500–1800* (Harmondsworth, 1984), pp. 13–16; Raymond Williams, *The Country and the City* (Frogmore, 1975), pp. 21, 71.

3 E. P. Thompson, *Customs in Common* (London, 1991), pp. 185–351; Joyce Appleby, *Economic Thought and Ideology in Seventeenth Century England* (Princeton, 1978), pp. 27–8; Keith Wrightson, *English Society 1580–1680* (London, 1982), pp. 175–9. Adolphus Speed, *Adam out of Eden* (London, 1659) is cited in Keith Tribe, *Land, Labour and Economic Discourse* (London, 1978), p. 59.

4 Roy Porter, 'Creation and Credence: The Career of Theories of the Earth in Britain 1660–1820', in B. Barnes and S. Shapin (eds.), *Natural Order* (Beverly Hills, 1979), pp. 97–124 (104–5).

5 William Lehmann, *Henry Home, Lord Kames and the Scottish Enlightenment* (The Hague, 1971), p. 111; Lord Kames, *The Gentleman Farmer* (Edinburgh, 1776), pp. 284–5.

6 Adam Smith, *An Inquiry into the Nature and Causes of the Wealth of Nations* (Edinburgh, 1814), ed. David Buchanan, 4 vols., II, p. 55; Thompson, *Customs in Common*, p. 281, n. 1.

7 Boyd Hilton, *Corn, Cash and Commerce* (Oxford, 1977), pp. 303–14; Thompson, *Customs in Common*, pp. 164–75; Richard Grove, 'Colonial Conservation, Ecological Hegemony and Popular Resistance', in John Mackenzie (ed.), *Imperialism and the Natural World* (Manchester, 1990), pp. 15–50.

8 Keith Thomas, *Religion and the Decline of Magic* (Harmondsworth, 1972), pp. 504–5.

9 Wrightson, *English Society*, pp. 180–1; Peter Burke, *Popular Culture in Early Modern Europe* (London, 1978), pp. 277–8.

10 Josiah Langdale, ploughman, cited in Margaret Spufford, *Small Books and Pleasant Histories: Popular Fiction and its Readership in Seventeenth-century England* (Cambridge, 1985), p. 30; John Evelyn to Thomas Browne, 1657, cited in John Dixon Hunt, *The Figure in the Landscape: Poetry, Painting and Gardening during the Eighteenth Century* (Baltimore, 1989), p. 28.

11 Samuel Hartlib, *Legacy of Husbandry*, 3rd edn (London, 1658), p. 38; Walter Blith, *The English Improver Improved*, 3rd edn (London, 1652), sig. d3^{v}. See Charles Webster, *The Great Instauration* (London, 1975), pp. 356, 471–3; Joan Thirsk, *Agricultural Change: Policy and Practice, 1500–1750* (Cambridge, 1990), pp. 121–2, 276–7.

12 Carolyn Merchant, *The Death of Nature* (London, 1980), pp. 42–68; G. E. Fussell, *Crop Nutrition: Science and Practice before Liebig* (Lawrence, 1971), pp. 57–9.

13 Gerrard Winstanley, *The Law of Freedom and Other Writings*, ed. Christopher Hill (Harmondsworth, 1973), pp. 20–5; for Harrington see J. G. A. Pocock, *The Machiavellian Moment* (Princeton, 1975), pp. 383–96; Buchanan Sharp, *In Contempt of all Authority: Rural Artisans and Riot in the West of England 1586–1660* (Los Angeles, 1980), pp. 244–5.

14 Cressy Dymock, 1649, cited in Thirsk, *Agricultural Change*, p. 282. See Charles Wilson, *England's Apprenticeship 1603–1763* (London, 1965), pp. 144–6 on 'conservative, illiterate and suspicions peasant farmers'.

15 Kenelm Digby, *Discourse Concerning the Vegetation of Plants* (London, 1661), p. 71; Robert Sharrock, *History of the Propagation and Improvement of Vegetables* (London, 1660), p. 86; William Clarke, *Natural History of Niter* (London, 1670), pp. 37–9.

16 R. V. Lennard, 'English Agriculture under Charles II: The Evidence of the Royal Society's "Enquiries" ', *Economic History Review*, 4 (1932–4), 23–45; Michael Hunter, *Establishing the New Science: The Experience of the Early Royal Society* (Woodbridge, 1989), pp. 105–14. See Mayling Stubbs, 'John Beale, Philosophical Gardener of Herefordshire: The Improvement of Agriculture and Trade in the Royal Society', *Annals of Science*, 46 (1989), pp. 323–63 (342–3). For Blith's fate, see Thirsk, *Agricultural Change*, pp. 290–1; for changes in the post-Restoration edition of Austen's *Treatise of Fruit Trees*, see J. R. Jacob, 'Restoration, Reforma-

tion and the Origins of the Royal Society', *History of Science*, 13 (1975), pp. 155–71 (170); for the neo-Harringtonian account of the past, see Pocock, *Machiavellian Moment*, pp. 416–17.

17 'Enquiries concerning Agriculture', *Philosophical Transactions*, 1 (1665), 91–4. For gentlemanly experience, see Steven Shapin, 'Pump and Circumstance: Robert Boyle's Literary Technology', *Social Studies of Science*, 14 (1984), 481–520.

18 John Evelyn, *Sylva*, 3rd edn (London, 1679), 'to the Reader'; John Worlidge, *Systema agriculturae*, 3rd edn (London, 1681), preface and pp. 1–2, 8, 13.

19 Merchant, *Death of Nature*, pp. 236–52 on Evelyn; Lindsay Sharp, 'Timber, Science and Economic Reform in the Seventeenth Century', *Forestry*, 48 (1975), 51–86 on Petty. For women in grain riots, see Natalie Zemon Davies, *Society and Culture in Early Modern France* (Cambridge, 1987), pp. 145–7 and Thompson, *Customs in Common*, pp. 233-4, 305–36.

20 John Houghton, *Collection for the Improvement of Husbandry and Trade*, nos. 3–9 (April–May 1692); see J. R. Jacob, 'Restoration Ideologies and the Royal Society', *History of Science*, 18 (1980), 25–38, and Stubbs, 'John Beale', pp. 352–5.

21 Evelyn, *Sylva*, p. 330; Newton on vegetation and condensation, 1675–6, in R. S. Westfall, *Never at Rest* (Cambridge, 1980), pp. 306–8. For Newton as Lord of the Manor, see *ibid.*, pp. 340–1.

22 W. Hiscock, *David Gregory, Isaac Newton and their Circle* (Oxford, 1937), p. 26; Henry Pemberton, *View of Sir Isaac Newton's Philosophy* (London, 1728), p. 245.

23 Thomas Manley, *Usury at six per cent. examined* (London, 1669), p. 10; for sacred physics, see Marjorie Nicolson, *Mountain Gloom and Mountain Glory* (New York, 1959), pp. 184–224.

24 Matthew Hale, *The Primitive Origination of Mankind* (London, 1677), p. 370; Robert Hooke, *Posthumous Works*, ed. Richard Waller (London, 1705), p. 427 (lecture of July 1699); John Ray, *The Wisdom of God Manifested in the Works of the Creation* (London, 1691), p. 113 and *Miscellaneous Discourses* (London, 1692), pp. 177–8.

25 Fussell, *Crop Nutrition*, p. 103.

26 Isaac Newton, *Opticks*, 4th edn (London, 1730, reprinted New York, 1952), p. 400; Isaac Newton in Thomas Birch (ed.), *History of the Royal Society*, 4 vols (London, 1757), III, p. 251 (9 December 1675).

27 Thomas Burnet, *The Theory of the Earth* (London, 1691; reprinted Fontwell, 1965), pp. 60, 148; M. C. Jacob and W. A. Lockwood, 'Political Millenarianism and Burnet's *Sacred Theory*', *Science Studies* 2 (1972), 265–79; Newton to Burnet, January 1681, in *The Correspondence of Isaac Newton*, ed. H. W. Turnbull, J. F. Scott, A. R. Hall and Laura Tilling, 7 vols. (Cambridge, 1959–77), II, pp. 329–34; Joseph Levine, *Dr Woodward's Shield* (Berkeley, 1977), pp. 25–6.

28 Levine, *Dr Woodward's Shield*, pp. 93–113 (for collections); Edwards to Woodward, 4 February 1697, Cambridge University Library MSS ADD 7647 f. 114; John Woodward, *Natural History of the Earth* (London, 1695), p. 165 (for supernatural power).

29 Levine, *Dr Woodward's Shield*, pp. 69–72; John Arbuthnot, *An Examination of Dr Woodward's Account of the Deluge* (London, 1697), p. 12.

30 Woodward to Edwards, 23 May 1699, Cambridge University Library MSS ADD 7647 f. 116; Woodward, 'Some Thoughts and Experiments Concerning Vegetation', *Philosophical Transactions*, 21 (1699), pp. 193–227 (213).

31 James Turner, *The Politics of Landscape* (Oxford, 1979), p. 165 on the 'taboo' against rural work in seventeenth-century verse; John Barrell, *The Dark Side of the Landscape* (Cambridge, 1980), p. 12 on Joseph Warton, *Works of Virgil* (London, 1753).

32 Jethro Tull, *The New Horse Houghing Husbandry* (London, 1731), pp. 38–9. See Tribe, *Land, Labour and Economic Discourse*, p. 65.

33 Tull, *New Horse Houghing Husbandry* (1731), pp. 107–9; A. Clow and N. Clow, *The Chemical Revolution* (London, 1952), p. 466.

34 G. E. Fussell, *Jethro Tull: His Influence on Mechanized Agriculture* (Reading, 1973), pp. 23–5, 49, 60–1.

35 Tull, *New Horse Houghing Husbandry* (1731), pp. xii, xx.

36 *Ibid.*, p. xxvi. For field trials, see Clow and Clow, *Chemical Revolution*, p. 471.

37 *Ibid.*, pp. 115, 124.

38 J. H. Plumb, 'The Walpoles: Father and Son', in J. H. Plumb (ed.), *Studies in Social History* (London, 1955), pp. 181–207 (184–5); F. N. Egerton, 'Richard Bradley's Understanding of Biological Productivity', *Journal of the History of Biology*, 2 (1969), 391–410, citing Richard Bradley, *A General Treatise of Husbandry and Gardening*, 3 vols. (London, 1721–4), II, p. 71.

39 Daniel Defoe, *The Life and Strange Surprizing Adventures of Robinson Crusoe* (London, 1719, reprinted Oxford, 1927), pp. 88–90; Williams, *The Country and the City*, p. 80.

40 For the Black Act, see E. P. Thompson, *Whigs and Hunters* (Harmondsworth, 1977). Robert Maxwell, *The Practical Husbandman* (Edinburgh, 1757) is cited in Fussell, *Jethro Tull*, p. 64. For the Society of Improvers and Tull, see Robert Maxwell, *Select Transactions of the Honourable the Society of Improvers* (Edinburgh, 1743), pp. 174–85 and Steven Shapin, 'The Audience for Science in Eighteenth Century Edinburgh', *History of Science*, 12 (1974), pp. 95–121 (102 and 118 n13).

41 Adam Smith, *Essays on Philosophical Subjects*, ed. W. P. D. Wightman, J. C. Bryce and I. S. Ross (Oxford, 1980), pp. 49–50, 66.

42 J. R. R. Christie, 'The Rise and Fall of Scottish Science', in M. Crosland (ed.), *The Emergence of Science in Western Europe* (London, 1975), pp. 111–26; A. C. Chitnis, 'Agricultural Improvement, Political Management and Civic Virtue in Enlightened Scotland', *Studies on Voltaire and the Eighteenth Century*, 245 (1986), 475–88.

43 Marie-Hélène Thévenot, 'Un magistrat au champs: Henry Home of Kames', *Etudes anglaises*, 35 (1982), 13–25; A. L. Donovan, *Philosophical Chemistry in the Scottish Enlightenment* (Edinburgh, 1975), pp. 67–72, 86–90; J. V. Golinski, *Science as Public Culture* (Cambridge, 1992), pp. 31–7; C. Withers, 'Cullen's Agricultural Lectures', *Agricultural History Review*, 37 (1989), pp. 144–56 (149). For Kames on 'custom', see Lehmann, *Henry Home Lord Kames*, p. 85 and Clow and Clow, *Chemical Revolution*, pp. 480–3; for the attack on the clans, see Ian S. Ross, *Lord Kames and the Scotland of his Day* (Oxford, 1972), p. 320.

44 For Highland management, see Malcolm Gray, *The Highland Economy 1750–1850* (Edinburgh, 1957), pp. 77–81; Eric Hobsbawm, 'Capitalisme et agriculture: les réformateurs écossais au 18e siècle', *Annales*, 33 (1978), 580–601; Ross, *Lord Kames*, pp. 316–18. For Walker, see Charles Withers, 'A Neglected Scottish Agriculturalist: the "Georgical Lectures" and Agricultural Writings of the Rev Dr John Walker', *Agricultural History Review*, 33 (1985), 132–46, p. 139; Roger Emerson, 'The Scottish Enlightenment and the End of the Philosophical

Society of Edinburgh', *British Journal for the History of Science*, 21 (1988), pp. 33–66 (50, 60).

45 Lehmann, *Henry Home, Lord Kames*, pp. 299–302; Steven Shapin, 'Property, Patronage and the Politics of Science: the Founding of the Royal Society of Edinburgh', *British Journal for the History of Science*, 7 (1974), pp. 1–41 (15).

46 Jean Jones, 'James Hutton's Agricultural Researches and his Life as a Farmer', *Annals of Science*, 42 (1985), 573–601.

47 James Hutton, 'Theory of the Earth', *Transactions of the Royal Society of Edinburgh*, 1 (1788), pp. 209–304 (291), and *Abstract of a Dissertation concerning the System of the Earth* (Edinburgh, 1785), p. 29.

48 Hutton, 'Theory of the Earth', pp. 291, 295 and *Theory of the Earth with Proofs and Illustrations*, 2 vols. (Edinburgh, 1795), II, p. 239. See R. Grant, 'Hutton's Theory of the Earth', in R. S. Porter and L. Jordanova (eds.), *Images of the Earth* (Chalfont St Giles, 1979), pp. 23–38.

49 Hutton, *Investigations of the Principles of Knowledge* (1794), cited in Maureen McNeil, *Under the Banner of Science: Erasmus Darwin and his Age* (Manchester, 1987), p. 173; Kames, *Gentleman Farmer*, pp. 34, 66; for (agri)cultural capital see Sarah Wilmot, *'The Business of Improvement': Agriculture and Scientific Culture in Britain 1700–1870* (Reading, 1990), pp. 22–3, 40–1 and McNeil, *Under the Banner of Science*, pp. 171–5, 197–9.

50 J. G. Gazley, *The Life of Arthur Young* (Philadelphia, 1973), pp. 151–4; Simon Schaffer, 'Measuring Virtue', in Andrew Cunningham and Roger French (eds.), *The Medical Enlightenment of the Eighteenth Century* (Cambridge, 1990), pp. 281–318 (291).

51 Gazley, *Life of Young*, pp. 268, 289, 312–18; Arthur Young, *Autobiography*, ed. M. Betham-Edwards (London, 1898), pp. 219–24; Christopher Bertelli, 'Theory and Practice: the Response of Farmers to Political Economy and Scientific Agriculture in early Victorian England', M. Phil dissertation, Department of History and Philosophy of Science, Cambridge, 1987, p. 25.

52 McNeil, *Under the Banner of Science*, p. 186; Thompson, *Customs in Common*, p. 140.

53 Thompson, *Customs in Common*, p. 217; Witold Kula, *Measures and Men* (Princeton, 1986), pp. 43–70.

54 Tribe, *Land, Labour and Economic Discourse*, pp. 73 (on Young), 105–6 (on Smith); G. E. Mingay, *Arthur Young and his Times* (London, 1975), pp. 84–6 for Young's experiments; William Marshall, 1779, cited in G. E. Fussell, 'The Technique of Early Field Experiments', *Journal of the Royal Agricultural Society*, 96 (1935), pp. 78–88 (86).

55 Humphry Davy, *Elements of Agricultural Chemistry* (London, 1813), p. 24; Morris Berman, 'The Early Years of the Royal Institution', *Science Studies*, 2 (1972), 205–40; Golinski, *Science as Public Culture*, pp. 198–9.

56 Pamela Horn, 'The Contribution of the Propagandist to Eighteenth-Century Agricultural Improvement', *Historical Journal*, 25 (1982), pp. 313–29 (328); *Autobiography of Young*, p. 242; Golinski, *Science as Public Culture*, pp. 199–201; Clow and Clow, *Chemical Revolution*, pp. 501–2.

57 Davy, *Elements of Agricultural Chemistry*, p. 233; W. Krohn and W. Schäfer, 'The Origins and Structure of Agricultural Chemistry', in G. Lemaine *et al.* (eds.), *Perspectives on the Emergence of Scientific Disciplines* (Paris, 1976), pp. 27–52 (32, 36).

EIGHT

THE ISLAND AND THE HISTORY OF ENVIRONMENTALISM: THE CASE OF ST VINCENT

RICHARD GROVE

THE King's Hill Forest Act passed on St Vincent in 1791 was a remarkable piece of legislation. Above all, it was based on a novel climatic theory, that deforestation might cause rainfall decline. The objective of the Act was to 'appropriate for the benefit of the neighbourhood the Hill ... and for enclosing the same and preserving the timber and other trees growing thereon in order to attract rain'.[1] The fact that the Act was unusual was clearly recognized at the time. Governor James Seton commented that the Act is 'of an unusual and extraordinary character', not least in the powers which the state arrogated to itself to control land and to impose penalties for its misuse.[2] In the language of today the Act thus conceived of two kinds of sustainability, at a local level, in terms of timber supply; and in a much broader climatic sense. It thus enshrined in legislation a highly sophisticated set of principles and was, in short, based on 'scientific' theory rather than on social structures or assumptions. The story behind the King's Hill Act is relevant not only to its later influence on colonial environmental legislation but also to the environmental crisis of today and to the special contribution which islands have played in bringing about the conceptualization of environmental problems on both local and global scales. There were two major innovative features of the King's Hill Forest Act. Firstly the Act dealt with the climatic consequences of environmental degradation and developed a conservationist solution to the problem. Secondly, this pioneer of environmental legislation developed in the very specific circumstances of an island. It was no accident that it did so. As we shall see, historically, oceanic islands have played a critical conceptual role in the emergence of modern environmentalism and in the emergence of modern ideas about conservation. St Vincent occupies a pivotal place in the origins of environmentalism, along with two other islands, St Helena and Mauritius.

How then do we set about understanding the context and origins of

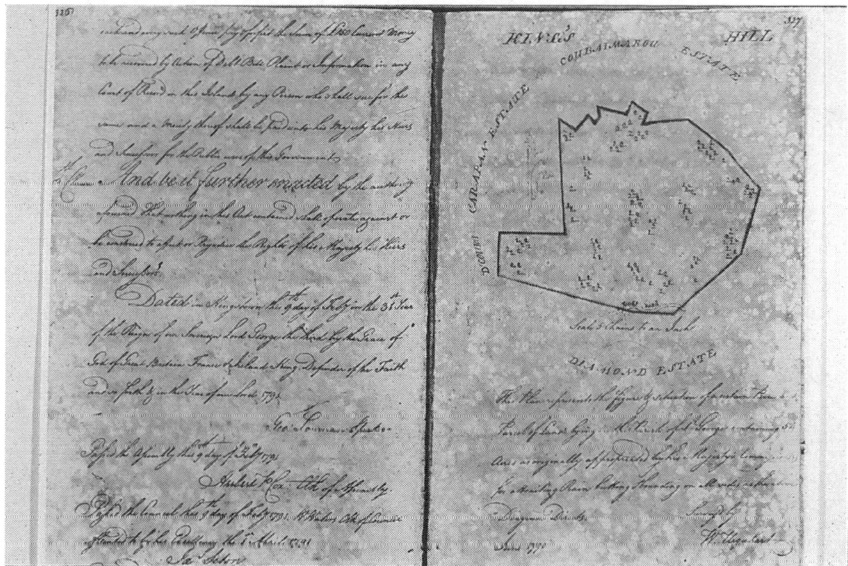

Figure 6 The Kings Hill Act of 1791.

the King's Hill legislation? First of all we need to question some of the more conventional histories of the emergence of environmental institutions. Most of these have promoted a history of conservation and environmentalism closely associated with the history of United States during the nineteenth century. According to these narratives George Perkins Marsh, Henry David Thoreau and John Muir were the originators and theorists of the 'gospel' of North American conservationism. In fact, recent research tends to indicate that conservation arrived rather late in European North America and that the main history of conservationist responses to environmental degradation developed much further 'south', in the context of the complex and largely destructive encounter between colonial expansion, tropical environments, the European imagination and indigenous environmental knowledge. Within these very broad categories the interaction between three much narrower phenomena need to be explored as a basis for understanding the late institutional basis of environmentalism as it came to fruition during the late eighteenth century. These three components are; the professionalization of science and particularly natural history; the emergence of global networks of botanical and other specialist information flow and, not least, the development of perceptions of the environmental degradation of oceanic islands. By the beginning of the 1790s (and a little earlier in the French colonial context) these combined phenomena had given rise to a coherent theory of 'desiccationism' connecting forest destruction to rainfall change and to a very specific kind of interest in tree-planting and afforestation. Both matters, it was considered, were a proper part of the concern of the state, in particular the colonial state. If they were not attended to, it was believed, social and economic chaos might follow. Of course, at the time of the King's Hill Act these ideas were only considered among a narrow circle of influential individuals. They were, as yet, weak in their impact, and only applied in actual policy terms in very few geographical locations. It should be noted, however, that highly interventionist environmental controls, especially in forest protection, were being pursued, often on a large scale, and quite independently of the European colonial regimes, by indigenous states and empires, by for example, the Chinese colonial power in Formosa, and by the Rajahs of Sind in North-West India, where enormous programmes of afforestation and game preservation were being pursued by 1730. Such indigenous interventions were often highly socially manipulative.[3]

In contrast, even as late as the end of the eighteenth century colonial environmentalism (as we may term it from hindsight) was confined to St Vincent, St Helena, Mauritius and to some very limited locations in India. It consisted, in practice, in limited forest reservation, timber licensing and tree planting programmes. Only in the three island colonies was environmental regulation based on scientifically-formulated fears of climate or precipitational change. However, it is on this development that we need to focus as desiccationism provided the basis for the coherent intellectual tradition behind the much larger programmes for later colonial conservationism, involving a series of ideas about anthropogenic effects on climate that has persisted and become very prominent today. The origins of colonial conservation legislation date back to the late seventeenth century, particularly at the Cape Colony and St Helena, and to a lesser extent in North America.[4] They were closely associated with the conditions of colonial rule. Capital intensive plantation agriculture, based on slave labour, promoted very rapid environmental change in terms of deforestation and subsequent soil erosion, flooding, gullying, local aridification and drying up of the streams and rivers. The first European colonies on the Canaries and at Madeira were devastated in this way by the effects of deforestation for sugar cultivation as early as the fifteenth century.[5]

The impact of introduced domestic stock was often rapidly felt, and we know that by the end of the sixteenth century severe soil erosion and pasture damage had occurred in large parts of Mexico.[6] Between 1600 and 1800 soil erosion became particularly acute on the Caribbean plantation islands and similar effects were being reported at St Helena by 1670. These phenomena were so serious and obvious on the restricted spaces of islands (or on isolated peninsulas such as the Cape of Good Hope) that local conservationist responses soon developed during the late seventeenth century into limited legislative attempts to irrigate land, prevent deforestation and carry out planting programmes. However these were strictly local responses for which previous precedents were not easily available, and there was very little diffusion of knowledge about soil erosion or conservation. Similar developments were taking place in Japan under the Tokugawa Shugunate, where urban and capitalist expansion promised effects similar to those of colonial plantation agriculture.[7] In general, however, until the end of the seventeenth century the tropical world was considered by Europeans to possess illimitable resources. This notion, which took a long time to dispel, was first questioned, in a highly empirical way, on island colonies threatened by the highly visible effects of plantation agriculture.

At this early stage in colonial expansion the notion of desiccationism started to make itself felt. Columbus is reported to have known that deforestation would cause rainfall changes. His thinking was probably based on the classical Greek writings of Theophrastus, which had first been printed in Italy in 1483. Columbus, who had witnessed the desiccation that had resulted from deforestation on the Canary Islands feared that the same developments might take place in the Caribbean. A century later we find the same concept elaborated in the work of Francis Bacon. It seems likely that Theophrastian concepts remained alive in Western thought after the Renaissance, although there are only scattered references to his ideas. However in the mid seventeenth century the desiccationist debate started to acquire some momentum, precisely in the context of island plantation agriculture. Deforestation in Jamaica was soon linked at this time to rainfall decline and, indeed, the theory was discussed by Sir Hans Sloane, who owned estates on the islands, in the *Philosophical Transactions of the Royal Society* during the 1670s.[8] Sir Edmund Halley, visiting St Helena at the same period, in 1676, made careful observations of the processes of soil erosion which were active on the island and theorized about the connections between rainfall, vegetation and runoff. Again, his observations were reported, although after a delay of some years, in the *Transactions* in 1691. In spite of these publications (which provide a clue to the way in which scientific associations would later develop an environmental debate) there was, at the beginning of the eighteenth century, virtually no way in which such knowledge could be easily diffused and transferred between colonies.

Figure 7 St Helena in *c.* 1570 during the Portuguese occupation, showing extensive deforestation. From *Jan Huygen Van Linschoten, his discours of voyages to Eeste and West Indies*, 1598.

So, for example, the local attempts made by officials to stop deforestation and plant trees on St Helena were studiously ignored or handicapped by the East India Company, which remained unaware or uninterested in the extent of environmental damage caused by its plantation policies. The case of the Dutch East India Company was somewhat different. Sharply aware of the problems of managing their home environment the Dutch selectively introduced forest management and tree-planting policies at the Cape and then in Java, where by the 1760s teak forests were being carefully managed, largely for naval purposes. VOC tree-planting policies at the Cape were important as they were later imitated by the French at Mauritius.[9] The Dutch made no attempt, however, to manage the Mauritius ebony forests in a similar way and by 1716 had actually abandoned the island. The most significant development in the Dutch context involved their deliberate fostering of botanical gardens and the fostering of botanical knowledge, botanical exploration and publishing. The establishment of botanical or 'Company' gardens (at, for example, Batavia, Peredeniya, Mauritius and the Cape) was essential for early experiments in plant transfer, particularly of spice and other plants to and from the West Indies. There were many different motives behind the establishment of botanical gardens by the colonial powers. However, the specialist skills needed to run networks of gardens and botanical exchange provided the basis for the employment of 'experts', most of whom were medical doctors, by all the colonial powers. The most significant development of this biological information system, essential to the emergence of eighteenth century environmental awareness, was a consequence of the very deliberate involvement of the French state in botanic garden development and systematic botanical exploration and collection. This involvement was sharpened by the rise of the 'agronomes' in France and the 'scientific' development of agriculture. Since the time of Colbert the French had become especially interested in English agricultural innovation and ideas about woodland management.[10] English agriculture had in turn gained much from the expulsion of the Huguenots from France and infusions of Dutch agricultural expertise.

By the 1760s the stimulus of systematic agricultural knowledge and early economic theory had crystallized in the evolution of the 'physiocratic' philosophies which became essential both to emergent French environmentalism and to proto-revolutionary thinking. By itself, however, this would not have enabled the growth of an environmental sensitivity. Emerging debates about the nature of the state, the foundations of economics, the management of agriculture and forestry and the workings of nature were all important to the evolution of environmental consciousness. When these debates came together with the empirical observations of the catastrophic effects of colonial plantation agriculture the results were decisive. The catalyst to the development of French colonial environmentalism was the appointment in 1766 of Pierre Poivre as Intendant of Mauritius. Poivre had already been extensively involved in attempts to transfer spice trees from the Dutch East Indies to Mauritius. In the course of trying to develop these and other objectives Poivre set up what was effectively a physiocratic state on the island. However, partly as a result of his experiments in plant transfer Poivre was already very interested in soil conditions and the effects of deforestation on moisture and local climate. He had developed these ideas in Lyons in the context of agricultural society meetings during the 1750s and in a paper written in 1763 made direct reference to what he thought were established connections between deforestation and rainfall change.[11] The provenance of these notions is not clear and further research would be needed to establish the source of Poivre's very definitive desiccationist convictions. The practical effects of the theory were soon apparent, however, particularly as Poivre had managed to persuade his physiocratic sympathizers in the colonial ministry in Paris of the seriousness of the deforestation issue. Poivre was not the first administrator of Mauritius to be concerned about the state of the island forests. This concern was not reinforced by the fear that a failure to control deforestation might result in rainfall decline. Moreover, Poivre was assisted by the services of Philibert Commerson as a professional and state naturalist. As a result the botanic garden was also much enlarged by the Intendant and was soon established as an unrivalled location for transferred plants and botanical expertise. In a law of 1769 and in later laws passed after Poivre had left the island in 1772 forest reservations were established on the basis of climatic arguments and to provide a sustainable timber supply. Meanwhile plans for state tree-planting were initiated, both to prevent soil erosion and, it was hoped, to promote rainfall. These plans were very ambitious in scale, one scheme of 1784 envisaging the planting of 500,000 trees. The complex environmental and botanical agendas pursued by the French on Mauritius stand out as the source of ideas for most subsequent conservationist initiatives in both British and French colonial contexts. Before investigating the way in which the methodology of Mauritius desiccationism was transferred to other parts of the world we need to look at another important aspect of eighteenth century environmentalism, the parallel development of state and colonial interests in tree-planting. Both developments were closely connected with the elaboration of botanical information and exchange networks during the latter half of the eighteenth century, particularly with the reinforcement of the French system by a British network centred on Sir Joseph Banks and his Linnaean exploring agents.

European tree-planting obsessions had devolved largely from concern about supplies of ship timber and the debate owed much to the contributions of John Evelyn, Buffon and Duhamel de Monceau. Tree-planting acquired a variety of potent meanings from the mid-seventeenth century onwards in both England and France, in economic terms and as an expression of power, order and improvement. Soon after its foundation the Society of Arts started to take a particular interest in arboriculture through the interests of its founder, William Shipley and in 1758 the Society started to award prizes for tree-planting. Significantly, Shipley and his colleagues were also much interested in exotic tree and plant transfer and in the establishment of botanic gardens as part of a wider improvement ideology. In 1762 this led the society to place an advertisement in its journal soliciting proposals for the establishment of a botanic garden in the West Indies.[12] It was this initiative by the Society of Arts that led Melville to establish the St Vincent gardens in 1763. In Scotland tree-planting had become a particular enthusiasm of the landed classes, above all in Fife. John Hope, Curator of the Edinburgh botanic garden, shared this enthusiasm, and was encouraged in it by his contacts with André Thouin and other tree-planting devotees of the Jardin du Roi in Paris. Hope in turn passed on his enthusiasm for tree-planting to his students, many of whom went on to become members of the East India Company Medical Service. One of them, William Roxburgh, as Superintendent of the Calcutta Botanic Garden, pioneered tree-planting programmes in north-eastern India.[13] In order to understand Roxburgh's tree-planting activities we need to shed a little light on the early pattern of the East India Company's worries about timber supplies. By 1761 Company officials at Fort William in Calcutta were already aware of the emerging French interests in conserving forests in Mauritius, and of their interest in the desirability of forest cover for defensive purposes. Throughout the 1760s the problems of timber supply at Calcutta for shipbuilding and urban supply became steadily more acute. So too did concerns about the degree of Company dependence on indigenous timber merchants. As a result, during the 1760s strenuous efforts were made to secure independent sources of supply from the Morangs region, on the northern Bihar border, whence supplies were floated down to Calcutta along the Kosi and Ganges rivers. Investigation of possible alternative sources was already reaching out as far as Burma and at this stage it became clear that the search for secure timber supplies away from indigenous control was becoming a major factor in East India Company expansion, not only in Bengal and Bihar but on the Bombay Presidency coast as well, where the desire to control timber sources contributed to Company involvement in the Maratha wars. On Prince of Wales Island and at Bassein in 1781 'indiscriminate cutting' was being openly put forward as a reason for the extension of political control.[14] However, it is also clear that the Indian forests were no longer being seen as inexhaustible sources of raw material supply, while the desirability of husbanding resources was already being canvassed by the colonial state.

On Mauritius the employment of a credible body of naturalists had bolstered the agendas of nascent state environmentalism. This kind of development was much delayed in India. Indeed it was an Indian ruler, the Nawab of Arcot, and not the East India Company, that first recognized the inherent value of professional naturalists, when the Nawab took Johann Koenig into his employ. Only as late as 1778 did the Company itself decide to employ Koenig, a Linnaean botanist from Schleswig-Holstein. William Roxburgh, who arrived in India in 1778, soon began the re-building of a Mughal garden, at Samulcottah, as a systematic botanic garden. However, this was a limited development. Further north, in Bengal, Robert Kyd, a Scotsman from Fife, started to replant several species of trees, some from the Himalayas, (as well as some imported cinnamon trees), in a private garden in Calcutta. This was partly a result of his shocked response to the famine of 1770 and what he saw as a need to establish alternative staple food plants. This led eventually to a proposal by Kyd in 1786 to establish a Company botanic garden in Calcutta.[15] In so doing Kyd was keenly aware of the precedents established at St Vincent and Mauritius. However he was also aware of the possibilities of developing tree stocks for plantations, an idea which he had probably also culled from the French in Mauritius. Until 1784 the East India Company Directors in London had failed to interest themselves in botanical matters. However in that year, with the appointment of the Board of Control, the situation was transformed, particularly with the rise to power of Henry Dundas as secretary of the Board of Control. Dundas was an agronomic and botanical enthusiast and an associate of Sir Joseph Banks. Indeed, after 1784 Banks was able to exercise considerable influence over EIC policy and to incorporate its servants into the global botanical network which he was now establishing. An early result of these changes was the appointment of Roxburgh to the Superintendency of the Calcutta Garden in 1792, in succession to Robert Kyd. The post gave Roxburgh the opportunity to develop an extensive tree-planting programme, carrying on the ideas of Kyd and John Hope as well as those of Pierre Poivre and his associates on Mauritius. From 1792 until 1820s it is possible to trace the pattern of a whole series of tree-planting initiatives developed in response to the deforestation of large parts of Bihar and Bengal. There is, however, no direct evidence that Roxburgh's agricultural zeal was fired by any well-defined climatic theory, even though he may have been acquainted with contemporary published works on the relationship between vegetation and moisture, particularly in the writings of Joseph Priestley. This is an area upon which further research may be able to shed some light.

However we do know that climatic theories had become very influential on St Vincent and St Helena between 1785 and 1795. The pattern of awareness that had developed on those islands was much more specially connected to the kinds of desiccationist interest in forest reservation which had emerged in Mauritius and which was ultimately decisive to the onset of state forest conservation in India. Roxburgh's geographically much larger afforestation efforts were, by contrast, eventually much less significant in the global development of conservation.

The connections between the Society of Arts, tree-planting and the establishment of the St Vincent Garden have already been alluded to, and the mere fact of the existence of a botanical garden on the island was clearly critical to subsequent developments there. The existence of the institution ensured that the environment of St Vincent would be monitored by individuals possessing a social and technical credibility that extended far beyond the bounds of the island, and who involved it in a network of globally-derived information from which precedent and experience could be derived. In this connection the appointment of Alexander Anderson was clearly significant in terms of the way in which he was able to articulate and apply environmental notions which had developed in very distant locations, above all in Mauritius. The connections with the latter island was strengthened by an existing pattern of contacts which had evolved in the course of numerous plant transfers. To some extent, then, the transfer of desiccationist notions to St Vincent was not derived substantially from local conditions but rather from imported technological assumptions. In the importation of environmental legislation, two factors stand out as having been significant; firstly the existence of expertise and a scientific discourse on the island, and secondly the evolution of environmental perceptions based on the mental constraints imposed by the island geography of St Vincent. In other words the notion of resource limitability was already present; it was simply not possible for planters to move on to a better situation, when an existing location had been degraded. It has to be said that the detailed administrative background to the introduction of the King's

Hill Forest Bill into the St Vincent Assembly on 13th November 1788 by William Bannatyne is still not fully understood.[16] Historically, however, the broader social and institutional context of the legislation can be stated with some confidence. The geological and climatic history of the island in 1788 was already well known and the vulnerability of its population to extreme events well appreciated. This impression is gained in particular from Alexander Anderson's paper published in the *Philosophical Transactions of the Royal Society* of 1785.[17]

In this article it is clear that Anderson was also keenly interested in cloud formation and the association between vegetation and moisture retention. He does not, though, go on to elaborate on the likely consequences of deforestation, emphasizing instead the bulk and impenetrability of the forest cover. Internationally, nevertheless, the causes of climatic change and meteorological alteration were already firmly on the international scientific agenda. Joseph Priestley had published his *Experiments and observations on different kinds of air* in London in 1774 and published an article on the subject in the Royal Society *Transactions* in the very year in which Anderson's article on St Vincent volcanism had appeared.[18] Only a year earlier Benjamin Franklin had put forward a theory linking volcanic dust to climatic change in the *Memoirs of the Literary and Philosophical Society of Manchester*.[19] Anderson would have been aware of such publications and thinking, as, of course, was Sir Joseph Banks himself. Banks had already, in his diaries, between particularly scathing about the extent of soil erosion on St Helena when he had visited the island in 1771. The colonists had, he said, 'made a desert out of a paradise'. However, these facts do not allow us to conclude that either Banks or Anderson played a decisive role in initiating the King's Hill Legislation, and indeed it would seem that even had Banks done so the only conceivable source for any fully developed precedent for desiccation-based forest legislation remained that gazetted in Mauritius in 1769 and subsequently renewed in 1777.

A partial clue to solving the problem of the origin of the King's Hill Act rests in the wording of the legislation, that it would 'be appropriate for the benefit of the neighbourhood', on the basis of the forests attracting rain. A passage in the Assembly minutes in March 1789 refers to the clearance of 'wild and unfrequented woods turned to cotton planting'. This, of course, reflects the wider economic background of the introduction of cotton cultivation into the island, an enterprise which Banks had sought to encourage through the introduction of new species of cotton seed from India. The environmental consequences of cotton plantation soon appeared to be serious, as an Assembly report of January 1790 indicates. Widespread gullying was described as a

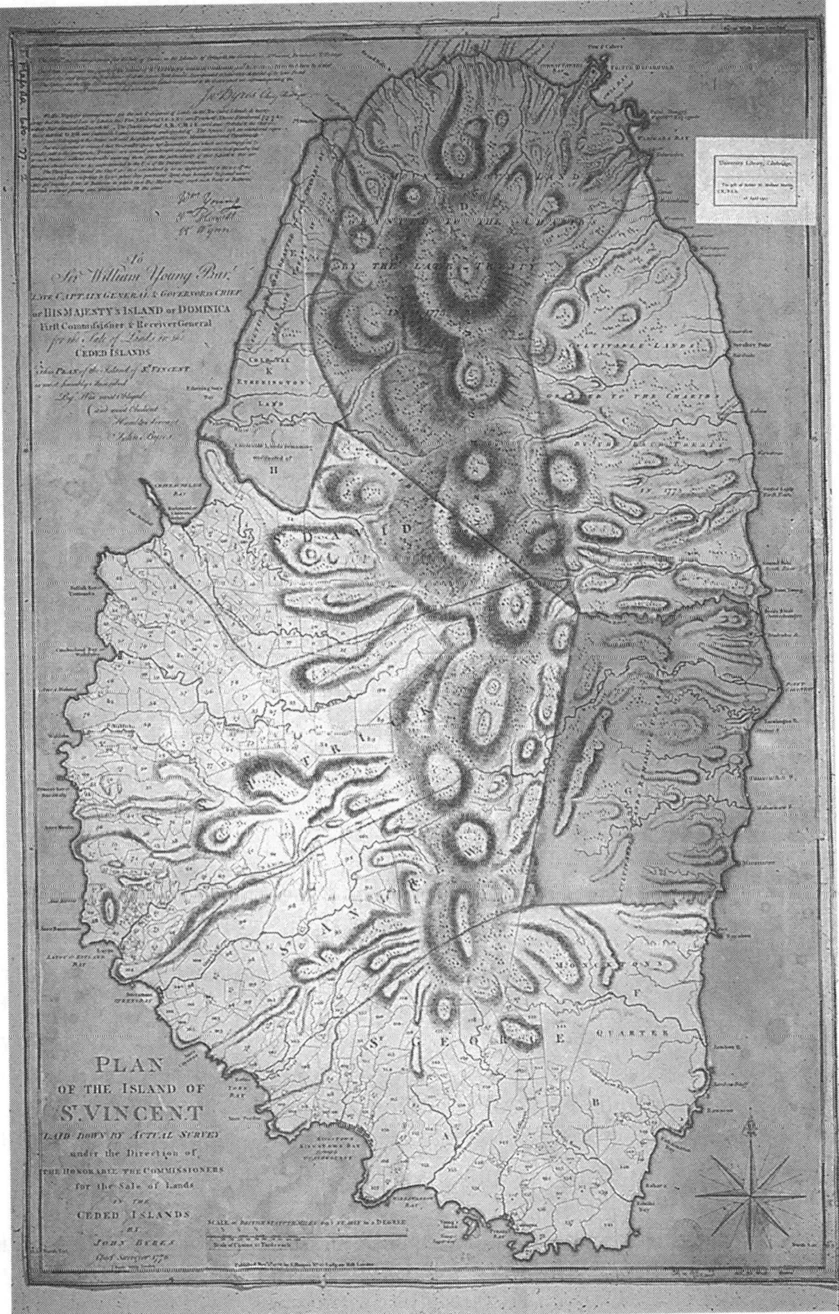

Figure 8 St Vincent *c.* 1800.

consequence of the new cultivation, some of the gullies being so wide that oxen could no longer cross them without the aid of wooden bridges.[20] These reports of gullying, a sign of well-developed overland-flow and soil erosion, echo contemporary descriptions of St Helena. They allow one to begin to understand why forest protection might suddenly have seemed attractive to the St Vincent colonists, particularly when one considers the impact which forest clearance for cotton might have had on what had originally been perennial stream channels. The slow three-year progress of the Act through the legislature was conspicuous, and it may well be that the Act reached the statute books only as a consequence of the rapid soil erosion recorded after the Bill had originally been laid on the table of the Assembly. Once made law, the King's Hill Act constituted one of the very earliest attempts at forest protection legislation in the English-speaking world based on climatic theory. While the exact nature of its connections with the French legislation of Mauritius still require detailed work it is a much easier task to identify the way in which the Act made its undoubted mark on the subsequent history of British colonial conservation legislation. By the time the King's Hill Act was passed Sir Joseph Banks had renewed his interest in the environmental status of St Helena, which was, unlike St Vincent, an East India Company possession. The immediate cause of Banks' concern was the establishment of a new botanic garden at St Helena in 1788. This appears to have led Banks to consider the serious water supply problems of the island, and during 1790 and 1791 he was frequently consulting official papers on St Helena at the specific request of the EIC Court of Directors.[21] At one stage Banks was even led to suggest that 'the cultivation methods and tenure system of Lincolnshire should be adopted to solve the island's agricultural problems'.

Clearly, by this stage Banks was casting around for a strategy for forest protection for St Helena. With the passing of the King's Hill Act he had found one, probably being briefed about the law by Henry Dundas who, during 1791, dealt with correspondence between Whitehall and Governor James Seton at St Vincent.[22] During 1791 and 1792 severe droughts were experienced in the Madras Presidency, on St Helena and on Montserrat. The coincidence of these events seems to have made a considerable impression on the East India Company and it may well be that alarm at such an apparently global incidence of drought stimulated it to more definitive action on St Helena, now vital to the transfer of botanical material between Calcutta, St Vincent and London. After much encouragement by Sir Joseph Banks the Court of Directors was eventually persuaded, by 1794, of the connections between rainfall decline and deforestation and was making anxious requests to the St Helena authorities to control deforestation and plant trees in order to maintain rainfall levels. As a result, after 1794 and particularly after the arrival of Alexander Beatson as Governor in 1808, tree-planting programmes were pursued on St Helena with direct Company backing from London.[23] By the mid-1830s, when the island was handed over to crown rule, it was generally agreed that rainfall levels had substantially increased as a result of the afforestation programme. These opinions were duly noted by Joseph Hooker when he visited St Helena and Ascension in 1843, and exercized a decisive influence on him when he came to advise Lord Dalhousie on the subject of tree-planting in India in 1847.[24] Dalhousie as in turn easily convinced of the climatic arguments for forest protection and this undoubtedly assisted him in the decision he made in 1854 to found an all-India forest service, a decision made at least partly on climatic grounds. Later on in the century the Indian model of forest management was adopted throughout much of the rest of the colonial and extra-colonial world, not least in the United States, which acquired a forest service's only at a relatively late date.

The Kings Hill Act can thus be seen to have played a critical role in bridging the gap between French physiocratic conservationism, as it was developed on Mauritius, and the evolution of a British colonial environmentalism. Undoubtedly the existence of close institutional links between the botanical gardens at Calcutta, Mauritius, St Helena, St Vincent and Kew played a vital part in enabling the development of the kind of embryonic global environmentalism so usefully symbolized by the Kings Hill Act.

NOTES

1 Public Record Office (PRO) CO2260/3 St Vincent Acts.

2 PRO CO263/21 St Vincent Assembly Minutes 12 January 1791, Letter from Governor Seton to the President of the Council.

3 For a survey of indigenous resistance to colonial and pre-colonial forest policies, see R. Grove, 'Colonial Conservation, Ecological Hegemony, and Popular Resistance; Towards Global Synthesis', in J. Mackenzie (ed.), *Imperialism and the Natural World* (Manchester, 1990).

4 See R. Grove, 'The Origins of Environmentalism', *Nature* (London), 3 May 1990, pp. 11–16.

5 A. Crosby, *Ecological Imperialism* (Cambridge, 1987).

6 E. Melville, 'Environmental and Social Change in the Valle del Mezquital, Mexico, 1521–1660', *Comparative Studies in Society and History*, 32 (1990), 24–53.

7 C. Totman, *The Green Archipelago; Forestry and Conservation in Seventeenth-Century Japan* (Berkeley, CA, 1989).

8 I have obtained the references to Sloane's comments from R. Moffat, *Missionary Labours and Scenes in Southern Africa* (London, 1884), p. 332.

9 P. Poivre, *Voyages d'un philosophe* (Paris, 1770).

10 A. J. Bourdes, *The Influence of England on the French 'Agronomes'; 1750–1789* (Cambridge, 1953).

11 Unpublished ms of P. Poivre, ref. no 575, Archives of Musée d'histoire naturelle, Paris, pp. 27–9.

12 L. Guilding, *The Botanic Garden at St. Vincent* (London, 1825).

13 Home Public Files, 1792–1820, National Archives of India, New Delhi.

14 Select Committee Proceedings, Foreign Department Files, Vol. 12, 1767. National Archives of India, New Delhi.

15 See R. Grove, *Green Imperialism; Colonial Expansion, Tropical Island Edens and the Origins of Environmentalism* (Cambridge, 1995), ch. 4.

16 The details of the laying on the table of Bannatyne's Bill are in PRO, CO263/21, 13 Nov. 1788.

17 A. Anderson, 'An Account of Morne Garou, a Mountain in the Island of St. Vincent, with a Description of the Volcanoe on its Summit (In a letter from Mr James [sic] Anderson to Mr Forsyth, His Majesty's Gardener at Kensington)', *Philosophical Transactions of the Royal Society*, 75 (1785), 279–309.

18 J. Priestley, 'Experiment and Observations Relating to Air and Water', *Philosophical Transactions of the Royal Society*, 75 (1785), 279–309.

19 B. Franklin, 'Meteorological Imaginations and Conjectures', *Memoirs of the Literary and Philosophical Society of Manchester*, paper read n 1784, published 11 (1785), 357–61.

20 PRO: CO263/21, 28 Jan 1790.

21 Letter to Thomas Morton, 8 Jan. 1791; Banks' Letters.

22 See, for example PRO: CO260/3 Miscellaneous correspondence; June 1791. During April 1791 the subject of the necessity of safeguarding the botanic garden was also frequently mentioned.

23 We now know that the global occurrence of droughts in tropical latitudes in 1791 and 1792 was due to a very severe El Nino/Southern Oscillation event in those years. For details of this see, Grove, *Green Imperialism*, and W. H. Quinn and V. T. Neal, 'El Nino Occurrences over the Past Four and a Half Centuries', *Journal of Geophysical Research*, 92 (1987), 1,449–61.

24 Hooker had been in close correspondence with Humboldt shortly before his departure for India. Humboldt had given him detailed instructions and it seems clear that these included remarks on the relationship between forest cover and rainfall retention: see Mea Allan, *The Hookers of Kew, 1785–1911* (London, 1967), p. 168.

NINE

ART AND NATURE IN PRE-CLASSICAL ECONOMICS OF THE SEVENTEENTH AND EIGHTEENTH CENTURIES

LARS HERLITZ

I

THE limited aims of this chapter should be stressed. It is about the history of economic thought. The thoughts are those of a small but eloquent minority of society. They date from centuries when progress in the knowledge of nature was considerable, while social sciences were only heralded by some brilliant ideas crucial to what were to become politology, sociology and anthropology.

But economics of this time were explicitly ideas about society and nature. Moreover, the development of these ideas from about 1620 to 1770 looks like a kind of cycle in the ways of conceiving the relations between society and nature.

The task of subordinating nature to man was an old one and inherited by mercantilists. They added that this purpose was served mainly by the development of arts, which was, in turn, made possible by the creation of a civil society that protected liberty and property. Nature was thus reduced to a constraint on man's craving for pleasure and profit, manifested by the scarcity of land and the privileges of landed property, to which was moreover assigned the task of stirring competition, appetites, industry and inventiveness. Confidence in the functional artifacts of man seems to have been shaken in the early eighteenth century. My cases are Mandeville on the deformations of human nature in civil society, and Cantillon on the absolute scarcity of land which indicated natural limits to population and consumption. These were dysfunctional elements announcing the revolt of nature in the late eighteenth century. Physiocracy means literally rule of nature. But to the French 'economists', the school of Quesnay and Mirabeau, nature was an order, within which man was reinstated to his superiority according to a preestablished hierarchy. And though human arts were now called sterile, they were so only when compared to the 'grand agriculture', run by wealthy farmers, who by means of heavy investments in tools, cattle and draught-animals and of free trade in grain raised the yield per unit of land.

2

Art belongs to the core of English mercantilist thought.[1] The general concept referred to an exclusive and ennobling faculty of man: his capacity to mould the objects of his activity into new forms and thus adapt them to his ends or needs. Artists and artisans were designers, who gave form to the matter in a way that was analysed by Aristotle.

The Aristotelian relation of form and matter was an internal one: they were opposites, though indissolubly united and necessary to each other. Their origins, art and nature, were also interdependent opposites, though more easily separated. Mercantilist thought, however, came to accentuate the opposition by extensively claiming independence for art as well as for artefacts.

Parallel to the relation between art and nature was that between labour and land. Common metaphors brought them closer to one another. The form-matter relation was applied to labour and land by Cantillon: 'Land is the source or the matter from which the riches are drawn; the labour of man is the form that produces them.'[2] Likewise, father and mother stood for artificialness and nature – as immortalized later by Goethe – but as used by Petty for labour and land.[3]

Art was however carefully distinguished from labour in general. To use the distinction of Locke: art did not belong to 'the labour of man's body', but to 'the work of his hands'.[4] Under his natural obligation to strive for happiness, man responded immediately to an original state of permanent need by a continued labour effort, which however could do no more than satisfy his most elementary wants of food, drinking, clothing and shelter. But the liberty of intellectual beings turned on their capability to suspend their prosecution of true felicity in particular cases, in order to find out by information and deliberation whether the desired objects did really lie in the way to their main end or did make a real part of their greatest good.[5] Knowledge, reason, and perhaps rationality were thus basic to those arts, which alone made human labour capable of creating plenty and convenience, and which, for Locke, embraced skill and technology, product and process innovations, divisions of labour and scale effects.

In the seventeenth century, the American evidence and its interpretations conferred an evolutionary meaning upon the interplay of art and nature. Francis Bacon pointed to the difference between men's lives in the most civilised countries of Europe, and in any wild and barbarous region of the new Indies. It was so immense that man might be said to be a god unto man. But their comparative states could not be attributed to differences in natural conditions as those of soil or climate. They were the results of arts.[6] This theme was elaborated by Locke, who noted that the inhabitants of a large and fertile part of the world, the West Indies, lived a poor, uncomfortable and laborious life and were for all their industry scarcely able to subsist. This was to him a sufficient instance of some more general truths. Nature furnished us only with materials, that for the most part were rough and unfitted to our use. Labour, art and thought were required to suit these materials to our occasions. And if the knowledge of men had not found out ways to shorten the labour and improve several things which seem at first sight to be of no use to us, we should spend all our time making a scanty provision for a poor and miserable life.[7] To Locke the use of iron seemed to be crucial. He found it obvious that, if this should be lost to the Europeans, they would very soon be unavoidably reduced to the wants and ignorance of the ancient savage Americans, whose natural endowments and provisions did in no way come short of those of the most flourishing and polite nations. The man who first made known the use of that contemptible mineral, might therefore be truly styled the Father of Arts, and the Author of Plenty.[8] Later, he emphatically put America at the point zero of general human development: 'Thus in the beginning all the World was America, and more so than that is now; . . .'[9]

The fertility of sixteenth-century America was perhaps less natural and more artificial than was recognized by the Europeans. Nevertheless the relative weakness of the Americans was used as evidence of the ascendancy of man over nature, and of the power of his arts, which made human development appear more independent of natural endowments and provisions. A relative independence of arts was convenient for the moral message of mercantilists, and appeared, towards the end of the seventeenth century, to be further endorsed by the palpable lessons of Holland and Spain.

The moral aspects were first only hinted at, but later developed into general statements on the proper conditions for the development of arts. An early definition of *natural* and *artificial wealth* was made by Thomas Mun in the early seventeenth century. The natural riches proceeded from the territory, while the artificial consisted of 'our manufactures and industrious trading with forraign commodities'.[10] The point was that natural riches could be attributed to the blessing of God, whereas the artificial ones were said to depend on the industry of the inhabitants.[11] Lewes Roberts praised earth for being the fountain and mother of all riches but warned in the next moment in general against an abundance that was not mobilized by trade, and particularly against the bad husbandry of landlords, farmers and tenants.[12] With the broad definition of Mun, the privileged supply of colonial raw produce imports to some European countries might well be called *artificial breed*, a designation used by the Swede Anders Bachmanson about 1730.[13] But with Davenant, the distinction was simplified: natural products were the fruits of earth, while the artificial ones were the manufactures.[14] Associated to this were some common ideas about what was a favourable environment to arts. Petty suggested that people, if few in number and in a position to live '*ex sponte creatoris*, or with little labour', remained wholly without art.[15] According to Temple, Holland was greatly favoured by a multitude of people crowded on a small compass of land: men of possessions were induced to parsimony; men without were forced to industry and labour, or else to want; vigorous bodies fell to labour, while others supplied their defects by inventions or ingenuity. The contrary was illustrated by Ireland, where plenty of soil and scarcity of people was the very plain ground of the laziness attributed to its inhabitants.[16] The sweeping statement was again Davenant's: where land was amply supplied and the inhabitants were few, there was nothing but sloth and poverty, but where great numbers crowded, necessity put them upon invention, frugality, and industry.[17]

The corollary was that nature's bounties were not only insufficient for, or when compared to the arts, irrelevant to the social evolution, but dangerous or even detrimental as well, because weakening the incentives to the development of arts. The Garden of Eden, America, and, by Temple, Ireland, could be brought forward as instances of that. But Spain, above all, was to become mercantilists' favourite lesson on the penalizing consequences of greedily gleaning the easy fruits of nature.[18] Man should eat his bread by the sweat of his brow, but he should also gain his bullion in no other way than by industrious trading and national savings in the form of export surpluses.

Thus nature and 'land' should be scarce. They were now well on the road to their place in classical economics and evolutionism: to represent the natural constraint, which stirred economic rationality, competition and selection. Some mercantilists from the end of the seventeenth century considered the rise of government, laws and commerce to be connected with a particular stage in social development when land had become scarce, landed property concentrated into the hands of great landowners, and the landless forced to vie with each other in industry, ingenuity and inventiveness when catering for landlords' demands.[19] Still more widespread was the idea of the complementary economic behaviour of extravagant landlords and acquisitive merchants, which was then elaborated by Hume and cleverly used by Smith. The always rent-seeking mercantilism was indeed very occupied with the rent of land as the true surplus income, and with the prospect, opened by landlord's prodigality, of getting part of it transferred to more productive use. For Cantillon, everybody lived at the expense of the landlords and their exclusive consumer sovereignty.

3

Now if nature was even negatively related to art – a constraint on man's striving for pleasure that should be relieved or overcome by his artistic and ingenious activity – what about the nature of man himself? The problem had been posed by Hobbes who made man's state of nature the very negation of social life, and thus of industry and arts as well. The idea of man's natural asociality was exemplary with regard to its bold objectification of human behaviour, but also very provocative, guardedly staved off by Pufendorf and Locke, and outright denied by the philosophers of moral sense. This discussion was evidently basic to the rise of social science, and of the 'natural history of man', in the eighteenth century, and could not fail to affect the mercantilist conceptions. A key figure here is Mandeville, who on one hand represented a consistent mercantilism, on the other tried to clean it from all strains of moralizing voluntarism and make it thoroughly naturalist. As the result, presented with a lot of irony and ambiguities, civil society appeared as the most excellent human artefact, which was, however, produced at considerable cost.

As against Shaftesbury, Mandeville claimed that man's sociableness did not arise from his good and amiable qualities in the Golden Age of Paradise, where indeed no reason or probability could be alleged why mankind should ever have raised themselves into large societies. Instead, it belonged to fallen and vicious man from the very moment after he lost the paradise, and derived from nothing but his wants, appetites and striving for pleasure, together with the obstacles put in their way by his natural environment. And nature was no less cursed. All the elements were man's enemies. Admittedly he escaped in general from such gigantic mischiefs as hurricanes, lions and earthquakes, but he was always persecuted, tormented and insulted by such trifles as a vast variety of insects, whose cruelty and contempt was so encroaching on his pity that they made laystalls of his head and devoured his young ones. Thus:

> There is nothing Good in all the Universe to the best-designing Man, if either through Mistake or Ignorance he commits the least Failing in the use of it; there is no Innocence or Integrity that can protect a Man from a Thousand Mischiefs that surround him: On the contrary every thing is Evil, which Art and Experience have not taught us to turn into a Blessing.[20]

Being an extraordinarily selfish and headstrong, as well as cunning animal, man was indeed very unfit for simply keeping together with many of his equals, as a herd of cows or a flock of sheep. But as he was moreover weak and duly timorous, he could be subdued by superior force or persuasion, and drawn from his savage state into a well-governed and cunningly managed civil society or body politic. Thus he became a disciplined creature that could find his own ends in labouring for others, by which Mandeville did not mean division of labour and market optimality, but reconciliation to social submission, or servitude construed to his own advantage.[21]

The Fable of the Bees provided a lot of famous instances of how to tame successfully man's evil nature and turn private vices into public benefits in a strong and powerful society. Progress was enforced by stirring passions, envy and competition. Luxury raised demand and employment – and Mandeville was anxious to dismiss the dangers from its emasculating effects by pointing out that all people of any substance had nothing to do with the wars but to pay taxes, whereas the hardships and fatigues fell upon the working slaving people, who bore the brunt of everything. Shows of virtue and courage, when needed, were elicited by playing on the pride of honour and the fear of shame. And the bulk of people were forced to hard and dirty labour by poverty and ignorance. But, as to please himself as long as he had the use of his faculties continued to be the nature of man, civil society was after all an artifice of hypocrisy:

> There is no difference between Will and Pleasure in one sense, and every Motion made in spite of them must be unnatural and convulsive. Since then Action is so confin'd, and we are always forc'd to do what we please, and at the same time our Thoughts are free and uncontroul'd, it is impossible we could be sociable Creatures without Hypocrisy. The Proof of this is plain, since we cannot prevent the Ideas that are continually arising within us, all Civil Commerce would be lost, if by Art and prudent Dissimulation we had not learn'd to hide and stifle them; and if all we think was to be laid open to others in the same manner as it is to ourselves, it is impossible that endued with Speech we could be sufferable to one another.[22]

For Mandeville parody was the general way guardedly to dissociate himself from the moral of his fable. But he also called upon a lion to plead the cause of evil nature against a Roman merchant, who tried to defend his right to live. Before devouring its prey the lion admitted that man, being a fickle timorous animal and a trifling atom of one great beast, was made by God for society and designed to compose by millions the strong *Leviathan.* But it denied his superiority of species, his vocation to rule over all other animals, and moreover his right to invoke any norm but his own principle of the reason of the strongest. In particular, his plead for pity recoiled on himself:

> Savage I am, but no Creature can be call'd cruel but what either by Malice or Insensibility extinguishes his natural Pity: The Lion was born without Compassion; we follow the Instinct of our Nature; the Gods have appointed us to live upon the Waste and Spoil of other Animals, and as long as we can meet with dead ones, we never hunt after the Living. 'Tis only Man, mischievous Man, that can make Death a Sport. Nature taught your Stomach to crave nothing but Vegetables; but your violent Fondness to change, and greater Eagerness after Novelties, have prompted you to the Destruction of Animals without Justice or Necessity, perverted your Nature and warp'd your Appetites which way soever your Pride or Luxury have call'd them.[23]

In the early eighteenth century, doubts were thus thrown by a convinced mercantilist upon the real fruits of man's art, among which were found unnecessary and pitiless destruction of nature, social class division and class rule, accompanied by moral hypocrisy.

His contemporary, Cantillon, was also decidedly mercantilist with regard to his aims, while naturalist by method, and his doubts were perhaps still more substantial as they concerned the demographic consequences of the scarcity of land. Cantillon linked up with the political arithmeticians Petty, King and Davenant, but found their long run demographic calculations 'far removed from the ways of nature' and thus purely imaginary and hazardous. Experience showed that trees, vegetables and animals multiplied according to the land devoted to their support. Likewise, men multiplied like mice in a barn if provisions were unlimited. Land being thus the scarce factor of production, the intrinsic value of every commodity, labour included, could be reduced to the acreages entering directly and indirectly into the production of one unit of the commodity. The value of labour, then, depended on the use of land, and on the standard of living. As for the use of land, Cantillon referred to the extensive one of North American hunters as one extreme, and to the intensive rice-cultivation of China as the other, suggesting that the simplest Iroquois demanded fifty *arpents* of land for his reproduction, whereas the Chinese margin, with nothing but rice and recurring famines, was no more than one tenth of an *arpent*. As for the standard of living, he distinguished between that of Middlesex where the peasant in general spent the produce of five to eight *arpents*, and that of the French Midi where one and a half *arpent* was enough to survive on. Given the yield of land and the standard of living, the population depended on the demand for labour created by the modes, tastes and humours of the proprietors, whose surplus income from scarce land was alone in allowing of consumer's choice. Cantillon refrained explicitly from deciding on the trade-off between standard of living and population number, but suggested that he who spent the produce of one and a half *arpent* might be more sturdy and brave than he who spent that of five or eight. The prospect of British population growth were not bright, as Englishmen consumed more produce of land than did their parents, but the population was greater than otherwise because of the coal mines, that saved land from forestry. In their American colonies, however, the Englishmen multiplied very fast, as they found there much new land for clearing, from which they drove away the savages.[24]

By stressing far-reaching implications of the simple truth that 'everybody has to subsist', Cantillon heralded the agromania of the middle of the eighteenth century. By this broad and almost Pan-European current nature seems to claim her due: there are good reasons to associate it with rising population and prices of agricultural products. But when turning to its culmination in the doctrine of Physiocracy, we meet with a surprisingly well-behaved nature.

4

'Physiocracy' suggests a naturalist or materialist approach, which was also articulated by leading physiocrats. Historians were criticized for telling stories about political events while ignoring the basic conditions on which rested the society concerned, or, more specifically, for describing warfare while disregarding the resources of the governments concerned.[25] The form of societies was said to depend on the more or less of properties which was owned by individuals and in need of protection.[26] Particularly the physiocrats connected physical and moral conditions. 'With and for us, everything is physical, and the moral derives from that', wrote Quesnay to Mirabeau.[27] In his preface to *Philosophie rurale*. Mirabeau promised the possibility to arrive at the haven of the moral truths by developing the physical truths. Man had always felt, he assured, by virtue and crime, by affection and remorse, that moral good and evil existed and were intimately connected to physical good and evil.[28]

The key to this relation was the dictum of Malebranche: the love of order is the principal, unique, fundamental and universal virtue, which alone makes virtuous the practices and dispositions of mind. The Natural Order was the basis and principle of Natural Right and Natural Law. The way of getting a sound knowledge about this order, said Mirabeau, goes through observing the physical world of matter and movement. Turning to what we touch is enough for learning to conform to the natural order and to cooperate in the performance of its laws. We will then discover our physical happiness in the invariable rules of movement impressed on matter. We will realize that, being a section embraced in the circle of this great law, we cannot refuse to play our part in the universal concert without involving ourselves and our species in revolt, misery, death, and chaos. The knowledge and consideration of his own interest will do for persuading man to contribute to the universal good, to the natural order.[29] Thus the moral epistemology of the physiocrats referred to man's learning, by experiences of happiness and misery, from being a part of the physical world governed by laws.

But there was also an ontology. According to Quesnay, the natural order was governed by laws that were instituted by a purposeful Supreme Being, and could be recognized as such by man because it was evidently optimal to him. The natural laws were physical and moral, the physical laws regulating the course of physical events, and the moral laws guiding human actions in conformity with the physical order. In every society physical laws governed the perpetual reproduction of goods necessary to the subsistance, preservation and convenience of men. This was fundamental to social order, and to realize that was to avoid confusion and arbitrariness. Positive laws should be deductions from or comments on the natural laws; thus the legislative as well as the executive power could and ought to be entrusted to a sovereign and unique authority, provided that public and private instruction on the natural order was instituted. Admittedly, the natural order was not optimal to other animals. But man's superiority belonged to the intelligence assigned to him by the Author of the nature, and authorized him always to make his part the best possible. Indeed, as man's natural right was never a right of everybody to everything but always limited to the enjoyment of what he acquired by research and labour, the scope of it was growing in the course of time with his physical and intellectual faculties, and was considerably extended by his acquisition of properties in societies under the protection of positive laws and a tutelary authority. Inequality between men with respect to natural rights followed from varying faculties, but did not justify anybody's usurpation on the rights of those who lived in a community of interest with him.[30]

The physiocrats hunted also for physical arguments for economic behaviour, social institutions, and indeed for the representation of the macroeconomic circular flow given by *Tableau économique*. The child starts spending immediately after birth and long before it can work for a living. Spending must in general precede labour and reproduction, and that is why economic analysis has to set out from expenditure.[31] Private ownership of land was a physical precondition of clearing and colonization, and safety of landed property was the conformable moral requirement for land values to be maintained.[32] Likewise, the accumulation of farmers' capital (*avances primitives*) was described as enforced by physical and moral laws. Cutting tools, strong draught-animals, manure and waggons were, in turn, physically necessary to the development of cultivation. But farmers work first of all for themselves: in spite of the greatest kings over the land, the last bushel of corn will be consumed by the last cultivator. The object is then to engage him in work for the subsistance of others. Freedom of cultivation and trade, by stimulating work and expenditure and allocating them profitably, has turned out to be the most easy and favourable means. The whole magic of an orderly society consists of everybody being or feeling free in his sphere and believing himself to work on his own while contributing to the universal good. Again, Mirabeau recognized this magic to be 'principles of economy and concord' given to us by the Supreme Being.[33]

The state of agriculture governed morals. When agriculture was deranged, morals became frivolous, men were forced by their needs to the most destructive moves, and the vicious circle ended in artifice, disorder, iniquity, quarrel, animosity, party spirit. Three instances were emphasized. One was the slavery of classical antiquity, a very denatured expedient, which had proved to be invalid for the great agricultural exploitations, disadvantageous to the nation, and ruinous to the state. Another was that idolatry of money, which created precarious properties and fictitious revenues by means of hoarding and usury, thus interrupting the flow of expenditure to the detriment of physical reproduction. Mirabeau denied that money could constitute properties, and Quesnay proposed that the rate of interest on money should be governed by the rate of return on investment in landed property.[34]

The third instance was the disastrous efforts, by the mercantile system, to expand the sterile sector, trade and industry, beyond the limits set by the state of agriculture. Against this the physiocrats maintained that agriculture alone was productive whereas trade and industry were sterile. But there were contradictions in the argument. Sometimes it seemed to be a matter of definition. Mirabeau said that the sterile class was very useful by procuring commodities and preparing goods for the various uses of life, and, moreover, saved time for the productive class which had otherwise been spent on necessaries of second place needs. But the Aristotelian distinction was simply turned back:

> We call it the sterile class because that is what it really is. In vain one has argued that it produces the form; to produce the form is to produce nothing, in the true sense that should be given to this word here, and in the reality of things.[35]

But as for matter, the physiocrats admitted of course, that land was nothing without the labour of man. Furthermore, they emphasized that no produce net of variable costs was to be got from land without great investments made by the farmers in strong draught-animals and heavy equipment. That is why the *Tableau économique* accounts for fixed capital within the productive sector, to which there is however no analogue within the sterile sector. Commenting on this specific difference, Mirabeau tried a reformulation of the relation between art and nature:

> As a matter of fact it is agreed that the activity gets the economic machinery moving. But the advances of agriculture derive mostly from the livestock, the effect of which is never inactive, because they consume and fatten every day even in times of rest, which cannot perhaps be said of a bale of silk or wool in the warehouse. Independently of the direction given by the employing hand, draught-animals have within themselves a motive force which gets them going and duplicates our impulsion. On the contrary, the works of art are dead and have no action but that which we lend to them. Briefly, as for current work, and for the advances as well, in the productive sector, labour directs but nature produces. From this alliance, and this treaty made with nature, derives the exclusive quality of being productive.[36]

With that, nature prevailed over art. But it did so at the cost of being domesticated into a natural order of material production, society and morals, guided and loved by man as the evidently best possible for him.

5

So the order was restored. Man became reconciled with the evil nature, which the art and experience of the economists taught him to turn into a blessing.

Against this idealization of nature, there were quite a few contemporary warnings, among them a characteristic one from Rousseau. But essential parts of the physiocrats' natural order was incorporated into classical economics. Mirabeau's magic principles of economy and concord reappeared as the invisible hand, together with the behavioural assumptions and *laissez-faire* principles of physiocracy.

The exclusive productivity of agriculture was of course denied. Adam Smith's suggestion that agriculture was at any rate the most productive sector was soon regarded as an oddity, and Ricardo argued versus physiocracy that rent was due to the niggardliness rather than to the bounty of nature. But Ricardo identified also nature with 'land', and purified it into a mere space, within which man was offered 'the use of the original and indestructible powers of the soil'. This was indeed a crucial success of the physiocrats' domestication of nature. Ricardian 'land' was then for long the third factor of production beside labour and capital. Later it was realized that, because of its being original and indestructible, it might as well, when accounting for growth, be subsumed under technological knowledge. By these steps, nature's own dynamics came to be effectively ignored within mainstream economics.

NOTES

1 E. A. J. Johnson, *Predecessors of Adam Smith: The Growth of British Economic Thought* (1937, repr. New York, 1960), pp. 259–77.

2 Cantillon, *Essai sur la nature du commerce en général* (INED, 1952), p. 1, cf. p. 18.

3 Petty, *Economic writings I*, ed. C. H. Hull (Cambridge, 1899), p. 68. The reference is to Goethe's famous account of his inheritance: 'Vom Vater hab' Ich die Statur, / des Lebens ernstes führen, / vom Mütterchen die Frohnatur / und Lust zu fabulieren'.

4 Locke, *Two treatises of government II*, ed. P. Laslett (Cambridge, 1960), §27, pp. 305–6.

5 Locke, *An Essay Concerning Human Understanding*, ed. P. H. Nidditch (Oxford, 1975), Book II, ch. 21, §52, pp. 266–7.

6 F. Bacon, *Novum organum*, ed. J. Devey (New York, 1902), Aphorism 129.

7 *An Early Draft of Locke's Essay, Together with Excerpts from his Journals*, ed. R. I. Aaron and J. Gibbs (Oxford, 1936), pp. 84–5.

8 Locke, *An Essay*, Book IV, ch. 12, §11, p. 646.

9 Locke, *Two Treatises II*, §49, p. 319.

10 Thomas Mun, *England's Treasure by Forraign Trade* (1664, repr. 1949), p. 7.

11 Mun, *A Discovrse of Trade from England vnto the East-Indies* (London, 1621), pp. 40–1.

12 Lewes Roberts, *The Treasure of Traffike* (London, 1641), pp. 5–6.

13 A. Bachmanson, *Arcana oeconomiæ et commercii* (Stockholm, 1730), p. 165.

14 *The political and commercial works of Charles Davenant I* (London, 1771, repub. 1967), p. 13.

15 Petty, *Economic writings I*, p. 34.

16 William Temple, *Observations upon the United Provinces of the Netherlands*, ed. by G. Clark (Oxford, 1972), pp. 109–10.

17 *The Political and Commercial Works of Charles Davenant I*, p. 73.

18 E.g., *The Political and Commercial Works of Charles Davenant I*, pp. 382–4; Mandeville, *The Fable of the Bees I*, ed. by F. B. Kaye (Oxford, 1924), pp. 194–7.

19 Locke, *Two Treatises II*, §§45–50, pp. 317–20; 'A discourse of the nature, use and advantages of trade' (London, 1694), pp. 1–7, in J. Child, *Selected Works 1668–1697* (Gregg Press, 1968).

20 'A Search into the Nature of Society', in Mandeville, *The Fable of the Bees I*, pp. 344–5.

21 *Ibid.*, pp. 347–8; cf. *The Fable of the Bees*, pp. 183–4.

22 'A Search into the Nature of Society', pp. 348–9.

23 *Ibid.*, p. 178.

24 Cantillon, *Essai*, pp. 22–3, 37–48.

25 'Hommes', in *François Quesnay et la physiocratie II* (INED, 1958), p. 520; *Les manuscrits économiques de François Quesnay et du marquis de Mirabeau*, ed. G. Weulersse, pp. 37, 85.

26 'Le droit naturel', in *François Quesnay et la physiocratie II*, p. 738.

27 *Les manuscrits économiques*, p. 122.

28 *Philosophie rurale I* (Amsterdam, 1764; repr. Aalen, 1972), pp. v, viii.

29 *Ibid.*, pp. xxxviff.

30 'Le droit naturel', in *François Quesnay et la physiocratie II*, pp. 731–41; 'Despotisme de la Chine', in *ibid.*, pp. 918–22.

31 *Philosophie rurale I*, pp. 2ff.

32 *Ibid.*, pp. 128–9.

33 *Ibid.*, pp. 20–1, 136ff.

34 *Philosophie rurale I*, p. 135, 269ff.; 'Observations sur l'intérêt de l'argent', in *François Quesnay et la physiocratie II*, pp. 763ff. Cf. Cantillon, *Essai*, pp. 110–22.

35 *Philosophie rurale I*, pp. 4–5, 7.

36 *Ibid.*, pp. 92–3.

TEN

THE URBAN AND THE RUSTIC IN ENLIGHTENMENT LONDON

ROY PORTER

INTRODUCTION

FALSTAFF's death-bed. His last words? Mistress Quickly tells us: he 'babbled of green fields'. Babbling of green fields, we might say, is *le vice anglais*. As H. G. Dyos, Mark Girouard, David Cannadine and scores of other scholars have insisted, the English have long had a penchant for thinking of themselves as country folk, living if not in stately homes at least in rose-rimmed thatched cottages, and, if not precisely huntin', shootin', and fishin', at least cultivating their window boxes.[1] Preoccupied with the National Trust or Heritage and crusading for conservation, Green Belts, parties and causes, the English indulge an arcadian escapism, preferring the past to the present, the country to the town, and basking in the world that never was.[2] 'Having country roots', Arthur Bryant explained not so very long ago, in an account in which description becomes prescription,

> we are constantly haunted by needs and cravings whose purpose is no longer clear to us. Our culture – to use a terrifying and much misused word – is a country culture; that is, such of it as is still left for us, for, though we have, since our emigration to the towns, lost and destroyed much of our own country culture, we have not as yet built up a civil structure to take its place.[3]

Bearing in mind the aura of the Lake poets or Constable-esque landscape painting, it makes some sense to say that English culture is a countrified culture, even, in dreams, a country-house culture. Yet the idea also promotes a blatant mystification, in that, for well over a century, most English people have lived in towns. Indeed, as Keith Thomas has stressed in *Man and the Natural World*, the English obsession with the glories of rusticity, with preserving wild plants, creatures and footpaths, is the fetish of a towns-dwelling bourgeois intelligentsia, oozing pseudo-pastoral nostalgia for a mythically Morrisy bucolic world of community and tradition: the *Wheelwright's Shop* rather than *Cold Comfort Farm*. Nostalgia for an imagined rural past was highly serviceable to a ruling order never entirely comfortable with its capitalist realities: urban, industrial, imperial.[4]

ANTI-URBANISM

Sentimentality towards nature has long blighted attitudes towards towns. Of course, such matters are complex. 'When a man is tired of London, he is tired of life', opined a great Midlander,[5] and it would not be hard to find many sharing Johnson's judgement, eager, echoing the Restoration wits, to expose the idiocy of rural life, with its Tunbelly Clumsys, all hicks out in the sticks. But the contrary chorus has probably been the stronger and shriller. When, some fifty years ago, John Betjeman wrote:

> Come, friendly bombs, and fall on Slough
> It isn't fit for humans now,
> There isn't grass to graze a cow
> Swarm over, Death![6]

wasn't he expressing, in modern idiom, long and deep-rooted attitudes of an earlier age? In *The Task* (1785), William Cowper damned 'gain-devoted cities', above all the metropolis:

> . . . thither flow
> As to a common and most noisome sewer,
> The dregs and faculence of every land.
> In cities foul example on most minds
> Begets its likeness. Rank abundance breeds
> In gross and pamper'd cities sloth and lust,
> And wantonness and gluttonous excess.
> In cities, vice is hidden with most ease,
> Or seen with least reproach; and virtue taught
> By frequent lapse, can hope no triumph there
> Beyond the achievement of succesful flight.
> I do confess them nurseries of the arts,
> In which they flourish most; where in the beams
> Of warm encouragement, and in the eye
> Of public note they reach their perfect size.
> Such London is, by taste and wealth proclaim'd
> The fairest capital of all the world,
> By riot and incontinence the worst.[7]

For William Blake as well as Cowper, London was Babylon:

I wander thro' each dirty street,
Near where the dirty Thames does flow,
And mark in every face I meet
Marks of weakness, marks of woe.[8]

– even if the capital might, one day, become the new Jerusalem – and it is surely no accident that in the early 1990s the British Labour Party adopted the Blake/Parry *Jerusalem* as its anthem, with its future perfect of a 'green and pleasant land'. Many besides Blake have found Georgian London hell. Defoe had dubbed it 'the monstrous city', the pioneer political economist Josiah Tucker judged it 'a kind of monster', 'no better that a wen'; and it was William Cobbett, who, damning all big towns as 'wens', anathematized the capital as the 'great wen'. This diagnosis of London as diseased and depopulating echoed through the eighteenth century, with its connotations of sterility and death. London supposedly tainted all it touched, sucking in the healthy from the countryside, and, as the Bills of Mortality proved, blighting far more than it bred. 'The Capital is become an overgrown monster', grumbled Tobias Smollett's character, Matt Bramble, 'which, like a dropsical head, will in time leave the body and extremities without nourishment and support'. According to the civic humanist critique of luxury, London seemed the culprit-in-chief for what the physician and pioneer demographer, Thomas Short, called the 'Waste of Mankind'. In Augustan moralizing, London exemplified iniquity. It was the headquarters of political gerrymandering and courtly decadence; its Grub Street was the high temple of Dulness; its Exchange spewed forth South Sea Bubbles; it was the poisoned spring of fashion and vice, the nursery of crime, riot, and all the other deformities lacerated in Samuel Johnson's Juvenalian satire, *London*. Not least, London was the hotbed of sickness. In the *Journal of the Plague Year*, Defoe reminded early Georgians that the great plague of 1665 had primarily decimated London. But they could see with their own eyes the festering rookeries of St Giles ('slum' was coined in Regency times to describe them) and sniff the stench of London's Cloacina, the Fleet Ditch, in Pope's phrase, that 'King of Dykes'.[9]

Anti-urban indignation and its accompanying pastoral nostalgia have long meant bad news for English cities. Millions flee them – perhaps working in city centres, but preferring to live in the country, or at least in a village or a significantly named garden city (no wonder the Town Planning movement this century, from Ebenezer Howard through Raymond Unwin and Barry Parker, with its aim of transferring population into the countryside, led indirectly to inner city decay).[10] The English love to rusticize their towns, with a penchant for gardens, boxes, pets and house-names like Brookside or Meadowbank. They think the city away. Even the metropolis, we are told, is not really a city but a cluster of hamlets. Following her *London Villages*, Nerina Shute published *More London Villages* (1981), with chapters on Richmond, Barnes, Kensington, Mayfair, St Giles and Bloomsbury, Charing Cross, Clerkenwell Green, Clapham, Bethnal Green and Hackney, arguing that 'to those of us who know and love it, the magic of London is connected with haunting memories of ancient villages and the ghosts of people who occupied cottages and mansions in the ways of romance and elegance. London is still a collection of villages, each with a story of its own'[11] – sentiments echoing the eighteenth century versifier, or falsifier, who wrote:

How bless'd the Swain of Bethnal-Green,
Who ne'er a Court beheld,
Nor ever rov'd beyond the Scene,
Of his paternal Field.[12]

No one would want to decry parks, commons and open spaces; and it has become standard, of course, amongst literary historians, to insist that English myths of rural wholeness are but bucolic bullshit. Country life was always idyllic about two generations ago. Like Nerina Shute, mythologists of sylvan purity always had to protest themselves too much. Near St. James's palace stood the original Buckingham House, built by the Duke of Buckingham (it was purchased in 1762 by George III). On the northern front of this early eighteenth-century red brick building, the precursor of the Palace, were inscribed the words '*Rus in Urbe*', the Georgian equivalent, I guess, of today's 'Glebe Cottage'. Rusticity even invaded gastronomy. 'All the geniuses of the age', explained Horace Walpole to his friend, Horace Mann in 1750, 'are employed in designing new plans for desserts'. One such was described by William Farington, at a function he attended in town *chez* the Duke and Duchess of Norfolk:

> after a very Elligant Dinner of a great many dishes ... The Table was Prepar'd for Desert, which was a Beautiful Park, round the Edge was a Plantation of Flowering-Shrubs, and in the middle a Fine piece of water, with Dolphins Spouting out water, and Deer dispersed Irregularly over the Lawn, on the Edge of the Table was all Iced Creams, and wet and dried Sweetmeats, it was such a Piece of work it was all left on the Table till we went to Coffee.[13]

(Presumably the confection had the same resonances as Sunblest Bread or Country Store muesli.)

TRUTH AND TOPOGRAPHY IN THE GEORGIAN METROPOLIS

A certain literal truth was conveyed, of course, by *rus in urbe.* From Buckingham House, open country stretched to the north as far as the Hampstead skyline, and there was a view southwards down to the Thames. Though, by 1700, the most populous city in Europe, London was still, by modern standards, staggeringly compact, and in Georgian times building sites abutted onto fields and afforded open views of Islington or the Highgate heights. Developments like the Foundling Hospital, in Bloomsbury, were on the very perimeter of the built-up area; the New Road, today's Marylebone, Euston and Pentonville Roads, was a bypass, yesteryear's M25, planned not least so that herds of cattle, being driven on the hoof from Wales and the west country to Smithfield Market, could be steered safely north of the elegant West End estates. Bayswater, Kensington and Chelsea were still villages, as were the new classy suburbs, like Camberwell and Streatham, where lived Johnson's friend, Henry Thrale the brewer. Doubtless London was shooting out its tentacles – in the 1720s Defoe was impressed to find 'Great Russell Street is a fair way to shake hands' with Tottenham Court, and sixty years later Horace Walpole reckoned 'there will soon be one street from London to Brentford' – but it never lost touch with orchards, milch cows, and duckponds.[14]

Yet this very fact brings out the myth of *rus in urbe.* Duckponds? Orchards? Yes, but much else as well that, from a different optic, threatened the arcadian fantasy. According to Charles Jenner's 'Town' and 'London' *Eclogues,* penned in the 1750s, virgin country was fast disappearing, eaten up by ribbon development:

> I spy no verdant glade, no gushing rill,
> No fountain gushing from the rocky hill.

Perambulating on the outskirts of expanding London, he reported:

> Where'er around I cast my wand'ring eyes
> Long burning rows of fetid bricks arise,
> And nauseous dunghills swell in mould'ring heaps
> While the fat sow beneath their covert sleeps.[15]

Gazing at Georgian prints of Paddington Green and maps of Marylebone, with their backgrounds of smiling fields and lowing herds, we must remember these were promotional literature, tourist guides. The ubiquitous brickfields, tips and shanties have been airbrushed out, such as painters scrubbed their landscapes squeaky clean of starveling peasants.[16]

Hardly a fact of nature, *rus in urbe* was an artifice, a stage set needing to be implanted and cultivated, rather in the manner of Marie Antoinette playing the milkmaid *à la mode.* In the 1770s, sheep were imported into Cavendish Square in the West End, where they grazed safely behind railings, prefiguring the fact that, within half a century, Regent's Park in turn would have its zoo. Grosvenor Square was originally given a formal layout, but in the 1770s it was relandscaped with naturalistic clumps of bushes; Portman Square was similarly replanted soon afterwards, and other squares followed suit. Late in his career, the redoubtable John Nash jumped on the fashion bandwaggon for *cottages ornées* by building two whole villages at the far north of Albany Street, on the eastern flank of Regent's Park. Composed of detached designer-villas, Park West and Park East have been judged by Sir John Summerson as 'the ancestors of all picturesque suburbia'. At about the same time, a pseudo-landowning, pseudo-gentry, was erecting villas with a country air in the new rustic commuterlands of Twickenham, Richmond, Kensington, and Primrose Hill.[17]

It is easy to see why the great aristocratic landlord developers of the Georgian age basked in the ideology of *rus in urbe*, for it reinforced *domini in urbe* or *equites in urbe*: in a nation where dominion was rooted in the shires, and the country house was still the power house, bringing the country into the city meant imposing upon the townscape the stamp of grandee glamour and authority – no difficult task, since the peerage owned the freeholds to the great estates around the old Cities of London and Westminster.[18] Indeed, many forces in the Georgian age were drawing the leaders of the landowning nation to town as never before: parliament and politics, shops and entertainments, the marriage market, money and mortgages, the pleasures of fashionable society and the Season. The metropolis was the site for the parade of superiority and the elegant expense of time and money.

If country grandees and gentlemen – those whose political ideology told them that true English liberties grew out of the clay of the shires – were to come to town, it is hardly surprising that they wished to bring at least some tokens of the countryside with them. But counter views always challenged such nonsense. The absurdity of the countrified town was often pointed out, as in *Critical Observations on the Buildings and Improvements of London* (1771), an anonymous work thought to be by John Stuart. Grazing sheep in Cavendish Square was plain silly. 'To see the poor things starting at every coach, and hurrying round their narrow bounds, required a warm imagination indeed, to convert the scene into that of flocks ranging fields, with all the concomitant ideas of innocence and a pastoral life'. The critic found almost all London squares 'tinctured with the same absurdity ... they are gardens, they are parks, they are sheep walks; in short, they are everything but what they should be. The *rus in urbe* is a preposterous idea at best; a garden in a street is not less absurd than a street in a garden'.[19]

In the light of such strictures, it is worth asking: did the elites that arrived to dwell, for the Season at least, in the newly elegant quarters of the Georgian metropolis, really want to think they were creating Little Mummersetshire-on-Thames? Hardly, because the cultural revolution that had come in with the Restoration and been consolidated by Addison, Steele and the *Spectator*, had convinced the Quality that if power lay in the shires, prestige and pre-eminence depended upon investing and excelling in a new culture of urbanity that was definitionally urban, a polish and politeness available only in Quality Street in the *polis*.[20]

There is no need to probe here the vogue for urbanity and politeness. Rather I want to examine how far a new tone of gracious living was embodied in, and spread by, building developments in London in the 'long eighteenth century' (from Restoration, through the Regency to the Reform age). Clearly this approach may beg many interpretative questions: how sure can we be that architectural and topographical styles genuinely expressed certain values? Or, if so, whose values? Those of lordlords? or the occupants? or speculative builders, double-guessing the tastes of buyers and lessees? Buildings, in any case, may long outlive tastes. Nevertheless, it must be a fair rule of thumb that architecture speaks languages widely understood and endorsed.

In Medieval, Tudor and early Stuart London, the great chose to build palaces, somewhat akin to the *hôtels* of the Paris of Henri IV, individual, detached structures standing in their own grounds, and generally walled around. Nobles' and bishops' palaces lined the strand, becoming the grandee palaces of Elizabethan and Jacobean times: Somerset House, the Savoy, Russell House, York House, Northumberland House. Many were built on a courtyard plan, their focus a great hall. Private palaces continued to be put up even after the Restoration and into the eighteenth century: Clarendon House in Piccadilly, erected by the Lord High Chancellor, the first Earl of Clarendon; Buckingham House, already mentioned, at the west end of Pall Mall; to the north, Chesterfield House, in the direction of the fast-expanding fashionable area of Piccadilly; Devonshire House, along Piccadilly itself; Burlington House, slightly to the East; Arlington House in St James's, built by the Secretary of State, Lord Arlington; Newcastle House in Lincoln's Inn Fields, Lansdowne House in Berkeley Square; and so forth.[21]

The basic fact about such structures, raised by the richest and most influential peers of the realm, is that they were standard piles, similar to their country cousins, the compact, rectangular, outward-facing houses without courtyards which set the trend in the Baroque and Classical ages. Clarendon House, Devonshire House, Chesterfield House – all could easily have been erected in the depths of the countryside. Indeed, the broadly Palladian preference in architecture in favour with the Whig oligarchs after 1714, made powerful statements about four-square country political values. A boundless admirer of Classical Rome and of the writings of Vitruvius, Palladio had expressed his commitment to order, geometry and rationality in his *Quattro Libri di Architettura*, and imported it to every site he planned. Architecture should be built upon fixed principles; geometry meant harmony, harmony meant beauty. The Whig grandees dominant after the accession of George I were Palladian to the core, and they used architecture to make propaganda statements in the style wars of the day. Enough of French and Dutch influences, enough courtly magnificence and frivolous frills; theirs would be a style erected upon the foundations of regularity, simplicity and a magisterial assurance. They would build solid. They would build to last. They would build with Nature, Antiquity and Euclid on their side. Palladio was their man. Holkham, Houghton, Stourhead, Wilton in the shires; Chiswick House nearer town; and in town itself, Burlington House in Piccadilly, the Horse Guards at Whitehall. These embodied a vision of immense stability.

Colen Campbell planned; William Kent designed; but the mastermind was the Earl of Burlington, a four-square Whig. A somewhat private figure, Burlington possessed sufficient seriousness of purpose, learning, devotion to the arts and high-mindedness to command the respect, even the admiration, of political foes and professional satirists such as Alexander Pope (who, just up river from Chiswick at Twickenham, was one of his neighbours). Pope praised:

> You show us, Rome was glorious, not profuse,
> And pompous buildings once were things of Use.

Following Burlington, Whig grandees planted their estates with solid, stately seats. Lesser gentlemen pioneered the particularly Palladian form of the villa, a squarish, geometrical construction, whose exterior commanded authority, but which, within, was perfectly suited to house that growing relish for informality, ease, and comfort which proved such a conspicuous feature of Georgian private lives. The English élite was collectively making a public affirmation of faith. Under the guidance of such cultural arbitrators as Burlington and his circle, political authority, moral authority and cultural authority would go hand in hand. Virtue, the virtuoso, and his virtuosity would make common cause. There were to be no more philistine rulers, no Popish fanatics, no bloodthirsty despots.

Palladianism was an Olympian vision. Like all that is grand, it relied heavily upon facades. Its pilasters and porticos have duly lasted in Norfolk and Northumberland; but it did not dominate the town. In fact, the English Palladians were rather indifferent to adapting their style, perhaps their values, to urban exigencies. Style books like William Kent's *Designs of Inigo Jones* (1727), and James Gibbs' *Book of Architecture* (1728) paid little attention to town-house design. The second volume of Colen Campbell's architectural designs included no town houses at all. The English Palladians ignored the problems of planning stately homes for urban sites. The indifference common amongst the grand architects to matching houses to sites – a foible not unknown today – is illustrated by the fact that when an engraving of Queensberry House was published in 1726, it was shown in a country setting.[22]

Yet other movements were afoot that upstaged country-house preferences in architecture. After 1660, all the great private palaces in the Strand area came tumbling down and were never rebuilt: Salisbury House, York House, Exeter House, Beaufort House, Norfolk House, Essex House, Hungerford House, Stanhope House, Wallingford House, and Bedford House. But as early as the 1630s, Inigo Jones was building Covent Garden for the Earl of Bedford. It was a piazza, based upon a great square in Livorno. The great house stood not alone, but was defined by a grouping of other planned, stylistically consistent buildings, including a church. Astonishingly, from an early stage, a street-market was licensed in the square, entering the optical space of the house. The Earl's residence was thus incorporated into what John Evelyn called 'a little town'. The point about the design – and precisely how far it was agreed between the architect and the patron cannot be documented – is that the aristocrat urbanized himself.[23]

ST JAMES'S AND THE WEST END

Something comparable happened in St James's, though in a far more piecemeal manner. Developed by the entrepreneurial skills of Henry Jermyn, the Earl of St Albans, one of Charles II's more astute courtiers, St James's Square was originally intended to involve a cluster of some thirteen or fourteen 'palaces', exceptionally distinguished and dignified dwellings, pointing in the direction of St James's Church, already a fashionable Piccadilly place of worship. Jermyn meant to erect a dazzling domicile for himself, while profiting handsomely from his development. Financial constraints, however, forced him to modify his plans, and he found himself completing his square by parcelling it up into more than half as many lots again than initially planned. Thus transfigured, St James's Square became the model for so much of the West End as a desirable residential quarter: more was crammed into less space, without sacrificing the goals of elegance, or making the ensuing houses less eligible to prospective buyers or lessees – an achievement rendered somewhat easier by the continuing buoyant demand for stylish accommodation in smart areas amongst those who recognized the indispensability of a fashionable address. St Albans's own house in the Square boasted a frontage of some 120 feet, and most a width of around 50 feet, but some had a frontage of as little as 27 feet. The message was clear: henceforth it would be possible to live fashionably in London in a very confined space.[24]

Under the late Stuarts, St James's Square set the social pace. When the Irish adventurer, James Butler, the first Duke of Ormonde, bought his house there in 1682, his son wrote a congratulatory letter: 'how ill it would look now you are an English duke to have no house there'. Rubbing shoulders with him in the Square were the first earl of Conway; Sir John Ernley, the Chancellor of the Exchequer; the fourth earl of Devonshire, Lord Steward of the Household; Lord Ossulston, Lieutenant of the Bodyguard; Lord Dartmouth, Master General of the Ordnance; the Early of Ranelagh, Vice-Treasurer of Ireland; the third earl of Suffolk, Earl Marshal of England; the first marquis of Halifax, the Lord Privy Seal; and the first earl of Essex, First Lord of the Treasury. By 1721 no fewer than six dukes – Chandos, Dorset, Kent, Norfolk, Portland and Southampton – lived there, as well as seven earls, a countess, a baron, and a baronet. You no longer needed a palace, a castle of your own, to live in style in London. It was becoming more chic to live in the sociability of a square, with its chaises and hackney carriages, its fine new street lighting and its visible comings-and-goings – by 1750 there were about 500 hackney cabs and 400 sedan chairs in London, and some 15,000 street lamps, meeting the needs of those who kept late hours.

The area had a different tone from anything previously experienced in London. 'When I consider this great city in its several quarters and divisions', remarked Richard Steele in 1714,

> I looked upon it as an aggregate of various nations, distinguished from each other by their respective customs, manners and interests. The Courts of two countries do not differ from one another as the Court and the City in their peculiar ways of life and conversation. In short the inhabitants of St. James's, notwithstanding they live under the same laws and speak the same language, are a distinct people from those of

> Cheapside, who are likewise removed from those of the Temple on the one side and those of Smithfield on the other by several climates and degrees in their way of thinking and conversing together.[25]

The St James's message was heeded elsewhere. With differing business rhythms, all the great aristocratic landlords – the Cavendishes, Devonshires, Portlands, Portmans, and so forth – who owned estates in Bloomsbury, around Soho and Piccadilly, and in Marylebone, began to build the look-alike squares so familiar today. A standard model was followed. Land would be leased to speculators – men in the mould of the notorious Nicholas Barbon – who would build for profit within strict guidelines of quality and architectural style to preserve the elegance, and hence the property values, of the ensemble. Houses could then be sold, or let on short leases, to tenants who might stay for just a season or two. Houses might differ in size, but the tendency was for them to join hands in continuous rows of terraces, and to conform to the layout and design norms of the quintessential Georgian town house. William Morgan's large-scale map of London and Westminster in 1682 shows that there were only about twenty-two great free-standing aristocratic palaces with gardens left in London, and by 1737, the total was down to ten.

With the erection of Southampton House, built by the fourth earl of Southampton, then Lord High Treasurer, and Montagu House, and the development of Great Russell Street in the reign of Charles II, Bloomsbury became a main site of development, and Bloomsbury Square developed early, around 1680.[26] And thence, while the submerged classes crammed sardine-like into the slums of Whitechapel, Clerkenwell and St Giles, elegance spread its golden grids. Bloomsbury Square was followed by Red Lion Square (1698), Golden Square (1699), Queen Square (1704), Hanover Square (1713), Cavendish Square (1717), Portman Square (1764), Bedford Square (1769), and Portland Place (1778), developed by Robert Adam with that delicate Rococo style that prettified the town. And all was crowned – literally, through the involvement of the Prince Regent – with John Nash's stuccoed swathe which snaked from Piccadilly, via Regent Street, to Marylebone and Regent's Park. Tight landowner control of ground plan, housing density and building standards, and the prohibition of warrens of lower-class tenements, workshops and markets, of course, prevented the development of the West End for commercial purposes as occurred in the rebuilt City of London after the Fire, and ensured the emergence of something rare in a European capital of the day: a high class, exclusively residential quarter.

In a sense, it was *rus in urbe*, if by that we mean that the West End reaped the benefits traditionally associated with rural surroundings – fresh air, greenery and open spaces – and escaped the penalties of traditional urban life: overcrowding, street squalor, filthy trades, slaughter-houses and the din of commerce. West End communities were deeply conscious of the desirability of amenities, paying rates and setting up committees to ensure piped water, drains, refuse collection, nuisance removal and street-lighting, measures embodied above all in the Westminster Improvement Act (1762) and the City Improvement Act (1766).[27] Contemporaries were impressed by urban housing that looked handsome and healthy. 'The stranger will be astonished', recorded William Hutton, in town from Birmingham in 1785,

> at the improvements which have been introduced during the last 35 years and how money could be procured to complete them. He will find every street and passage in the whole city, and its environs, has been paved in one regular and convenient stile; [as] the people of Birmingham ... must observe the conveniency arising from open streets, the centers of which are regularly paved and the sides, from one foot to sixteen, according to the width of the street, laid with flat stones, for the benefit of the passenger, it is surprizing they do not, at a humble distance, wish to imitate the Metropolis.[28]

And physicians declared it worked. 'In the airy parts of this city and in large, open streets', commented Dr John Coakley Lettsom in 1773, 'fevers of a putrid tendency rarely arise ... In my practice I have attentively observed that at least forty-eight of fifty of these fevers have existed in narrow courts and alleys.'[29]

With ground space at a premium, houses lost their sideways spread and became vertically oriented. This proved a major innovation. High society pursued, for the first time, a mode of high-rise living. Whereas medieval homes had rarely been more than two storeys high, great ingenuity was now devoted to packing accommodation into dwellings five storeys high, built on deep narrow sites. Houses were erected on a service basement, used for the kitchen and servants' hall, and commonly extending under the pavement in front of the house used as a coal cellar. Above this, the front portion of the plot typically contained three floors for the family, and an attic for servants' bedrooms, wrapped round a staircase, commonly top-lit. Often there was a wing behind the main block, which overlooked a garden, at the bottom of which would be the laundry block and the stables connected to a mews, running parallel to the street or the side of the square. At first vertical living seemed peculiar. Visiting the duke of Ormonde's house in St James's Square in 1712, Jonathan Swift jokily described its novelty to Stella:

> Today in the morning I visited upwards; first I saw the Duke of Ormond below stairs ... then I went up one pair of stairs and sate with the Duchess; then I went up another pair of stairs and paid a visit to Lady Betty; and desired her woman to go up to the garret, that I might pass half an hour with her, but she was young and handsome and would not.[30]

These Quality town houses may initially have felt cramped: there was less space than in the country or in a nobleman's Parisian *hôtel.* But people were prepared to put up with overcrowding in town, partly because they could lavish conspicuous consumption in buildings, gardens, parks, and lakes at their country seats. In town, the nobility, observed Horace Walpole in 1743, had 'contracted themselves to live in coops of a dining room, a dark back room with one eye in a corner, and a closet'. Englishmen of rank continue to consider their estates their real residences', a foreigner observed a few years later, 'and their houses in London as a kind of pied-à-terre. Many who have revenues of £20,000 and more live in London with hardly a dozen rooms. Consequently, they and their numerous servants are rather crowded.' 'Very few persons of rank have what we on the Continent call a palace in London', noted another foreigner in 1823: 'Their palaces, their luxury and grandeur are to be seen in the country.'[31]

URBANIZING THE CITY

The magical art of London living was to make a pleasure out of necessity. It meant developing, on the one hand, a variety of public spaces – the street, the shops, the theatre, the assembly, the club – where social life could flourish, while, on the other hand, utilizing space to maximum advantage at home through appropriate social rituals, which compensated for, or hid, the relatively cramped conditions.

How were these tricks achieved? In part the secret was developed by the Brothers Adam with their interiors, creating illusions of spaciousness in houses on confined sites, like Wynn House, Derby House and Home House, all around forty-odd feet wide, interiors that represent, in Summerson's view, 'the highest point of imagination and artistry in the handling of the London House. They are not mere repositories of delicious ornament; the basis of their splendour is their minutely considered arrangement.'[32]

The top-lit staircase, for one thing, proved tremendously space-saving, while securing the light and airy feel the Georgians valued. Adam also excelled in designing the reception rooms *en suite*, to provide vistas in different directions, and in varying the height and shape of apartments to create surprise and diversity. In Wynn House, he installed a staircase hall that rose the full height of the house. Being only a single bay wide, however, an illusion of capaciousness was obtained by cutting a deep apse in the south wall on both the ground and first floors. And these motifs were echoed with oval rooms and domed rotundas, and rooms with semi-circular recesses, the curves suggesting depth and subtlety of space, all echoed by a barrel-vaulted ceiling.

Many other designers alongside the Adams were skilled in the theatricalities of handling the confined space of the town house. And developments in the social round went with eye-catching changes in domestic layout and function. Metropolitan life prized a sociability which was demanding and unceasing, yet was also, or was also meant to seem, informal, familiar and flexible, involving much casual visiting, dropping in, briefly, for tea, or supper, or paying one's respects. Homes needed to be arranged to meet the needs of streams of callers from dawn to dusk. 'In the morning', wrote Madame du Bocage, visiting London in mid-century,

> breakfasts, which enchant as much by the exquisite viands, as by the richness of the plate in which they are served up, agreeably bring together both the people of the country and strangers. We breakfasted in this manner today at Lady Montagu's ... A long table covered with the finest linen, presented to the view a thousand glittering cups, which contained coffee, chocolate, biscuits, cream, butter, toasts, and exquisite tea. You must understand that there is no good tea to be had but at London. The Mistress of the house ... poured it out herself.[33]

Designed to meet such social demands, Norfolk House led the field, signalling, as Girouard has suggested, a significant change in fashion, a move away from the habit of exclusive formal dinners, to the desire to entertain, however briefly and superficially, as much of the *crême* as possible.[34] Erected, from 1748, on the east side of St James's Square, Norfolk House suited the needs perfectly. Its unpretentious facade led a contemporary observer to comment: 'Would any foreigner, beholding an insipid length of wall broken into regular rows of windows ... ever figure from thence the residence of the first Duke of England?' But the interior dazzled. A top-lit staircase in the centre of the building afforded a flood of light that accentuated a suite of sumptuous reception rooms, each with a different colour scheme and decorative style, allowing guests to feast the eyes while moving from room to room. The dining room was relatively unimportant, but the first floor double drawing rooms were perfect for parties, balls, or an after-dinner rout, providing spaces where people could take tea, play cards, dance or drink wine.[35]

Norfolk House provided the form for new kinds of entertainments. Visitors were duly impressed. 'Everyone who was there', wrote Captain William Farington of the Indian Army to his sisters, having attended the 'first night' party, 'agreed that Norfolk House was infinitely superior to anything in this Kingdom ... and to most things they had seen in Europe'. 'There were', he reported, 'in all eleven rooms open, three below, the rest above, every room was furnished with a different colour, which used to be reckoned absurd, but this I suppose is to be the Standard'. In such ways, a new town architecture helped create an urban interior geography tailor-made for a full and animated social calendar, creating sensation, exhilaration, gaity, vivacity. The *rout* was the very epitome of this social *multum in parvo*. 'One of the social pleasures of London is a rout', wrote the German, Christian Goede, in 1802, drawing attention to the crush,

> When the apartments are not sufficiently capacious for the company, temporary rooms are created in the yard, and most elegantly fitted up ... on entering the temple of pleasure, nothing is presented to the view but a vast crowd of elegantly dressed ladies and gentlemen, many of whom are so overpowered by the heat, noise and confusion, as to be in danger of fainting. Everyone complains of the pressure of the company, yet all rejoice at being so divinely squeezed. The company moves from room to room and the most an individual can do, on meeting a particular friend, is to shake hands as they are hurried past each other [at supper] not one fifth of the guests can be accommodated ... behind each chair, are ladies standing three or four deep, others are enclosed in the doorway, unable to advance or retreat.[36]

In his *Anecdotes*, James Malcolm told the same tale of fashionable metropolitan parties. At the rout, he wrote, 'there is pleasure, there is amusement, and the inexpressible delight of languor, even fainting through exertion, heat and suffocation; the company endeavours to compress themselves for obtaining a space to dance in'. Or, as Louis Simond put it, 'no cards, no music, only elbowing, turning and winding from room to room'.[37] This was very metropolitan madness, but foreigners could not help but be impressed by the beauty and liveliness. 'The East end', noted the Prussian, Wilhelm von Archenholz, in 1780:

> especially the houses along the bank of the Thames, is composed of old ruins; the streets are narrow, obscure, and badly paved ... The contrast betwixt that and the western parts of the metropolis is astonishing: the houses there are almost new, and of an excellent construction; the squares are magnificent, the streets are built in straight lines, and perfectly well lighted: no city in Europe is better paved. If London were equally well built, no place in the whole world would be comparable to it.[38]

In the world the Georgians made, one of new polish and politeness, oriented to new opportunities for sociability and consumption, it was necessary for anybody who was somebody to come to town, but not essential to plant their main residence there – the country still had its attractions, and a palatial dwelling in London would have been astronomically expensive. Compact residences were sufficient, because of new lifestyles that spelt out – perhaps for the first time – an eligible town life for the gentry. Edward Gibbon caught the metropolitan bug early. In his early twenties, he spent a year in London and was enchanted:

> The metropolis affords many amusements which are open to all: it is itself an astonishing and perpetual spectacle to the curious eye; and each taste, each sense may be gratified by the variety of objects that will occur in the long circuit of a morning walk. I assiduously frequented the Theatres at a very prosperous aera of the stage, when a constellation of excellent actors both in tragedy and comedy was eclipsed by the meridian brightness of Garrick, in the maturity of his judgement, and vigour of his performances.[39]

His throw-away conclusion – 'the pleasures of a town life, the daily round from the tavern to the play, from the play to the coffee-house, from the coffee-house to the —— are within the reach of every man who is regardless of his health his money and his company' – rhetorically masked the fact that, on the death of his father, he sold up the family estate, Beriton, in Hampshire, and rented a bijou bachelor residence at 7 Bentinck Street, just off newly developed Bond Street, then the *ne plus ultra* in fashion, installing his library, servants and pet parrot, bossing the upholsterer, drooling over the fine shag flock-paper he had chosen, light blue with a gold border, and purring at his good fortune:

> I had now attained the solid comforts of life, a convenient well-furnished house, a domestic table, half a dozen chosen servants, my own carriage, and all those decent luxuries whose value is the more sensibly felt the longer they are enjoyed. These advantages were crowned by the first of earthly blessing, Independence: I was the absolute master of my house and actions: nor was I deceived in the hope, that the establishment of my library in town would allow me to divide the day between Study and Society. Each year the circle of my acquaintance, the number of my dead and living companions, was enlarged. To a lover of books the shops and sales in London present irresistible temptations ... By my own choice I passed in town the greatest part of the year.[40]

Gibbon didn't want the idiocy of rural life, or even a country house and country charms. He wanted to be a town mouse, to enjoy *urbanitas in urbe* – though in the end it burnt a hole in his pocket, and he had to decamp to Lausanne. Many wanted such a life; and the building of the West End in the Georgian age provided an architecture, an urban topography, a social ritual, to meet such desires. It marks a high point in urban ideals that has never, in Britain at least, been fully recaptured.

CONCLUSION

In these days of ecocrisis, it is tempting to contrast the country and city, and to assume a radical opposition between them, the one natural (or, as Cowper would have said, divine), the other man-made. This has been the tendency of much environmental history.[41] To think in such terms, however, this paper has suggested, would be a grotesque oversimplification; indeed, it would be to perpetuate certain aristocratic prejudices reformulated in time in the language of Romanticism. Man has made the country no less than he has made the town, and from this it follows that the historical relations between town and country are contingent, expressions in part of changing images of the urban and the pastoral – images that must themselves, in turn, be seen as expressions of the complex interplay of economic forms and political domination. Highly urbanized societies with aristocratic élites often cultivate myths of pastoral; by contrast, agrarian societies may prize civic values. The comparative history of urbanism is an enticing field, or rather piazza, ripe for further study.[42]

NOTES

1 H. J. Dyos, 'Agenda for Urban Historians', in H. J. Dyos, *The Study of Urban History* (London, 1968), 1–46; and 'A Castle for Everyman', *The London Journal*, 1 (1975), 118–34; and *Exploring the Urban Past: Essays in Urban History* (Cambridge and New York, 1982); Mark Girouard, *The English Town* (New Haven, 1990); David Cannadine, 'The City in History', *Encounter*, 61 (1983), 45–9.

2 For this myth-mongering, see Eric Hobsbawm and Terence Ranger (eds.), *The Invention of Tradition* (Cambridge, 1983); Tom Nairn, *The Enchanted Glass: Britain and its Monarchy* (London, 1988); Raphael Samuel (ed.), *Patriotism. The Making and Unmaking of British National Identity*, 3 vols. (London, 1989); and Samuel (ed.), *The Myths We Live By* (London, 1990); Pierre Nora, *Les Lieux de Mémoire* (Paris, 1984–6); J. Le Goff and P. Nora (eds.), *Faire de L'histoire*, 3 vols. (Paris, 1974); Roy Porter (ed.), *Myths of the English* (Cambridge, 1992).

3 Quoted in David Cannadine, *The Pleasures of the Past* (London, 1989), p. 35.

4 Keith Thomas, *Man and the Natural World* (London, 1983; Harmondsworth, 1984). It would be inappropriate in this paper to explore in any detail rural myths as expressions of the hegemonic ideology of England's emerging capitalist ruling class. But see Perry Anderson, *English Questions* (London, 1992); P. Corrigan and D. Sayer, *The Great Arch: English State Formation as Cultural Revolution* (Oxford, 1985); and E. P. Thompson, *Customs in Common* (London, 1991).

5 For Samuel Johnson, see Richard B. Schwartz, *Daily Life in Johnson's London* (Madison, WI, 1983).

6 *John Betjeman's Collected Poems*, compiled and with intro. by the Earl of Birkenhead (London, 1958), p. 21.

7 Cowper's poem is discussed in Raymond Williams, *The Country and the City* (1973; 1985) pp. 126, easily the most important analysis of English pastoral myths. For a text drawing upon Williams's pioneering work, see John Lucas, *England and Englishness. Ideas of Nationhood in English Poetry 1688–1900* (London, 1990).

8 Geoffrey Keynes (ed.), *Blake: Complete Writings* (Oxford, 1972), p. 216.

9 These ideas are developed and references at greater length in Roy Porter, 'Cleaning Up The Great Wen: Public Health in Eighteenth-Century London', *Bulletin of the Society for the Social History of Medicine*, 35 (December, 1984), 24–5.

10 Ebenezer Howard, *Garden Cities of Tomorrow* (London, 1902); W. Ashworth, *The Genesis of Modern British Town Planning: A Study in Economic and Social History of the Nineteenth and Twentieth Centuries* (London, 1954).

11 Nerina Shute, *London Villages* (London, 1977); and *More London Villages* (London, 1981).

12 Quoted in Williams, *The Country and the City*, p. 90.

13 C. S. Sykes, *Private Palaces* (New York, 1986), p. 35.

14 For basic introduction to the topography and growth of Georgian London, see Jack Lindsay, *The Monster City: Defoe's London, 1688–1730* (London and New York, 1978); M. D. George, *London Life in the Eighteenth Century* (Harmondsworth, 1966); George Rudé, *Hanoverian London, 1714–1808* (London, 1971).

15 Charles Jenner, *Town Eclogues* (London, 1772), Eclogue IV, 'The Poet', pp. 27–8.

16 John Barrell, *The Idea of Landscape and the Sense of Place, 1730–1840: An Approach to the Poetry of John Clare* (Cambridge, 1972), and *The Dark Side of the Landscape: The Rural Poor in English Painting, 1730–1840* (Cambridge, 1983).

17 For these developments, see Sir John N. Summerson, *Georgian London* (London, 1970), ch. xii; and *The Life and Work of John Nash Architect* (London, 1980); and 'The Beginnings of Regent's Park', *Architectural History*, 20 (1977), 56–62; and 'London, the Artifact', in H. J. Dyos and Michael Wolff (eds.), *The Victorian City: Images and Realities* (London and Boston, 1973), I, pp. 311–32.

18 This is well evoked in Lawrence Stone, 'The Residential Development of the West End of London in the Seventeenth Century', in Barbara C. Malament (ed.), *After the Reformation* (Manchester, 1980), pp. 167–212.

19 [Anon.], *Critical Observations on the Buildings and Improvements of London* (London, 1771), pp. 8, 10–11. This work is believed to be by John Stuart. See Mireille Galilou (ed.), *London's Pride: The Glorious History of the Capital's Gardens* (London, 1990).

20 There are valuable discussions of the implications for town life of this new urbanity in Peter Borsay, *The English Urban Renaissance: Culture and Society in the Provincial Town 1660–1770* (Oxford, 1989) and Paul Langford, *Public Life and the Properties Englishmen 1689–1798* (Oxford, 1991); and *A Polite and Commercial People: England 1727–1783* (Oxford, 1989).

21 For much of what follows, see Christopher Simon Sykes, *Private Palaces: Life in the Great London Houses* (New York, 1986).

22 For a brief discussion, see Roy Porter, 'Palladian Man Deconstructed', in *Essays*

to Honour Stephen Lock (London: Keynes Press, 1991), pp. 60–4; and Sykes, *Private Palaces*, pp. 89f.

23 See Sir John N. Summerson, *Inigo Jones* (Harmondsworth, 1966); Edwin Beresford Chancellor, *The Annals of Covent Garden and its Neighbourhood* (London, 1930).

24 For this and what follows, see B. H. Johnson, *Berkeley Square to Bond Street* (London, 1952); Edwin Beresford Chancellor, *Memorials of St. James's Street, Together with the Annals of Almack's* (London, 1922); Arthur Irwin Dasent, *The History of St James's Square and the Foundation of the West-End of London: With a Glimpse of Whitehall in the Reign of Charles the Second* (London and New York, 1895); Joan Glasheen, *St James's, London* (Chichester, 1987); Charles Lethbridge Kingsford, *The Early History of Piccadilly, Leicester Square, Soho and their Neighbourhood* (Cambridge, 1925).

25 Richard Steele, *The Spectator*. For much of the preceding, see Christopher Simon Sykes, *Private Palaces: Life in the Great London Houses* (New York, 1986), pp. 45f.

26 Donald J. Olsen, *Town Planning in London: The Eighteenth and Nineteenth Centuries* (New Haven & London, 1982); G. S. Thomson, *The Russells In Bloomsbury 1669–1771* (London, 1940).

27 Francis Sheppard, *Local Government in St. Marylebone, 1688–1835: A Study of the Vestry and the Turnpike Trust* (London, 1958).

28 L. Jewitt (ed.), *The Life of William Hutton* . . . (London, n.d.), pp. 69, 154.

29 Quoted in C. Creighton, *A History of Epidemics in Britain: with Additional Material by D. E. C. Eversley (and others)*, 2nd edn (London, 1965), II, pp. 133–4.

30 See Sir John N. Summerson, *Georgian Houses* (London, 1970); and Christopher Simon Sykes, *Private Palaces: Life in the Great London Houses* (New York, 1986), pp. 45f.

31 For the above, see Sykes, *Private Palaces*, pp. 54, 221.

32 Summerson, *Georgian London*, ch. x.

33 Quoted in Sykes, *Private Palaces*, p. 129. Sykes offers a useful discussion.

34 See Mark Girouard, *The English Town* (New Haven and London, 1990), pp. 130ff.

35 See Dan Cruickshank and Neil Burton, *Life in the Georgian City* (London, 1990), pp. 45ff. I have relied heavily on this admirable book.

36 Christian August Gottlieb Goede, *The Stranger in England* (London, 1807), II, pp. 99–102, quoted in Cruikshank and Neil Burton, *Life in the Georgian City*, p. 46.

37 See James Malcolm, *Anecdotes of the Manners and Customs of London During the Eighteenth Century* (London, 1808), p. 489, quoted in Cruickshank and Burton, *Life in the Georgian City*, p. 47.

38 J. W. von Archenholz, *A Picture of England* (Dublin, 1791), p. 77.

39 Edward Gibbon, *Memoirs of My Life*, ed. G. A. Bonnard (London, 1966), p. 183; see also Patricia Craddock, *Young Edward Gibbon: Gentleman of Letters* (Baltimore, 1982).

40 Gibbon, *Memoirs*, p. 154.

41 See for instance Donald Wooster, *The Wealth of Nature. Environmental History and the Ecological Imagination* (New York, 1993).

42 See Donald J. Olsen, *The City as a Work of Art: London, Paris, Vienna* (New Haven, 1986), and Anthony Sutcliffe (ed.), *Metropolis 1890–1940* (Mansell and London, 1990), which offer an interesting start.

ELEVEN

SCIENCE, SOCIETY AND CULTURE IN THE ROMANTIC *NATURFORSCHUNG* AROUND 1800

DIETRICH VON ENGELHARDT

DURING the development of science in modern times and, especially of the eighteenth and nineteenth centuries, the period of Romanticism and idealism in Germany possesses great importance: for itself, with regard to the general situation of science around 1800 and the internal as well as external causes of its change, and also with regard to contemporary reflections on science and society, on the relationship between natural and human sciences, as well as on the attitude of man toward nature.[1]

One can characterize the modern development of science as an expansion of knowledge of phenomena, as an increasing specialization, as a growing of empiricism with technico-practical consequences, as an institutionalization of science and dominance of research, as an emancipation from theology and philosophy, as a separation from the humanities or a loss of historico-theoretical interests within the sciences. The period of Romanticism and idealism in Germany was an engaged and substantial reaction of several naturalists (*Naturforscher*) and physicians against this development – a reaction as correction and complement, not as contrast or alternative.

Generally one can differentiate for the time around 1800 the following positions: (a) an empirical science with a corresponding theory and methodology of science, (b) the transcendental philosophy of nature (Kant), (c) the speculative philosophy of nature (Schelling, Hegel) and (d) Romantic *Naturforschung* (nature study) with a variety of positions.

Above all Kant and Schelling influenced the Romantic nature movement, but other philosophers and earlier positions also provided stimulation. Exponents of this movement include Eschenmayer, Novalis, Ritter, Görres, Schubert, Steffens, Oken, Oersted, Windischmann, Troxler, Carus. The dependence was not constant, changes in the biographical development, combinations of different principles were common. Romantic natural science is not itself a unity; specific features and individual developments have to be noted; divergent conceptions of nature, science, history and society; different responses to the victory of positivistic natural science in the nineteenth century. The typification of the Romantic positions and their changes in the first decades of the nineteenth century remain an important task for future research.

Goethe represents a specific position with his combination of aesthetics, science, philosophy and biography, with his proximity and distance to Romantic and speculative *Naturphilosophie* (nature philosophy). Hegel describes Goethe's position as 'thoughtful contemplation of nature' (*Sinnige Naturbetrachtung*) in difference to his own 'notional comprehending of nature' (*begreifendes Erkennen*).[2] Alexander von Humboldt also occupies a specific place between empiricism, art and philosophy; his aim is in his own words an 'empirical view of *nature as a whole* in the scientific form of a *portrait of nature*'.[3] Schopenhauer too occupies a specific position in this spectrum around 1800. He criticizes Hegel and contemporary science as materialism, he acknowledges the search of the Romantic scientists for a 'basic type' (*Grundtypus*) of nature, but rejects their 'hunt for analogies'.[4]

The systematization of these different positions finds its confirmation through the self-description of the naturalists and *Naturphilosophen* of that time. *Naturphilosophie* is not natural science or scientific theory or methodology of research. According to Schelling and Hegel *Naturphilosophie* does not compete with natural science. *Naturphilosophie* according to Schelling 'is nothing but physics, but it is only *speculative* physics'.[5] The correctness of the philosophical constructions is demonstrated by the 'coincidence of the product appearing in experience with that which has been constructed'.[6] Hegel constantly emphasizes the difference and identity subsisting between philosophy and natural sciences: 'It is not only that philosophy must accord with the experience nature gives rise to; in its formation and in its development, philosophic science presupposes and is conditioned by empirical physics. The procedure involved in the formation and preliminaries of a science is not the same as the science itself however, for in this latter case it is not longer experience, but rather the necessity of the notion, which must emerge as the foundation.'[7]

The Romantic naturalists themselves underline their distance to the speculative form *Naturphilosophie* – despite the unquestionable influence especially of Schelling of their metaphysical understanding of nature. According to Ignaz Paul Vitalis Troxler (1780–1866), the Absolute which underlines nature and the spirit cannot be grasped – neither by 'intellectual contemplation' nor by 'belief in reason'; any word in favour of the Absolute is only a 'sign' of it.[8] Also Johann Wilhelm Ritter (1776–1810) confirms: 'The *highest* deduction a priori is a misunderstanding, and man is not its master'.[9] In addition to understanding faith, feeling and dreams can contribute to natural science, but their findings have to be confirmed by experience; the Romantic naturalist does not glorify the irrational.

Naturphilosophie of all types as well as the Romantic *Naturforschung* evoke rejection during all the years around 1800. According to Georges Cuvier (1769–1832) *Naturphilosophie* or Romantic *Naturforschung* is a 'jeu trompeur de l'espirit'.[10] The naturalists of the Romantic line formulate their critique of positivistic science, of Kant's transcendental philosophy of nature, and of the speculative method of Schelling and Hegel. In the eyes of the Romantic naturalists, contemporary science is lost in senseless details, its characteristics are crude empiricism and futile theory.

The sceptical or negative judgements of Schelling and especially Hegel about the Romantic concepts are no less distinct, further, they express their distances from Kant and positivistic science. For Hegel the essential deficiency of the Romantics lay in their inability to interrelate notional and phenomenal dimensions immanently; in his view they possess only 'a dim concept of the idea, of the unity of notion and objectivity, and of the fact that the idea is concrete'.[11] With regard to the misunderstanding and distortion of his philosophy of nature, Schelling renounces in 1807 further publications in this field: 'Since I have seen the misuse which is made of the ideas of *Naturphilosophie*, I have resolved to keep to verbal communication over the whole matter until a time when that no longer is a concern'.[12]

In this chapter, only an overview of the concept of nature, science and society of Romantic *Naturforschung* around 1800 and not of the other types of *Naturphilosophie* and science will be given.

The scientific development of modern times depends on socio-cultural changes and corresponds at the same time to changes of concepts of society and culture. The relationships were manifold and differently narrow and up to now for the period around 1800 neglected by historical research.

The concepts of the Romantic naturalists – or in the language of that time: the philosophical naturalists, applied *Naturphilosophen*, or just *Naturphilosophie* – regarding society and history are directly connected with their concepts of nature and science. In contrast to present scientific publications, observations and experiments in the natural sciences of the Romantic period were combined with reflections on history, arts, philosophy and religion. The stress was on different points and disciplines, the union was realized more successively or simultaneously, more in one work or in several publications – but always the universal claim, the transprofessionalistic perspective was maintained.

Scientists are considered uncultured who devoted themselves to only one science, governments which didn't support this universality are criticized. History and natural science belong to each other, man ought to be naturalized, nature ought to be humanized. Natural sciences could be declared central, Lorenz Oken (1779–1851) wishes to take the natural sciences as basis for his journal *Isis* because especially through them man gains his 'proper culture' (*eigentliche Bildung*), because especially they teach him, 'where is his place and the place of the environment', whereas theology and jurisprudence should not be included, because they retreated from humanity.

In general the attitudes of the Romantic naturalists to society and history to Antiquity and the Middle Ages, the Renaissance and the Enlightenment, the political events of their time, the French Revolutions of 1789 and 1848, Napoleonic France, the German struggle for independence, the constitutional movements have not yet been studied. It would be interesting to compare the social and historical concepts of these natural scientists with those of the poets, historians and philosophers of that time. Our knowledge of the interrelations, the mutual influences of the sciences and humanities around 1800 is limited.

A history of science and medicine during modern times and especially during the eighteenth century, which does not describe and analyze the Romantic *Naturforschung* and medicine around 1800, does not correspond with the historical reality – this movement was in quantity and quality too important to be passed over.

CONCEPT OF NATURE AND SCIENCE

Romantic *Naturforschung* understands itself as a counterposition to the development of science in modern times, at the same time also as the immanent fulfillment of this development and not as its total negation. *Romantic* ideas are not at all entirely free of absurd or extravagant notions, but they cannot be characterized as an alternative to empiricism, to experiment and mathematics. Central moments of modern science ought to be carried on, others overcome or relativized.

The interpretations of nature were guided by metaphysical and mathematical principles, by formal categories like differences and identity, analogy, polarity, potency and metamorphosis, but also by specific phenomena and processes of particular spheres of nature. All philosophical understanding must depend on science, on empirical facts. 'Speculativeness' which does not mean irrational or poetic deduction of nature and reality – and here lies the difference between the naturalists of Romanticism and Schelling and Hegel with their speculative

Naturphilosophie – exceeds the capacities of man; faith, revelation, intuition, *Ahnung* (presentiment) were opposed to the means of notion and intellectual perception of contemplation.

The conceptions of the Romantic naturalists of nature and science are based on the identity of nature and spirit; the laws of nature are supposed to correspond to spiritual laws. The 'Deduction of the living organism' of 1799 by Adam Carl August von Eschenmayer (1768–1852) depends on the presupposition 'that precisely this object comes under the necessary conditions of self-consciousness'.[13] The correspondence between nature and spirit follows according to Troxler from the fundamental 'animation of nature'. In this perspective Henrik Steffens (1773–1845) declares: 'Do you want to know nature? Take a look inside yourself, and in your gradual intellectual enlightenment, you may have the privilege of looking on nature's stages of development. Do you want to know yourself? Observe nature, and her works are of the same essence as your mind.'[14]

Nature in the perspective of the Romantic naturalists must be conceived as a union and interrelationship of all phenomena and processes, dependent on metaphysical principles and immanently combined with the world of man. Gotthilf Heinrich von Schubert (1780–1860) is guided above all by the principle of a link between natural phenomena: 'The history of nature has to do not just with individual, finite, before long perishable beings, but with an imperishable and unifying cause giving life to all that can be seen.' The task of the naturalist is to study and elucidate not only the individual natural phenomenon but also the linkage in nature 'from fixed stars to the ephemeral insect'.[15]

The specific character of the organic or the organism was underlined. Often the proofs of the unity of nature rely on a translation of organic categories into inorganic. The whole nature was conceived as an organism. Each absolutization of the principle of mechanics was criticized – in the natural sciences as well as in medicine, for example in the interpretation of disease and therapy. Besides causality (*causa efficiens*), finality (*causa finalis*) was not to be neglected. The central point was the union of nature and spirit, of body and soul. The insights into the unconscious, into irrationalism and the nature of dreams, gained in that time especially by Schubert and Carl Gustav Carus (1789–1869), were more fundamentally studied in the twentieth century (Freud, Jung).

Without a philosophical basis no science and scientific progress ought to be possible, without this basis nature, man and society equally should be endangered. Empiricism should be combined with theory, physics with metaphysics. Essential observations and inventions derive from

Romantic naturalists, but they cannot form the central point or value of this movement.

In its essence history of science is neither apology nor condemnation. But unfortunately the one-sided judgement of Romantic science by the scientists of the positivistic nineteenth century dominated also the historiography of science; up to the present time historians of science have to frequently adopted the premises and ideological convictions of the victorious sciences they have studied.

To understand nature as a total organism is to conceive its genesis, its genetic development. Nature has a history, in the same way as history is nature. All natural phenomena know development, have changed with the time. These changes must be understood according to the Romantic scientists always in combination with the ideal systematics of nature and its forms and processes; furthermore they should correspond with the systematics of the psychical faculties and mental capacities of man and the phases of the history of science. The historization of nature is connected with the historicization of the knowledge of nature, or the objective and the subjective dimensions of the historical knowledge (as one can say), are brought by the naturalists of the Romantic movement into a union; the separation of the history of science and empirical scientific research – a result of the nineteenth century and generally accepted in our days – was not the concept of science of the Romantic naturalists.

The development of nature was conceived as an ideal evolution, as metamorphosis of ideas, as *Idealgenese* and not as *Realdeszendenz*, an evolution in the Darwinian sense. Steffens developed in 1801 an 'Evolutions-Theorie', a 'theory of evolution', where he deduces the multiplicity of plants and animals from a dynamism of expansive and contractive forces, through which the 'Totalorganisation' of nature is realized. Oken explicitly rejects the conception of a real change: 'To say that earth and metal evolved to coral conveys as little as to say that earth as such really changed into coral, just like the above assertion that it became metal, or air became sulphur ... everything is to be taken in a philosophical sense.'[16] Changes, death and new formation are only the surface, the manifest and external side of nature, in the essential, substantial sphere no real beginning and ending are possible.

Schelling and Hegel too reject the idea of real transformation. Evolution pertains according to Hegel to notion and its development, not to real phenomena and their changes: 'Thinking consideration must reject such nebulous and basically sensory conceptions as for example the so-called emergence of plants and animals from water, and of the more highly developed animal organizations from the lower etc.'[17]

CONCEPT OF SOCIETY AND HISTORY

In numerous publications the naturalists of the Romantic period outlined their concepts of society and history, and left this area not at all to philosophers and historians, as it is so common in our days. By this fact the epoch of Romanticism offers the possibility of studying the relation of concepts of nature with concepts of society in the consciousness and language of the scientists themselves, and not only by means of a systematic or logical analysis from the historical standpoint.[18]

According to the Romantic naturalists, history is nature in the same way as nature is history. The understanding of man and society without taking account of scientific knowledge, without considering the natural basis must remain insufficient. The development of the individual and social being is subject to change, to history. Also in the human area expansions and contractions guide the development, are responsible for stagnations and accelerations, for revolutions and turning points in human history. Society derives according to Steffens from a moving force, which he identifies with the formative or dynamic force (*Bildungstrieb*) of nature. Particularity is justified but, at the same time, must serve the whole.

As in nature, there exist in society the individual and the genus. Man can be in his world 'recluse' and 'worldly'. The organic functions serve as a model or metaphor for the political life and human history. The inorganic is often compared or identified with a lack of freedom, the 'machine-man' (*l'homme machine*) is contrasted with the living man. The relation between the individual and the state is illustrated by the example of the organism and the relation of its parts to the whole. The hierarchy of the Estates has its analogy in the kingdoms of nature.

The history of mankind, of races and peoples, is combined with nature through the metaphysical identity of nature and spirit as well as through real phenomena and concrete processes. Each epoch of history has its relative value, decisive is the idea of the total evolution. The 'dark' Middle Ages gain a new estimation. At its end history turns back to its beginning, the whole is realized, the Kingdom of God (*Reich Gottes*) will dominate the World of Nature (*Naturwelt*), through the historical development art, science and religion are unified with life.

As for the natural development, ideas are responsible for human development. Concrete factors are acknowledged, but are not decisive, finalism overcomes causality; history in its essence history of ideas. Steffens denounces those historians who trace the stream of history 'up to the dirtiest puddles' (*bis zu den schmutzigsten Pfützen*), and that sort of historiography 'they call research based on sources' (*und das nennen sie Quellenstudium*).[19]

Society and political progress are influenced by the sciences and their progress. The new sense of nature, the sense of the Romantic naturalists, is promoted by art, philosophy and religion, and should fundamentally transform human life, should destroy old forms of society and help to build up new social conditions, should produce morality. Natural science should be able to fortify the health of the psyche, have emotional and intellectual consequence. Gottfried Reinhold Treviranus (1776–1837) thinks biology particularly suitable for educating human beings: there is probably hardly any other 'science which keeps the understanding and at the same time the power of imagination so active and therefore is so appropriate for bringing people to humanity'.[20] In 'equal respect for nature and the spirit' lies, according to Carus, 'the key to every true art of living'.[21] Ignaz Döllinger (1770–1841) pleads for an interest of his times in natural knowledge, which 'penetrates deeply into education, has an effect on the development of spiritual capacities (*Entwicklung der Geisteskräfte*), to which maxims of government (*Regierungsmaximen*) correlate and, perhaps, cannot remain completely unnoticed even in the regulation of affairs of states (*Bestimmung der Staatenverhältnisse*).'[22] In the view of the Romantic naturalists the governments and states close their minds too much against the new, ideal, and philosophical understanding of nature, and their resistance finds an ally in the antimetaphysical contemporary science.

Around 1800, Romantic science and political radicalism were repeatedly identified. The Romantic naturalists were reproached for confusing students and misleading them into errant activities, for promoting mental illnesses, atheism, political terrorism and revolution. Hegel's appointment to Berlin is legitimated because of his distancing from Romantic *Naturforschung*. Officials tried to keep Oken's philosophical *Naturforschung* out of the Prussian universities. Oken is considered as one of the 'wild professors' (*verwildertern Professoren*), who together with the seduced students practised vandalism and intolerance at the *Wartburgfest*. There Oken didn't participate in the burning of writings by Ancillon, v. Haller, Kotzebue v. Kamptz, and also of the *Code Napoléon*. He postulated in a speech the universal student, who stands above all parties and associations of compatriots and, with the other students, encompasses as an educated Estate (*Stand*) the whole state and achieves unity, which can be found also in nature and will lead one day to German unity.

The differentiation of Estates and political representation are defined with regard to nature and spirit. Oken bases Estates on the nature of man on his central faculties: 'the physical, the spiritual, and that which is a combination of both, mind or courage (*Gemüt* oder *Mut*)' – these faculties correspond with the feeding, teaching and military Estates (*Nährstand*, *Lehrstand* and *Wehrstand*); they are natural and cultural Estates, 'appointed by nature, philosophy, and all history'.[23] Eschenmayer, more religiously influenced in his concept of nature and society than Oken, supports the development of an inner balance between political forces, 'where democracy, aristocracy and autocracy each has its own influence without disturbing one another and the general welfare'.[24] Eschenmayer's arguments were not without importance for the drafting of the new Constitution of Württemberg.

The state is limited and spiritualized. Its historical development is for Joseph von Görres (1776–1848) 'a permanent oscillation from absolute despotism to anarchical freedom'.[25] One of the central insights of the time is that of Steffens that the state and freedom 'may never fight against and limit one another, that the most open pursuit of the real determination of each calls forth the inner most union in the purest separation' (*in reinster Trennung die innigste Vereinigung*).[26]

The state and the spirit must acknowledge their spheres and their limitations. The individual cannot be the norm for the organization of the state if one wishes to avoid the fanaticism and anarchism of the French Revolution of 1789, at the same time the state should not be allowed to reign and control the world of the spirit, if one wishes to avoid despotism and loss of culture. For Steffens the highest legitimations of the state are science and art, which ought not be sacrificed to an ideal of an 'empty political freedom'.[27]

INTERRELATIONSHIP BETWEEN NATURE AND CULTURE

Nature has a history and history is nature. The history of man depends in the eyes of the Romantic naturalists on the history of nature and vice versa the history of nature on the history of man. The mediated history of man and nature should lead to a new history of man and nature. This new history will realize a fundamental, original identity of nature and man, of being and consciousness, which was in the beginnings at the basis of everything. The concepts of integration are different, they follow from different philosophical and religious positions.

Nature and man share the same destiny. Man is a natural being, in man nature unfolded into the spirit. By understanding nature man conceives more and more of his union with nature, and begins now to care for her cultivation. History had its beginning with a period of an identity of nature and spirit, the second period was the separated development of natural history and history of mankind, and this twofold development should now pass to an epoch of union and freedom a process of naturalization of man and humanization of nature. Exploitation and destruction of man should be as impossible as psychical reductionism and denial or neglect of nature in social concepts.

Man has a special responsibility for nature, which serves at the same time his own development. For Novalis (1772–1801) the mission of man is the 'cultivation of the earth' (*Bildung der Erde*);[28] nature will become completely spirit through man. According to Ritter nature can reach through man 'the supreme presence and self-awareness' making 'man part of a blessedness which is like that of nature itself'. Then he urges: 'to integrate nature is the purpose of his existence'.[29] Johann Ferdinand Koreff (1783–1851) speaks, in regard to the destruction of Italy by human beings, of a 'sarcasm of nature at the tombs of history'.[30] This destruction of nature confirms Carus in his opinion that 'not only man needs the earth for his life and activity, but also the earth needs man'.[31] The relationship between nature and man cannot be only or essentially guided by the concept of power (Bacon, Descartes) – it should combine natural teleology with anthropocentrism.

The concepts of society and the political commitments of the natural scientists of the Romantic period vary considerably, and also change with time. Oken took part in the *Wartburgfest*, Eschenmayer gave the Württemberg Constitution legitimacy inspired by *Naturphilosophie*. More substantial, however, is the hope common to all Romantics – for the 'Kingdom of God', 'everlasting peace', the 'Golden Age' – this hope combines utopia, history and the present.

The usual alternatives of restoration and revolution, change and continuity, history and progress do not correspond with the thoughts of the naturalists of the Romantic movement. History and system are considered always together, in the realm of nature as well as in the world of society and culture. Development is related to ideas which are realized in a temporal succession and can be brought into a systematic order. History is not only movement as progress towards the future but through this movement history reverts to the beginnings of nature and society. Progress and regress combine.

History restores the origin on a higher level, actualizes potency; Görres conceives of a 'regressive progress' and 'progressive regress' respectively; he is convinced 'that after the progress from the sensual to the supersensual has reached its point of culmination, the progress turns on itself and becomes regression'.[32] History is birth and precipitate delivery inwards (*Sturzgeburt nach innen*) which also leads the true historian 'to seek the rule and the law of the future in the present and the past'.[33] On this ground historians are able to analyze the present and give prognoses, history has a duty toward the future, it is an important factor of future developments. This historian is according to Novalis a prophet.

GENERAL CONCLUSION

The hopes and expectations of Romantic *Naturforschung* were emphatic and universal; they failed to be realized even if some influences can be observed during the nineteenth and twentieth centuries, especially in medicine and psychiatry. The controversy between the different positions of *Naturphilosophie* and natural sciences was not solved by arguments but decided by scientific facts and practice. The advances in knowledge in the natural sciences with an abundance of technical-industrial results, the radiation of the scientific specialization and the institutionalization of science with an imperative of research, the academizing of philosophy and theology sealed the fate of *Naturforschung* and *Naturphilosophie* of Romanticism and idealism in Germany.

The historiographic scheme by which all natural sciences around 1800 passed through a phase of Romanticism and idealism does not correspond to historical reality, and is not even correct with respect to the German-speaking countries. One cannot write an accurate history of science and medicine of the eighteenth and nineteenth centuries without describing and analysing the Romantic *Naturforschung*, that is true, but one should not exaggerate its significance. Romantic *Naturforschung* is a special and unsuccessful reaction against the scientific evolution, which had become more and more powerful since the Renaissance and which also existed and prevailed around 1800 and soon in the course of the nineteenth century gained hegemony. Nevertheless, the Romantic movement in science can further our historical knowledge, our understanding of the transition from the eighteenth to the nineteenth century.

Romantic *Naturforschung* is an important phase in the subjectivity of past science, a subjectivity of natural pathos and scientific scepticism. With their emphasis on man and his relations to nature, with their naturalizing of culture and humanizing of nature, the Romantic concepts may be viewed as corresponding in central points to current critiques of science and progress, and to contemporary searches for new concepts of nature and a new understanding of man – and it is with this perspective in mind that one may judge their relative importance.

Without doubt natural science influenced by Romanticism and idealism can still provide today categorical stimulations. But restitution and imitation are not possible for science and daily life have changed too radically in the meantime.

The victory of positivistic science over Romantic science – which was at the same time a victory over the speculative *Naturphilosophie* of Schelling and Hegel – decisively contributed to the separation of natural and human sciences. The uncritical use or application of the concept of evolution, including, the one-sided critiques of the humanities by the natural sciences have contributed to the growing disinterest of natural scientists in history and philosophy.

The fact of the existence of Romantic *Naturforschung* around 1800 demonstrates that the general sociocultural conditions at the end of the eighteenth century did not produce only one type of science. One needs further historical differentiation; the multiplicity of positions requires a concrete social history of Romantic *Naturforschung*, a socio-psychological analysis of its adherents, an institutional analysis of the universities they attended and which gave them the possibility of teaching and research. Through such historical studies one will get new insights into the relationship between internal and external factors of the scientific changes during the eighteenth and nineteenth centuries, including the concepts of nature, science and culture.

NOTES

1 R. Ayrualt, *La Genèse du romantisme allemande* (Paris, 1961–76), I–III; R. Benz (ed.), *Lebenswelt der Romantik. Dokumente romantischen Denkens und Seins* (Munich, 1948); R. Brinkmann (ed.), *Romantik in Deutschland* (Stuttgart, 1978); U.. Cardinale (ed.), *Problemi del romanticismo* (Milan, 1983), I–II; A. Cunningham and N. Jardine (ed.), *Romanticism and the sciences* (Cambridge, 1990); D. v. Engelhardt, 'Bibliographie der Sekundärliteratur zur romantischen Naturforschung und Medizin 1950–1975', in R. Brinkmann (ed.), *Romantik in Deutschland* (Stuttgart, 1978), pp. 307–30; D. v. Engelhardt, 'Romantische Naturforschung', in D. v. Engelhardt, *Historisches Bewußtesein von der Aufklärung bis zum Positivismus* (Freiburg i.Br. and Munich, 1979), pp. 103–57; A. Faivre, 'La philosophie de la nature dans le romantisme allemand', in Y. Belavel (ed.), *Histoire de la philosophie* (Paris, 1974), III, pp. 14–45; A. Gode-von Aesch, *Natural Science in German Romanticism* (1941; New York, 1966); R. Huch, *Die Romantik* (Leipzig, 1898/1902; Tübingen, ³1964), I–II; W. Leibbrand, *Die spekulative Medizin der Romantik* (Hamburg, 1956); A. O. Lovejoy, 'The Meaning of Romanticism for the Historian of Science', in *Journal of the History of Ideas*, 2 (1841); R. Porter and M. Teich (ed.), *Romanticism in National Context* (Cambridge, 1988); H. Prang (ed.), *Begriffsbestimmung der Romantik* (Darmstadt, 1968); K. E. Rothschuh, 'Naturphilosophische Konzepte der Medizine aus der deutschen Romantik', in R. Brinkmann (ed.), *Romantik in Deutschland* (Stuttgart,

1978), pp. 243–66; Th. Steinbüchel (ed.), *Romantik. Ein Zyklus Tübinger Vorlesungen* (Stuttgart, 1948).

2 G. W. Fr. Hegel, *System der Philosophie. Zweiter Teil. Die Naturphilosophie* (Stuttgart, 1958), para. 246, pp. 45ff.

3 A. v. Humboldt, *Kosmos* (Stuttgart, 1844), I, p. 33.

4 A. Schopenhauer, *Die Welt als Wille une Vorstellung* (1819; Wiesbaden, 1978), I, p. 171.

5 F. W. J. Schelling, 'Einleitung zu dem Entwurf eines Systems der Naturphilosophie', in *Werke* (1799; Munich, 1927), II, p. 274.

6 F. W. J. Schelling, 'Ueber den wahren Begriff der Naturphilosophie', in *Werke* (1801; Munich, 1927), IV, p. 30.

7 G. W. F. Hegel, *Philosophy of Nature* (London, 1970), I, para. 246, p. 197.

8 I. P. V. Troxler, *Elemente der Biosophie* (Leipzig, 1808), pp. 228–9.

9 J. W. Ritter, *Fragmente aus dem Nachlasse eines jungen Physikers* (1810; Heidelberg, 1969), II, p. 173.

10 G. Cuvier, *Histoire des progrès des sciences naturelles* (Paris, 1826), I, p. 7.

11 G. W. F. Hegel, 'System der Philosophie. 1. Teil. Die Logik', in *Werke* (Stuttgart, 1964), VIII, para. 231, p. 441.

12 F. W. J. Schelling, 'Kritische Fragmente', in *Jahrbücher der Medicin als Wissenschaft*, 2 (1807), 303.

13 A. C. A. v. Eschenmayer, 'Dedukzion des lebenden Organismus', in *Magazin zur Vervolkommnung der theoretischen und praktischen Heilkunde*, 2, 3 (1799), 327–290.

14 H. Steffens, 'Ueber die Vegetation', in Steffens, *Alt und Neu* (Breslau, 1821), II, p. 1022.

15 G. H. Schubert, *Allgemeine Naturgeschichte* (Erlangen, 1826), p. 4.

16 L. Oken, *Abriss des Systems der Biologie* (Göttingen, 1805), p. 53.

17 Hegel, *Philosophy of Nature*, I, para. 249, p. 212.

18 Some bibliographical references: A. C. A. v. Eschenmayer, *Reflexionen über den Württembergischen Landtag* (Stuttgart, 1817); G. D. Kieser, sociopolitical observations in his *System der Medizin*, 2 vols. (Halle, 1817–19); G. D. Kieser, *Konstitutionelle Monarchie oder Republik?* (*Jenaische Zeitung*, 1 April 1848); L. Oken, numerous articles in *Isis*; H. Steffens, *Abhandlung über Universitäten* (Berlin, 1809); H. Steffens, *Ueber das Verhältniss unserer Gesellschaft zum Staate* (1812); H. Steffens, *Ueber die Bedeutung eines freien Vereins für Wissenschaft und Kunst* (Frankfurt, 1817); J. J. Wagner, *Der Staat* (Erlangen, 1815; Ulm, [2]1848); Autobiographies of Schubert, Steffens, Ringseiss, Carus, also the letters of the Romantic naturalists.

19 H. Steffens, 'Ueber die Bedeutung eines freien Vereins für Wissenschaft und Kunst, in *Alt und Neu* (1817; Bresslau, 1821), I, p. 150.

20 G. R. Treviranus, *Biologie* (Göttingen, 1802), p. 6.

21 C. G. Carus, *Lebenserinnerungen und Denkwürdigkeiten* (Weimar, 1966), I, p. 257.

22 I. Döllinger, *Von den Fortschritten, welche die Physiologie seit Haller gemacht hat* (Munich, 1824), p. 4.

23 L. Oken, in D. G. Kieser, *Das Wartburgfest am 18. Oktober 1817* (Jena, 1818), p. 113.

24 A. C. A. Eschenmayer, 'Reflexionen über den württembergischen Landtag', in *Heidelberger Jahrbücher der Literatur* (1817), p. 107.

25 J. v. Görres, 'Wachstum der Historie', in *Gesammelle Schriften* (1808; Cologne, 1926), III, p. 376.

26 H. Steffens, 'Ueber das Verhältnis der Naturphilosophie zur Physik unserer Tage', in Steffens, *Alt und Neu* (Breslau, 1821), I, p. 135.

27 H. Steffens, 'Ueber die Bedeutungeines freien Vereins für Wissenschaft und Kunst', in Steffens, *Alt und Neu*, I, p. 157.

28 Novalis, 'Vermischte Bemerkungen und Blüthenstaub' in *Schriften* (1798; Darmstadt, 1965), II, p. 427.

29 J. W. Ritter, *Die Physik als Kunst* (Munich, 1806), p. 14.

30 J. F. Loreff, 'Ueber die in einigen Gegenden Italiens herrschende böse Luft', in *Magazin für die gesamte Heilkunde* (1821; lat. Berlin, 1817), IX, p. 152f.

31 C. G. Carus, 'Von den Naturreichen, ihrem Leben und ihrer Verwandtschaft', in *Zeitschrift für die Natur- und Heilkunde* (1820), I, p. 72.

32 Görres, 'Wachstum der Historie', III, p. 372.

33 *Ibid.*, p. 379.

TWELVE

THE ANTI-ROMANTIC ROMANTICS; NATURE, KNOWLEDGE, AND IDENTITY IN NINETEENTH-CENTURY NORWAY

NINA WITOSZEK

IN the spring of 1794 Henrik Steffens, a young Danish-Norwegian stipendist of The Natural Science Association in Copenhagen, stood on the deck of a ship approaching the coast of Bergen. He had returned to his fatherland to undertake a geognostic-mineralogical research of certain rock specimens and collect molluscs on Norway's coast. As soon as the shore line came into view and he could distinguish 'the confusing mountain mass', he was overwhelmed by a mixture of angst (how could he ever comprehend its 'terrible beauty'?) and ecstasy. When he stepped on land, tears rolled down his cheeks. He was back at his birthplace, the *terra sacra* of his dreams. 'It was as if the earth opened before me the most secret core of its arsenal. As if the fertile earth, with its flowers and forests, was but a light and lovely cover which hid a multitude of treasure.'[1]

Steffens, who believed that Schelling's *Ideen zu einer Philosophie der Natur* was written exclusively for him, and who was soon to become one of the most intriguing transcultural apostles of nature philosophy, was a Romantic from head to toe. As a young boy he sank to his knees in the worship of trees, his pulse, he insisted, 120 beats per minute. Later, as a Romantic polymath, natural scientist, writer and philosopher of nature, he indulged in transcendental fusions. He wanted a science which would be poetry and poetry which would be a science. He insisted that 'Nature was an invisible spirit and spirit an invisible nature'. Nature philosophy was an alchemical brew of history, art, natural science, religion and patriotism. 'Like a new Ansgarius he set before himself the task of converting our gentle spirits and philosophers in the North from superstition to the right faith', wrote his friend, the Danish poet Oehlenschläger.[2]

He failed abysmally. In 1802 he held a series of hypnotic lectures at the University of Copenhagen which instantly made him the *bête noire* of the rationalist establishment. The Danish Crown Prince Frederik was to announce: 'You have good brains which we might use indeed, but lecture thou shalt not. You make my subjects crazy in their heads.'[3] Rejected by Copenhagen, which offered the vacant chair of philosophy to the sceptical Norwegian empiricist Niels Treschow, and rebuffed by his sober Norwegian compatriots, Steffens went on to teach transcendental idealism at the University of Halle and to become a German savant.

Steffens' unromantic odyssey to regions which were, at the time, the official *mundus imaginalis* of European Romanticism, is instructive. In some respects his experience was not so very different from the experience of a modern anthropologist who, upon arrival in Buddhist Sri Lanka, expects to find ecophilosophical natives but meets instead pragmatic materialists. An inexorable split between outside projections and native self-image, between the local tradition of knowledge and the myths about it, marks just about every culture which has been 'discovered' and created as Europe's utopian *alter ego*. The Nature Steffens constructed, however enticing to Danish students, was not in tune with the Nature sanctioned by the establishment. The Danish *Naturfilosofi* of the day was a Sunday philosophy, one which could be cultivated without surrendering Christianity or one's bourgeois proclivities. Norway – the locus of that primordial felicity, wildness and simplicity which reduced Steffens to romantic tears – was still caught in its time-warp, unable either to accept the new philosophy nor to reject it.

The question remains: why did Steffens' Nature find its disciples or adherents in Prussia and not in the Kingdom of Denmark-Norway? If, as Mary Douglas claims, 'each environment is a mask and support for a certain kind of society',[4] what lay beneath the Norwegian mask?

Norwegian Romantic nature mystique makes a particularly interesting case study. As a symbolic-iconic *fons et origo* of Romantic ideas of nature – an epitome of a land where 'natural man' lived for centuries in a 'natural state' – Norway has provoked and absorbed so many outside projections and tropes that even modern native scholarship has not yet managed to shrug off the sweet burden of flattering fictions. It is especially the period 1814–1850, customarily described as *Nasjonalromantikken*, which demands a radical rereading. How romantic precisely were the native perceptions and experiences of the natural world? What cosmology really underlay the sublime hymns to the mountain peaks and the national folktales about trolls? What concept of man and nature dominated nineteenth-century Norwegian science and philosophy? And how did the 'imagined Nature' of the natives relate to the nature imagined in Steffens' second homeland with which Norway once shared a common Germanic cosmology and a common story of roots and origins?

In what follows I wish to review briefly three significant nineteenth-century Norwegian traditions of knowledge informed by ideas about nature: that of the cultural nationalists, that of the philosophers and that of the people at large. Such a review, I believe, is important for two reasons: firstly, it may clarify some of the meta-myths about *Naturromantikken* which, today, is frequently (mis)taken as the main source of contemporary Norwegian attitudes to nature and to society.[5] Secondly, it will draw attention to the significant ways in which, what I take to be the Norwegian tradition of thinking about nature and man, departed from German *Naturphilosophie.* As I hope to demonstrate, there existed in Norwegian culture powerful mechanisms for recoding European constructions of nature. They were set in place both by particular socio-political conditions and by pre-nineteenth-century native categories and schemata.

THE NATURE OF THE NATIONAL ELITE: A CASE OF ROMANTIC VENTRILOQUISM

In the 1994 volume *Norwegian Literature over a Thousand Years*, 'National Romanticism' rules supreme: in one of the contributions it is a ubiquitous, even cannibalistic aesthetic category which devours everything in sight. Besides National Romanticism, Norway has had 'liberal romanticism', 'vitalist romanticism', 'social-realist romanticism' and 'regional romanticism', to mention but a few species.[6] There is hardly anything left, so romantic is Norway's cultural heritage and so rhapsodic her people.

The spectre of Romanticism which haunts Norway is, like most nineteenth-century spectres, a very problematic, protean being, which requires closer inspection, if not ghostbusting. Much of the confusion in modern discussions of Norwegian Romanticism springs from two related *quid pro quos*: The first one has to do with the omnipresence of nature (not necessarily Romantic – just nature in any 'style') as a semiotic referent of Norwegian identity in the nineteenth century and later. The second confusion springs from the fact that notions of the North as the quintessence of 'Romantic Nature' were largely a creation of more southernly latitudes.

Madame de Staël, who is increasingly burdened with the 'invention of Romanticism', established a powerful and durable cliché of the North as the quintessence of Romantic landscape: eschatological, metaphysical, inhabited by ghosts and by passionate, angst-ridden heroes engaged in permanent rebellion.[7] For Maurycy Mochnacki, the leading Polish romantic historian and philosopher, the superior nature of the North embodied *natura naturans* (i.e. active, creative force) while that of the South, was merely *natura naturata* (i.e. passive nature).[8] For Herder and Heine, and later Baudelaire, the religion of nature concealed in runic hieroglyphs was to be found only north of the Baltic Sea.[9] Mary Wollstonecraft was so inspired by these peans that, in the best tradition of religious pilgrimage, she undertook a journey to the Northern mecca of freedom to check for herself.

Her travel diary is an interesting document of sober demystification. It speaks of a 'manly race; for not being obliged to submit to any debasing tenure ... they act with an independent spirit'. The independent spirit, however, she finds a bit puzzling, for they 'sing republican songs but are attached to a [Danish] prince royal'. Nature is a spiritual anti-climax: The forests are 'full of philosophers rather than nymphs'. Equality is a diluter of excellence, since a 'mistaken moderation which borders on timidity, favours the least respectable of the people'. In a rather self-revealing passage, Mary Wollstonecraft concludes: 'I am, therefore half-convinced that I could not live very comfortably exiled from the countries where mankind are so much further advanced in knowledge ...'[10]

How did the Nature and knowledge of the native élite measure up to these outside representations?

What is clear is that by the mid-nineteenth century, nature and nature-related imagery were recognized as a 'totemic' possession of all Norwegians. ('The mountains are, in the last instance, our best Norwegians', proclaimed Wergeland in satirical exasperation.[11]) What is much less clear is the romantic provenance of these representations. For while it is true that nature is the orbit around which everything else moves in nineteenth-century Norwegian writing, the movement itself follows a curiously unromantic trajectory.

There was virtually no contemporary appreciative audience for the only true national romantic, Henryk Wergeland, and his erotic *biodicy*. Wergeland's kisses bestowed on the mouths of flowers, his gambollings with animals and plants and his poetic raptures were more an embarrassment than anything else. The most famous attack: 'How long will you fume against Reason?'[12] clearly indicates that the rejection of Wergeland by his contemporaries (and his *post-mortem* beatification) was not merely the old story of misunderstood genius, as in the later case of Ibsen. It was a blow from a culture which had no room and no time for Romanticism.

The majority of the cultural élite of the day received Romanticism as an anomaly, a violation of native cultural codes of perception and expression, an ethics and aesthetics of excess which very few were prepared to stomach. With the exception of Wergeland, neither romantic formal experiments in literature nor the iconoclastic Faustian-Promethean mythology found real Norwegian followers in the first half of the nineteenth century. The proliferation of such myths was curbed both by Christian ontology and anthropology and by the native, largely peasant tradition which, for all its 'radicalism', offered a conservative resistance to untried novelty and large scale social revolutions. *Vidar*, a noteworthy journal of the Intellectual Party in 1830s,[13] devoted most of its columns to an extensive critique of the new aesthetics and the corresponding world view. Leading Norwegian writers and historians (A. Schweigaard, J. P. Welhaven, J. Collett and P. A. Munch), who were also the trend-setters of the day, spent a great deal of ink condemning almost everything European Romanticism prized: the priority of emotions (read 'emotional muddle'), formal experimentation (read 'formlessness'), fascination with evil ('moral licence') and spirituality ('indulgence in hypochondrias').[14] The aesthetic tastes of most Norwegian 'romantics' were mostly classical-realist, fixated on faithfulness, clarity and accuracy in the representation of national reality. That procreative marriage between mind and nature, so ecstatically proclaimed in Schiller, Novalis and Wordsworth, was in Norwegian literature a rather down-to-earth, low-voltage marriage of convenience, documented more by realistic description than by mystic incantations. Neither the habit of 'exaggerating people into beasts and half-gods' nor 'the chimeric pictures of the Germanic past' held any appeal for Welhaven's generation.[15] The obligatory semiotic inventory of Romanticism – 'forest-cathedrals', 'proud free peasants' and 'sacred mountains' – were more often than not a romantic facade concealing a rational-pragmatic mindscape. The Nature of most Norwegian 'Romantics' – Mauritz Hansen, J. P. Welhaven, Andreas Munch, Peter Chr. Asbjørnsen, Ivar Aasen and A. O. Vinje – was nature as we find it in a dogmatic and enormously influential definition of Tertullian: 'It is the rational element [in man] which we must believe to have been innate in the soul from its beginning, as the work of an Author who is himself "rational"; the non-rational element is not properly called "natural"'.[16]

The principle 'what is natural is rational' applied both to nature itself and to the approved protagonists of nineteenth-century Norwegian narratives. A fascinating, if overlooked, aspect of the Norwegian narrative creation of the 'peasant mystique' is, precisely, its flight from Romantic stereotypes. The national peasants as celebrated by Moe, Brun and Vinje were more the bearers of the Enlightenment and the old classical virtues than of a *pensée sauvage*. The 'free and proud' Norwegian peasant was not a 'noble savage' but something of a village encyclopaedist. Jacob Aall gives an account of the *bønder*[17] in Telemark who, with 'their knowledge of the sagas prepared the ground for rationalist theology'. Henrik Steffens exulted over the 'the power of rationalism' in the Opplands' countryside.[18] Similarly Wergeland praised the peasants of the sagas not because they were bearers of a wild spirit but of the '*classical* virtues of freedom'.[19] The image of the enlightened freeholder keeping Snorre's *Eddas* on his shelves – after the fashion of an Indian peasant reading Valmiki's *Ramayana* – exists in Norwegian literature alongside that of the auto-didactic religious revivalist. It is not the Romantic, spiritual peasant at one with Nature but the rationalist *bonde* which is elevated into a cultural hero.

What is novel about the Norwegian *Naturlyrikk* – and what often makes it misleadingly Romantic – is that it harnesses nature in the service of national sentiment. Nature is not merely a source of personal and artistic salvation – as it is with other European traditions – it evokes national pride and assuages national anxiety as well. The sublimity of nature relieves Norwegians from having to apologize for their lack of cities, castles, ruins and libraries. The vast reserves of mountains, fjords and forest function as equivalents of castles and cathedrals, i.e. as national heritage.

Nineteenth-century Norwegian patriotism celebrated Nature as a source of national identity, as an arbiter of moral justice, even as the basis of national military achievement and triumph. In popular tradition, the memory of the 1718 confrontation with the Swedish army in the Tydal Mountains or the 1808 battle of Trangen was inseparably connected with nature which helped the patriotic cause either by freezing the enemy to death or by ensuring that the victory went to ski-borne Norwegian troops. Wergeland was to write: 'Even in war, Norwegian Nature fights for the people.'[20]

Paradoxically, the celebrations of Nature and *Naturfolk*, intended as they were to function as a rhetorics of solidarity bridging the gap between classes, cultures and subcultures, contributed to a growth in tension. So strong was the equation between nature and nationality that in the 'politically correct' images of Norwegianness of the time, there was little room for an urban imaginary. Unlike Lewis Mumford, for whom the city is a 'fact in nature, like a cave, a run of mackerel or an ant-heap',[21] for the Norwegian patriots of the nineteenth century the city was a parasitopolis despoiling native ground. The contest: nature against culture, countryside against the city was as fervent as it was confounding, if only because the city hardly existed. At the time of this *kulturkamp* Christiania was a capital with 20,000 souls and a theatre called by Welhaven an 'institute for catching moral and physical colds'.

The city as a symbol of progress and enlightenment, the Wordsworthian 'place of wonder and obscure delight', was something that the true patriots felt like disowning. Urban culture, associated with extraterritorial (i.e. Danish) clergy, bureaucracy and townsfolk,[22] was alien to the folk spirit. It was nature, not culture that was national. It was outside, amidst the splendours of the forest, the fjord, and the valley that the morals, manners and mores of true Norwegians were shaped, not in the modest (by European standards) *borgerskapet's* salons of Christiana or Bergen.

Such perceptions go some way to explain the pervasiveness of dichotomous thought in cultural narratives at the springtime of the nation – and indeed up to this day. In Norway, the opposition city *vs* countryside and the revivalist celebration of nature and the peasantry were not just a 'national pastoral', a rhetoric of lost authenticity as described by Raymond Williams.[23] Neither did the worship of the simple life of *Naturfolk* conceal a world of oppression and dispossession, as in the case of England. What was significantly absent from the Norwegian countryside was the experience of serfdom and of the dehumanizing machinations of state bureaucracy and officialdom. What was present – and unique in comparison with other peasant societies – was the sense of individual rights and freedoms fostered by the allodial property system. For centuries the legally free peasantry – even under tenancy conditions – had felt themselves to be answerable only to God and King. Freedom, democracy and egalitarianism were ideas which may not have had a strict institutional basis at the beginning of the nineteenth century but, as has been frequently noted, they functioned as an intrinsic part of social practice and communal ethos centuries prior to the democratic Constitution of 1814.[24]

In the Norwegian frame of remembrance, it was nature which was history, a cachet of the 'storied residence' of the nation; the city was a foreign growth and a place of amnesia. If the purpose of Blake was to build Jerusalem 'in England's green and pleasant land', the aim of Norwegian nationalists was to prevent the townfolk from imposing their cultural and political hegemony on the rest of Norway. In very few countries of Europe did culture (understood not so much as 'high culture' but as whatever was urban and cosmopolitan) come to be so synonymous with alien power; in very few places did Nature become oppositional to such a degree. For the nationalists who embarked on cultural cleansing, things Norwegian, including language, had their home in nature, not in culture. The true Norwegian speech was to be found 'in peasant cottages in our valleys and on our seashore'.[25] When Ivar Aasen (a 'scholar gypsy' who collected native plants and dialects), concocted *nynorsk*, a synthetic Norwegian based on Western dialects, he bound it up forever with the myth of *naturfolk*: the myth which has haunted the urban élite ever since.[26]

It would not be too much to say that in the nineteenth century Norwegian nature became so emotionally and ideologically charged that, for the Norwegians, it has never recovered its pristine detachment from questions of nation and identity. Such an intensive, national appropriation of nature can easily be confused with the 'Romantic' enterprise of re-enchantment. My argument is that the discovery of nature as an *objet d'art* and as an ideologically charged national emblem was carried within a cosmological framework which was less a break with Enlightenment values and more a continuation of the rationalist-pragmatic tradition which remained the centre that held.

THE NATURE OF PHILOSOPHERS: NORDIC LIGHT AGAINST GERMANIC *GÖTTERDÄMMERUNG*

The utilitarian, realist aspect of Norwegian literary representations of nature is corroborated by the budding native science and philosophy.[27] Although it is difficult to generalize from a vast body of texts and *bons mots*, Norwegian thought in the period 1814–1850 dissociated itself from the romantic nature mystique. For A. Schweigaard, the influential social economist, editor and the pioneer of liberalism, objective knowledge was possible because 'the same conditions at the same stage of objective development produce similar results ... And inasmuch as Nature is reasonable, shouldn't one explore it in order to know what it says, and in order to control it, shouldn't one listen to it?'[28] These largely pragmatic, rationalist perceptions were tempered by a strong sense of the organic interconnection of things. The Cartesian image of nature as machine was never fully assimilated by native thinkers. 'Nature is no mechanics', argued Christopher Hansteen, mathematician, physicist and astronomer. For him the world was a manifestation of energy, in which light, heat, magnetism and other forces were all the expression of one principle in different forms. Similarly for Niels Treschow, the key philosopher of the 'Romantic' period, 'all things hang together: Everywhere everything has the same root: divine is our provenance and infinite our purpose'.[29]

A typical savant of the transition from one paradigm to another, Treschow was a post-Voltaire Christian and a Darwinist *ante* Darwin.[30] Though he distanced himself from Monbodo's theory of the orang-utan as a forefather of humanity, he certainly saw development from the perspective of a natural scientist: the divine aspect of all creation notwithstanding, the science of embryology showed that human foetal development included stages resembling these of plants and animals. (This model, based on a 'bottom to top' approach differed from the speculative, poetic philosophy of Schelling and Steffens which adopted the 'top to bottom' perspective.)

What is perhaps a most intriguing, and hitherto overlooked, aspect of Treschow's philosophy, is the way in which it attempts to restrain and counteract both the sinister implications of holism and the temptations of the new positivism. Thus the purpose of nature is revealed in individuality. Only the revolutionary fanatic will sacrifice an individual for the wellbeing of the whole. 'The particular or the individual is not a means or a tool through which to reach the universal but the goal itself.'[31] For Treschow, civilization is a product of growth and development. In contrast with Condorcet, however, progress which is synonymous with the scientific and technological control of nature is but a *fata Morgana*. It will, in effect, 'tie leaden blocks under our wings instead of boosting our flight. The earthly paradise which we imagine will show itself to be a 'glorious misery'.[32] The characteristic, anti-utopian strain in Trechow's thought is inseparably connected with his anthropology: ultimately it is not the scientific but the spiritual progress of mankind which will keep the barbarians at bay.

The best *résumé* of the nineteenth-century perceptions of nature – organic, pragmatic and Christian – and their extension into the 'practice of everyday life' – is to be found in a school book by Nordhal Rolfsen:

> People who daily struggle against the harshness of Nature will be schooled in the comprehension of nature's greatness and of the unity of all things. On the bottom of the sea, in the stars of the sky, in the pollen of the flowers and the life of cells, in the paths of ocean streams, will the young comprehend the economy of the world and its laws and the creative omnipotence which stands behind everything.[33]

The singularity of Norwegian thinking about nature and man in the period 1800–1850 becomes especially striking in the comparative context of a dominant German *Naturphilosophie*. The crux of the German Romantic representation of man and nature, the kernel around which everything else was elaborated, was the idea of separation and strife. All evil and wickedness were due to an alienation of man from nature, his setting himself in opposition to the outside world. 'So long as I myself am identical with nature', argued Schelling, 'I understand what a living nature is as well as I understand my own life . . . As soon, however, as I separate myself . . . from nature, nothing more is left for me but a dead object.'[34]

This two dimensional fission between man and external nature and between the mind and its own natural instincts and desires, had an ambivalent ring to it. However negative, the man–nature split was the *sine qua non* condition of speculative philosophy whose aim was to reconcile oppositions and restore unity.[35] However painful, the ever-evolving process of oppositions, reconciliations and renewed oppositions was a constructive movement in humanity's *Bildungsgeschichte*. For Schiller, the separation from nature was a *felix divisio*: for it is culture (*eine höhere Kunst*) which will lead us back to nature again.[36] In the extreme, ominous vision of Hölderlin, all the suffering and evil ensuing from the separation from nature were necessary to achieve a new higher synthesis: 'Men fall from thee, O Nature, like rotten fruits; oh let them perish, for thus they return to thy root; so may I too, O tree of life, that I may grow green again with thee.'[37]

These matters are worth rehearsing if only to see that the main ideational premise for romantic philosophizing about nature (i.e. the divorce of humanity from nature), was largely absent from the experience of nineteenth-century Scandinavians. Certainly in Norway the pauperism of metropolitan culture deprived discursive forays into nature of their necessary antithesis and compelling *raison d'être*. There was simply no negative foil against which to construe a truly romantic narrative of return to an 'authentic, rooted existence' or indeed to inspire mystical rapture over a living tree.

The Norwegian reception of German romantic philosophy reveals further discrepancies. It is striking that, from the very beginning, the point of heightened sensitivity in Norwegian responses to German *Naturphilosophie* was, paradoxically, its very 'unnaturalness'. Nature that submitted so readily to the terrorism of language, to the German passion for unintelligible truths and pompous verbiage, was not glorified but annulled. Already in the eighteenth century a Norwegian poet sneered: 'Germany, oh Germany, in Hermans awash / how deep you are sunk in nonsense and tosh.'[38] Irritated and repelled by the German philosophical baroque, Norwegians studying philosophy and theology in Copenhagen felt a redoubled nostalgia for the sweet simplicity of their native idiom and cast themselves ever more zealously into the other extreme: the salty Holbergian rationalism of the dwellers in the fjords.

The native assault on German romantic philosophy intensified in the 1830s. For the leading national poet J. S. Welhaven, Hegelianism was but a 'play with auxiliary verbs'.[39] A. Schweigaard declared German nature philosophy remote from reality and therefore un-Norwegian (*unorsk*) in the extreme.[40] In particular, he scoffed at the *a priori* school which proceeded 'without entering into any relation to the outer world, without deriving from it, without enriching itself with facts and experience'.[41] Treschow lacerated German philosophers for not following English empiricism. Most Norwegian writers sided with Goethe, a staunch opponent of romanticism which he defined as a sickness.[42] The message was clear: The Norwegians embraced nature and reality, the Germans, for all their *Naturphilosophie*, betrayed it. The Norwegians cultivated healthy common sense, the Germans went for 'Apfelstrudel in the sky'. So unequivocal and comprehensive was the native rejection of Germanic *romantische Schwärmerei* that, for some Danish literati, Norwegian steadfast common sense became a hallmark of 'true healthy nordicity' which in Denmark itself was in imminent danger of Germanization.[43]

There are many indications that, in spite of the later impact of Hegelianism, the Norwegian élite's early self-image of themselves as guardians of Enlightenment values against the dark energies of the German romantics proved to be a durable component of the national self perceptions. The pragmatic tradition of knowledge which naturalized Reason (i.e. regarded cognitive processes as a species of biological ones) and yet refused to demote it, created its own buffer against the seductions of irrationalism. A confidence in the unsullied authority of Reason as an agent of benevolent forces within nature, remained dominant in the Norwegian intellectual tradition for the most part of the nineteenth century. It may well be that, prosaic and realist as it was, it effectively discouraged a shift of interest, if not of loyalties, to other natural forces, such as Will, instinct or race. Not until the *fin de siècle* generation of isolated vitalist writers fascinated by the twilight of the gods (*vide* Hamsun), did nature usurp the role of Reason and forced it to bow to the deeper wisdom of community and tradition, to blood, soil and the subterranean forces of the psyche. As late as 1905 Hjalmar Christensen declared self-righteously: 'In our history Schweigaard is a representative of the clear and quiet power of judgement, *The healthy realism which we also possess*.'[44]

THE NATURE OF THE *FOLK*: THE 'TAO' OF ASKELADDEN

From the perspective of Norwegian freeholders the attempt to declare one's identity in and through nature did not require any mystifying strategies – nature, after all, was all around, *à l'outrance*, both threatening, benign and all-encompassing. The hills and forests which so magically 'opened their treasures' to Steffens, made great tracts of the country inaccessible for most part of the year. (In the period 1804–1836, for example, Provost N. Hertzberg, who kept a register of all travellers in Hardanger, counted only twenty-three Norwegian travellers: three university teachers and twenty students.[45]) For the natives, the primary environment was nature rather than other people. they lived on the margins of the possible, cocooned for generations in deep isolated valleys, fighting against the stinginess of the soil or the cruelty of the sea, against snow and stone avalanches and the long, arctic darkness in the regions of permafrost. So profound was the isolation that, when discovered in the nineteenth century by scientists and ethnologists, Norway turned out to be an amazing mosaic of pocket-universes with their own idiosyncratic dialects, model of communication, sexual ethos, consumption patterns, architectural design, even sense of humour.[46] The Telemark housing design – launching defiant, sculptured cottages to counterpoint the dramatic environment – and the typical *Jærhuset* of the West coast – growing from or melting into the landscape – illustrate the various 'grammars' of adaptation: They testify as much to regional difference and individuality as to traditions which 'listened to nature', and were compliant with its moods and demands.

The hill-and-forest-and-seashore people were an egalitarian *communitas* held together by religion, tradition – and by the struggle against incalcitrant elements. Overshadowing formal class and sex distinctions was the struggle for survival which turned men, women and animals into a community of interest and interdependence.[47] In such a community values, of necessity, had to be resilient under pressure, while hierarchy was a fragile construct prone to collapse in the face of common adversity. Daily life relied on a practical, experiential knowledge of nature: its rhythms, regularities, warnings and boundaries. The sky, landscape, work-day, feasts and ceremonies created a continuum. Human life imitated natural rhythms; everything, from reeling fish-nets to bearing the body to the churchyard had to follow the sun. Things had to be done at the right time and in the right place (many place-names in Norway still refer to these traditionally prescribed activities[48]). The cycle of the sea was different from the cycle of the soil, the time perspective of a farmer different from that of a fisherman, socializing in a seascape (reading weather, wave and stream patterns) different from that in the valleys. From the organic perspective of dwellers in the land, their natural surroundings were less a romantic landscape and more a 'task-scape', to use Tim Ingold's phraseology, a dynamic man-in-nature gestalt imbued with action.[49] Their view of nature was pragmatic, 'pre-positivist' even, based on close observation from which to infer law and pattern. The supernatural world of folk tales – lascivious forest huldras stealing men from their wives, malicious trolls kidnapping babies or musical watermen luring innocent souls to their perdition – was invoked to explain the extraordinary and the abnormal rather than to describe daily routine. The core paradigm of action and morality was shaped equally by Christian teaching as by the 'Book of Nature'. Nature was not just God's handiwork replete with messages that people must discern the better to live by God's will. More often than not, the order of God and the order of Nature were in competition with one another, proposing their own heroes and standards of performance.[50] Their adequacy was determined less by the power of dogma and more by what might be called 'adaptive efficiency'. The shocking custom of *nattefrieri* (i.e. pre-marital tests of sexual prowess), observed by Eilert Sundt in certain regions, was but one of many instances where Christian mores were dropped in the interest of biological survival.[51]

The popular tradition of knowledge based on a direct experience of nature fostered its own heroes and exemplary models of action. If we follow James Hillman, who has suggested that each community has its own 'heroic centre' which is less 'a single monad, an inner replica of a single God, than a group ethos',[52] the collective totemic ancestor of the Norwegian countryside is Askeladden. His adventures, recorded in countless folk tales, are perhaps the most illuminating imaginative testament to the popular native *codex natura* and the way it has influenced national ethos and models of action.[53]

Askeladden is one of three sons of a poor couple living in a miserable cottage in the depths of the Norwegian forest. An incorrigible lazybones, he sits by the fire all day, poking and fiddling with the ashes. Out there on a farm lives a peasant king who is troubled by hostile natural phenomena (a tree which refuses to be cut down, a well which refuses to yield water, etc.) as well as by a sharp-tongued daughter whom he invariably promises as a reward to the lad who can solve his problems. Provoked and prodded by the elder brothers, Askeladden reluctantly joins the competition. Without a great deal of sweat or tears, through his own resourcefulness and with nature's support (streams, trees, nuts, horses prompt him in the right direction) he wins half of the kingdom and the princess.

Although rife with motifs familiar from folktales elsewhere, the story of Askeladden is exceptional in the way it implicitly outlines an ecological protagonist (a comic surviver) and a corresponding code of action. As a narrative epitomizing the essence of national role models and action patterns, 'Askeladden' proposes a lazy, anarchic, but also highly pragmatic lad whose success depends on both on his own resourcefulness and on the favour of nature. The principle underlying Askeladden's behaviour recalls the Taoist *wu wei*, i.e. 'action in inaction', or action in accordance with the laws of nature. In contrast to the *yu wei* (forceful striving), exercized by his brothers, Askeladden wins because the basis of his action is less violent intervention than close, sober observation of, and cooperation with, nature.[54]

It is here, in the Askeladdian ecological exemplum, that nature as imagined by the people at large conflates with the nature of the national writers and philosophers. It is Nature seen not through romantic, but through pragmatic lenses, a nature which will deliver as long as we heed her and know exactly the horizon of limits to our interventions.

CONCLUSION: THE NORWEGIAN 'ECOHUMANIST' TRADITION

It is one of the meta-ironies of Romanticism that while nineteenth-century Europe was romancing the North as a Gothic nature utopia, the North itself embraced values which suggested the classical ethos of Greece and Rome. It espoused the ancient 'middle course' in which brains were certainly more precious than blood. It evoked nostalgia for a comprehensible, rational, ecologically 'simple and natural' world. It embodied the Romantic ideal without being quite Romantic, like a Pre-Raphaelite beauty with the soul of a milk-maid.

To speak of 'Nordic classicism' – the designation which has occasionally been invoked to describe the nineteenth-century national renewal[55] – is to impute a derivative character to what was basically a native 'nature tradition'. For there was a normative code, traceable to peasant folktales, which effectively 'hijacked' the Norwegian Romantic poetry and *Naturfilosofi*. This code and this tradition, I suggest, might be tentatively described as 'ecohumanist'.[56] Ecohumanism in this case refers to a cosmology based on humanist ideals, but one in which the symbolic referents of identity derive from nature imagery and from affective ties with a particular place. The basic premise of humanism, the recognition of the inherent dignity and of the equal and unalienable rights of all members of the human family, is here corrected by values springing from man's experience of nature. It is the art of the *via media* and *via activa*, based on the knowledge of nature's ways and moderated by the awareness of limitations inherent both in nature and in society. The 'eco-' prefix, we may say, protects humanism from its own excesses.

The eco-humanist tradition of knowledge is forged less by the lore of the city and more by the 'wisdom of the open air': it promotes realism rather than extravagance, equality rather than hierarchy and, though it launches organic, holistic perceptions of nature, it measures the value of the environment and culture in utilitarian rather than in romantically idealist terms. After all, pragmatism, as William James remarked, 'means the open air and the possibilities of nature, as against ... dogma, artificiality and the preference of finality in truth'.[57]

The above attempt to point to a 'Pragmatist's Progress' as an important narrative strain in Scandinavian cultural history is not merely to de-romanticize a tradition which still employs nature as an emblem of identity; it is to suggest that the dominant system of values which in the last 200 years empowered social change in Norway has been based on a pragmatic, ecohumanist code of action. Although there is no doubt that this code was not shared equally by all classes, it has nevertheless constituted a crucial axiological reference system. Nobody who has aspired to political or cultural leadership could afford to ignore it in the past century.

NOTES

1 Henrich Steffens, *Forelesninger og fragmenter.* 'Norsk filossofi i det 19. århundre' series, (Oslo, 1967), p. 16.

2 See Harald Beyer, 'Henrich Steffens', in E. Beyer *et al.* (eds.), *Norsk Biografisk Leksikon* (Oslo, 1962), pp. 463, 465.

3 *Norsk Biografisk Leksikon*, p. 465.

4 Mary Douglas, 'Environments at Risk', in *Implicit Meanings: Essays in Anthropology* (London, 1993), p. 247.

5 Norwegian historians and literary scholars have not only scrutinized myths of the Norwegian Revival; they have also created myths *about* it. Those meta-myths derive in large part from an all-too-easy transfer of European categories to the Norwegian situation where they serve to obscure rather than to illuminate the particularity of the Norwegian tradition.

6 See Asbjørn Aarseth, 'Norsk litteratur ut verda, 1864–1905', in Fidjestøl *et al.* (eds.), *Norsk litteratur i tusen år* (Oslo, 1994), pp. 316, 328 45. Aarseth's extended concept of romanticism is, he tells us, not only justified by an eternal heroic-nationalist-idealist agenda lurking behind various literary programmes but also by the demands of constructivist hermeneutics.

7 See Madame de Staël's chapter on 'De la poésie classique et de la poésie romantique' in *De l'Allemagne*, ed. Comtesse Jean de Pange (Paris, 1958). On de Staël's alleged 'invention' of Romanticism, see A. Isbell, *The Birth of European Romanticism: Truth and Propaganda in de Staël's De l'Allemagne* (Cambridge, 1994).

8 See Maria Janion and Maria Zmigrodzka, *Romantycyzm i Historia* (Warsaw, 1978), p. 289.

9 Herder wrote:

> However rude, the civilizations of the Northern coasts were long forced to remain, however rough their climate and manner of life – there was nevertheless hidden in them, mainly because of their seafaring habits, a germ which in milder environments was quickly capable of shooting beautifully blossoming springs. Bravery and vitality, dexterity and skill in the arts which were later called knightly, a great appreciation of honour and noble

descent, together with the well known Nordic respect for the feminine sex as the prize of the bravest, handsomest and noblest men – these were qualities which in the South were certain to make the Scandinavian sea-robbers much beloved.

See J. G. Herder, *Ideen zu einer Philosophie der Geschichte der Menschheit* (Berlin, 1965). Quoted in J. Kurschner (ed.), *Deutsche nasjonal Literatur*, 77 vols. (Stuttgart, n.d.), XVIII, ch. 4, pp. 754–5. See also Charles Baudelaire, *Curiosités esthétiques. L'Art romantique, et autres oeuvres critiques* (Paris, 1962).

10 See Mary Wolfstonecraft, *Letters Written During a Short Residence in Sweden, Norway and Denmark* (London, 1796), pp. 76, 79, 110, 117. Wollstonecraft's sober observations were, however, completely eclipsed by the later eruption of Carlyle's fervid worship of Northern *Übermensch* as an antidote against enervating civilization. We may add here that the image of healthy teutonic biologism did not die in English literature with Carlyle. It lives in a subdued form in the work of the British poet laureate, Ted Hughes. As Tom Paulin argues, 'the entrepreneurial side of the British imagination identifies with the Nordic, or the Teutonic blood ... Vikings are really a proleptic cultural code for Protestant individualism'. See Tom Paulin, *Minotaur* (London, 1944), p. 265.

11 Cited by F. Paasche in *Norges litteraturhistorie* (Oslo, 1970), III, p. 236.

12 This thundering reprimand, authored by J. S. Welhaven, (Wergeland's chief literary and ideological opponent) was published anonymously in the Norwegian daily, *Morgenbladet*, on 15 August 1830 in response to Wergeland's poetic masterpiece 'Creation, Man and Messiah'. Welhaven's assault on Wergeland as 'A poet marked by all poetry's mortal sins: perfect lack of clarity in perception and level-headedness in realization; most exaggerated affectation ... and uncontrollable anarchy', was repeated *ad nauseam* in various combinations and permutations in the national journals and newspapers throughout the poet's life. Cited by Reidar Amundsen Næss in *Norsk Biografisk Leksikon*, p. 408.

13 The programme of the 'Intellectual Party', led by Welhaven and Schweigaard, was based on the assumption that Norway, having received her civilization from abroad, must make up for the '400 years' night' by drawing on the best, foreign and native resources. The 'Patriots' on the other hand, with Wergeland at the lead, insisted that Norway must invest in her own national tradition based on the values of the countryside.

14 See the debate in *Vidar* (Christiania), especially issues 1–9 (1832–1834).

15 When Welhaven called for matching Norwegian political radicalism with a literary one, he argued for realism, not for romanticism: 'It is in our acknowledgement that we cannot express something clearer and better than what we ourselves experienced and achieved that the fruit of romantic protest is contained.' See Welhaven, *Cyclus Forelæsninger over vort Sprogs skjønne Literaturs Historie*, published in *Den Constitutionelle* (Christiania, 1837), nr. 98, p. 255.

16 See Tertullian *De anima* (Amsterdam, 1947), p. 16. The very term *anima*, as used by Tertullian, refers to a faculty through which 'natural truths are apprehended' and which makes man the 'rational animal', capable of thought and knowledge. See also J. P. Welhaven, *Samlede skrifter*, VIII, pp. 43, 46.

17 The Norwegian *bonde* (pl. *bønder*), i.e., 'peasant' in a strained English translation, denotes a freeholder or a fisherman (*fiskebonde*) whose legendary free status and

property rights were quite unique in pre-nineteenth century Europe. See Øyvind Østerud, *Agrarian Structure and Peasant Politics in Scandinavia* (Oslo, 1978).

18 See Paasche, *Norges litteraturhistorie*, pp. 109–10.

19 Johan Sannes, *Patrioter, Intelligens og Skandinaver: norske reaksjoner på skandinavismen før 1848* (Oslo, 1948), p. 122.

20 See Wergeland, *Samlede Skrifter*, 'Blaamyra 23' in *Digte*, vol. I, ed. H. Jæger and D. A. Seip (Christiania, 1918–40), p. 279.

21 Lewis Mumford, *The Culture of Cities* (New York, 1938), p. 5.

22 To be precise, many of the townspeople were of rural origin but a large percentage also traced their lineage back to citizens of Denmark, Schleswig Holstein, Holland and Scotland.

23 See Raymond Williams, *The Country and the City* (London, 1979).

24 Øyvind Østerud talks about the 'old communitarian fellowship based on strongly egalitarian norms'. *Agrarian Structure and Peasant Politics*, p. 129. See also Østerud, 'Nasjonalstaten i Norge – en karakteriserende skisse', in *Det norske samfunn*, ed. L. Aldeen, N. Rogoff Ramsøy og M. Vaa (Oslo, 1986).

25 Ivar Aasen, 'Om vort Skriftsprog' (1836), published in *Skrifter – Eit Utvalg*, ed. Olav Hr. Rue (Oslo, 1976), p. 197.

26 Even today environmental activists in Norway often perceive *nynorsk* as the language of grassroot revolt in opposition to the educated Dano-Norwegian which is associated with the evils of civilization.

27 There exists no analytic integrative study of nineteenth-century Norwegian thought. Hjalmar Hegge in a series of summary reviews confirms that there was very little interest for German idealism early in the century. It is only in the 1850s and 1860s that Hegel made any impact on the thought of the leading Norwegian philosopher M. J. Monrad. See Hjalmar Hegge, 'Strømninger og brytninger i norsk tenkning fra 1700-tallet til annen verdenskrig' in *Essays og Debatt* (Oslo, 1993). Hegge's argument that idealist philosophy was more representative of the Norwegian *Zeitgeist* because it underlay the writings of Wergeland, Steffens and later Monrad is, however, misleading. Firstly, it attempts to read *modern* perceptions of Steffens and Wergeland into the past, forgetting that both savants were very much sidetracked by their Norwegian contemporaries during their lifetime. Secondly, it underestimates the actual weight and influence of 'the cold soberness and scepticism' of the Intellectual Party around Schweigaard in the period 1814–1850.

28 A. M. Schweigaard, 'De la philosophie allemande', *La France Litteraire* (Winter 1834/Spring 1835).

29 See Niels Treschow, *'Philosophiske Forsøg' og andre skrifter*, in A. H. Winsnes (ed.), *Niels Treschow* (Oslo, 1927), p. 23.

30 And a socialist *ante* Marx as well. Treschow believed that the state should take over the production of goods and their distribution. See Anthon Aall, 'Filosofien', in *Det Kongelige Frederiks Universitet 1811–1911*, Festskrift (Oslo, 1911), II, p. 395.

31 Niels Treschow, 'Gives der noget Begreb eller nogen Idee om enslige Ting? Besvaret med Hensyn til Menneskeværd og Menneskevel', in A. H. Winsnes (ed.), *Philosophiske Forsøg*, pp. 175–99.

32 Niels Treschow, 'Om nogle Grunde, tagne af vore Tiders Aand, til at frykte et nyt Barbarie', avhandling, cited in Winsnes (ed.), *Philosophiske Forsøg*, p. 29.

33 Nordahl Rolfson, *Læsebog for folkeskolen*, fjerde del (Christiania, 1894), p. 4.

34 Friedrich Schelling, *Ideen zu einer Philosophie der Natur*, *Sämtliche Werke* (Stuttgart, 1856–61), Pt. I, II, pp. 57–8.

35 For Schelling, all philosophizing consisted in 'recalling the condition in which we were at one with nature'. See Schelling, *Allemeine Deduktion des dynamischen Process* in *Sämtliche Werke*, Pt. IV, p. 77.

36 Friedrich Schiller, *On the Aesthetic Education of Man* (1795), trans. E. M. Wilkinson and L. A. Willoughby (Oxford, 1967), pp. 39–43.

37 F. Hölderlin, *Hyperion*, in *Sämtliche Werke* (Stuttgart, 1944–62), III, p. 159.

38 See Zetlitz, 'Lore', cited in Theodor Caspari, *Norsk naturfølelse i det nittende aarhundrede* (Christiania, 1917), p. 2.

39 Cited by Anthon Aall in 'Filosofien', *Det Kongelige Frederiks Universitet*, p. 398.

40 After a research trip to Berlin, Schweigaard complained about the *charlatanisk bombast* of the academy and insisted he had never seen 'so many sublime trivialities and indigestible crudities growing in that part of Germany that calls itself most urbane and educated'. See L. M. Aubert (ed.), *Anton Martins Schweigaard's barndom og ungdom: 1808–1835, breve og erindringer* (Christiania, 1883), p. 137.

41 See Schweigaard's, 'De la Philosophie Allemande'. His lecture in Studenterforbundet in 1833 ('*Om falske Idealer, Systemtvang og Goethes Kunstbestrebelse som begge modsat*') elaborated some of his critique. See also Anton Martin Schweigaard, *Ungdomsarbeider* (Christiania, 1904), pp. 243, 233.

42 Goethe wrote: 'There is nothing natural or original in Romanticism – rather it is contrived, affected, intensified, exaggerated, bizarre, even distorted and caricature-like.' See J. W. v. Goethe to Fr. W. Reimer (letter of 28 August 1808), in *Goethe's Gespräche*, ed. W. Herwig (Zurich, 1969), I, p. 328.

43 L. Dietrichson, *Omrids af den norske Poesis Historie. Norges Bidrag til Felleslitteraturen.* (Kjøbenhavn, 1866), p. 9. Already at the end of the eighteenth century Heiberg, who contrasted the Danish poet Ewald (inspired by German Romanticism) with the 'Norwegian school of poetry', argued that the latter was purer and more national. (Dietrichsen, p. 151)

44 Hjalmar Christensen, *Kulturkamp i Norge* (Christiania, 1905), p. 17, italics mine. According to Moltke Moe, who attempted to sum up the nineteenth-century upheaval at home. Norwegian Romanticism was more 'healthy' than the German. Even Fridtjof Nansen, although he shared Haeckel's monism, was more a follower of the Anglo-American 'school of nature' (J. S. Mill and Emerson) than of German *Naturphilosophie*. See Moltke Moe, *Samlede Skrifter* (Oslo, 1927), III, p. 366. See also Fridtjof Nansen 'Videnskap og moral' published in *Samtiden* in 1908, rpt. in *Nansens Røst. Artikler og taler av Fridtjof Nansen* (Oslo, 1908), II, pp. 372, 376.

45 Caspari, *Norsk naturfølelse*, p. 15.

46 One of the pioneering anthropological studies of Norway is Eilert Sundt's *magnum opus* on the national building styles, soberness and chastity. Sundt's research trip across Norway undertaken in 1850–60 revealed both striking differences and similarities: on the whole Sundt was surprised to see how 'extremely similar were the houses and the everyday life of both the prosperous and the poor peasant'. See Eilert Sundt, *Om Bygningsskikken paa Landet i Norge* (Christiania, 1862).

47 Andreas Holmsen points to a *familiesamfunn* in which strong individualism was curbed and controlled by the tradition of cooperation and solidarity which cancelled social distinctions. See A. Holmsen, *Gard, Bygd, Rike* (Oslo, 1966). See also Holmsen, *Nye studier i gammel historie* (Oslo, 1976).

48 See Anne Grete Ljøsne, *Naturen og menneskeverket* (Oslo, 1993), p. 62.

49 See Tim Ingold, 'The Temporality of Landscape', ms, University of Manchester, 1993, (prepared for a special issue of *World Archeology* on *Conceptions of Time in Ancient Society*, ed. R. Bradley).

50 The competition between the 'god of Nature' and the 'god of Culture' has been powerfully captured in Ibsen's *Brand.* There a Nietzschean priest who decides that the true God dwells not in the church but up in the open, among the mountain peaks, perishes on the icy mountainside while climbing to his Lord.

51 See Eilert Sundt, *Om Sædelighetstilstanden i Norge* (Christiania, 1859; rpt. Oslo, 1968).

52 See James Hillman, 'Psychology, Self and Community', in *Resurgence* (Sept./Oct, 1994), p. 20.

53 See P. Ch. Asbjørnsen and J. Moe, *Norske folkeeventyr* (1841), rpt. in *Samlede eventyr* (Oslo, 1957).

54 For the review of the main axioms of Tao, see Chung-ying Cheng, 'On the Environmental Ethics of the Tao and the Ch'i', *Environmental Ethics*, 8, 4 (Winter 1986), 351–70.

55 See for example Carl W. Schnitler, *Slegten fra 1814* (Christiania, 1911); see also Sigmund Skard, *Vinje og antikken. Studier i norsk aandshistorie* (Oslo, 1938); Skard, *The Classical Tradition in Norway* (Oslo, 1980).

56 The concept of 'eco-humanism' deployed in this study is used in a metaphorical sense; it designates a set of phenomena which were prior to the proper discovery of the environment and the establishment of the science of ecology. It is a result of a struggle to name, and thereby to come to terms with, a distinctive tradition of knowledge which was heavily influenced by the dynamics of man's relationship to nature. The prefix 'eco' must be then treated as a modifier of images and ideas which Norway shared with or acquired from Europe but which were either reworked or contested by the native, nature-oriented, holistic world view.

57 See William James, *Pragmatism* (Cambridge, MA, 1975).

THIRTEEN

THE WORDY WORSHIP OF NATURE AND THE TACIT FEELING FOR NATURE IN THE HISTORY OF GERMAN FORESTRY

JOACHIM RADKAU

I

RECENTLY I had an encounter which gave me the idea for this title. One day when I travelled by train, I happened to sit in a compartment together with two women. The one was young and smiling and had an intellectual appearance; the other was old, looked gloomy and appeared to be petty-bourgeois. Of course, I tried at first to get into conversation with the first woman, and that turned out to be very easy. Immediately she began to talk incessantly about nature. We must live with nature, we must listen to the voice of nature, human beings have left the path of nature, we must listen to the voice of nature, human relations nowadays have become unnatural – greed for money is destroying nature, only the children still keep a sense for nature, nature will take revenge on mankind, sooner or later the human species will perish because of the neglect of nature ... And so forth. Nature, nature, nature ... At first, her talk on nature awoke my sympathy. After some time, however, I felt that I began to hate this woman. She talked and talked like a computer programmed with all the environmental phrases of the last twenty years, and she did not listen to any remark of her fellow-travellers. Her evocation of nature lacked any dialogue, any experience of life. In no way it was based upon a real interest in her present environment which she did not even seem to perceive. Even worse, she apparently enjoyed the outlook of a future ecological catastrophe! I was deeply relieved when she finally left.

Just at this moment, the old woman changed her face and began to smile. Obviously she was also relieved. Now I got into a long and lively conversation with her, and after a short time, I became really enthusiastic. She had had a long life with a lot of hard work, but with many happy days, too, having not only husband and children, but managing a country inn for forty years. She had an immensely rich experience of life and with people. She liked her family, her friends, her home and her meals, and she had a sharp eye for all details of her natural and social environment. She never used the term 'nature'; but she probably lived much closer to nature than the young woman – if a life close to nature exists at all. When I said good-bye to her, I felt I had made an experience with symbolic meaning.

II

This story leads on to three main points of my chapter: (1) The term 'nature' can be a mere pretext for dogmatism, a justification for an apodictic style of pronouncement. (2) A real feeling for nature is not always expressed by high-sounding words on nature; sometimes one has to search for it elsewhere. (3) A reasonable concept of nature has to be based upon dialogue, upon experience, upon sensibility for the nature and social environment. I think these three points mark serious problems connected with the concept of nature: problems which we are meeting today, but met already in the past, too. The history of the term 'nature' is not a pleasant one throughout; maybe that is one of the reasons why the modern environmental movement is showing so little inclination for history on the whole. As Fernand Braudel stated, the French revolutionists had a predilection for 'nature', because an argument based upon 'nature' did not tolerate any objection.[1] For the same reason, the French pressure towards the Rhine, the Alps and the Pyrenees was justified by nature: by the so-called natural frontiers; this concept of nature resulted in many wars. Moreover, the whole ideal of nationalism meant that political units were based upon nature[2] and were endowed in this way with an obligatory, compulsory character. In Germany, the Nazi movement founded its violently militant character upon a Darwinist concept of nature: the conviction that nature means struggle, and that a *Volk* is obliged to struggle externally in order to survive. Today, the dark chapters of nature's history seem to be often neglected in order to keep the concept of nature clean and peaceful.

But these considerations should not be understood as arguments for rejecting the concept of nature radically; on the contrary, they should underline the urgency to investigate the idea of nature and to make it fruitful for environmental history. At first, however, it is important to confront the problems which are involved with this idea. Forest history seems to be a useful example in order to reveal the difficulties of the concept of nature in the course of history, but it is useful, too, for opening some ways to solve these problems.

Forestry history, if considered from a present-day environmentalist outlook, frequently appears as a confusing story. Often it is not easy to decide where to find true environmental consciousness. If one meets the term nature, it is important to note exactly what the appeal to nature concretely means, and which interests, attitudes and actions are involved. For instance, the late eighteenth and early nineteenth century marked a high-tide for the term nature in both science and literature and in politics. But if we look at forestry, we face a paradox. The philosophical faith in nature was usually connected with the conviction that nature can never be destroyed. Therefore, at that time, the concept of nature generally did not promote environmental consciousness in the modern sense but, on the contrary, was often turning away attention from human destructions of nature.[3]

To be sure, philosophical neglect does not mean that people about 1800 did not perceive the destruction of woodlands. On the contrary, exactly at that time we meet a real flood of complaints about deforestations and imminent timber famine.[4] There was even a tendency to overstate the danger and the degree of deforestation. But these complaints did not originate from a philosophy of nature, but originated from practical experiences and economic interests. As to the German Romantic *Naturphilosophie*, it had a highly speculative character and was insufficiently connected with empirical research. If we think that the genuine feeling for nature has to be based upon experience, much of the *Naturphilosophie* existed far away from nature.

Around 1800, for many contemporaries the woodlands became the embodiment of nature. In Germany, the great reafforestation movement was starting exactly at that time. But nature did not belong to the forest terminology at the beginning of the nineteenth century. On the contrary, one gets the impression that the contemporary leading German forestry teachers – Hartig, Cotta, and Hundeshagen – were somewhat suspicious of the idea of nature. Indeed, they were interested to make sure that the forest should not be considered as a gift of nature but should become the object on which the work of forestry is performed. At the time of forest reforms, imitation of nature and love of natural woodlands were rather old-fashioned attitudes typical for the elder generation of foresters who were more hunters than tree-planters and who laughed at theory.[5]

Now, where do we find the true environmentalists? Indeed, it is not easy to pin down environmentalist outlook among the interested parties in the history of forestry. Some kind of environmental consciousness – especially an intimate cognition of the interior of the woodlands and a strong emotional affinity towards the old wooded landscape – can be discovered within the soul of the old hunters. Another kind of consciousness, reflected in an active engagement in the reconstitution of forests, can be found embodied in the new reformers. If environmental consciousness is to provide for a far-away future, the forest reformers undoubtedly possessed it to a high degree because they planned a sustainable forest economy for more than 100 years. But a critic such as Wilhelm Pfeil mocked these centennial plans by pointing to the continuous change of conditions, and he blamed sharply the rigid rules which Hartig had decreed both in neglect of history and nature.[6]

Again and again, it is not easy to identify environmental consciousness in the past. To be sure, even if the forest reformers avoided the term nature as they frequently did, one must not necessarily conclude that they lacked any feeling for the nature of the forest. When they advocated the high forest with extremely long-term cutting-circles, they justified this policy by rational economic arguments asserting that high woods produce the biggest crops not only of timber but also of firewood.[7] Today, however, we know on the basis of a really rational outlook, that the cutting-circles of the so-called forest classics were much too long-term. As early as 1830, Wilhelm Pfeil stated that the advantage of the high forest in producing firewood existed only theoretically but not effectively, and he ridiculed the predilection for old oaks as a sentimental bias.[8] Later on, foresters were repeatedly blamed for not being really economically minded. Indeed one can presume that the predilection for the high forest with long-term cutting circles was not rationally based[9] but had something to do with a veneration of big old trees, and the feeling that a good tree should have a whole life and should die only when it is old. We can recognize in the background a feeling of partnership with nature. Besides another motive was probably important, too: only a high forest policy with long cutting-circles was appropriate to justify an independent and well-established forest administration and to defend it against the rising liberalism.

But the feeling for the nature of the woodlands is certainly not confined to modern educated foresters. There exists a tacit feeling for the natural regeneration of the wood which stems from long-time experience and from close affinity to the woodlands. One can recognize it by discovering the silent history of the so-called *Plenterwirtschaft*,[10] a kind of forestry typical for the peasant who used to cut only single trunks according to their specific need. This method of wood-cutting created a mixed wood of different species and ages with natural regeneration without the necessity of planting trees. The forest reformers condemned the *Plenterwald* as a *Plünderwald* (plunder forest). But today we know that a deliberately managed *Plenterwald* excels in economical stability. Already in the course of the nineteenth century several foresters, shocked by the instability of the recently established monocultures, rediscovered the virtues of the old *Plenterwirtschaft* which had been outlawed and prohibited by the first generation of forest reformers. August Bernhardt, a leading German forest historian of the late nineteenth century, who became a friend of the *Plenterwald*, emphasized that the return to the old *Plenterwirtschaft* happened very quietly: Hardly anybody dared to say loudly that this nearly despised, long time overcome type of forestry was being reintroduced.[11] This state of affairs continued until the mid-twentieth century when an official rehabilitation of the *Plenterwald* appeared suitable.

Until today the history of woodlands has too often been written as a mere history of forest regulations, which tended to stabilize the ecology of the woodlands: when, for instance, the peasants were shooting game, they drove their cattle into the forests, refused to collect the knags and knots and obstructed the afforestation of conifers. The revolutionary events of 1848 present a particularly amusing example. Most of the contemporary foresters perceived only the destruction done to the woods by the peasants at the time of the Revolution when the police did not dare to venture into the depth of the forests. When the poor peasants, however, trespassed on the forests and shot all game they could come upon, they rendered possible the upgrowth of beautiful broad-leaved mixed forests.[12] It is a nice example of *natura naturans*, nature as an actor on the historical scene.

Considering events of such kind, one can draw the general conclusion that, writing environmental history, we should not only focus on the observance or *non*-observance of administrative regulations, but we should also try to think in terms of self-regulating systems, in accordance with the new trends of system theory which could prove to be more fruitful for historians than the old static system model. In the same way we should not so much think in terms of a stable balance fixed once and for all between man and nature, but rather in terms of a flowing equilibrium (*Fliessgleichgewicht*) which is restored by dynamic processes and even by conflicts. Only the pattern of flowing equilibrium seems to portray truly the relation between man and nature in the past. But in forest history the processes by which flowing equilibrium is restored are frequently not well documented in the records, but have to be read between the lines.

III

We can find a dynamic idea of sustainable forestry already in the writings of Wilhelm Pfeil (1783–1859), a pioneering but always controversial Prussian forestry teacher. He sharply attacked the rigid rules which Georg Ludwig Hartig, the long-time head of the Prussian forest administration came to impose upon state-forestry. In contrast to Hartig, Pfeil frequently appealed to nature, though mostly during his later years. For the fighting Pfeil, nature was used as a polemical concept, a concept against general theories and general rules. In the *Kritische Blätter* (which he edited) he attacked most contemporary forestry writers. In 1849 he even advised the forester to forget all theories and to go to the school of nature.[13] Pfeil's phrase – Ask the trees for advice: they will teach you the best forest – was frequently quoted. Again and again he emphasized that all good forestry was adapted to local conditions.

But let us be cautious with Pfeil and his enthusiasm for nature. When he spoke of local conditions, he meant not only natural but also economic conditions. In practice, Pfeil often advocated a kind of forestry which was strongly guided by financial interests. When he attacked general rules, he pleaded for the freedom of private owners in the management of their woodlands even if that freedom was used to cut down woods and convert them into arable land.

Did Pfeil not recognize that contradiction between his enthusiasm for nature and his liberal forest policy? He seemed to have been confident that man had a natural love for the nature of the wood, and that therefore the permanent fear of forest destruction was groundless. Pfeil's deep emotional adherence to forests was closely connected with his pleasure in hunting and he liked to say that only the passionate hunter possessed an intimate feeling for the forest. But it was exactly the excessive protection of game promoted by powerful hunting interests which did great damage to many forests. Its unintended effect was usually the decline of broad-leaved forests. Again, the environmental historian should pay attention not only to the *idea* of nature and to verbal enthusiasm for nature but also the actions and their unintended consequences, too.

In 1842 when German high forest policy began to be adopted by the French government, a French conservative writer called upon to defend nature by warning against German theory.[14] But again one should be wary of the worship of nature because this writer was probably not defending the interest of nature, but the interest of French ironmasters who preferred coppices to high forests. However, in early nineteenth-century France, more than in Germany, a true philosophy of nature detached from mere economic interests was sometimes advanced in favour of a reafforestation policy on a large scale.[15] Presumably soil erosion and inundations, resulting from deforestation, constituted a danger much more imminent in southern parts of France than in most

German regions. The same holds true for the Alpine regions of Switzerland which were troubled during the early nineteenth century by a wave of floods. These catastrophes were attributed to deforestation and gave rise to a strong forest protection policy. In 1849 the leading Swiss forester Marchand put the 'economy of nature' against the short-sighted economy of *laissez-faire*.[16]

But again we should not applaud too unconditionally this worship of nature. As Swiss historians recently pointed out, it is neither proven nor even probable that wood destruction done by people living in mountain areas was really responsible for the inundations. Accusations of this kind have rather to be understood within the context of Swiss power-play: environmental complaints served as a means for the dominating Swiss lowlands to get control over the mountain forests. In France the whole situation was quite similar.[17] In fact it can be assumed that the ecological and cultural value of forests was invented during the early nineteenth century when the old fear of imminent wood famine was no longer strong enough to justify governmental forest protection in the face of rising liberalism and advancing coal and steel production.

IV

In Germany we find an early expression of a passionate spiritual worship of the natural woodlands explicitly detached from economic interests in a booklet published in 1815 by Ernst Moritz Arndt, one of the founding fathers of German nationalism. The booklet contains ideas which appear deeply environmentalist today: Man and nature make each other mutually; to the extent man spoils nature, the earth becomes inhuman; the axe which fells the tree threatens to become an axe which 'cuts down the whole people'.[18] But this cult of nature had nothing to do with the afforestation movement of that time; at least, there was no direct influence. Of course, German foresters could only be frightened when confronted with a philosophy which condemned the axe! Arndt's appreciation of the woodlands must be understood as symbolic behaviour without real connection with an effective conservation policy. This lack of practical significance: is it a typical feature of high-sounding appraisals of nature?

By the mid nineteenth century, much more important than Arndt, for the German romanticizing of woods, was Wilhelm Heinrich Riehl (1823–97), a popular social scientist who exerted considerable influence upon the German worship of nature as well as the development of German nationalism. 'Nature' was one of Riehl's favourite themes.[19] And the nature he loved was the wilderness: when he praised forests he meant the wild woodlands. He seemed to be unaware that German woods were formed under human influence lasting many centuries. He cultivated a typical romantic illusion which is still popular today though the first lesson one has to learn about forest history is that our forests are not untouched nature but a product of more than 1,000 years of human economic activities. But for Riehl, nature and woodlands had a high symbolic value; therefore he needed to have faith in the wild German woodlands. For him there existed a close connection between nature and society in general, and between wild woodlands and German society in particular. Based upon this assumption, Riehl could write *The Natural History of the German People* (1854). And he wrote: 'The German people need the wood as man needs the wine.'[20] Riehl warned that if the Germans lost their woodlands, they would lose their happiness. He declared the woodland to be the natural and spiritual base of the German people. He connected German forests with peculiar German kind of freedom, whereupon Karl Marx asked ironically: What is the difference between the history of *our* freedom and the (history) of the freedom of the wild boar, if one can find it only within the forest?[21]

But here and there, Riehl presents a remarkable combination of environmental and social philosophy especially when he states that good human society needs social niches: resources open for everybody which are not totally controlled and exploited in an exclusive manner. In some way he was even realistic when he asserted: 'The forest alone guarantees in a genuine medieval way a contribution to the living of the peasant which is untouched by the rush of competition (*Hetzjagd der Konkurrenz*).'[22] Sometimes he appears to be inconsistent when he praises the old German freedom of the forests but condemns, at the same time, the freedom of forest use which occurred during recent revolutions. The contradiction, however, could be resolved by assuming that in old times people used their freedom in accordance with the nature of the woods. As Riehl stated 'the phantasy of every natural human being' is deeply horrified by the idea that each place on the earth should be exploited by mankind.[23]

In any case, freedom of the forest is a very ambiguous idea, even more ambiguous from an environmental viewpoint. German Romantics meant the freedom of roaming and the freedom of phantasy, sometimes the freedom of love; so did Riehl, and moreover, he meant the freedom of children playing in the loneliness of the woodlands. On the other hand, as Riehl knew well, the poor peasant demanding free use of the forests meant above all freedom of collecting firewood and litter for the stable *Streunutzung*. Especially the collecting of litter, was an important controversial issue throughout the eighteenth and nineteenth centuries;

if done excessively, it caused impoverishment of the forest soil. Freedom of the forest, understood in this way, clashed sharply with the aims of the afforestation movement. And indeed Riehl's ideal, wild woods, was far away from the ideals of reformed forestry! Again, the popular idea of nature had little to do with effective conservation of nature.

Surely one can draw the general conclusion that the idea of wilderness and of nature's own right is chiefly a symbolic attitude, not a pattern for practical behaviour, at least outside the limited areas of nature protection. That holds true at least for a country like Germany which is nearly devoid of real wilderness; maybe it does not hold to the same degree for Scandinavian or North American countries which seem to possess great areas of wilderness. But are these areas really untouched by human beings? Surely in German regions only concepts which combined ecological with economic considerations were able to exert real influence upon the course of events in forests. Sometimes, however, symbolic behaviour may exert considerable influence as well. It is possible to imagine that the cult of the wilderness contributed to bringing about a public consensus in favour of reafforestation though the wild woodlands German Romantics were dreaming of were not identical with the well-managed forests which were the aim of the forest reformers. The relationship between German forestry and German wood Romanticism still contains open questions!

V

Since the late nineteenth century, the idea of the 'natural forest' (*naturnaher Wald*) has gained growing popularity in German forestry teaching. But again we have to scrutinize the practical effect of this ideological trend. It would be erroneous to identify the history of forestry *ideas* with the real history of the forests. Sometimes ideas are a negative picture of reality. The idea of nature in German forestry arose foremost as a critical reaction against misfortunes caused by rigid general rules, by clear-cutting and by coniferous monocultures. In the mid-nineteenth century the revival of the idea of nature was especially a reaction against the challenge of the so-called *Bodenreinertragslehre* (doctrine of net land yield), consistently oriented toward short-term financial gains. The stronger commercial forestry became in reality, the stronger the notion of nature became in the ideational sphere. Sometimes the idea of nature appears like a symbolic compensation for the factual course of events! Seen in the sociopolitical context, the rising significance of the idea of nature in forestry was a conservative reaction against the growing liberal and capitalistic *Zeitgeist*. But it did not indicate that German forests became really more 'natural'.

To be sure, *naturnaher Wald* meant opposition against clear-cutting, against monoculture and against predominance of pinewood; but it was not so easy to define positively the term 'natural forest'. In any case *naturnah* ('close to nature') meant 'adapted to local conditions'; but local conditions could be interpreted in different ways. The passionate adherents of the natural forest like to paint a vivid picture of their ideal; but this pattern was not adapted to every place. During the early Nazi years, Walter von Keudell, the *Generalforstmeister* (Head of the Forest Service) newly appointed by Hermann Göring, tried to enforce his own concept of natural forest economy (*naturgemässe Waldwirtschaft*) upon the whole German forestry; but even under Nazi dictatorship such a rigid concept could not get carried through against powerful landowning interests.[24] But even if it had been enforced by the state, it is not certain whether that kind of policy would have created really good environmental forestry because Keudell's concept of *naturnaher Wald* was not adapted to local conditions.[25]

The Nazi concept of natural forestry reflected the Darwinist selectionist outlook, expressed in the principle: 'The bad tree falls, the good tree stays upright'. From an economic viewpoint, this principle is sheer nonsense: a forester would become very unhappy if he were be allowed to sell only bad trees. But also from an environmental viewpoint, the selections principle is not advantageous in any case. Economic and environmental interests are not necessarily contradictory. In the late nineteenth century, Karl Gayer, the founder of the doctrine of 'natural forestry', tried to combine ecological and economic considerations when he recommended growing adiversity of trees not only because he regarded it to be natural, but also because it was possible to predict demands and future market developments.

A reference to the idea of nature is included in the term *Naturverjüngung* (natural regeneration) without artificial seeds and planting. *Naturverjüngung* gained growing popularity during the twentieth century. Again one has to scrutinize what are the true motives and effects of *Naturverjüngung* in each specific case – not always has it to do with nature. We should not be seduced by the suggestive effect of the term 'nature'! Especially during the recent decades when forest owners were confronted with strongly rising wages, the main motive of *Naturverjüngung* seems to have been the interest of saving costs for tree-planting and tree-cultivation.[26] Not everywhere is *Naturverjüngung* the best way in order to achieve ecologically rich and stable forest conditions. But a convergence of economy and ecology seems to be imaginable in the forests today.

Rising wages must not lead to over-mechanization of forest exploitation but can lead back to natural types of woodland.

Critics object that the appeal to nature in forestry conceals unclear thinking and the lack of a distinct concept for action, or even non-admitted interests. Sometimes, this criticism seems to be convincing. Heinrich Wilhelm Weber (1868–1934), a forestry teacher at the University of Giessen, criticized the concept of the so-called *Dauerwald* (permanent forest) – a forerunner of the 'natural forest economy, which was based upon the idea that the forester should follow the lessons of nature. Weber commented, 'The study of the law of woodland nature does not give any answer to the question: what is the aim?' He ridiculed the manner of speaking about the so-called want (*Bedürfnis*) of the woods when he remarked: 'If the woods really had a want, they hardly had the want for man's axe!'[27]

Walter Kremser, the author of a voluminous forest history of Lower Saxonia, concludes his chapter on the origins of the doctrine of natural forestry with the statement: 'The sources of ecological understanding in forestry are always a communication based on empathy.'[28] Indeed, environmental consciousness cannot be founded merely upon doctrines but has to be generated by discussion, by experience and by sensibility. When we investigate the history of environmental awareness, we should study not only the history of ideas and doctrines, but also the practical effects of these principles and ideas, and moreover the history of everyday life and habits. Perhaps the history of the relation between man and nature had more to do with everyday customs than with high-sounding ideas. Therefore, the environmental historian has frequently to read between the lines and, being distrustful of words – even of the term 'nature' – he has sometimes to become a kind of detective. He should not only look back at former ideas of nature but investigate also the non-articulated experience with nature. At this final point, we may remember both women in the train!

NOTES

1 Fernand Braudel, *Frankreich, Vol. I: Raum und Geschichte* (Stuttgart, 1989), p. 330.

2 Otto Dann, *Nation und Nationalismus in Deutschland 1770–1990* (Munich, 1993), pp. 45ff.

3 Wolf Lepenies, 'Historisierung der Natur und Entmoralisierung der Wissenschaften seit dem 18. Jahrhundert', in Hubert Markl (ed.), *Natur und Geschichte* (Munich, 1983), pp. 263–88.

4 Joachim Radkau, 'Holzverknappung und Krisenbewusstsein im 18. Jahrhundert', *Geschichte under Gesellschaft*, 9 (1983), 513–43; and 'Zur angeblichen Energiekrise des 18. Jahrhunderts: Revisionistische Betrachtungen über die

Holznot', *Vierteljahrschrift für Sozial- und Wirtschaftsgeschichte*, 73 (1986), 1–37; and 'Warum wurde die Gefährdung der Natur durch den Menschen nicht rechtzeitig erkannt? Naturkult und Angst vor Holznot um 1800', in Hermann Lübbe and Elisabeth Ströker (eds.), *Ökologische Probleme in kulturellen Wandel* (Paderborn, 1986), pp. 47–78; Ingrid Schäfer, *Holz. Ein Naturstoff in der Technikgeschichte* (Reinbek, 1987), pp. 149–60.

5 Radkau, 'Warum', pp. 57–8.

6 Karl Hasel, *Studien über Wilhelm Pfeil* (Hanover: Mitteilungen aus der Niedersächsischen Landesforstverwaltung Heft 36, 1982), pp. 157ff.

7 Heinrich Rubner, *Forstgechichte im Zeitalter der industriellen Revolution* (Berlin, 1967), p. 120.

8 Hasel, *Studien*, pp. 292, 268.

9 Andrée Corvol, *L'Homme et l'arbre sous l'Ancien Régime* (Paris, 1984).

10 Felix von Hornstein, *Wald und Mensch, Waldgeschichte des Alpenvorlandes Deutschlands, Österreichs und der Schweiz* (Ravensburg, p. 59).

11 August Bernhardt, *Geschichte des Waldeigentums, der Waldwirtschaft und Forstwissenschaft in Deutschland*, vol. III (1875; Aalen, 1966), p. 221.

12 Karl Hasel, *Auswirkungen der Revolution von 1848 und 1849 auf Wald und Jagd, auf Forstverwaltung und Forstbeamte, insbesondere in Baden* (Stuttgart, 1977), p. 14.

13 Hasel, *Studien*, p. 167.

14 Rubner, *Forstgeschichte*, p. 101.

15 Radkau, 'Warum', pp. 63f.

16 *Ibid.*, p. 67.

17 Andrée Corvol, *L'Homme aux Bois. Histoire des relations de l'homme et de la forêt XVIIe–XXe siècle* (Fayard, 1987), p. 305.

18 Radkau, 'Warum', p. 65.

19 George L. Mosse, *Ein Volk, ein Reich, ein Führer. Die völkischen Ursprünge des Nationalsozialismum* (Königstein, 1979), p. 27.

20 Wilhelm Heinrich Riehl, *Die Naturgeschichte des deutschen Volkes* (Stuttgart, 1935), p. 76.

21 Hubertus Fischer, 'Dichter-Wald. Zeltsprünge durch Silvanien', in *Waldungen. Die Deutschen und ihr Wald* (Berlin, 1987), p. 23.

22 Riehl, 'Naturgeschichte', p. 75.

23 *Ibid.*, p. 76.

24 Heinrich Rubner, *Deutsche Forstgeschichte 1933–1945* (St Katharinen Scripta Mercaturae, 1985), pp. 101ff. sequ.

25 Gerhard Mistscherlich, *Wald, Wachstum und Umwelt, Eine Einführung in die ökologischen Grundlagen des Waldwachstums* 2nd edn, vol. 1 (Frankfurt, 1978), p. 116.

26 Victor Dieterich, *Gesammelte Aufsätze, insebesondere zur forstlichen Wirtschaftslehre*, ed. Karl Hasel (Stuttgart, 1976), pp. 231ff., 256ff.

27 Walter Kremser, *Niedersächsische Forstgeschichte. Eine integrierte Kulturgeschichte des nordwestdeutschen Forstwesens* (Rotenburg, 1990), p. 795.

28 *Ibid.*, p. 723.

FOURTEEN

'LET US BEGIN WITH THE WEATHER?': CLIMATE, RACE, AND CULTURAL DISTINCTIVENESS IN THE AMERICAN SOUTH

MART A. STEWART

IN his widely publicized and circulated anniversary address before the State Agricultural Society of South Carolina in 1848, William Elliott defended the way of life and the institution of slavery in the American South as

> an affair of climate ... [that] will endure as long as the climate which called it into being; which sustains it, and at the same time justifies it, in the opinion of all unprejudiced men. This climate is of God's making; and so long as it continues fatal to the white race, so long will the countries subject to it, continue to be cultivated by men of vast African stock.

This argument from climate, which became a key part of the defence of that peculiar institution and a fundamental of Southern nationalism as it was asserted again and again by leading Southerners in southern journals and magazines and in addresses before agricultural societies and political meetings in the years before the Civil War, was already a commonplace. The belief that climate and race were bound together inexorably had, in any case, long been a convention among Southerners. Elliott was simply reminding his audience what they already assumed, that Southern society was unique to the place, had an organic integrity, was God-created, and was part of the natural order of things.[1]

Historians and commentators on the South have recognized, even if indirectly, the potency of Elliott's claims. The question of the relationship between climate and culture in the South has been a perennial one for them. Many journalists, geographers, novelists, and historians, recent and past, have all, along with the historian U. B. Phillips, 'begun with the weather.' Some have credited the climate, especially when it was 90° in the shade, for the dietary habits, slurred speech, aptitude for porch-sitting, traditions of leisure and hospitality, and lack of interest in matters of the mind among Southerners. Others have, like Phillips, approximately followed the argument made by Elliott and other Old South apologists, and have hitched together the cultivation of certain plants, the institution of slavery, and a climate they also deemed 'peculiar'. Because of the climate, staple crop agriculture was the best adapted to the region; because of this agriculture, the plantation was the best unit of organization for growing staple crops; because of plantations, slavery was the best labour system, because Africans had been imported as plantation labourers and, according to some variants of the argument, were better suited for labour in the long, hot summers; because of all three, the South possessed an economic and cultural uniqueness. With Phillips, they have argued that climate 'has been the chief agency in making the South distinctive'.[2]

Others have taken seriously the possible causative link between climate and culture in the South in order to refute it, to point out, as Edgar Thompson did in a 1941 essay on climatic determinism in Southern history, that an argument that the plantation and the institution of slavery followed necessarily from the climate of the South was a kind of a 'divine right' theory that put the cart before the horse. More recently, several historians have reconsidered the tradition and have offered an approval of a qualified link between climate and Southern distinctiveness, though they have not extended that approval to the 'peculiar institution.'[3]

None of these has focused on what *antebellum* Southerners themselves were saying about the 'peculiar climate', however. Scholars have largely been discussing the possible link between climate and culture in overarching terms of the causative force of climate, and have ignored the perceptions of the Southerners they have been studying. They have consequently largely denied, as Edgar Thompson observed, agency to the people they have been studying. How did *antebellum* Southerners perceive this connection and how did they act upon it? If Southerners have traditionally believed that climate and culture in the region are connected, where did this belief come from and what form did it take in their discussions with each other?[4]

Throughout the period, the perceptions of and conceptions about climate and the weather by Southerners – indeed, by Americans in other regions as well – were intricately interwoven with their understanding of agricultural rhythms and of patterns of health and disease. Moreover, Southerners who were most keenly aware of the weather may have agreed with Elliott or later with Phillips, that climate provided an organic mould for culture, but were mainly interested in only the climate and culture in their own neighbourhoods. Later in the period, however, reforming Southerners advocated the study of meteorology and the systematic gathering of climate data for larger regions, to identify patterns that would allow Southern planters and medical men to manage both agricultural and medical practices more successfully. Though they continued to argue that climate was something that was visited upon them and that had to be lived with, they allowed, or at least implied, that humans who understood patterns of climate had much more latitude, options, and even control in learning to live profitably with climate.

Was the notion promulgated by Elliott and other leading Southerners related to these efforts by mid-nineteenth-century agricultural and medical reformers to identify the statistical parameters of the relationships between climate and the behaviour of both plants and humans? If the defence from climate was designed for political purposes, how sharply did it connect with or diverge from the interests of agricultural and medical reformers in meteorology? Most significantly, was the argument by Southern nationalists that the society of the American South was distinctive, partly because of climate, a matter of experience or a conceit of belief? What was, then, the relationship between climate and culture in the perceptions and conceptions of *antebellum* Southerners?

A residue of environmental determinism from the Enlightenment continued to influence the thinking of *antebellum* Americans about climate and culture.[5] Early-nineteenth-century Americans also commonly drew upon an ancient medical model that assumed an organic connection between climate and health and disease: in the general sense, between temperature and temperament (both physical and moral) and more specifically, between temperature, moisture, soil-type, plant cover, certain pathogens, and individual temperaments in combinations particular to each person and place. Most early nineteenth-century general reports of climate measured it by both temperature and mortality rates. Further, just as Americans traditionally judged the soil of the place by what naturally grew on it (although this was quickly changing in the 1820s and 1830s, with the introduction of Justus Liebig's soil chemistry to America), they described the climate by what grew in it. For agriculturalists, climate was a force that usually arrived in discrete phenomena and was always connected to the particular content of the seasons and growing cycles. Any farmer or planter who sought success paid the closest attention to patterns of heat, cold, and moisture in his neighbourhood, and to variations from field to field. Few *antebellum* Americans, even those who were interested in a more specialized meteorology and who were more attentive to separating out and quantifying components of the weather – temperature, barometric pressure, wind direction and velocity – conceived of climate in terms that excluded this organic connection between plants, human bodies (and the relationships between them), and the weather.[6]

The assertion by leading Southerners that an organic unity existed between the natural order and the social and political one, then, was not only compatible with older traditions of environmental determinism, but derived from medical and agricultural practice and from systems of common sense prevalent in America in the early nineteenth century. Nothing in these practices, however, led to the conclusion that the South was a region with any climatic homogeneity. Indeed, the meteorology of doctors and farmers and planters moved in the other direction, toward the identification of the characteristics of neighbourhood climates and the unique climatic traits of each locale, and usually in terms that could not be easily generalized.[7]

Those farmers and planters who kept records – and many of them often recorded notes about the weather in their farm and plantation journals – have left rich documentation of their perceptions of and interactions with the weather, and also of the extraordinary diversity of climates in the region. Hard freezes in Virginia in the late winter that stalled the ploughing, a good 'season' (the right combination of heat and moisture to cause the seeds to germinate) for planting in the Piedmont, alarming fluctuations in the water levels of bayous adjacent to sugar plantations in Louisiana, the dangerous coincidence of a strong northeast wind and a high tide during the harvest on low country rice plantations: these, and a regular and reassuring, but always particular, cadence of germinating showers, obscuring clouds, crop-damaging winds, droughty weather and so on, all woven into observations of agricultural rhythms and work, were common in *antebellum* farmer and planter journals. These perceptions were individualistic and relatively self-contained, though planters also swapped weather anecdotes beyond their neighbourhoods in letters to each other and to agricultural journals.[8]

When Southern farmers and planters – or their slaves – attempted predictions of weather patterns, they played out equally unique understandings of the weather. They also assumed a vibrant, organic relationship between observer and observed. In practice, they read the weather any way they could. They were attentive to changes in the phases of the moon, to animal behaviour and plant growth patterns that were 'signs' of weather change, to variations in light and cloud patterns, and to the prognostications in widely distributed almanacs. Educated planters sometimes spoofed or dissected and explained this folk meteorology in agricultural journals and at the same time pronounced themselves exceptions to the rule.[9] A widely circulated almanac testimony by one amateur meteorologist, which a prominent low country Georgia planter fastened on the first page of his weather journal, gives some indication of the spectrum of natural clues to changes in the weather that farmers and planters observed:

> Many a time ... have I watched the heavens with anxiety; examined the different appearances of the morning and evening sun, the phases of the moon, the scintillations of the stars, the course and colour of the clouds, the flight of the crow and swallow, the gambols of the colt, the fluttering of the ducks, and the loud screams of the seamew, not forgetting the hue and croaking of the frog. From the little knowledge I had derived from close observation, I often ventured to direct our agricultural operations in reference to the coming days, and was seldom much mistaken in my reckoning.[10]

Farmers and planters left a significant shadow of evidence that they consulted or took seriously the weather predictions in almanacs. They bought almanacs by the thousands throughout the period, and often recorded meteorological observations on the blank pages interleaved within many of them.[11] Even if farmers and planters did not take seriously those almanac predictions that were organized around astrological formulas, they continued throughout the period to associate changes in phases of the moon with changes in weather and in growth patterns.[12]

Farmers regarded these signs and pointers only as guides, however, and did not expect accuracy or complete understanding. They engaged in an intuitive dialogue with the weather to attempt to forestall disaster in the fields, and acknowledged indirectly that the weather, and more generally, climate, were largely providential in both origin and effects and were not subject to rational comprehension and management. Adaptation was a day-to-day and deeply felt process, and was never either precisely executed nor comprehensively mastered. This fatalism about weather and climate, which was common in pre-modern agricultural societies, operated on a local level and tended to emphasize extraordinary phenomena over regular patterns. Farmers and planters who read weather signs also talked about the weather with descriptions that were vernacular to the locale, and that did not easily bloom into larger understandings of climatic patterns. Their interaction with the climate was a practical meteorology for the neighbourhood, and one that made no claims to larger patterns of understanding and management.[13]

Southern medical practitioners were also more attentive to the unique qualities of climate in each locale than to larger patterns. As

John Harley Warner has explained, they commonly adhered to the doctrine of 'specificity' in their therapeutic practices. Practising American physicians of all regions commonly shaped and applied medical therapy in terms of the specific conditions of patient and environment, instead of aiming mainly and routinely only at the disease. Each patient in each place and in each environment required a different application of medical principles, this doctrine held. The consequence at first for medical practitioners was again an emphasis on the neighbourhood.[14]

In the 1840s and 1850s, partly in a defensive response to economic and political challenges in the region and partly to fine-tune therapeutic practices that would fit Southern conditions better, but also by way of participation in influential national trends, leading planters and medical men sought reform of prevailing practices in the direction of a larger and more scientific manipulation of the physical world. Medical men connected to the newly formed or revivified Southern medical societies or to several prominent medical institutions organized the data of individual record-keepers or themselves conducted careful studies in medical topography in small, often only county-wide locales throughout the South, in order to develop a medicine that was more closely adapted to local Southern conditions. A careful attention to the weather was part of their effort: 'Knowing [the] constants [of maxima and minima temperatures] for any locality', Dr W. L. James of Athens, Georgia explained, 'It would be easy to trace the relations between them and the diseases incident to it.' These studies also looked at the soil, terrain, and vegetation, water-flow and moisture patterns, dominant economic and agricultural practices, and common diseases of each patch of the South they surveyed. They were often detailed, here measured and there impressionistic, inclusive essays that were sometimes more physical biography than scientific treatise, but that included formulas of investigation and description familiar to medical researchers.[15]

Many of these studies were published in southern medical journals or were available in unpublished form, where some researchers organized them to another level of generalization in studies of larger areas, such as Daniel Drake's study of the Mississippi Valley, *Principal Diseases of the Interior Valley of North America*, published in 1849. These studies aimed to locate the relationships between physical geography and disease patterns, so that medical men could better understand the etiology of diseases and could better treat them. They tended towards a larger understanding of weather patterns – and Drake's *Principal Diseases* was the best example of a comprehensive medical topography – but still did not mark out the South as a climatic region. Drake identified mean temperatures and compared them from place to place, sketched out isothermal patterns, and discussed climate in terms of the northern limits of certain kinds of plant growth. The interaction of airs, places, and waters in the Mississippi Valley was his focus of investigation, however, rather than the more ephemeral unit – for the purposes of medical topography – of the South.[16]

Improving planters also sought a more systematic understanding of local climatic environments through a more systematic gathering of data. Many of the agricultural societies that improving agriculturists organized in the 1830s and 1840s to respond to economic and political challenges and that dabbled, sometimes quite seriously, in scientific agriculture, also sponsored efforts to study meteorology and to gather records of the weather.[17] Southern agriculturists declared, in articles and correspondence in agricultural journals and in specific initiatives through the burgeoning agricultural societies, a general interest in the study of climate and in the use of instruments to measure the weather. They commonly expressed a more deliberate scientific concern with the relationships between plants and temperature and other components of climate and in the problem of acclimation. Some also advocated a systematic study of the seasons, especially of 'the time to plant', or of local variations in the interactions of soil and atmosphere. Many of these efforts proceeded haphazardly. Some planters collected a run of temperature readings that were submitted to the group in an annual ritual, or recorded reflections, sometimes punctuated with thermometer readings, on the weather in correspondence to the editors of agricultural journals. Others attempted to create a consistent and cumulative statistical record that might eventually allow them to identify larger climatic patterns in the locale and in relationship to patterns elsewhere.[18]

Like Southern medical reformers, improving planters who were interested in meteorology appropriated a universal descriptive language of abstraction and the Baconian inductive method, and a language and a method that scientific investigators elsewhere were also using, to learn more about local conditions. Their efforts often followed significant national and international trends. The best and longest run of records, those kept by the Black Oak Agricultural Society in South Carolina, was patterned after the national data-gathering network organized by the Smithsonian Institution in Washington, D.C. Henry William Ravenel, the prominent South Carolina mycologist and planter who joined the Smithsonian network of observers soon after it was established in 1848, was prominent in setting up the local system. The statistics that could be compiled by the Black Oak planters, he explained in a paper he presented before the Society in 1849 on the connection of meteorology and agriculture, would teach them about 'those causes which affect us injuriously'. Organized in tabular form and 'adapted to the cotton months', these statistics would help them to correlate precisely the 'production of crops' with the 'condition of the seasons'. Later, after South Carolina had seceded from the Union, when Ravenel was seeking to establish a network of weather observers in the Confederacy similar to the Smithsonian one, he was plain about the importance of gathering weather data: 'Agriculture is our natural calling, and meteorology is the handmaid of Agriculture.' And statistical data was the handmaid of meteorology; in the precarious exchange between agriculture and climate, the data bank would be a rock Southern planters could hold to, and one that promised eventual understanding and a more precise adaptation and management.[19]

The language and the form of investigation made Ravenel and the Black Oak planters akin to the larger 'statistical community' of Smithsonian data-gatherers and calculators of means, but their purpose was a more parochial one. Indeed, the data from most of the efforts by reform planters remained self-contained and seldom integrated into banks of data from other locales, largely because they remained fixed more on variation than on pattern. Like the medical topography studies, climate records gathered by improving agriculturists marked out an extraordinary variety of local climates, rather than demonstrated a larger regional homogeneity or unity.

More significant than the variations in local weathers that the data quantified, however, was the variety of meteorology that these improving planters appropriated. When planters organized these data, they did not strip away entirely the organic connections agriculturists had traditionally maintained with climate, but they regarded climate as a complex interaction of physical forces, many of which could be measured and quantified. They assumed, like Ravenel, that more information – and information of a statistical sort – would teach them how to fine-tune and control their adjustment to climate. They remained ambivalent about a form of understanding that no longer had clear connections with providential forces, but proceeded to pursue it nonetheless. 'How much more worthy of idolatry is this little instrument than all the deities ever offered to Pagan worship?' said Edward Barton, a medical man who promoted the study of meteorology to agriculturists, about the thermometer. 'By its means we can foretell when flowers are to bloom, fruits to ripen, and the rich harvest to reward the labour of the husbandman. By its means we become acquainted with most of the climatic conditions that add to the well-being ... of our race [and] plainly see the operation of the great laws of deity.'[20]

By its means, Barton also explained, the South could continue to fulfill its promise as a prosperous and civilized region. This added note of justification harmonized with the most common and distinctive chord in the efforts of improving planters and medical men to better understand the weather and the climate. The probing of the workings of providence with the thermometer and other instruments and the gathering of statistical data about the weather by these amateur meteorologists was hardly distinctive, but followed national and international trends. Yet reform planters and medical men justified their efforts in a distinctive manner. A study of the weather would demonstrate the healthiness of the region and the natural suitability of the South for expanded agricultural production. Few went as far as Bennett Dowler, who sought justification for Southern society in a 'Meteorological, as well as Political Economy ... and not on theories based on false legislation, national prejudice, egotism and sophistry'. But by the 1850s, planters and medical men who talked about meteorology and who studied the weather customarily sought to strengthen the region, to make it healthier, more prosperous, and more independent. By the end of the decade, the study of the weather had become another strident defensive reflex in the intensifying struggle between North and South.[21]

Many of the arguments for the distinctiveness and promise of Southern agriculture and institutions that included the 'peculiar climate' of the 'sunny South' as a fundamental component did not contain all the elements of Elliott's. Some merely mentioned the 'peculiar climate' and its advantages. Some, like the prominent apologist for the South, George Fitzhugh, explained that warm climates had always produced high cultures. Others pointed out that, historically, great civilizations had emerged in the global latitudinal and climatic band that bounded the South. Some pursued the longstanding belief among Southerners that only African-Americans could labour in the hot summers of the region.[22]

The peculiar trajectory of this last belief in the decades between 1830 and 1860 included yet another development in the considerations of the relationships between organisms and climate in the South and deserves emphasis. A strong shadow of the eighteenth-century doctrine that environment, and especially climate, caused racial differences, persisted in America well into the *antebellum* period and was not challenged until the 1830s and 1840s. Ethnologists alone did not hold and advance this doctrine; the belief that a causal link existed between climate and racial characteristics was deeply ingrained in the popular mind. For Southerners, an important racial trait that had been shaped by climate was the ability to sustain hard field labour in the long, hot, Southern summers. That Africans could apparently could endure such labour better than whites was proof positive to some that different climates had moulded the races differently and to others at least that Africans were historically better 'acclimated' to hot climates. This observation also served as justification for the labour system that Southerners had created.[23]

In the 1840s and 1850s, the challenge to climatic determinism as an ethnological doctrine gathered force in the efforts of several ethnologists and medical men to prove the immutability – beyond climatic or any other environmental influence – of races and the separate origin of Africans. The most prominent advocate of the latter view, Josiah C. Nott of Mobile, gained a public forum in the 1850s in *De Bow's* and other publications and through converts who popularized the argument. Of these converts, Samuel Cartwright was most certainly the most influential. In 'Slavery in the Light of Ethnology', included in the 1858 collection of proslavery arguments, *Cotton is King*, and other essays, Cartwright promoted and explained the doctrine of polygenesis and the 'natural history' basis of the inferiority of blacks.[24]

Cartwright did not question the conventional wisdom about the unique ability of blacks to do hard labour and thrive in hot, humid climates. He explained,

> Negroes glory in a close, hot atmosphere; they instinctively cover their head and faces with a blanket at night, and prefer lying with their heads to the fire, instead of their feet. This ethnical peculiarity is in harmony with their efficiency as labourers in hot, damp, close, suffocating atmosphere – where instead of suffering and dying, as the white man would, they are healthier, happier, and more prolific than in their native Africa – producing, under the white man's will, a great variety of agricultural products, besides upward of three million bales of cotton, and three hundred thousand hogsheads of sugar.

Africans did not have this ability because they had developed it in a long interaction with tropical climates, however. They had it because they were created differently. Acclimation was now evidence of permanent and immutable differences, rather than of a process of differentiation. 'Negroes . . . are proved to belong to a different species from the man of Europe or Asia', pronounced Cartwright. Slavery, the perfect institution for civilizing and managing an inferior race and the perfect labour system for the production of the South's staple crops, was perfectly adapted to the South's climate. And it always had been and always would be, this proslavery argument implied.[25]

Whatever the configuration of the defence of the South in its relationship to the 'peculiar climate', was the climate that apologists for slavery and for *antebellum* Southern society called upon the same climate that reform doctors and improving planters had discovered? Elliott knew about these efforts: reform-minded planters were the audience for his 1848 address. Other apologists for the South's peculiar climate and distinctive culture were also familiar with the interest among science-minded doctors and planters in using instruments to measure and to collect data about climate. Discussion of these and monthly records appeared regularly in several widely circulated Southern publications late in the *antebellum* period. The assertion of Elliott and others of a providential and organic cause-effect relationship between climate and culture was not incompatible with the notion that climate could be understood by gathering measurements of components of it that could be quantified. Such a hybrid of exact, almost-mechanical investigations along with assumptions of less distinct organic connections was common in mid-nineteenth century science; developments in ethnology provided an example close to home.

William Elliott, George Fitzhugh, Samuel Cartwright, and other defenders of the South who called up climate as a cause or as part of a justification were likely all attuned to the new interest in scientific meteorology. Their arguments had an urgency and rhetorical dimension, however, that ignored the precision of the reformers' investigations, especially by way of the assumption that the South was a climatic unit. At the same time, their arguments meshed with the parochial motives and defensive fever of the reforming medical men and agriculturists. By the late *antebellum* period, when political temperatures were rising to the boiling point, most inquiries into the nature of the South were made to serve Southern nationalism. Whatever the climate revealed, described, or alluded to by both scientific reformers and proslavery ideologues, it became a fundamental point in an ideological defence, a note in a common chord struck to reinforce the commitment of leading Southerners to slavery and to Southern society.[26]

Southerners were not unique in legitimizing a political ideology by grounding it in the natural world; arguments that claimed a deterministic force for climate were a common Enlightenment residue. Moreover, other Americans in other regions have commonly attached cultural meanings to the most general aspects of regional climates. New England Puritans in the late seventeenth century perceived a climate of calamities and harsh winters as a clear indication that their mission had strayed from the path. Americans regarded the Great Plains as an arid desert with a climate that only Native Americans could live in in the first half of the nineteenth century; in the latter half, settlers saw the region as an agrarian frontier of great promise when they accepted the belief that planting trees would make the rain come. Commentators on the climate of the Pacific Northwest have often claimed that the long season of mist and rain has instilled a characteristic 'quiet and introspective moderation' in its citizens. The configuration of ideology and nature Southerners created was even more unique and certainly more fully developed. And the regional weather they made was more distinctive than the weather they got. Indeed, when Southerners used climate to legitimize a social order, they did not *begin* with the weather, but *ended* with it, and ended with it with an argument of such force and conviction that it long survived the storm of the Civil War.[27]

NOTES

1 William Elliott, *The Anniversary Address of the State Agricultural Society, of South-Carolina* (Charleston, 1849), p. 43.

2 U. B. Phillips, *Life and Labor in the Old South* (Boston, 1936), pp. 3–6; Clarence Cason, *90° in the Shade* (1935; Alabama, 1983); Avery O. Craven, *The Growth of Southern Nationalism, 1848–1861* (Baton Rouge, 1953), pp. 7–10. For a summary of the debate over the 'plantation school' and of twentieth-century discussions that have linked climate and Southern culture, see James O. Breeden, 'Disease as a Factor in Southern Distinctiveness', in Todd L. Savitt and James Harvey Young (eds.), *Disease and Distinctiveness in the American South* (Knoxville, 1988), pp. 1–6.

3 Edgar T. Thompson, 'The Climatic Theory of the Plantation', in *Plantation Societies, Race Relations, and the South: The Regimentation of Populations* (Durham, 1975); p. 82. See also Rupert Vance, *Human Geography of the South* (1935; New York, 1968), pp. 351–74; William A. Foran, 'Southern Legend: Climate or Climate of Opinion?', *Proceedings of the South Carolina Historical Association* (1957), 6–22; David L. Smiley, 'The Quest for the Central Theme in Southern History', *South Atlantic Quarterly*, 71 (Summer 1972), 311–13; Raymond Arsenault, 'The End of the Long Hot Summer: The Air Conditioner and Southern Culture', *The Journal of Southern History*, 50 (November 1984), 597–628; A. Cash Koeniger, 'Climate and Southern Distinctiveness', *Journal of Southern History*, 59 (February 1988), 21–44. For a study of perceptions of the South during the colonial era, see Karen Ordahl Kupperman, 'Fear of Hot Climates in the Anglo-American Colonial Experience', *William and Mary Quarterly*, 3rd ser. 16 (April 1984), 213–40.

4 Both Breeden and Koeniger are partial exceptions to this; both glance at the perceptions of nineteenth-century Southerners. The question of the interaction between the physical environment and considerations of it by specific cultures has also become a central one for environmental historians. Several have looked at the relationship between nature and culture in connection to changing perceptions of 'wildness', forest fires, wildlife, watersheds and rivers, or particular landscapes, in terms of those who were doing the perceiving and the social or cultural meaning of those perceptions. The study of the relationship between climate and regional or national cultures is also a core problem for them, especially at a time when we are attempting to understand the cultural and

political implications of definitions of global climate change. Some of these works and the prospects for environmental history are discussed in Donald Worster, Alfred Crosby, William Cronon, Richard White, and Stephen Pyne, 'Environmental History: A Roundtable Discussion', *Journal of American History*, 77 (March 1991), 1087–47. See also William Cronon, 'A Place for Stories: Nature, History, and Narrative', *Journal of American History*, 78 (March 1992), 1347–76.

5 See James Breeden's discussion of Jefferson, for example, in 'Disease as a Factor', pp. 3–4, and Alexis de Tocqueville, *Democracy in America*, Henry Reeve text rev. by Frances Bowen and Phillip Bradley (New York, 1989), p. 369.

6 Charles Rosenberg, 'The Therapeutic Revolution: Medicine, Meaning, and Social Change in Nineteenth-Century America', *Perspectives in Biology and Medicine*, 20 (1977), 485–500. See the discussion of diseases in and mortality rates in, for example, Thomas M. Logan, 'On the Climate and Health of Charleston', *Southern Literary Journal and Monthly Magazine*, 2 (July 1836), 348–56. For an example of qualified connections between climate and culture, see M., 'Habits and Privileges of Sea Islands Planters', *Southern Cultivator*, 15 (October 1857), 200.

7 'Systems of common sense' is a deliberate usage, and alludes to Clifford Geertz's discussion of 'common sense' as a cultural creation. 'Common sense' here, as elsewhere and about other matters, fits Geertz's analysis of it as 'historically constructed and ... subjected to historically defined standards of judgement': 'Common Sense as a Cultural System', in *Local Knowledge: Further Essays in Interpretive Anthropology* (New York, 1983), p. 76.

8 I have looked at a couple hundred of these for several projects. Representative samples include: 'Extracts from the Diary of Leven Covington', in Ulrich B. Phillips (ed.), *Plantation and Frontier, 1699–1863* (New York, 1969), I, pp. 231–44; 'Diary of a Mississippi Planter (M.W. Phillips), January 1, 1840–April, 1863', in *Publications of the Mississippi Historical Society*, ed. Franklin L. Riley (Oxford, 1909), IX, pp. 311–481; Thomas Walter Peyre Plantation Journal, 1812–1851', in *Records of Antebellum Southern Plantations*, ed. Kenneth Stampp, Series B, Reel 5, Microfilm; Walter Price Talmage Diary, Hargrett Rare Book and Manuscripts Room, University of Georgia, Athens; Philip N. Racine, *Piedmont Farmer: The Journal of David Golightly Harris. 1855–1870* (Knoxville, 1990); William Gordon Plantation Journal, 1845–1857 & George E. Grymes Manager's Journal, 1855–1857, *Records of Antebellum Plantations*, ed. Stampp, Series E, Reels 34 & 38.

9 For examples of weather signs and local reckonings of the weather and climate, see W. J. Wintemberg, 'Dogwood Winter', *Journal of American Folk-Lore*, 20 (1907), 235–6 and 'The Union of Water with the Atmosphere', *American Cotton Planter*, 3 (December 1855), 355–8.

10 Roswell King, Jr. Diary, 1838–1845, Special Collections, Louisiana State University Libraries, Baton Rouge.

11 Paul W. Gates, *The Farmer's Age: Agriculture, 1815–1860* (New York, 1968), p. 339; Merchant, *Ecological Revolutions*, pp. 139–45; Richard Beale Davis, *Intellectual Life in the Colonial South, 1585–1763* (Knoxville, 1978), II, p. 884; Robb Sagendorph, *America and her Almanacs: Wit, Wisdom and Weather, 1639–1970* (Boston, 1970), pp. 150–70. For the persistence of a belief in astrology and the influence of the planets on matters on earth, see Herbert Leventhal, *In the Shadow of the Enlightenment: Occultism and Renaissance Science in Eighteenth-Century America* (New

York, 1976), pp. 13–65. The Wymberly DeRenne library in coastal Georgia contained a representative sample of southern almanacs all of which contained astrological tables for telling the weather. For an indication of the enormous number of almanacs available in the South during the period, see the state-by-state lists in Milton Drake, comp., *Almanacs of the United States* (New York, 1962), part I, pp. 1–4, 152–61, 187–91, 454–8, and part II, pp. 858–70, 1246–82, 1313–51.

12 A belief in the effect of the moon on weather and growth patterns was very common then and continues to have its adherents. For example, see: 'The Moon – Her Influence on Vegetation, &c.', *Southern Cultivator*, 18 (June 1860), 175; 'Planting by the Full Moon: Is it a Bright Idea, or is it Lunacy?', *New York Times* (2 May 1991).

13 This notion of a 'pre-modern' understanding of the weather owes much to Carolyn Merchant's discussion of 'the animate cosmos of the colonial farmer' in *Ecological Revolutions*, pp. 112–45. Obviously, a very strong shadow of this 'cosmos' persisted well into the nineteenth century, perhaps especially in the South, though sometimes alongside more 'modern' views. An excellent expression of both, underpinned by an assumption of the providential nature of natural forces, is found in a letter to the editor of *Cotton Planter and Soil* by W. C. Tally of Notasulga, Alabama in 1858, which contains a strong caution on the importance of acknowledging the local manifestations of the seasons and at the same time an eloquent reprimand to scientific agriculturists who would attempt to transcend them: 'On the Absurdity of Winter Plowing', *Cotton Planter and Soil*, 2 n.s. (July 1858), 214–215.

14 Warner, 'The Idea of Southern Medical Distinctiveness: Medical Knowledge and Practice in the Old South', in Ronald C. Numbers and Todd L. Savitt (eds.), *Science and Medicine in the Old South* (Baton Rouge, 1989), pp. 185–9.

15 James also sketches out an agenda for a well-conducted medical topography: 'On the Relations Between the Climate and Diseases of Our State', *Southern Medical and Surgical Journal*, 6 n.s. (1850), 528–32 (p. 529). For examples of published medical topographies, see: John M. B. Harden, 'Observations on the Soil, Climate, and Diseases of Liberty County, Georgia', *Southern Medical and Surgical Journal*, 1 n.s. (October 1845), 545–69; C. E. Lavender, 'On the Topography, Climate, and Diseases of Selma, Alabama', *New Orleans Medical and Surgical Journal*, 6 (November 1846), 342–8.

16 John Harley Warner, *The Therapeutic Perspective: Medical Practice, Knowledge, and Identity in America, 1820–1885* (Cambridge, MA, 1986), p. 91; Warner, 'The Idea of Southern Medical Distinctiveness', pp. 197–8; Daniel Drake, *A Systematic Treatise, Historical, Etiological, and Practical on the Principal Diseases of the Interior Valley of North America as They Appear in the Caucasian, African, Indian, and Esquimaux Varieties of its Population* 2 vols. (1849; New York, 1971). Again, the efforts of Southern physicians were part of a national trend. The reference to 'airs, places, and waters' is an allusion to the influential classic by Hippocrates, which provided Southern medical men with a philosophical basis for a regional medicine.

17 For a discussion of this agricultural reform movement, see William K. Scarborough, 'Science on the Plantation', in Numbers and Savitt (eds.), *Science and Medicine in the Old South*, pp. 79–106.

18 These records were similar to the temperature and barometric pressure records that Southern medical men had long been collecting. For discussions of climate by agriculturists, general interest features in agricultural journals included: 'The Difference of Climate Between the Eastern Side of the Continent of North America and Europe', *Southern Agriculturist*, 9 (March 1837), 142–52; 'Climate of the United States (from Lorin Blodget, *Climatology of the United States*)', *De Bows Review*, 23 o.s. (October 1857), 506–21. For praise or explanation of instruments, see 'A New Barometer', *Southern Cultivator*, 18 (December 1860), 391; 'Rain Gauges and Their Uses', *American Cotton Planter*, 5 n.s. (August 1860), 351. For acclimation, see any discussion of plants for the South and the mission statement of *Southern Agriculturist*, 2 n.s. (December 1849), 4. For discussions of atmosphere and soil and the seasons see, for example: 'Air – How Invaluable to the Successful Husbandry of the Soil and its Produce, Animal, and Vegetable', *Southern Cultivator*, 17 (January 1859), 9–10. Also see the monthly calendars for plantation work that were a traditional commonplace in these journals.

19 For information about the Smithsonian network and the participation of Southerners in it, see James Rodger Fleming, *Meteorology in America, 1800–1870* (Baltimore, 1990), pp. 75–93, 175–84. H. W. Ravenel, 'A Paper on the Subject of Meteorology in its Connection with Agriculture', in Black Oak Agricultural Society Constitution and Minutes, 1842 and 1847–48, South Caroliniana Library, Columbia, S.C. For Ravenel's programme for a national network of weather observers in the Confederacy, see his letter to the editors, *Charleston Daily Courier*, 8 July 1861, printed in full in Robert Croom Aldredge, *Weather Observers and Observations at Charleston, South Carolina* (Historical Commission of Charleston, n.d.), pp. 251–2. The term 'statistical community' is from Daniel Boorstin, and is his chapter heading for his discussion of the growing army of statistics-gatherers of all sorts in mid-nineteenth century America: *The Americans: The Democratic Experience* (New York, 1973), pp. 165–73. I use it to mark out only one small part of this community. See the more thorough discussion of the national development of a penchant for quantitative knowledge and statistics, in Patricia Cline Cohen, *A Calculating People: The Spread of Numeracy in Early America* (Chicago, 1982).

20 Dr E. H. Barton, 'The Influence of Climate on Agricultural Productions, Health, Etc.', *DeBow's Review*, 20 (June 1856), 721, 734. Barton praises the usefulness of other instruments and gauges and makes an approving nod to the data compiled by the Smithsonian network in 'The Influence and Connection of Meteorology with the Pursuits of Agriculture', *DeBow's Review*, 27 (July 1859), 100. The number of notes and essays about aspects of meteorology proliferated in agricultural and medical journals in the late 1850s.

21 Bennett Dowler, 'Researches on Meteorology', *New Orleans Medical and Surgical Journal*, 4 (January 1848), 411–34, quote on 412.

22 For examples of celebration of the 'peculiar' climate, see: John Brisbane, 'An Address Delivered Before the St. Andrew's Ashley and Stono Agricultural Association', *Southern Agriculturist*, 3 (February 1843), 44; C. G. Edwards, 'An Essay Read Before the L. & S. Society of Selma', *American Cotton Planter* 1 o.s. (September 1853), 268; William Daniel, 'An Address Delivered at the Opening of the Convention to Organize an Agricultural Association of the Slaveholding

States', *American Cotton Planter*, 2 o.s. (February 1854), 38. For Fitzhugh's ideologizing, see George Fitzhugh, 'Make Home Attractive', *De Bow's Review*, 38 o.s. (May 1860), 636–7. For assumptions of the immutable connection between the climate and the institution of slavery using Africans, see E.G., 'Slavery in the Southern States', *Southern Quarterly Review*, 11 (October 1845), 343–4, 354, 360; L., 'Philosophical View of Southern Agriculture', *Southern Cultivator*, 16 (September 1858), 265–7; L. B. Mercer, 'Laborers for the South', *American Cotton Planter*, 2 n.s. (October 1858), 298, 300.

23 For a discussion of environmentalism that modifies Winthrop Jordan's contention that environmentalism disappeared much earlier in the period and for a discussion of the ethnological doctrine that replaced it, see George Fredrickson, *The Black Image in the White Mind: The Debate on Afro-American Character and Destiny, 1817–1914* (New York, 1971), pp. 2, 72–96. Fredrickson disagrees with two other prominent accounts of scientific racism during the period that are, nonetheless, useful: William Sumner Jenkins, *Pro-Slavery Though in the Old South* (1935; Gloucester, 1960), pp. 42–84; William Stanton, *The Leopard's Spots: Scientific Attitudes Toward Race in America, 1815–59* (Chicago, 1960), pp. 9–196. Jenkins's account is elegantly useful for connecting developments in ethnology and the nationalist, pro-slavery argument. The belief among planters that only Africans could endure summer labour in the Southern climate permeated the discussion of Southern agriculture throughout the period. For an example of a full expression of this belief by a prominent planter that is also an early expression of Southern nationalism, see John Henry Hammond, 'J. H. Hammond Defends Slavery, 1836', in Sean Wilentz (ed.), *Major Problems in the Early Republic, 1787–1848* (Lexington, Mass.: D. C. Heath, 1992), pp. 489–90.

24 Nott's discussion of the connection between polygenesis and the differences in 'adaptation' of races to climates can be found in 'Thoughts on Acclimation and Adaptation of Races to Climates', *American Journal of the Medical Sciences* (October 1856), 320–34. George Fredrickson convincingly refutes William Stanton's argument that Nott was outside the pro-slavery movement, because his beliefs appeared to be a scientific counter to Biblical doctrine. Nott's ideas were widely published in leading Southern journals and won influential converts like Cartwright, John H. Van Evrie, George S. Sawyer, and even, on the eve of the Civil War, George Fitzhugh. He must be considered a prominent pro-slavery ideologue. See Stanton, *The Leopard's Spots*, pp. 65–72, 198; and Fredrickson, *Black Image in the White Mind*, pp. 78–88. On Nott and the marriage of scientific racism and Southern nationalism in the 1850s, see John McCardell, *The Idea of a Southern Nation: Southern Nationalists and Southern Nationalism, 1830–1860* (New York, 1979), pp. 78–83.

25 S. A. Cartwright, 'Slavery in the Light of Ethnology', in E. N. Elliott (ed.), *Cotton is King, and Pro-Slavery Arguments* (Augusta, 1860), pp. 704–5, 707, 717–21. See also Jenkins, *Pro-Slavery Thought*, pp. 248–9; and Fredrickson, *Black Image in White Mind*, pp. 87–9. Some apologists qualified this defence by arguing that the climate and the production of tropical staples had made African labour necessary in the beginning, but that whites were learning to live in the climate and were increasingly applying their aptitude for industry to Southern agriculture and to the general improvement of the region: 'The Relations of Labor and

Climate', *The Southern Cultivator*, 15 (April 1857), 106–7. Nott's doctrine remained controversial and was not accepted by many medical men, who claimed that 'acclimation' was a matter of seasoning, and that some people were more successful in the process than others: see E. D. Fenner, 'Acclimation; and the Liability of Negroes to the Endemic Fevers of the South', *New Orleans Medical and News and Hospital Gazette* (1858–9), 78–87. Cartwright's commitment to the doctrine may have also been qualified, though the pro-slavery argument in the late 1850s was, in the hands of some ideologues, a hothouse blend in which distinctions became blurred.

26 Drew Faust's argument that the addresses made by improving planters before conventions of the agricultural societies of South Carolina during the period, that calls for scientific agriculture were largely ideological formulations and part of rituals that leading Southerners engaged in to buttress their commitments to the values and institutions of Southern society, is relevant here: see Drew Gilpin Faust, 'The Rhetoric and Ritual of Agricultural in Antebellum South Carolina', *Journal of Southern History*, 45 (November 1979), 541–68. Faust has also argued that reformers and pro-slavery defenders were an alienated elite, who pushed reform as a program for the South that would also improve their status. The relationship between popular belief and sophisticated scientific or political expression in regard to climate was more complex than Faust's argument allows, and needs to be considered more fully. See 'A Southern Stewardship: The Intellectual and the Proslavery Argument', *American Quarterly*, 31 (1979), 63–80; and *A Sacred Circle: The Dilemma of the Intellectual in the Old South, 1840–1860* (Baltimore, 1977), pp. 112–31.

27 Karen Ordahl Kupperman, 'Climate and Mastery of the Wilderness in Seventeenth-Century New England', in *Seventeenth-Century New England*, ed. David D. Hall and David E. Allen, *Publications of the Colonial Society of Massachusetts*, vol. 63, 3–37; Martyn J. Bowden, 'The Great American Desert and the American Frontier, 1800–1882: Popular Images of the Plains', in Tamara K. Hareven (ed.), *Anonymous Americans: Explorations in Nineteenth-Century Social History* (Englewood, 1971), pp. 48–77; Richard Maxwell Brown, 'Rainfall and History: Perspectives on the Pacific Northwest', in G. Thomas Edwards and Carlos A. Schwantes (eds.), *Experiences in a Promised Land: Essays in Pacific Northwest History* (Seattle, 1986), pp. 13–27. For a discussion of the racial theory that Phillips draws upon in his discussion of the natural compatibility of Africans to hot climates, as part of his defence of slavery in *American Negro Slavery*, see John David Smith, *An Old Creed for the New South: Proslavery Ideology and Historiography, 1865–1918* (Westport, CN, 1985), p. 256.

FIFTEEN

WILD WEST IMAGERY: LANDSCAPE PERCEPTION IN NINETEENTH-CENTURY AMERICA

GERHARD STROHMEIER

Mais il est plus difficile qu'on ne croit de recontrer aujourd'hui le désert.

Alexis de Tocqueville, 1831

LANDSCAPE AS WILDERNESS: CULTURAL AND POLITICAL METAPHORS

IMAGES of cowboys roaming through vast prairies and movie pictures of cavalry wars with Indians, both of which were favourite themes of Ronald Reagan's nationalist rhetoric, are part of the enduring imagery of the Wild West. Another important part of this imagery is the American West as a landscape of nature and wilderness. The landscape of the Wild West is imagined as open lands and mountains, free to roam about. It is a basic mental landscape still guiding a special mode of the perception of space in the United States and influencing the feelings of Americans towards the land. Historically, the imagery of the West was drawn over real landscapes of the American continent like a filter of perception. A symbolic landscape was produced: one that not only had aesthetic importance to artists but also was guiding landscape perception in American culture.

The term 'symbolic landscape' is used synonymously with the term 'spacing image';[1] although the theoretical base of these terms is different in some ways, the meaning is basically the same. These terms convey the idea that in every society, at every historical moment, a specific mode of landscape perception is culturally produced in images. Images are built up by manifold complex metaphors. Religious, political, economic and social conceptions of the world – world views – are set up as metaphors and are projected into society, people, buildings and landscapes.[2] They transfer values and meanings. Essentially, we perceive and value what the images indicate to us as relevant. Space images, for example, are very complex preconditions of our relation to the land.

Although it is commonplace in social science for images, signs and symbols to play an important role in guiding and forming social behaviour, research in the imagery and myth of landscapes is rather marginal.[3] The reasons might be that empirically oriented social science asks for exact cause–effect relations and easily neglects the 'soft' influences of images on behaviour. There also is a strong critique of mentality research in social science: it is doubted if ideas and images have any influence on real behaviour. But reverse the hypothesis: Assume that mental images have no impact on behaviour!

My contribution is to show the American West's landscape images, signs and symbols, to explain parts of its background, and to try to trace their influence on American attitudes towards the land. It is a case-study of the mentalities, created by the way of space images. It is not meant to present a general theory of space images.

The questions are these. What kinds of space-images of the American West were constructed? What kinds of metaphors did they consist of? Who constructed this imagery? What was the cultural and social background? How did the landscape imagery of the American West influence individual behaviour? What is its importance today?

THE NEW WORLD: UTOPIAN LANDSCAPES

The real landscape of the nineteenth-century America was perfectly suited to becoming a symbolic landscape. The nature and wilderness of the vast continent with its fascinating geographical and climatical characteristics and the general lack of trustworthy information made these landscapes susceptible to utopian landscape imagery.

The Louisiana-Purchase doubled the size of the United States at the beginning of the nineteenth century. It was a great challenge for the young independent nation to explore, discover and subdue the new land, most of which was viewed as 'virgin-land'. Since the land itself was seen from a European perspective as unburdened by history, tradition and culture, Americans found themselves in a position to write their history into this land by ways of images, signs and symbols: 'It invites us ... to impose literary ideas about the world.'[4]

The world learnt about the new American history, written heroically into the landscape to excel all its previous history. Literature and the arts brought the idea of America to Europe,[5] where the image of the great American landscapes met a large fabrication of fantasies, which had already created an image of the New World: long before it was settled by Europeans America was invented as an utopian idea.[6] Dreams of vast, endless and fertile lands, blended with the political conception of the free liberated individual and the self-made-man, swept over Europe. The waves of migration to the United States cannot be explained on economic grounds alone. Undoubtedly there were economic reasons, but the motivation to go came from a utopian impulse which was energized by the imagery of America. The migrants' utopian hopes were for free and fruitful lands, hopes presented to them with cultural, economic and political metaphors, woven into the symbolic landscape, the space image of the American West.

IMAGERY TO 'ANIMATE THE MANY HUNDRED MILLIONS'

From the first settlements on the North American continent, the land has been a source of ambivalence. New arrivals had dreamed of paradise, but experienced wilderness. In the first steps on the new continent, wilderness meant two different things. It was the earthly paradise discovered, the promised land in the covenant of the first settlers with their Lord. But settling there also meant hardship, drudgery, and danger. This can be seen as the first and fundamental ambivalence in American culture towards nature and wilderness. There are many written complaints about the hardships of settling in the New World. Instead of the paradise, a 'cursed wilderness' was found, experienced by hundreds of thousands of early settlers. From the religious perspective, it was an evil wilderness to fight against. The test of Puritan virtue was to overcome wilderness and turn it into 'a Garden of Eden'.[7] But in general the letters, reports and literary documents addressed to Europe tend to be apologetic. They are individual justifications for the migration, a testimony of the first settlers' achievements in overcoming wilderness, and an invitation for relatives and friends in Europe to come over.

In the eighteenth century the rhetoric of the New World's landscapes became more differentiated and complex. In two famous descriptions, we find a new rhetoric of landscape. These accounts are St John de Crèvecoeur's 'Letters from an American Farmer', and Thomas Jefferson's 'Notes on the State of Virginia'.[8] Their landscapes still contain the old ambivalence. The wilderness landscape is a projection of a utopian earthly paradise, on the one hand, and it was perceived and described as a threat to the spreading of civilization, on the other. But as a new notion landscape now was based on an agrarian ideal, confronting the wilderness. Here pastoral land and cultivated soil, rather than natural wilderness, were portrayed as the garden of Eden.

The term 'middle landscape'[9] is used for the new image of land that is set between the East, the decadent and sinful Old World of Europe, and the West, the wild, barren wilderness. In 1785 the British minister Richard Price put it in words: 'The happiest state of man is the middle state between the *savage* and the *refined*, or between the wild and the luxurious state.'[10] Jefferson was the most notable promoter of the 'middle landscape': It 'is a real place located somewhere between *l'ancien regime* and the western tribes'.[11] Crèvecoeur painted a literary motive in a geographical tryptich, a threefold image: 'Eastwards it reaches to Europe, encompassing *l'ancien regime*, an oppressive social order of great lords who possess everything, and of a herd of people, who have nothing.' In the West he saw the dark frontier of the forest wilderness where the pioneer-farmer was in permanent danger. It was both physical danger and the threat of mental defeat by the wilderness – that is, becoming a raw and uncivilized frontier man who had lost his religious faith and his civilized manners. The middle made the farming landscape and the social virtues. The farmer – along with this image – is put right in the centre of society; he is to guarantee religious faith, political reason, and economic prosperity. The importance of agricultural (as against industrial) farming is stressed in the pastoral ideal because it is associated with caring for the soil and the stable rooting of man in his landscape. Thomas Jefferson saw the farmer and his 'rural virtues' as the opposite of the modern 'homo oeconomicus': he does not strive for growth and wealth, but for 'sufficiency, happiness and permanence of government'.

An allegory of American geography, the pamphlet *The Golden Age*, published in 1785, also uses the difference between the images of the East and of the West. Celadon, an American citizen, had a vision while resting on the bank of a river with 'murmuring waters below and sighing winds above' – a vision in which an Angel brought him to the top of a high mountain in the middle of the continent. From this place he could see all over the continent: To the east 'spacious cities ... thriving towns ... a thick conjunction of farms, plantations, gardens ... laden with every kind of fruit!' The Angel then turns Celadon westwards. He is 'equally surprised at the wide extended landscape. This western part of America, is as yet but an uncultivated desart [*sic*]; the haunt of savages; and the range of wild beasts. – But the soil in general is much richer than that of the eastern division ...'. The pamphlet ends with a vision of a beautiful world rising out of the wilderness.[12]

At the beginning of the nineteenth century, the landscapes of the American West already had developed an image that carried religious, aesthetical, moral, and political values. It was an image of a landscape, vast and grand, with fertile soil, ready to be taken by the yeomen-farmers, but as yet in the condition of wilderness. Wilderness was envisioned primarily in the West. Between the wild western lands and the eastern civilization was the frontier set by the American Census Office, which moved westwards of the speed with which Americans settled land.[13] Frederick Jackson Turner stressed the notion that the frontier between the civilized world and the wilderness was essential for the American character.[14] 'The frontier is ... determined by the reactions between wilderness and the edge of expanding settlement.'[15] According to Turner's theory, the confrontation with nature as wilderness and all the efforts in the struggles along the wilderness frontier strongly influenced American culture and society. The experience of wilderness supported and strengthened a common political and economic understanding and created a kind of 'Kollektives Gedächtnis'[16]: 'Out of his wilderness experience, out of the freedom of his opportunities, he fashioned a formula for social regeneration – the freedom of the individual to seek his own.'[17]

During the nineteenth century a new rhetoric of landscape was connected to the first settlers' metaphor of the natural wilderness as God's creation. It was the 'sublime landscape', a visual perception of landscape as a way to come closer to God and his grandeur. The sublime was part of the aesthetical value of the landscape. It emerged in a new attitude towards the landscape: 'The arts of travel, poetry, painting, architecture, and gardening ... fused into a single art of landscape.'[18] A broad discussion started in philosophy and the arts about the beauty of the wild landscape. Three main notions were discussed in aesthetic theory and practice: the beautiful, the picturesque, and the sublime. How to find the beautiful, how to imagine it and how to worship the creation of God became central questions in the landscape's aesthetic. Imagination and visualization was supported by John Locke's sensualistic philosophy, which was widely known and popular at this time. The look of the landscape was declared an emotional source of wisdom and joy. Aesthetic knowledge was disseminated to improve ways of seeing and to enhance visual sensuality. The real landscape was to be contemplated as a source of aesthetic pleasure. Members of the urban upper class started journeys to the western mountains and to extraordinary land formations. One of their utensils was the 'Claude-Glass', named after the landscape painter Claude Lorrain. It was gold-tinted and framed the spectator's vision with an engraved frame; this way they could see the landscape as a painting, as a masterpiece of art.[19] It was a space image, imposed directly on the landscape. Seeing the land as a golden-toned landscape painting was not just a single, individual way of perception. It was the cultural and societal image, set up by an extensive production of western landscape images interwoven with the fabric of American ideology.

Around the middle of the century one of the main actors in the production of western landscape images was the American Art Union. A German travel report of 1853 mentioned a noteworthy interest in art: 'Art Associations are well established in big cities. The Art Union of New York numbers more than 20,000 members and spends $120,000 annually for the acquisition of art works.'[20] Historians estimate that between 1840 and 1852 Art Union exhibitions attracted up to three million visitors.[21] With a New York population of about 400,000 in the 1850s, this meant a remarkably high number of spectators of art works presented by the Art-Union, even if one takes in to account multiple visits and tourists who visited the exhibitions on a trip to New York. The founders and functioneers of the Art Union were leading merchants, bankers, lawyers, and politicians of New York, 'patrons for expansionist ideology'.[22] They tried to disseminate their images not only by exhibiting paintings but also by putting on a lottery. The membership fees included $5 for a lottery ticket. In this way, members of the Art Union could win paintings that were purchased with lottery funds. These prizes were printed and described in the Bulletin of the Art Union. In 1849 the Art Union had 18,960 members who were subscribers to the bulletin; in that year, 460 pieces of art were distributed to winners.[23] The presentation of paintings at exhibitions, the publication of prints in the Bulletin, and the allotment of art works by the lottery, reached a great many Americans. The imagery created in this way became an essential part of American culture. In the words of William Gilpin, the mission of the Art Union was 'to . . . animate the many hundred millions'.[24] The American Art Union encouraged artists to choose themes and motifs '. . . illustrative of American scenery and American manners',[25] in order to spread American nationalism and patriotism. So the space images of the Art Union entered American culture through attractive visualizations of landscapes which were connected to highly valued cultural metaphors.

Paintings were not the only source of such imagery. We also find an exuberance of literary images which supported the space image of the American west.

KEY METAPHORS OF THE WILD WEST'S LANDSCAPE IMAGES

Cultural conception and perception of land was dominated by three distinctive metaphors: the religious metaphor of the *Promised Land*, connected with the deeply rooted notion of the religious mission of the American Nation; the political metaphor of the *Manifest Destiny*, which was created to lead American expansionism towards the West and the South-West; the economic metaphor of *This Mighty Machine of Nature* as the foundation of the American economy.

The Promised Land

One of the central topics of American image production, fundamental to settlement, was the religious vision of the Promised Land.[26] In the utopian hopes of the religious migrants to the New World, the landscapes of America were imagined as the Promised Land of the Bible long before they made their journey across the ocean.[27] 'The Lord is bringing you into a fertile land – a land that has rivers and springs ... a land that produces wheat and barley, grapes, figs, pomegranates, olives and honey.'[28] The Bible provided them with one of the most famous phrases of American land imagery: 'A land of milk and honey.' But within the wilderness perception there was also the ambivalence of the *wilderness as a desert*[29] and the *wilderness as a sanctuary*.[30]

The myth of landscape as sanctuary, as sacred space, was expressed in the notion of the 'sublime landscape'. The sublime landscape was the grand, wide, deep, vast land in its original wild condition. It was the romantic grandeur of nature seen in the landscape. As the urban upper classes formed this romantic mode of landscape perception, the industrial destruction of landscapes was already on its way. While Henry Thoreau retreated to Walden Pond in the 'sublime silence of nature', he found the first locomotives hissing and puffing through the forests of Concord.

Georg Caleb Bingham's painting 'Daniel Boone Escorting Settlers Through the Cumberland Gap' (1851) provides an example of the spiritual landscape.[31] 'Bingham's Boone leads his people forward through a hostile environment like a latter-day Moses *en route* to the Promised Land ... the woman on the white horse ... symbolizing the gentle, civilizing influences necessary to develop frontier culture.'[32] The landscape on both sides of the trail is dark, suggesting danger; the painter has placed destroyed trees next to the settlers, symbolizing the annihilating power of the wild. But the foreground is lit, as if by a fire column, according to the way God gave light to the Israelites fleeing Egypt toward the Promised Land. The axe and the rifle in the middle of the track represent the struggles well known in the wilderness. The faces of the settlers show a keen forward-looking spirit, a secure mind ready to be guided along the right path.

The religious legitimation of the movement towards the West can also be found in literary images. Samuel Bowles, editor of *The Springfield Republican*, Massachusetts, travelled west in 1866 by horse coach and reported directly to his newspaper. Later he published all of his reports in the book *Across the Continent.*[33] He wrote about the wagon trains travelling west: 'The Wagons are covered with white cloth – each is drawn by four to six pairs of mules or oxen – and the trains of them stretch frequently from one-quarter to one-third of a mile each. As they move along in distance, they remind one of the caravans described in the Bible and other Eastern books.'[34] Bowles, like Bingham, based the meaning of his image on religious motives. Here it was the activity of moving to the West into the wilderness landscape that was supported by religious metaphors.

The perception of landscape itself, its vision, was also based on religious notions. C. W. Dana published the book *The Garden of the World, or the Great West* in 1856. He puts the biblical motive in a prime position in his introduction: 'The land of promise, and the Canaan of our time, is the region which, commencing on the slope of the Alleghenies, broadens grandly over the vast prairies and mighty rivers, over queenly lakes and lofty mountains, until the ebb and flow of the Pacific tide kisses the golden shores of the El Dorado.'[35]

Manifest destiny

With the Louisiana Purchase in 1803, a huge territory was opened up for discovery. Although the land purchase attracted a great deal of controversy, images of the new lands reinforced a mood of expansionism. It was directed against doubts within the United States about rapid expansion, especially in the South-West. A strong movement formed, opposing both the annexation of land in the South-West and the Mexican War. As a countercritique and as a promotion of expansionism a new political rhetoric was developed: America's 'Manifest Destiny'. John O'Sullivan, editor of *The New York Morning News*, found the words: 'Our Manifest Destiny [is] to overspread and to possess the whole of the continent which Providence has given us for the development of the great experiment of liberty and federated self-government entrusted to us.'[36] A powerful phrase was created for justifying the move to the West. Ray Allen Billington describes the reception of this phrase in the American population: 'Manifest Destiny! There was a pulsifying phrase indeed. Overnight the magic word swept the nation. Congressmen fastened upon them. "The right of our manifest destiny", declared one.'[37]

The rhetoric of 'Manifest Destiny' made the continent and its land an object for acquisition. The West stood for wealth and large resources: 'It was the West. But it was not just the West of geography. It was also the West of the mind, the spirit, a concept for generations had reassured the Americans of a future, of a place to go ... Somewhere out there in the general direction of the Pacific Ocean lay a depository of unending resources, imperfectly described or understood, and a source of *Lebensraum* that often was one more of imagery than of substance.'[38]

The imagery of 'Manifest Destiny' was created by a large number of paintings and literary works. Painters who had viewed the landscapes of the West only on short trips became great aesthetic promotors of Western landscapes. They painted the West in their studios in Manhattan, in Hoboken, or in other urban areas, or even in Düsseldorf, Germany. Numerous paintings anchored the expansionist idea in the minds of the American people. An example is John Gast's 'American Progress', painted in 1872. It was ordered for the cover of the travel guide-book of George A. Crofutt, *Crofutt's New Overland Tourist and Pacific Coast Guide*. Crofutt himself gave a description of the painting:

> ... a beautiful and charming female ... floating westward through the air, bearing on her forehead the 'Star of Empire'. She has left the cities of the East far behind, crossed the Alleghenies and the 'Father of the Waters', and still her course is westward. In her right hand she carries a book – common school – the emblem of education and the testimonial of our national enlightenment, while with the left hand she enfolds and stretches the slender wires of the telegraph, that are to flash intelligence throughout the land.[39]

The image of progress as a movement in time and space towards a better world was projected into the landscape of the American continent. Even in Henry Thoreau's work we can trace the imagery of 'Manifest Destiny'. He condemned the aggressive expansion in the South-West, as a criminal action, yet he promoted the annexation of Western lands in powerful words. In his essay 'Walking', he described a force that originates from natural instincts and leads him unerringly towards the West:

> When I go out of the house for a walk, uncertain as yet whither I will bend my steps, and submit myself to my instinct to decide for me ... I turn round and round irresolute sometimes for a quarter of an hour, until I decide, for a thousandth time, that I will walk into the southwest or west. Eastward I go only by force, but westward I go free. Thither no business leads me. It is hard for me to believe that I shall find fair

> landscapes or sufficient wildness and freedom behind the eastern horizon ... I must walk toward Oregon, and not toward Europe ... We go westward as into the future, with a spirit of enterprise and adventure.[40]

Thoreau envisions the movement to the West as natural: man naturally strives for 'business' and 'adventure' in the West. In the East he can find neither business nor freedom. Thoreau uses landscape for the projection of key terms of modern society: 'business', 'enterprise', 'adventure'. A symbolic space was produced and loaded with ideas, which led far into the future and into a global social space. In global imaginations the 'West' still symbolizes these ideas.

The imagery that led to the quick and celebrated victory in taking western lands had used the image of the western landscapes as abundant natural resource designated to the American Nation and open for the entrepreneurial individual. 'A dream world [was created] in which personal greed and the national good became magically associated.'[41]

This Mighty Machine of Nature

The railway played an essential role in the production of an industrial image of landscape. With breathtaking speed, the construction of railroads penetrated the wilderness of the West; it took only a few years in mid nineteenth century for a revolutionary change in the transit system of the United States. In the first big growth of the railway system, the length of the railroads grew from 4,828 km in 1840 to 48,279 km in 1860. By 1900, the total length of the railroad was 305,767 km.[42]

The development of the railway system not only made the transport of goods and people easier but also changed the perception and experience of nature and wilderness. The city had developed a strong tool – the rails and the locomotive – to subdue the landscape fundamentally. This tool made it possible to cross easily land which was not resourceful in an economic sense. It made possible a romantic vision of wilderness landscapes, enjoyed from the safety of a railcar as it sped through the landscape. Landscapes, which a few years ago had been difficult and dangerous to cross, became beautifully framed when viewed from the train. In its literary image of the machine in the garden, a small event was dramatically loaded with its future impact on the landscape and society. Emerson wrote in his diary: 'I hear the whistle of the locomotive in the woods ... It is the voice of the civility of the Nineteenth century saying, "Here I am".'[43] You could not ignore 'the little event, which introduces the industrial world in wilderness America'.[44]

The railway was the most important instrument in American expansion across the continent. Samuel Bowles wrote in 1866: '... To build the railroad is the cheapest, surest and sweetest way to preserve our nationality, and continue the Republic a unit from ocean to ocean.'[45] 'Cheapest', 'surest' and 'sweetest' are perfect attributes to colour the basic assumptions underlying the interests of the nation in constructing railways. This rhetoric helped bring about railway boosterism. In the long run it was cheap and reliable – both technically and economically. It was sweet, in a romantic sense, to look at the ease with which the railway crossed the American wilderness and made the American people its master.

The railway itself played an important role in the production of images. Pictures were made along with the mapping and planning of the railway routes. From 1853 to 1855 the Secretary of War, Jefferson Davis, commissioned seven expeditions to map the economically and technically best route for a transcontinental railway. Twelve artists accompanied the expedition, '... creating a new category of western pictorial imagery'.[46] The pictures they drew show a landscape perfectly suitable for the construction of railway tracks.[47] The landscapes were modelled as gardens to meet the expectations of – most of all – the investors in railway companies. The pictures show '... gently rolling hills, readily adaptable to agriculture, pasturage and railroad routes'.[48] Americans preferred to see a landscape which made it easy to push railway construction. It was the wish for an easy crossing of the wilderness in the West to the Pacific.

After East was joined to West, the image of the locomotive in the landscape changed. The majestic, grand landscape surrounded the railway. The grandeur of landscapes crossed by train underlined the technical and industrial masterpiece. The breakthrough of the railway through the wilderness was seen as the great achievement of the whole American nation. It was American expansionism glorified.

In the painting by Andrew Melrose, 'Westward the Star of Empire Takes Its Way', the headlight of the locomotive beams directly into the eye of the spectator. The 'Star of Empire' thunders through the wilderness; next to it is a clearing with a log cabin. Tree stumps catch the rays of a low sun, symbolizing the hard work of clearing the forest. The thin smoke from the hearth of the log cabin shows the settled farmer: it symbolizes a slow backward world compared to the light and rapid movement of the train through the wilderness. Nature and wilderness is represented by deer crossing the train tracks in their flight. The modern man now travels through wilderness without any risk. The image tells that society is in control of the wilderness.

Basic to American society, the very important notion of nature finds its expression in the connections between machine and nature in the image of the railway, the 'grand machine': The railway '... epitomizes the motion of the spheres, that roll throughout the universe ... this mighty machine of nature'.[49] The locomotive set into the landscape was seen as a tool which sprung out of the industrious nature of man as an 'empire' and as an 'epic'. The machine seems to become a sort of superior nature: 'And the Iron Horse, the earthshaker, the fire-breather, which tramples down the hills ... and breaks down the gates of the mountains, he too shall build an empire an epic. Shall not solitudes and waste places cry for gladness at his coming?'[50]

THE RELEVANCE OF SPACE IMAGES IN SOCIETY

Space images become relevant in two ways. The first is through their immediate influence on the way people perceive land and act upon it. The second is through their transportation of values across time.

The space image of the American West in the nineteenth century consisted of religious, political and economic metaphors. These metaphors were deeply connected with central values of the American society. In particular the space image had the function of relating cultural notions to the land. It helped develop a land perception that suited prevalent conceptions of societal development. In this function it clearly influenced and helped us form land-related behaviour. It is not easy to find precise proof for this very general thesis. As we have seen already, the images produced in the nineteenth century found a large public. I traced space images in the perception of people through their expression in biographical notes and presented some of the findings in a recent article.[51] Diaries and letters from trails to Oregon and California contain accounts of the impact of paintings and literary works both on the decision made by the writers to move to the West and on their perception of the landscape. In one note a landscape was compared with 'Catlin's view over the Mississippi'. The sublime was recognized in landscapes ('... was awfully sublime'). Clearly the writers of diaries were members of an educated upper class, but their ideas found innumerable outlets through education and by other paths of societal communication and acculturation.

The ecological debate provides a long and continuous influence of space images. Cultures and societies produce not only dominant images but also contradictory ones, and the relation between the two sets can be highly significant.[52] One example is still important in today's ecological debate. In the nineteenth century, the imagery of western landscapes gave rise to conflicting ecological images. These images rest on an early ambivalence which still influences ecological thinking:

the wilderness is to be cleared and turned into a civilized world;

the wilderness is God's creation, the sublime landscape.

At the end of the nineteenth century it became obvious that the clearing of the wilderness and the reckless exploitation of natural resources could have disastrous socio-economic results. 'With a considerable sense of shock, Americans of the late nineteenth century realized that many of the forests which had shaped their national character were disappearing.'[53] First it was an urban upper class worry about dangers for the supply of resources for further growth (in almost all cases, the concern was about forests and water). Thus, the idea of wilderness protection was started in the cities. One of the well-known exponents of the utilitarian idea of protection of wilderness areas was Gifford Pinchot.[54] His arguments connected the idea of overcoming wilderness with the good of the nation. Based on another idea, an opposing way of arguing for wilderness protection was developed. Its rhetoric came from the transcendentalist philosophy of Ralph Waldo Emerson and Henry Thoreau. It was based in the religious, ethical and political values that were imbedded in the landscape. The argument was to protect wilderness as a spiritual and intellectual resource for the American nation: 'Why should we not ... have our national preserves ... in which the bear and panther, and some even of the hunter race, may still exist, and not be "civilized off the face of the earth" – our forests ... not for idle sport or food, but for inspiration and our own true recreation.'[55] Nature and wilderness should be conserved to underline the grandeur of the American nation which should be visible even in the future. And they should also be kept as a collective memory of the New World the American people had created: '... let us keep the New World new, preserve all the advantages of living in the country'.[56]

As an example I will refer to the Hetch Hetchy Valley. Wilderness preservation in the USA has a remarkable history: in 1864 the Yosemite Valley was given to California as a 'Federal Grant' to establish a park 'for public use, resort and recreation'.[57] In 1872 the first National Park, the Yellowstone National Park, was set up; in 1885 a 'Forest Preserve' was protected in the Adirondacks with the goal that it 'shall be kept forever as wild forest lands'.[58] But the first important controversy about the protection of wilderness land was the struggle for the protection of the Hetch Hetchy Valley. The wilderness imagery and its metaphors already discussed were used in the arguments around this controversy. Political and economic metaphors dominated the attitude of changing wilderness to suit society and economy as the utilitarian concept of relating to nature. Religious metaphors dominated the other idea of wilderness preservation, derived from the ethical notion of wilderness and the adoration of the sublime landscape.

The fight against the water reservoir in the Hetch Hetchy Valley, intended to supply San Francisco with water, lasted several years from 1906 to 1913. Located in Yosemite National Park, the Hetch Hetchy Valley had been protected since 1890. The fight was far more important than the fate of this particular valley, it was a struggle against economic land use in a land preserve.

As a promotor of the dam project, and as an expert appointed by the government, Gifford Pinchot, the Nation's forester, argued for the needs of the people: 'Put it to that use in which it will serve the most people.'[59] Even more clear was the position of President Theodor Roosevelt: 'Forest protection is not an end in itself; it is a means to increase and sustain the resources of *our country* and *the industries* which depend upon them.'[60]

The outstanding personality of the opponents, who in the end lost their battle, was John Muir. He fought against the dam project using fundamentalist religious rhetoric. In his words the dam-project was a violation of God's temple: 'To dam Hetch Hetchy! As well dam for water tanks the people's cathedrals and churches!'[61]

Muir's religious images transported ideas, which later were formulated by Aldo Leopold in his *Land Ethic*. We can find his approach still active in today's ecological debate around the value of wilderness. We can discover it in the 'deep ecology' of Naess and others,[62] and in the works of those who promote a new 'connectedness' between the human society and nature.[63]

NOTES

1 Detlev Ipsen, 'Raumbilder', *Informationen zur Raumentwicklung*, 11/12 (1986), p. 926. 'Raumbild', the German term for space image can be found with basically the same meaning in Ernst Bloch, *Experimentum Mundi* (Frankfurt, 1985), p. 107. A theoretical explanation of the term space image is Gerhard Strohmeier, 'Das Raumbild des Amerikanischen Westens', *Zeitschrift für historische Anthropologie*, 1 (1993). The term 'space-image' is also related to 'ecological image', which stresses the element of nature (Leo Marx, *The Machine in the Garden* (Oxford, 1964), p. 42). I also refer to the theoretical approaches of an 'imagerie culturelle', and the 'Bilderfabrikation'. Both terms are used by Manfred S. Fischer, 'Literarische Imagologie am Scheideweg, Die Erforschung des "Bildes vom anderen Land" in der Literatur – Komparatistik', Günther Blaicher (ed.), *Erstartes Denken, Studien zu Klischee, Stereotyp und Vorurteil in englishsprachiger Literatur* (Tübingen, 1987), p. 61.

2 David Harvey, *The Condition of Postmodernity* (Oxford, 1989), pp. 220, 221. See also: David Harvey, 'The Nature of Environment: The Dialectics of Social and Environmental Change', *The Socialist Register* (1993), 1–51.

3 There is developing interest in imagery in social geography. The works of J. B. Jackson and Yi-Fu Tuan, for example, found broad acceptance in the 1960s; A. Pred, in Germany, D. Ipsen, G. Hard, and also D. Harvey are nowadays connected to part of the old tradition. Meanwhile critics have argued that influences of the images on social behaviour are not explained sufficiently, e.g. R. W. Chambers, 'Images, Acts and Consequences', in: A. Baker and M. Billinge (eds.) *Period and Place* (Cambridge, 1982), who asks for biographical proof. I have tried to show the relevance of the image of the American West to social action by analysing biographical notes of the journey westwards: G. Strohmeier, 'Das Raumbild des Amerikanischen Westens', *Zeitschrift für historische Anthropologie*, 1 (1993), 63.

4 Henry James, cited in Marx, *Machine*, p. 352.

5 Literature's portage of the idea of America is the theme of Ray Allen Billington, *Land of Savagery. Land of Promise* (Norman, 1985).

6 On the early creation of an image of the New World, see Manfred S. Fischer, 'Komparatistische Imagologie', *Zeitschrift für Sozialpsychologie*, 10 (1979).

7 Richard Münch, *Die Kultur der Moderne* (Frankfurt, 1993), pp. 258. See also P. Miller, *Errand into the Wilderness* (Cambridge, 1956), and Roderick Nash, *Wilderness and the American Mind* (New Haven and London, 1967), p. 40.

8 Quoted and analyzed in Marx, *Machine*, p. 73. Also in Martin Christadler, 'Heilsgeschichte und Offenbarung, Sinnzuschreibung an Landschaft in der Malerei der amerikanischen Romantik', in Manfred Smuda, *Landschaft* (Frankfurt-o-M., 1986).

9 Marx, *Machine*, p. 121. The term is also used by Yi Fu Tuan, *Topophilia* (New York, 1974), p. 104.

10 Marx, *Machine*, p. 104.

11 Marx, *Machine*, p. 120.

12 Marx, *Machine*, S107. To recall a similar passage in the Apocalypse of St John: 'And he carried me away in the Spirit to a mountain great and high, and showed me the holy city of Jerusalem, coming down out of heaven from God, having the glory of God.'

13 The frontier was located in the West although the actual settling of the American Continent was more of a 'demographic swirl' than a continuous stream from the East to the West. I have to thank Mart Stewart for this comment.

14 A good discussion of the Turner thesis appears in Margaret Walsh, *The American Frontier Revisited* (London, 1981).

15 Frederick Jackson Turner, *The Significance of Sections in American History* (New York, 1932), p. 183, cit. in Nash, *Wilderness*, p. 146.

16 Maurice Halbwachs, *Das kollektive Gedächtnis* (Frankfurt, 1985).

16 Frederick Jackson Turner, *The Frontier in American History* (New York, 1920), p. 1.

17 Marx, *Machine*, p. 89.

18 Marx, *Machine*, p. 89.

19 Gottfried Menzel, *Die Vereinigten Staaten von Nordamerika mit besonderer Rücksicht auf*

deutsche Auswanderung dahin nach eigener Anschauung beschrieben (Berlin, 1853), p. 230. Translation by the author.

20 Patricia Hills, 'Picturing Progress', in William H. Truettner (ed.), *The West as America. Reinterpreting Images of the Frontier* (Washington and London, 1991), p. 104.

21 Hills, 'Picturing Progress', p. 104. Some examples of the leading functioneers of the Art Union: Francis W. Edmond, artist, professionally active as a banker and director of the New York and Erie Railroad Company, Jonathan Sturges was an art collector, a merchant and director of the Illinois Central Railroad, Charles M. Leup, was a merchant and director of the Tradesmen's Bank and the Erie Railroad.

22 Hills, 'Picturing Progress', p. 106.

23 Cited in Hills, 'Picturing Progress', p. 102.

24 Hills, 'Picturing Progress', p. 106.

25 Hills, 'Picturing Progress', p. 106.

26 Christadler, 'Heilsgeschichte', p. 135.

27 On the world-views of religiously motivated migrants to America see Charles L. Sanford, *The Quest for Paradise* (New York, 1979), p. 94.

28 Deuteronomy, 8.

29 Roderick Nash, *Wilderness and the American Mind* (New Haven and London, 1967), p. 14: 'The Old Testament reveals that the ancient Hebrews regarded the wilderness as cursed land ... when the Lord of the Old Testament desired to threaten or punish a sinful people, he found the wilderness condition to be his most powerful weapon.'

30 Nash, *Wilderness*, p. 17: '... wilderness retained its significance ... where spiritual catharsis occured.'

31 Hills, 'Picturing Progress', p. 113.

32 Hills, 'Picturing Progress', p. 114.

33 Samuel Bowles, *Across the Continent* (Springfield, 1865), p. 14; cit. in Hills, 'Picturing Progress', p. 121.

34 Bowles, *Across the Continent*, p. 14, cit. in Hills, 'Picturing Progress', p. 121.

35 Hills, 'Picturing Progress', p. 114.

36 John O'Sullivan, in *The New York Morning News*, 27 December 1845. Two of the most comprehensive studies to the ideology of 'Manifest Destiny' are: Albert K. Weinberg, *A Study of Nationalist Expansionism in American History* (Baltimore, 1935), and Dennis E. Berge, *Manifest Destiny and the Historians* (Lincoln and London, 1983).

37 Ray Allen Billington, *The Far Western Frontier* (New York, 1956), p. 149. And even in the foreword to Billington's book we can find the apologetic comment about the American expansion westwards: '... what is most impressive about the American Expansion is the ease, the simplicity and the seemingly inevitability of the whole process.'

38 Robert G. Athearn, *The Mythic West in Twentieth Century America* (Kansas, 1986), p. 10.

39 Hills, 'Picturing Progress', p. 134.

40 Henry D. Thoreau, *Selected Writings on Nature and Liberty*, ed. Oscar Cargill (New York, 1952), p. 117.

41 William H. Truettner, 'Ideology and Image', in Truettner (ed.), *West*, p. 31.

42 Lewis Paul Todd and Merle Curti, *Rise of the American Nation* (New York, 1977), pp. 253, 408.

43 R. W. Emerson, cit. in Marx, *Machine*, p. 12.

44 Marx, *Machine*, p. 17.

45 Bowles, *Across the Continent*, p. 225, cited in Hills, 'Picturing Progress', p. 127.

46 Hills, 'Picturing Progress', p. 115.

47 Good examples are the pictures by John Mix Stanley who accompanied an expedition, of the Teton Valley. Hills, 'Picturing Progress', p. 117.

48 Hills, 'Picturing Progress', p. 117.

49 Marx, *Machine*, p. 161.

50 Marx, *Machine*, p. 196.

51 Gerhard Strohmeier, 'Das Raumbild des Amerikanischen Westens', *Historische Anthropologie*, 1 (1993).

52 For the idea of conflicting images I have to thank the members of a seminar at the Historical Department of the Western Washington University, summer 1993.

53 Nash, *Wilderness*, p. 45.

54 Gifford Pinchot, *Breaking New Ground* (New York, 1947).

55 Henry Thoreau, *Maine Woods*, *Writings 3*, p. 212.

56 Henry Thoreau, *Journal*, ed. Torrey and Allen (Boston, 1906), pp. 12, 387.

57 Nash, *Wilderness*, p. 106.

58 Nash, *Wilderness*, p. 108.

59 Gifford Pinchot in a hearing in the House of Congress, cited by Nash, *Wilderness*, S171.

60 Cit. in Nash, *Wilderness*, p. 162.

61 Nash, *Wilderness*, p. 167.

62 Arne Naess, *Ecology, Community, and Lifestyle* (Cambridge, 1989), whose ideas are fundamentally based on Spinoza. Also George Sessions and Bill Devall, who worked towards a new ecological philosophy, based on Naess' notion of deep ecology.

63 To name only two of the many exponents of the ecological notion of 'connectedness': Wendell Berry for the rural part of the USA (Wendell Berry, *What are People For?* (London, 1990)) and Tony Hiss for urban America (*Experience of Place* (New York, 1990)).

SIXTEEN

ON HUMAN NATURE: DARWIN AND THE ANTHROPOLOGISTS

ADAM KUPER

IN 1838 Darwin wrote the famous note: 'Origin of man now proved. – Metaphysic must flourish. – He who understands baboon would do more towards metaphysic than Locke.'[1] In the event, however, metaphysics continued to flourish without reference to primatology. More surprisingly, even the scientific anthropology that emerged in the 1860s was not entirely Darwinian in its orientation.

In the two decades following the publication of *The Origin of Species*, in 1859, a series of monographs appeared that dealt in a fresh and urgent manner with primitive society, the evolution of marriage and the family, and the rise of magic, religion and science. The authors of these books (who included Maine, Fustel de Coulanges, Lubbock, McLennan Morgan and Tylor) referred to each other's work and quickly developed a coherent new discourse. While they differed on many issues, they generally agreed upon a crucial organizing premise: that a direct progression could be established from primitive society through various intermediate stages to modern society. When anthropology became established in universities in the twentieth century, and histories of the discipline began to be written, these pioneer anthropologists were conventionally grouped together as 'evolutionists'.

In 1966, however, in his masterly *Evolution and Society*, J. W. Burrow protested against the ritual invocation of Darwin's name to explain the emergence of a new anthropology in the second half of the century. 'Darwin was undoubtedly important', he concluded, 'but it is a type of importance impossible to estimate at all precisely. He was certainly not the father of evolutionary anthropology, but possibly he was its wealthy uncle.'[2] Burrow emphasized other sources of the new anthropology, and in particular he pointed out the continuing influence of the progressive world histories of the Scottish Enlightenment. As he remarked, Spencer had drawn on this tradition to protect Utilitarian theory from the challenge of cultural relativism, arguing that institutions, moral principles, forms of happiness, were appropriate to specific levels of development. By profession, the pioneer anthropologists were lawyers, classicists and theologians. It is therefore not altogether surprising that they were more susceptible to influence from historians and philosophers than from natural scientists. But Burrow also showed that in so far as they did take account of scientific advances, they were more impressed by the lessons of uniformitarian geology and comparative philology than by evolutionary biology.

Reacting, in part, to Burrow, George Stocking in his *Victorian Anthropology* emphasized the ways in which the Darwinian revolution obliged intellectuals to reconsider the place of human beings in nature and in time. Some experienced a traumatic shock as a myth of divine election was challenged by a natural history of the human species. Yet the new ideas about human origins did not necessarily undermine the established rationalist ideas about cultural progress. 'Indeed, in a sense it might even be said that while Darwinism gave man a new place in nature, classical socio-cultural evolutionism reasserted a traditional one; for if in origin man was part of nature, and controlled by it, the progress of civilization removed him from nature and won him control over it.'[3] Moreover, this older tradition offered a welcome alternative to the disturbing Darwinian view that the course of change might have no obvious direction, that natural selection was the law of higgledy-piggledy. As Bowler remarks, 'there is little evidence that [Darwin] was able to disturb his contemporaries' faith in teleology'.[4]

Even as a wealthy uncle, Darwin was, of course, a major influence on the nascent anthropology, but Darwinian theory offered a number of distinct leads, and it was possible to pick and choose among them. Moreover, some of the most important Darwinian principles had only doubtful relevance to social and cultural history.

Burrow identified 'three specific implications of Darwinian theory which were relevant to evolutionary anthropology':

> The first was that man, by his kinship with animals, is part of nature, not outside it ... Secondly, Darwinism seemed to justify social theorists in accounting for racial differences in terms of environmental differences over a long period, rather than regarding them as ultimate and unaccountable data ... Finally, there is the question of natural selection ...
>
> (pp. 114–15)

The first principle, common descent, was generally accepted by British biologists and anthropologists, at least after 1871. Its acceptance raised the question of how (by what uniform processes) human civilization had developed from a common primate starting-point. But the acceptance of common descent did not explain these processes of development. Nor did every expert accept that all humanity had shared a common ancestor: each 'race' might have evolved separately, as a distinct species. Even if monogenesis was accepted, some anthropologists were inclined to the view that environmental pressures had shaped racial differences over a long period, so that the cultural history of the various races might have been quite different. There was much disagreement on that question even in Darwin's inner circle, and Darwin himself became more favourable to racialist views in the 1880s.

There was even less agreement about Darwin's theory of natural selection, which was, in any case, much disputed by biologists, even Huxley remaining a sceptic. The anthropologists found it of little interest. 'Neither Maine, nor Tylor, nor McLennan made much use of the theory of natural selection and Spencer used it only as a garnish for a theory he had already developed.'[5] McLennan perhaps came closest to a Darwinian model, with his vision of primitive foragers engaged in a perpetual gang-war. Yet as late as 1876 he felt he could afford to ignore Darwin's views on mating. His writings on primitive marriage by capture and female infanticide reflect rather the direct influence of Malthusian thinking.[6]

Lubbock, Darwin's country neighbour, and Galton, Darwin's cousin, commented more substantially on Darwinian theory, but developed it in contrary directions. Lubbock's main contribution was to introduce and adapt Scandinavian models of archaeological 'stages' into the argument on historical development. Galton's central concern was the selection of intelligence – 'genius' – and its role in competition between 'races'.

Other leading figures were more remote from Darwinian preoccupations. Maine came late and briefly to Darwin, in the 1880s, invoking Darwin's critique (in the second edition of *The Descent of Man*) of his own rivals, McLennan and Morgan, but his writings were firmly in the Germanic tradition of philology and legal history, and he was hostile to the emerging consensus (represented especially by Lubbock and Tylor) that all human populations went through the same stages of historical development. Perhaps no anthropologist of his generation was less touched by Darwinian theory. In the eighties and nineties, however, such leading evolutionists as Robertson Smith and Frazer were also apparently indifferent to Darwinian ideas. A recent, authoritative biography of Frazer includes only three glancing references to Darwin in the index.[7]

Even the self-confessed Darwinians among the anthropologists treated Darwinian theory as an *à la carte* menu. In his biography of E. B.

Tylor, the father-figure of British anthropology, whom he knew well, Marett insisted that while he was an orthodox Darwinian 'whenever he has to pronounce on the physical problems relating to human descent', his Darwinism did not otherwise run deep:

> Though he occasionally used ... the rather high-sounding phrase 'evolution' which Darwin had taken over from Herbert Spencer, perhaps without paying much heed to its philosophical implications, Tylor decidedly prefers to speak simply of the 'development' of culture. Probably he realizes, though subconsciously, that the growth of culture is a distinct, if analogous, process as compared with that involved in biological evolution in the sense of such race-propagation as makes for an increasing complexity.[8]

In his own textbook *Anthropology*, written in 1911, Marett insisted that 'Anthropology is the child of Darwin', but he too stressed common descent, and had next to nothing to say about heredity and natural selection. 'What is the truth that Darwinism supposes? Simply that all the forms of life in the world are related together; and that the relations manifested in time and space between the different lives are sufficiently uniform to be described under a general formula, or law of evolution'.[9] However, for Marett this general formula of evolution was in practice virtually identical to the familiar Whig principle that progress was inevitable. Marett's Cambridge counterpart, Alfred Haddon, who began his career as a biologist, made just two brief references to Darwin in his *History of Anthropology* (1934), and, like Marett, he concluded that Darwin's main contribution had been to establish the natural origin of the human species.

Burrow was surely right: the direct influence of Darwinian theory on the theoretical thinking of the first generation of anthropologists was diffuse and often superficial. Moreover, it can be argued that there were good reasons for the uncertainties of the anthropologists. Formidable difficulties confronted an aspiring Darwinian historian of social and cultural institutions. This is apparent if one considers Darwin's own interventions in the debates of the social and cultural evolutionists, an aspect of his intellectual history that has been relatively neglected.

I shall consider three episodes in the development of Darwin's anthropology: his ethnography of the Fuegians; his views on race, selection, and mental progress, as they developed during the years of the American Civil War, and in the local context of an institutional split in the anthropological community; and his intervention in the debate about primitive marriage. The exercise will help to make clear why Darwin's ideas did not revolutionize the understanding of social and cultural history, for even Darwin found that he could be a Darwinian only intermittently when he reflected on the course of human history.

DARWIN AS A PRE-DARWINIAN ETHNOGRAPHER

Darwin's commander on the *Beagle*, Robert FitzRoy, had encountered the Fuegians on an earlier voyage (1826-30). Greatly troubled by thieving, he took hostages, but this strategy back-fired. The miscreants kept his goods, and he was left with three Fuegians on his hands. A fourth was purchased for a pearl button and named Jeremy (Jemmy) Button.

FitzRoy decided to take the Fuegians back to England with him, where they would be exposed to civilization and Christianity, eventually returning them to spread the good word to their people. One died from smallpox, but the survivors were educated with the help of the rector of Walthamstow. They absorbed English and Christianity, one even picking up some Spanish and Portuguese on voyage, and they were presented by FitzRoy to the King and Queen. When he set sail on the *Beagle* again in 1831, one of his objectives was to return the Fuegians (Jemmy Button, York Minster, and a woman, Fuegian Basket) to their homes. Darwin was on board, and so was a missionary who had elected to work among the Fuegians.

Darwin's first direct encounter with what he called 'untamed savage' Fuegians came on the morning of 19 December 1832, and as he remarked in his diary and in letters home, it impressed him profoundly. Writing to his sister Caroline from the *Beagle* in 1835, Darwin listed 'the three most interesting spectacles I have beheld since leaving England – a Fuegian savage. – Tropical Vegetation – & the ruins of Concepcion –'[10] When he returned to the islands a year later he wrote: 'Viewing such men, one can hardly make oneself believe that they are fellow creatures placed in the same world'.[11] Fuegian homes were rudimentary, they slept 'on the wet ground, coiled up like animals', their food was miserable and scarce, they were at war over means of subsistence with their neighbours. 'Captain FitzRoy could never ascertain that the Fuegians have any distinct belief in a future life.' Their feelings for home and hearth were stunted. Their imaginations were not stimulated, their skills 'like the instinct of animals' were not 'improved by experience'.[12] 'Although essentially the same creature, how little must the mind of one of these beings resemble that of an educated man.' And yet: 'There can be no reason for supposing the race of Fuegians are decreasing, we may therefore be sure that he enjoys a sufficient share of happiness (whatever its kind may be) to render life worth having.

Nature, by making habit omnipotent, has fitted the Fuegian to the climate and productions of his country.'[13]

As Janet Browne argues, there was little to distinguish Darwin's reflections from those of Captain FitzRoy, a more representative man of his time, if anything a rather conservative man of the thirties.[14] To be sure, there were signs of Cambridge deism, and of the liberalism of the Darwins. The evocation of Nature's purpose is consistent with Paley's deism, in which Darwin had steeped himself while at Cambridge. His curious harping on the question of happiness should alert us to the fact that this is also the discourse of a Utilitarian. But FitzRoy, for example, was willing to consider the Fuegians as the equivalent of the ancient Britons:

> Disagreeable, indeed painful, as is even the mental contemplation of a savage, and unwilling as we may be to consider ourselves even remotely descended from human beings in such a state, the reflection that Caesar found the Britons painted and clothed in skins, like these Fuegians, cannot fail to augment an interest excited by their childish ignorance of matters familiar to civilized man, and by their healthy, independent state of existence.[15]

This anticipates Darwin's most famous reflection on the Fuegians: 'The astonishment which I felt on first seeing a party of Fuegians on a wild and broken shore will never be forgotten by me, for the reflection at once rushed into my mind – such were our ancestors.'[16]

Darwin and FitzRoy also agreed that while savages were very different indeed from Victorian Englishmen, they were capable of rapid improvement under missionary guidance. FitzRoy's party of Fuegians had quickly absorbed English culture. When the Fuegians were set ashore with the missionary, Matthews, in February 1833, Darwin reflected that 'in contradiction of what has often been stated, 3 years has been sufficient to change savages into, as far as habits go, complete & voluntary Europeans'.[17]

Indeed, Darwin worried rather that the Fuegians would not be unable to adapt again to a savage life, and he was pleasantly surprised by what transpired. When, in March 1834, the *Beagle* returned to the camp of their Fuegian party, Fitzroy found Jemmy Button much thinner, but he assured the captain that he was 'hearty, sir, never better', and that he was contented and had no desire to alter his present way of life. Moreover, civilization was evidently catching. It was generally agreed, the captain noted, that Jemmy's family 'were become considerably more humanized than any savages we had seen in Tierra del Fuego'. Perhaps one day a shipwrecked seaman might be saved by Jemmy's children 'prompted, as they can hardly fail to be, by the traditions they will have heard of men of other lands; and by an idea, however faint of their duty to God as well as their neighbour'.[18] Equally, it seemed that a civilized person could also revert happily to a state of savagery. Darwin himself wrote in his diary, noting the farewell signal fire that Jemmy lit as they sailed away, 'I hope & have little doubt he will be as happy as if he had never left his country; which is much more than I formerly thought.'[19]

In short, both Darwin and FitzRoy were agreed that the Fuegians stood low on the scale of civilization – on the lowest rung, Darwin believed. Nevertheless, there was no intrinsic reason why individual Fuegians should not very quickly be 'civilized'. 'These Indians appear to have a facility for learning languages . . . which will greatly contribute to civilization or demoralization: as these two steps seem to go hand in hand.'[20] Lack of intelligence did not seem to be the explanation for their apparent backwardness:

> Although the Australian may be superior in acquirements [to the Fuegian], it by no means follows that he is likewise superior in mental capacity: indeed, from what I saw of the Fuegians when on board, and from what I have read of the Australians, I should think the case was exactly the reverse.[21]

It is remarkable that the one speculation Darwin made on the cause of their backwardness was purely sociological. The Fuegians bartered freely and shared everything – 'even a piece of cloth given to one is torn into shreds and distributed; and no one individual becomes richer than another'. This insistence on exchange (which so tormented their English visitors) was based on the assumption of equality. And it was precisely this equality that held them back.

> The perfect equality among the individuals composing the Fuegian tribes, must for a long time retard their civilization. As we see those animals, whose instinct compels them to live in society and obey a chief, are most capable of improvement, so is it with the races of mankind . . . On the other hand, it is difficult to understand how a chief can arise till there is property of some sort by which he might manifest his superiority and increase his power.[22]

Conversely, Darwin attributed the relative sophistication of the Tahitians to their hierarchical social order.

To sum up, Darwin's account of the 'untamed savages' took for granted current ideas about human development, conceived as the consequence of reasoned choices, expressed institutionally in civil order and private property. All humans possess reason, and the development of this faculty depends on the stimulus provided by the environment, on exposure to sources of enlightenment, and upon the existence of an ordered social hierarchy.

THE NATURALIZATION OF REASON

The theme that pervades Darwin's 'Notebook on Man', which he opened in 1838, is that all mental activities are reducible to states of the brain. Even love of the deity was a function of the organization of the brain – 'oh, you Materialist!'[23]

Only, perhaps, after prodding from Huxley did Darwin reach the conclusion that the evolution from apes to humans was itself a result of the growth of the brain. Huxley contributed a special note that was published as an appendix to chapter 7 of the second edition of the *Descent of Man*, in which he compared the brain of humans and those of other primates, and established their structural similarity. The main difference was one of size and, presumably, complexity. 'As the various mental faculties gradually developed the brain would almost certainly become larger', Darwin concluded. 'No one, I presume, doubts that the large proportion which the size of man's brain bears to his body, compared to the same proportion in the gorilla or orang, is closely connected with his higher mental powers.'[24]

The specialization of the brain was a consequence of natural selection, but Darwin allowed for a feedback between nature and culture. The individuals best suited to use language and tools would be those with the most active brains, and their cultural success would bring them gains in the procreative stakes. 'We can see, that in the rudest state of society, the individuals who were the most sagacious, who invented and used the best weapons or traps, and who were best able to defend themselves, would rear the greatest number of offspring. The tribes, which included the largest number of men thus endowed, would increase in number and supplant other tribes' (p. 196). Similarly, the moral and social qualities (which Darwin reckoned of greater importance than the purely intellectual) were to be found among other animals. Their high development among human beings was the result of natural selection 'aided by inherited habit'. Populations in which these qualities were most developed would be successful in competition with their rivals. 'Thus the social and moral qualities would tend slowly to advance and be diffused throughout the world' (p. 200).

It has often been remarked that the conception of natural selection shifts subtly but significantly in this argument. The classical Darwinian view is that natural selection operates on individuals. Each individual has unique features, and these features may help it or handicap it in competition with other individuals, of their own species and of other species. The better adapted are relatively more successful in terms of procreation, and so their particular features spread in the population. This still held true, Darwin thought, so long as civilization remained undeveloped: Savages are known to suffer severely from recurrent famines; they do not increase their food by artificial means; they rarely refrain from marriage, and generally marry whilst young. Consequently they must be subjected to occasional hard struggles for existence, and the favoured individuals will alone survive. (p. 906)

However, when writing about more civilized human populations – and sometimes more generally about other gregarious species – Darwin allowed an element of group selection. When treating what he termed the 'moral qualities' which distinguish human beings, he argued that their yield was social rather than individual. Being a good citizen might have a high cost for the individual, but it benefits the community.

> It must not be forgotten that although a high standard of morality gives but a slight or no advantage to each individual man and his children over the other men of the same tribe, yet that an increase in the number of well-endowed men and an advancement in the standard of morality will certainly give an immense advantage to one tribe over another. A tribe including many members who, from possessing in a high degree the spirit of patriotism, fidelity, obedience, courage, and sympathy, were always ready to aid one another, and to sacrifice themselves for the common good, would be victorious over most other tribes: and this would be natural selection. (p. 203)

On this argument, it is the tribe that adapts, as a community, rather than the tribespeople as individuals. Competition between groups is stressed, rather than between individuals. It is societies, perhaps even 'races', that compete, sometimes to the death.

Why did Darwin flirt with group selection? Most obviously, it suggested one answer to the puzzle of how selfless and risky modes of behaviour were transmitted to later generations. A community benefited if moral individuals 'sacrifice themselves for the common good'. But why should individuals put the community interest before their own – and how was a tendency to such self-destructive behaviour passed on to the next generation? Darwin argued that the community rewarded people for behaving in ways that served the public interest. Apparently selfless conduct had its selfish rewards, although Darwin did not suggest that these were measured by procreative success. Moreover, as societies became more civilized, so they were better able to inculcate moral, unselfish values through education.

Acceptance of the principle of group selection – at least for civilized human populations – shifted the emphasis from the evolution of the brain itself to the effects of education: from nature to nurture. 'The more efficient causes of progress seem to consist of a good education during youth whilst the brain is impressible, and of a high standard of excellence, inculcated by the ablest and best men, embodied in the laws, customs and traditions of the nation, and enforced by public opinion' (p. 220).

But if a critical role was conceded to social institutions, to values, to education, this could only dilute the power of the natural selection of physical modifications to shape human evolution. Darwin approvingly cited Wallace's views on this question:

> Mr Wallace ... argues that man, after he had partially acquired those intellectual and moral faculties which distinguish him from the lower animals, would have been but little liable to bodily modifications through natural selection or any other means ... He invents weapons, tools, and various stratagems to procure food and to defend himself. When he migrates into a colder climate he uses clothes, builds sheds, and makes fires; and by the aid of fire cooks food otherwise indigestible. He aids his fellow-men in many ways, and anticipates future events. Even at a remote time period he practised some division of labour. (pp. 195–6)

Indeed, cultural developments might in the long run work against natural selection. Human beings had become essentially a domesticated species. They shielded their own weaker members from the effects of natural selection. This could bring about a deterioration of the stock, particularly since, Darwin complained, men chose wives on frivolous grounds.

In short, Darwin took the view that, after the initial phase of human evolution, any advantage that one population enjoyed over another was by and large the consequence (positive or negative) of what we would now call cultural factors. Natural selection, classically conceived, became less decisive, group selection increasingly important. He sometimes even rhetorically set 'races' in competition with one another, but did not necessarily believe that this competition would be settled by the biological qualities of each race. There was, however, room in this conception of human history for a more forthright racism, if (as he came to argue with some force in the 1880s[25]) brain capacity varied between racial groups.

Darwin wavered on the question of race. It was one of the most sensitive political issues of the 1860s, and its split the nascent anthropological community. The members of the Anthropological Society largely supported the race-determinism of Knox, propagated by their leader, the Tory pro-slavery publicist John Hunt. The Darwinians allied themselves with the rival Ethnological Society, dominated by Whigs and faithful to its origin in the Aborigines Protection Society. The central issue that divided the parties was that of the single or multiple origin of human beings: the Ethnologicals, for Darwinian reasons or, in some cases, theological reasons, favouring monogenesis. But even some who believed in the single origin of the human species nevertheless argued that racial differences were very ancient, and caused differences in mentality and behaviour.

Darwin devoted a long and balanced chapter in *The Descent of Man* to the question of race, and concluded that racial differences were relatively insignificant, and that they did not correspond with substantial intellectual differences:

> The American aborigines, Negroes and Europeans are as different from each other in mind as any three races that can be named; yet I was incessantly struck, whilst living with the Fuegians on board the 'Beagle', with the many little traits of character, shewing how similar their minds were to ours; and so it was with a full-blooded negro with whom I happened once to be intimate.

Ethnography suggested the same conclusion. 'He who will read Mr Tylor's and Sir J. Lubbock's interesting works can hardly fail to be deeply impressed with the close similarity between the men of all races in tastes, dispositions and habits.'[26]

What then explained the differences between the races? The causes, he now argued, were to be found not in environmental pressures and natural selection but in sexual selection. There was no apparent survival value in being bearded rather than beardless, red-haired rather than blond, thick-lipped rather than thin-lipped. These variations – which in the long run produced 'racial' differences – were produced by chance, local aesthetic preferences, which guided men and women in choosing their mates.

Wallace, who might have claimed priority in the statement of the theory of natural selection, was dismissive: everything Darwin attributed to sexual selection was better explained in terms of natural selection. Perhaps a majority of Darwin's contemporaries conceived of competition in terms of a struggle between races, and assumed that racial differences (particularly differences in the capacity of the brain, which were signalled by differences in skull shape) explained differential cultural development. Darwin himself frequently remarked that the eventual elimination of the 'lower races' by the 'highly civilized races' was in the long run inevitable.'[27]

But this opening to a racial theory of history was seldom fully exploited, since it was in conflict with the Enlightenment tradition that history was a story of rational advance, a road followed, albeit at a different pace, by all peoples. Darwin's writings on the course of human evolution were hardly calculated to revolutionize the well-established ideas current among social and cultural evolutionists. Far from unequivocally 'naturalizing' reason and history, he sometimes endorsed the traditional dichotomy between biological forces and moral, intellectual, what we might call cultural forces. The cultures of the different 'races' might represent stages in a single process of evolutionary advance from magic through religion to science, from promiscuity to monogamy, from stone tools to factories.

MATING AND MARRIAGE

The slight influence of Darwinian thinking on anthropological argument is very evident when one considers the main debate – indeed, in some ways the founding debate – within the community of anthropologists. Concerned with the origins of marriage and the family, it began with the publication of Henry Maine's *Ancient Law* in 1861 (two years after *The Origin of Species*) and reached a climax with the publication of Lewis Henry Morgan's *Systems of Consanguinity and Affinity of the Human Family* in 1871, the year in which *The Descent of Man* appeared.[28] Although the issue was marriage, this was not for Darwinian reasons. The protagonists had nothing to say about heredity or sexual selection, and seldom referred back to primate analogies. Rather, they were concerned with the origins of moral principles and social institutions.

In *Ancient Law*, Maine began with a conventional idea, that the original human institution was the patriarchal family (as described in the Old Testament and by Homer). He represented this aboriginal political system as a primitive tyranny, in which there was no individual freedom at all. All power lay with the father. If one considered the various Indo-European speaking peoples, it was evident that all were still patriarchal and patrilineal, but some had advanced beyond others, and introduced individual liberties, private property, and the right to enter into contracts in place of the old rule that one had to accept one's birth-status. This history, Maine argued, proved the falsehood of Rousseau's speculation about the state of nature. According to Rousseau, our natural condition was one of freedom and equality. This heritage had been betrayed by our rulers. Maine insisted that on the contrary we were born in chains and had been freed through the development of law, private property and the state.

A radical Scottish lawyer, J. F. McLennan, set out to counter this new conservative myth of origin. His main strategy as to deny that the aboriginal human institution was the patriarchal family. On the contrary, in the beginning human beings lived like animals, promiscuously. Brothers and sisters lived in the same band, and the men shared the women. However, these bands were in competition with each other – as Spencer, for example, had insisted, along with Darwin. In order to fight more effectively, some jettisoned their women-folk, perhaps practising female infanticide (as Malthus had speculated). They then captured women from their enemies when they wanted to have children. In these conditions nobody could know who had fathered a particular child, and therefore the only kinship tie that was recognized was that between a child and its mother. It was only after great technological changes led to the development of private property that men began to claim a monopoly of sexual access to their wives, and to establish relationships with their sons, who would inherit from them.[29]

McLennan's ingenious thesis was illustrated with a striking variety of ethnographic instances, in the style of the Scottish speculative historians rather than the European Indo-Europeanists. But what counted as evidence? McLennan argued that modern savages tended still to be promiscuous and to trace descent in the female line, but he had to concede that there were probably no peoples who still lived the woman-stealing, child-killing lives of the original warrior bands. However, the memory of these practices was preserved, McLennan argued, in the rituals and ceremonies of contemporary 'savages'. If a bride ritually protested against being moved from her parent's home, for example, this was a throwback to the institution of marriage by capture.

McLennan made it clear that this argument did not derive from Darwin, but his thesis might have appealed to Darwinians on the grounds that it stressed competition and mating; and some may have been attracted by the parallel he drew between morphological and cultural fossils. However, an American anthropologist, Lewis Henry Morgan, who was more directly influenced by Darwin, bitterly attacked McLennan's hypothesis, mainly on methodological grounds.[30] The true fossils of past institutions were to be found in language. Kinship terms preserved the outlines of ancient forms of family organization. And this approach revealed no trace of marriage by capture. On the contrary, all primitive social systems were based on collective marriages, first between a group of brothers and their own sisters, later, as morality advanced, between a group of brothers and a set of women to whom they were not related; and finally, with the introduction of private property, human beings progressed to monogamy.

Competition played no part in Morgan's argument, but when Tylor reviewed the debate between McLennan and Morgan he invoked competition to explain the evolution of marriage forms. 'Again and again in the world's history, savage tribes must have had plainly before their minds the simple practical alternative between marrying-out and being killed out.'[31] However, he rejected McLennan's thesis that primitive mating was dependent on the capture of foreign women, arguing instead that a peaceful exchange of women between groups was the normal basis for alliances. But once marriage by alliance was instituted for diplomatic reasons, its further development was explained by Tylor in conventional terms, as the consequence of moral advances, and the development of private property. Lubbock took a great interest in this debate, but his main concern was to endorse the view that the first human populations had lived promiscuously.[32]

In the second edition of *The Descent of Man* Darwin himself reviewed the debate. The context was his discussion of the relative effect of sexual selection and natural selection on early or primitive human populations. Among 'the causes which prevent or check the action of sexual selection with savages' he listed 'so-called communal marriages or promiscuous intercourse; secondly, the consequences of female infanticide; thirdly, early betrothals; and lastly, the low estimation in which women are held, as mere slaves'.[33]

If savages were promiscuous, as McLennan, Morgan and Lubbock believed, then it followed that sexual selection could not have been a significant factor in early human evolution. Yet there may have been some confusion, Darwin thought, as to what marriage and promiscuity involved. A naturalist was quite happy to use the term 'marriage' to mean any exclusive mating relationship that lasted at least for a breeding season. If this usage was accepted, then it could hardly be denied that even savages tended to marry. So long as there was some selection of breeding partners, then sexual sexual selection could operate.

To the extent that promiscuity was general, the effect of sexual selection would be reduced, but Darwin doubted that something very near promiscuity did reign originally in human communities. Sir Andrew Smith, a respected scientist who had written about the native peoples of Southern Africa, 'expressed to me the strongest opinion that no race exists in which woman is considered as the property of the community' (p. 897). Moreover, among other animals, including the apes, adult males were extremely jealous, and the strongest males tended to accumulate mates whom they monopolized.

Sexual selection may therefore have been significant, although Darwin allowed that female infanticide (posited by Malthus and

McLennan) would have reduced its impact, particularly if in consequence a female would have to mate with all of a group of brothers, by whom, moreover, she had been captured. Early betrothals, too, would reduce the element of choice in mating, and so work against sexual selection. So would the valuation of women purely for their labour power.

Natural selection would also have operated in the earliest stages of human history.

> At a very early period, before man attained to his present rank in the scale, many of his conditions would be different from what now obtains amongst savages. Judging from the analogy of the lower animals, he would then either live with a single female, or be a polygamist. The most powerful and able males would succeed best in obtaining attractive females. They would also succeed best in the general struggle for life, and in defending their females, as well as their offspring, from enemies of all kinds. (p. 906)

Darwin's intervention was by no means decisive. McLennan (*Studies in Ancient History*) ducked Darwin's criticisms of his thesis in *The Descent of Man*. Maine naturally enough claimed Darwin as an ally against Morgan and McLennan. The patriarchal family, he now suggested, was obviously based upon the Darwinian principle of male jealousy.[34] Freud was to seize later upon Darwin's image of gorilla bands. Young males were driven off by the father-leader when they reached maturity, an arrangement that limited inbreeding but might, Freud speculated, provoke resentment and rebellious plans to kill and supplant the father.[35]

But although anything that Darwin had to say was being taken very seriously by the loose community of anthropologists in the last three decades of the century, it must be evident that even on the crucial question of human mating his theory offered little direct illumination. Darwin's most important contribution to the debate on primitive marriage was to suggest that primate forms of mating might have been carried over to the earliest forms of human marriage, and that therefore the first humans would not have been promiscuous. The one pioneer anthropologist to develop this speculation was the Finnish scholar Edward Westermarck, whose *The History of Human Marriage* was published only in 1891.

CONCLUSION

The founding generation of British anthropologists and ethnologists established itself just at the moment when Darwinism became a major intellectual force in Britain, and yet the influence of Darwinism on their thinking was diffuse and often superficial. As the 'wealthy uncle' of British evolutionism, Darwin helped to legitimate their projects, but they continued to draw upon a well-established tradition of socio-cultural evolutionism. His theories of common descent, natural selection and sexual selection did not obviously resolve the problems of cultural development.

Moreover, Darwin's own anthropology was rather conventional. He was prepared to adopt a progressive thesis on human history that was quite foreign to his theory of biological evolution, and in general he too accepted the ideas that had guided writers in this field for over a century. Most strikingly, he was prepared to compromise his materialism, shifting the emphasis from the growth of the brain (which was, he came to believe, the most significant single factor in the emergence of the human species) to the development of forms of knowledge and moral principles (which explained the subsequent progress of humanity); and knowledge and morality, he argued, were learnt rather than inherited. He insisted upon the primate origin of human beings, but allowed them thereafter to enjoy a good Victorian Whig destiny, fighting their way up a ladder of moral improvement using the weapons of hierarchy, order and education. When it came to human history, in short, even Darwin wrote quite often as a traditional evolutionist, rather than as a Darwinian.

NOTES

A draft of this paper was read by Peter Bowler and James Urry, who both made helpful suggestions for improving it. I am grateful also to Janet Browne for allowing me to refer to an unpublished paper.

1 Howard E. Gruber, *Darwin on Man: A Psychological Study of the Scientific Creativity* (London, 974), p. 281.

2 J. W. Burrow, *Evolution and Society: A Study in Victorian Social Theory* (Cambridge, 1966), p. 114.

3 George W. Stocking, *Victorian Anthropology* (New York, 1987), p. 325.

4 Peter J. Bowler, *The Non-Darwinian Revolution: Reinterpreting a Historical Myth* (Baltimore, 1988), pp. 150–1.

5 Burrow, *Evolution and Society*, p. 115.

6 J. M. McLennan, *Primitive Marriage: An Inquiry into the Origin of the Form of Capture in Marriage Ceremonies* (Edinburgh, 1865); and *Studies in Ancient History* (London, 1876).

7 Robert Ackerman, *J. G. Frazer: His Life and Work* (Cambridge, 1988).

8 R. R. Marett, *Tylor* (London, 1936), p. 19.

9 R. R. Marett, *Anthropology* (London, 1911), pp. 8–9.

10 F. Burckhardt and S. Smith (eds.), *The Correspondence of Charles Darwin, Volume 1 (1821–1836)* (Cambridge, 1984), p. 434.
11 R. D. Keynes (ed.), *The Beagle Record* (Cambridge, 1979), pp. 222–3.
12 Charles Darwin, *Journal of Researches into the Geology and Natural History of the Various Countries visited by H.M.S. 'Beagle'* (London, 1839), cap. X.
13 Keynes (ed.), *Beagle Record*, pp. 222–4.
14 Janet Browne, 'Missionaries and the Human Mind: Charles Darwin and Robert FitzRoy', in Roy MacLeod and Philip F. Rehbock (eds.), *Darwin's Laboratory: Evolutionary Theory and Natural History in the Pacific* (Honolulu, 1994), pp. 263–82.
15 Robert FitzRoy (ed.), *Narrative of the Surveying Voyages of H.M.S. Adventure and Beagle Between the Years 1826 and 1836* (London, 1839), pp. 120–2.
16 Charles Darwin, *The Descent of Man, and Selection in Relation to Sex* (1871), 2nd edn, revised, 2 vols. (London, 1874), pp. 919–20.
17 Keynes (ed.), *Beagle Record*, pp. 141–2.
18 Fitzroy (ed.), *Narrative*, pp. 323–7.
19 Keynes (ed.), *Beagle Record*, p. 221.
20 *Ibid.*
21 Darwin, *Journal of Researches*, ch. X.
22 *Ibid.*
23 Adrian Desmond and James Moore, *Darwin* (London, 1991), p. 250.
24 Darwin, *Descent of Man*, p. 81.
25 Peter J. Bowler, 'From Savage' to 'Primitive': Victorian Evolutionism and the Interpretation of Marginalized Peoples', *Antiquity*, 66 (1992), 721–9.
26 Darwin, *Descent of Man*, p. 276.
27 Desmond and Moore, *Darwin*, p. 653.
28 Adam Kuper, *The Invention of Primitive Society: Transformations of an Illusion* (London, 1988).
29 McLennan, *Primitive Marriage*.
30 Lewis H. Morgan, *Systems of Consanguinity and Affinity of the Human Family* (Washington, DC, 1871).
31 E. B. Tylor, 'On a Method of Investigating the Development of Institutions: Applied to Laws of Marriage and Descent', *Journal of the Anthropological Institute*, 18 (1889), 267.
32 John Lubbock, *The Origin of Civilization and the Primitive Condition of Man* (London, 1870).
33 Darwin, *Descent of Man*, pp. 889–90.
34 Henry Maine, *Dissertations on Early Law and Custom* (London, 1883).
35 Sigmund Freud, *Totem and Taboo* (German edition, 1913) (London, 1918).

SEVENTEEN

THE SIREN OF EVOLUTIONARY ETHICS: DARWIN TO WILSON

PAUL LAWRENCE FARBER

IT would seem a reasonable claim that the sciences which explore the behaviour of humans, the functioning of the brain, or the evolutionary history of *Homo sapiens*, have relevance for discussions on human nature. In spite of some tendentious opposition, many philosophers, anthropologists, and psychologists believe that science can yield information useful for constructing a modern conception of human nature. When the topic is raised of how that scientific knowledge is to be used, however, disagreement mounts. For example, the ambitious claims by proponents of the Genome Project that their research will uncover the genetic basis of alcoholism, homosexuality, and criminality, have unleashed a storm of protest from critics who argue that early twentieth-century eugenics stands now as a stark historical reminder of how easy it is to read our own values into nature.

Even more heated has been the continuing debate over the implications of sociobiology. What social or moral lessons can we draw from an evolutionary perspective on our behaviour? The issue is hardly new, for the attempt to understand the nature of man from an evolutionary point of view is as old as the theory of evolution itself, and has engendered a lively, century-old debate.

I have been looking at one aspect of that controversy, the attempt in the Anglo-American world to use the theory of evolution as a foundation for ethics, or what is called evolutionary ethics.[1] Below I sketch that overall history, which I divide into three main periods, and point out a few of what I take to be its implications.

Evolutionary ethics in the Anglo-American tradition began with the writings of Darwin and Spencer. Both were quite important. Let me start with Darwin.

CHARLES DARWIN

Early in his career Charles Darwin realized that if his attempt to account for how species come into being was to be convincing it would have to account for that most singular species: *Homo sapiens*. The physical aspects presented no difficulty, rather it was man's behaviour that appeared to be the obstacle. In typical Darwinian fashion, he set out a reading programme on 'human nature'. Although the list of books and articles he read was extensive, Darwin soon realized that the subject of man's behaviour was *not* well known from a scientific point of view, and he wisely skirted the issue of man in *The Origin of Species* (1859).

But he returned to it in *The Descent of Man* (1871), where he discussed man's moral capacity – which he, and many others, considered to be the main chasm between man and the animals: 'I fully subscribe to the judgment of those writers who maintain that of all the differences between man and the lower animals, the moral sense or conscience is by far the most important.'[2]

Darwin tackled the issue from the perspective of natural history – like the problem of the adaptation of the giant sloth to its environment or the origin of the human eye. He used his *standard* technique – that is, depicting a particular unusual phenomenon as a part of a continuum, i.e., not focusing on its unique characteristics, but rather viewing it as a part of a series. Seen this way, the moral sense was a natural development in the intellectual faculties of social animals: 'any animal whatever, endowed with well-marked social instincts, would inevitably acquire a moral sense or conscience, as soon as its intellectual powers had become as well developed, or nearly as well developed, as in man'.[3] It might be a different moral sense, perhaps, but still it would be a moral sense, i.e., it might differ in degree but not in kind.

To arrive at this position Darwin utilized information from two fields related to natural history: ethnography and psychology. From the expanding literature on ethnography he was led to believe that there existed a set of universal ethical norms, and that there was a continuum in both time and space between rude barbarism and high civilization. Ethnographers and travellers had amassed observations and studies which suggested that underneath the diversity of cultures, all humans shared a basic set of ethical beliefs. Some of these cultures had attained greater sophistication than others, and they could be ranked from crude to highly civilized – Great Britain, for example, was highly civilized, even if their invasion of China in 1841 (the 'Opium War') to force the emperor to allow the English to sell dope to his subjects struck some less civilized people as dubious.

Psychology in Darwin's day accounted for moral habits by 'sympathy' of individuals for others, and by the internalization of society's punishment of deviant behaviour. Darwin added to these ideas the concept of natural selection, which for him was the main force of progress in the organic world. The resulting picture of the moral development of man was something like this: with increased intelligence early man became capable of having certain sentiments (sympathy, fidelity, courage) which gave advantages to his group. Groups with such sentiments survived better than others. Finally, 'a highly complex sentiment, having its first origin in the social instincts, largely guided by the approbation of our fellow-men, ruled by reason, self-interest, and in later times by deep religious feelings, confirmed by instruction and habit, all combined, [and] constitute our moral sense, or conscience.'[4]

Darwin was confident that further investigation of the universal norms that ethnographers uncovered, would reveal their adaptive value, and that natural history, therefore, would 'resolve' the issue of the basis of ethical systems by relating individual codes to their environment and history. In his published work Darwin was satisfied to leave the issue there. His ethical position was not totally reductionist. He recognized, for example, that higher civilizations gave rise to humanitarian impulses and concepts that were not adaptive. He also noted that 'the strangest customs and superstitions' had become powerful over vast parts of the globe. The issues were not of particular importance, however, because he did not pursue the ramifications of his position. That is, he was satisfied simply with an understanding of the *origins* of the moral sentiment.

HERBERT SPENCER

In contrast, *Herbert Spencer*, whose early published writings on ethics predated Darwin's, wanted not only to establish the origin of the moral sense, but to elaborate what the ethical standards of society *should* be.

Ethics was central to Spencer's thinking (one could reasonably say that the goal of his entire efforts was ethical-political).[5] He began his career with a consideration of how man ought to live (*Social Statics*, 1850) then, after a number of volumes surveying – in a truly Leibnizian fashion – the necessary background, i.e., cosmic, physical, psychological, and social evolution, plus an investigation of the laws underlying those processes, he returned to the topic of proper living (*Principles of Sociology*, 1876–97, *Principles of Ethics*, 1879–93).

Spencer's ethics centred on the individual who sought his own happiness in the exercise of his faculties. Since man was a social animal, this necessarily presupposed freedom of action, so long as it did not infringe on the equal freedom of others.

As Spencer was quick to note, such a position was not practical. Rather, it was the ultimate towards which we were striving, and the standard in ethics and in politics by which we could make judgements. Actions or policies that took us closer to the ultimate were good ones. Spencer described the ultimate state towards which man was evolving in the following words:

> The ultimate man will be one whose private requirements coincide with public ones. He will be that manner of man who, in spontaneously fulfilling his own nature, incidentally performs the functions of a social unit, and yet is only enabled to so fulfill his own nature by all others doing the like.[6]

Spencer's ethical writings were both predictive and prescriptive. He tells us what the future will be like, and he tells us what actions we ought to take to bring us closer to that ideal state.

Darwin and Spencer believed that ethical systems had evolved from human interactions. They both relied on a naturalistic approach (rather than employing any supernatural factors), used biological metaphors, and favoured material and mechanical explanations.

But there were significant differences between them. Spencer was more Lamarckian that Darwin in the sense of giving greater emphasis to acquired characteristics and of conceiving an overall goal toward which evolution was headed. For Spencer, the outcome of human evolution was clear: a utopian industrial society where duty became pleasure, mutual aid replaced competition, and the greatest possible individual freedom existed. Darwin held a much more open-ended view of man. He saw duty as adaptive, and he was less predictive, less prescriptive, and a little less optimistic (not that Spencer was a simple-minded Pollyanna, as he is occasionally portrayed).

Evolutionary ethics, then, from the very beginning had different interpretations. And, it is not surprising that it developed in a variety of directions and elicited a range of reactions. It was incorporated, co-opted, opposed, altered, but rarely ignored in the last quarter of the nineteenth century by those who were interested in the nature of man and the moral sentiment.

Evolutionary ethics received attention in large part because of the timing of its appearance. As intellectual historians have noted, beginning in the 1870s there was a 'crisis of conscience' in Victorian thought, or – another way of phrasing it – there was an intense re-examination of the basic assumptions of society. In attempting to understand the origin of this intellectual upheaval, historians point to the dramatic development of nineteenth-century science, the influx of 'higher criticism' from Germany, and the massive social consequences of the industrial revolution, all of which undermined a literal interpretation of Scripture, and in the opinion of many at the time, the entire framework of Christianity and its associated morality.

It was, philosophically, an exciting time (chaos seems conducive to philosophizing), and many different intellectual currents were competing for attention. Evolutionary ethics was one. For such men as John Fiske in the United States and Leslie Stephen in England, evolutionary ethics was a vital component of what they hoped would be a new worldview. Fiske, an ardent admirer of Spencer, believed that evolution pointed the way to a reborn Christianity.[7] Stephen, who was more Darwinian, looked to evolution for a foundation of an agnostic, liberal morality.[8]

All the proponents of evolutionary ethics capitalized on the popularity of the theory of evolution. There were, however, many questions raised about the validity of basing ethics on evolution. Ironically, two of the important critics were leading protagonists of the theory of evolution: Thomas Henry Huxley and Alfred Russel Wallace. They opposed evolutionary ethics for different reasons, however.

THOMAS HENRY HUXLEY

One would, I think, have expected Thomas Henry Huxley to be sympathetic to evolutionary ethics: after all, he was known to argue for naturalistic interpretations in general, and took particular delight in theology-bashing. But quite to the contrary, Huxley was very unhappy with attempts to use evolution as a moral guide. In his Romanes Lecture (1893) he stated that nature was no guide for ethics: 'Let us understand, once for all, that the ethical process of society depends, not on imitating the cosmic process, still less in running away from it, but in combating it.'[9]

Although typical of Huxley's rhetoric, these remarks were very surprising from one of the leading proponents of naturalism, and historians have tended to focus on his political views (reform liberal) to explain his position. They have pointed out how he was offended by Spencer's espousal of a free reign of natural law in the human domain, and was equally bothered by socialist doctrines that claimed an evolutionary foundation.[10]

Huxley may have had political views that explain his antipathy to evolutionary ethics, but he also had very strong intellectual reservations, and he used *them* as the justification for his opposition. Those ideas were of considerable historical importance because they entered the debate on evolutionary ethics and were extensively quoted.

Huxley went back to the writings of Hume to make the point that describing what 'is' does not give us leave to proscribe what 'ought' to be (the famous is/ought distinction). Of perhaps greater interest, he elaborated on his view that man had a dual nature. That is, humans were physical beings, but ones that possessed freedom, consciousness, and moral intuition. It was an awkward intellectual position. Seventeenth-century writers who held a dual nature of man had been working in a tradition where the supernatural was a part of natural history. Huxley's commitment to naturalism created a dilemma, for unlike his seventeenth-century forebears he renounced the use of a deity from which to suspend the human mind and morality. Intuitive morality had been regarded as a key component of Victorian religious sentiment, and when science and religion were divorced, as Huxley believed proper, morality was orphaned. So Huxley was in the uncomfortable situation of holding that the evidence for God's existence was inconclusive and therefore could not be the font of morality, but also holding that nature was not a replacement for God in establishing morality. He was left with the unsatisfactory legacy of his evangelical background, that morality is an intuitive emotion. In a work on Hume (1878) Huxley wrote:

> In which ever way we look at the matter, morality is based on feeling, not on reason; though reason alone is competent to trace out the effects of our actions and thereby dictate conduct. Justice is founded on the love of one's neighbor; and goodness is a kind of beauty. The moral law, like the laws of physical nature, rests in the long run upon instinctive intuitions, and is neither more nor less 'innate' and 'necessary' than they are.[11]

Thomas Henry Huxley was not alone in his rejection of evolutionary ethics. Other naturalists with equally strong evolutionary credentials were also unhappy with it. Alfred Russel Wallace, for instance, was quite outspoken. He disagreed with the attempts of Darwinians to use natural selection to account for human progress as the basis of human action. He also disagreed with Spencer's materialistic teleology, and instead saw in spiritualism the answer to man's moral meaning. Wallace was but one of several scientists who were drawn to spiritualism at this time.[12] To consider the history of spiritualism would take us too far from our subject. All that is necessary for present purposes is to note that from the very beginning the issue of man was highly problematic for evolution theory: humans undoubtedly had a physical nature, but how to account for their cultural development was not clear.

EARLY DEBATES OVER EVOLUTIONARY ETHICS

The reception of evolutionary ethics is a complicated story, for to do the subject justice we need to consider more than a few major intellectual figures. And when we look at what was written on the subject between, say, 1870 and 1890, we encounter an interesting aspect of the early history of evolutionary ethics, i.e., it was a multifaceted debate with no central forum. One cannot easily locate a 'debate' over evolutionary ethics. If one looks for books or articles on the topic there are few. Yet the subject was discussed, usually in the context of related issues such as eugenics or social reform.

In part, this lack of a defined form was a consequence of the fact that modern intellectual disciplines (e.g., philosophy) were just coming into being. It was after all, only in the period between the 1860s and 1880s that in England what is called the 'revolution of the dons' took place – i.e., teaching and scholarship became serious professions in the university. Formerly most university positions were temporary steps in an ecclesiastical career.[13] The specialization that has come to characterize modern academia was unknown. This may make some of us nostalgic for the good old days of the generalist, but it does not make it easy to map the intellectual terrain. The only simple part of the story seems to be that there was wide consensus on what the 'received morality' was. The main issue was to justify it.

What was opinion like on evolutionary ethics? If we judge the reception from the literature of the time, we can distinguish a broad range of ideas. For convenience, I have divided the reaction of the reading public into the general public, the intellectual circles, and the professional philosophers.

The *general reading public* held that the topic of morality was the prerogative of the church. Needless to say, there was not much agreement on what that meant. The more educated among the general population regarded the morality of Scripture to be incompatible with their sense of moral justice (i.e., they believed man could be improved and was not the depraved creature Christianity often made him out to be), and therefore they wished to reform religious teaching on ethics. The majority, however, continued as it had for decades: with common sense guides to socially sanctioned action plus conformity to specific creeds.

Although the growing secularism of the century eroded the place of the church in people's lives, what replaced it was not a faith in rationality (as intellectual historians might hope) but rather an amalgam of ideas: typically a mix from early religious education plus the maxims of popular writers (like Samuel Smiles) on the norms of industrial society. One gets unlikely (and unconscious) combinations of Comte, Paley, Spencer, plus the Golden Rule (rather than converts to Kant, Mill, or evolutionary ethics. Not surprisingly, then, when one encounters a reference to evolutionary ethics it is generally negative.

The *intellectual public*, i.e., the well-educated part of the population, whose opinions are reflected in the high quality reviews, was equally unenthusiastic. Although there was no direct debate over evolutionary ethics, none the less it was an important component of general discussions on ethics, positivism, science and religion, utilitarianism, etc. In articles on such topics, Darwinian positions were not generally distinguished from Spencerian ones, and both were treated critically. For example, if one looks at the issues of the *Contemporary Review*, a review with a broad range of perspectives, between 1866 to 1900, one finds that three quarters of the discussions of evolutionary ethics were unfavourable.

What about the *professional philosophers*? Philosophers were nearly unanimous in rejecting evolutionary ethics. The leading moral philosopher at Cambridge in last quarter of nineteenth century was Henry Sidgwick. He was a philosopher of major importance in the history of ethics, and is often described as the transitional figure between classical utilitarianism and modern moral philosophy. His most famous work, *Methods of Ethics* (1874), surveyed the major positions in ethics and attempted to synthesize them. In that book, he noted that he had

> avoided the inquiry into the Origin of the Moral Faculty ... [for] If it be admitted that we now have the faculty ... it appears to me that the investigation of the historical antecedents of this cognition, and of its relation to other elements of the mind, no more properly belongs to Ethics than the corresponding questions as to the cognition of Space belong to Geometry.[14]

He could be quite biting in his dismissal of evolutionary ethics, e.g., he wrote of it:

> Current philosophical notions characteristic of the most recently accepted system or manner of thought in any age and country are apt to exercise over men's minds an influence which is often in inverse ratio to the clearness with which the notions themselves are conceived, and the evidence for the philosophical doctrines implied in their acceptance is examined and estimated.[15]

(One can only imagine what he would have said about post-modernism.)

Although Sidgwick may have disdained evolutionary ethics (especially Spencer's version), good academic that he was, he was careful in his analysis. Indeed, most of the standard arguments against evolutionary ethics originated with him. His major objections were that justification of evolutionary ethics consisted of either (1) going from the description of moral belief to a belief in its validity or (2) going from a description of the 'natural state' of things (man, society, etc.) to using that state as the foundation for ethics. The first, Sidgwick said merely tells us about customs, and is of no value to ethics. The second (still hotly debated among philosophers), he argued, is a confused view because any impulse, desire, tendency, is 'natural'. How then do we choose what we take as significantly natural without some prior justified criterion? As for Spencer's 'future' perfect state, the future holds no sanction for us: what will be, will be – good, bad, indifferent, and we are under no obligation to help bring about any particular future state (unless we have some justification for doing so).

Sidgwick defined ethics as the systematic examination of right/wrong with an eye towards constructing a rational system of moral ideas. According to his view, evolutionary ethics was not an ethical system or method since it tended to focus on the origin of the moral sentiment and the history of customs, rather than the construction of a systematic, rational justification for action. To him it was an annoying popularized notion, not quite as vulgar as patent medicine, but no more to be trusted.

At Oxford, Thomas Hill Green was equally critical.[16] Although a personal friend of Sidgwick's, Green was far removed from him philosophically. Green was an Hegelian, which might lead us to think he would look favourably on a developmental ethical position, but Green was searching for a divine plan in human history, not a naturalistic ethic. Of greater importance, Green believed that moral obligation was a matter of man freely choosing to conform to *the* divine plan. Since Sidgwick and Hill were the leading figures in moral philosophy in the last quarter of the nineteenth century, it is not surprising that evolutionary ethics never made any significant inroads in academic philosophy (in Great Britain or in the United States).

By the early part of the twentieth century, it looked like the entire subject of evolutionary ethics would be consigned to that great dustbin of the mind, labelled, 'merely of historical interest'.

There were some popular writers who took up evolutionary ethics, e.g., Benjamin Kidd (Great Britain) and Dr Woods Hutchinson (United States), each of whom developed widely read versions.[17] But philosophers were relentless in their disdain. In Cambridge, G. E. Moore tried to silence forever any variety of evolutionary ethics with an assault on the general topic of naturalistic ethics.[18] On the American side of the Atlantic, pragmatists like Dewey stressed the importance of evolution for an understanding of man, but rejected it as a guide for behaviour. Although Dewey recognized the evolutionary background of the moral sentiment, he held that morality existed only when an individual freely chose the good. The criteria for judging what was the 'good' did not rest on determining whether or not it led to the greatest good, the survival of society, etc., but rather had to be evaluated in its specific context and with an eye to how it solved the immediate problem at hand.[19]

In spite, then, of seemingly fatal intellectual wounds, academic ostracism, and guilt by association, evolutionary ethics did not disappear. This shows the danger of prediction in intellectual history, and why historians are loath to make them. One certainly would have expected evolutionary ethics to have sunk into oblivion during the twentieth century: in addition to all the above, evolutionary explanations in general were on the wane. For example, in anthropology 'functional explanation' tended to replace evolutionary ones; in psychology, the experimental approach and the rise of behaviourism was hostile to evolutionary explanation; and ideas of 'progress', which were linked to evolutionary ethics were seriously called into question after the First World War.

Evolutionary ethics, however, was picked up after the war by a few biological scientists, who were committed to creating a humanist world-view founded on evolution, and who believed that evolutionary ethics was an important component of such a view. These individuals also were influenced by the psychoanalytic movement, which they believed gave them a new way to deal with moral obligation, one hopefully that would surmount the objections of academic philosophers.

JULIAN HUXLEY AND C. H. WADDINGTON

The principal figures in this second chapter of the history of evolutionary ethics were Julian Huxley and C. H. Waddington. Huxley was the more important of the two. He was, of course, one of the main architects of the Modern Synthesis, the neo-Darwinian theory that reasserted Darwin's original emphasis on natural selection of small, random variation as the central driving force of evolution. But Julian Huxley had greater ambitions. In Spencerian fashion he envisioned a grand synthesis to fill the spiritual void that he, and his brother, Aldous, saw as resulting from the collapse of the Victorian world-view after the war, and the decline of the validity of organized religion in the face of modern science. Intellectuals like the Huxleys confronted an unsettling array of new cults, which were competing to replace the declining new creeds. Widespread economic and social unrest underscored the problem as one that was more than just of academic interest.

Julian Huxley believed that evolution was a progressive process, and that it had cosmic, biological, and psycho-social stages. Human evolution, the final stage, was unique in that it involved the development of a single species, and was not the result of any biological trend. Rather human evolution was due to rapid cultural evolution based on cumulative, transmitted knowledge. Huxley – through a rather tortured argument – claimed that human progress was the only possible avenue of progress left in the entire evolutionary process. The responsibility of future progress was left to man.

Human evolution, according to Huxley, was not measured in terms of adaptation, but rather was judged by the fulfilment of human possibilities and the formation of values. Ethics, then, featured very centrally in Huxley's overall scheme.

Fifty years after his grandfather, Julian Huxley gave the Romanes Lecture, and like Thomas Henry Huxley, he stated that there was a discontinuity between man and the rest of nature. Julian Huxley, however, thought that he could explain our 'intuitive' sense of right and wrong, and in his lecture he discussed moral obligation and ethical standards from a psychological and evolutionary point of view.[20]

Huxley explained our sense of moral obligation by tying it to the Freudian concept of the super-ego. From this perspective an internalized authority permitted our sense of guilt to repress aggression, and was the source of our sense of 'wrong' and of 'duty'.

Huxley realized that his account of obligation in terms of individual psychology left open the question of group standards. These he argued should be based on what leads to human fulfilment i.e., what humans judge of intrinsic value (not adaptive value). Huxley, of course, had very specific ideas about what would promote the fulfilment of man, and elaborated a liberal vision of a democratic society guided by rational and scientific knowledge.

Huxley's utopian vision never caught on. I suspect that the reason is simple: the position was intellectually bankrupt. Leaving aside the issue of the acceptance of Freudian psychology, a psychological account of why we 'feel' obligation has nothing to say about its validity. Even Huxley realized this, stating that our sense of guilt had to be rationally tempered otherwise we become psychologically abnormal.

His treatment of ethical standards was equally flawed. Huxley claimed that our standards should be based on the pursuit of 'intrinsically valuable' goals. But questions immediately arise: intrinsically valuable to whom and in what sense valuable? Huxley's position was clear: he was referring to aesthetic, spiritual, and intellectual experiences. They were the avenues where future progress would lead. But those experiences are part of what we call 'high culture'. Such 'culture' can be viewed very differently: as tools of repression, products of vanity, commodities, etc. Jerry Falwell, Jacques Derrida, Dan Quayle, William Bennett, and Noam Chomsky (to name just a few) would probably differ with Julian Huxley about the significance of high culture as well as what was 'intrinsically valuable'.

Although Huxley sketched a lofty vision in his attempt to create a twentieth-century secular myth, his writings did little to further the acceptance of evolutionary ethics. Nor did those of C. H. Waddington who recognized the circularity of Julian Huxley's view and attempted to go beyond it by stating that the 'good' was what furthers human evolution. By human evolution, Waddington meant human cultural evolution. But this criterion was hardly an improvement over Huxley's, for 'furthering human evolution' was too broad a standard. Man's history was filled with change; which changes were good? As might be suspected, according to Waddington they were the ones he valued.[21]

E. O. WILSON

Evolutionary ethics, then, had a second chance to die a natural death. But, phoenix-like, it reemerged in the 1970s. This time it was associated with the synthesis of animal behaviour and evolution theory, or what is popularly called *Sociobiology*.

E. O. Wilson's classic text (1975) by that name is a brilliant discussion that pulls together research from the Modern Synthesis, population biology, and ethnology. The central thesis of the book is that behaviour is adaptive and can be understood best from an evolutionary perspective.

Nor just animal behaviour, but, according to Wilson and other writers inspired by him, human behaviour, human values, and (of importance to us) ethics. Wilson wrote in the final chapter of *Sociobiology*: 'Scientists and humanists should consider together the possibility that the time has come for ethics to be removed temporarily from the hands of the philosophers and biologicized.'[22]

Well, by this point, the historian is ready to throw up his floppy disks and scream, 'hasn't anybody been reading about what's been said on this topic during the past hundred years?' The adaptive value of behaviour (or genes, or behavioural tendencies, or cultural units) whether we think of it in terms of inclusive fitness, tooth and claw competition, or whatever, has no intrinsic philosophical significance, and even if it did, is so all-encompassing as to be ethically meaningless.

Although the new evolutionary ethics avoids some of the circular reasoning of earlier versions, none the less the basic thrust is to relate behaviour to evolutionary genetics, and accordingly, as part of our instinctive mental make up morality is thought to have an adaptive function. E. O. Wilson is blunt about his assumptions. He writes: 'The essence of the argument ... is that the brain exists because it promotes the survival and multiplication of the genes that direct its assembly. The human mind is a device for survival and reproduction.'[23]

Central to the discussions of the evolutionary significance of morality is the nature of altruism – unselfish behaviour. Various compelling explanations of altruism, based on the idea that such behaviour is in the best interest of increasing copies of our genes in the next generation are widely accepted. And, leaving aside the question of accuracy in using terms like 'selfish' and 'altruistic' in situations where conscious choice is not a factor, we can see the temptation of trying to gain insight into human actions based on what we hypothesize about animals.

But such an extrapolation raises the issue of the origin of culture, for any discussion of altruism, values, kin-relationship, etc., has to be related to the cultural milieu in which it occurs. Here the subject clouds over. Sociobiologists differ in their assessments, and these differences are quite important. Most sociobiologists do not believe that human culture is directly determined by our genes, but many hold that either through some genetic-cultural interaction, or through 'tendencies' that individuals inherit, perhaps we can better understand existing moral codes. Richard Alexander, for instance, believes that an 'evolutionary analysis can tell us much about our history and existing systems of laws and norms, and also about how to achieve any goals deemed desirable'.[24]

But the key issue, let us not forget, is can evolution be a guide? Many sociobiologists are sceptical. Richard Alexander, just quoted above, for instance, immediately adds to his statement on the value of evolutionary analysis that it 'has essentially nothing to say about what goals are desirable, or the directions in which laws and norms should be modified in the future'.[25]

Wilson, and those who want to fashion a new evolutionary ethics, however, claim more for the insights of sociobiology. Although he admits that cultural evolution can include non-Darwinian dimensions (i.e., we cannot explain all morality in simple reductionist terms), Wilson makes the following statement:

> Can the cultural evolution of higher ethical values gain a direction and momentum of its own and completely replace genetic evolution? I think not ... Human behavior – like the deepest capacities for emotional

> response which drive and guide it – is the circuitous technique by which human genetic material has been and will be kept intact. Morality has no other demonstrable ultimate function.[26]

How does this translate into a plan of action? That is, what can the biologist provide moral discourse? Wilson is adamant that, 'ethical philosophy must not be left in the hands of the merely wise ... only hard-won empirical knowledge of our biological nature will allow us to make optimum choices among the competing criteria of progress.'[27] He tells us that in spite of the 'hodgepodge of special genetic adaptations to an environment largely vanished', man can break through the human predicament by an 'exercise of will':[28]

> The principal task of human biology is to identify and to measure the constraints that influence the decisions of ethical philosophers and everyone else, and to infer their significance through neurophysiological and phylogenetic reconstructions of the mind ... In the process it will fashion a biology of ethics, which will make possible the selection of a more deeply understood and enduring code of moral values.[29]

In practice, what Wilson does is to derive his own American liberalism from evolutionary premises. Whether or not there is a crypto-conservative edge to this position, or a latent racism, sexism, vegetarianism, or whatever, is really beside the point. What he has done suffers from the philosophical flaws of earlier systems, and is just as patently *ad hoc*. The post-Vietnam period has witnessed a spectacular growth of the life sciences, and public figures increasingly have been tempted to seek quick fixes to intractable social problems by looking to science. It is, therefore, not surprising that the popular press has drawn attention to attempts at understanding human nature in biological terms. But given today's stringently analytical philosophy community, it should come as no shock that its silence on Wilson, *et al.* has been deafening. There are a few exceptions, e.g., Michael Ruse. But statements of his like 'morality is a collective illusion foisted upon us by our genes'[30] have not done much to convince other philosophers, or the general educated public. So, once again, the restless spirit of evolutionary ethics has the opportunity of eternal rest.

WHAT DOES THE STORY TELL US?

I think that the history of evolutionary ethics shows that evolutionary theory, has provided a powerful 'invitation' to develop an ethics. Theories that tell us of our origin often map our destiny. But the theory of evolution has not helped us much with human values. Although a crisis in Anglo-American ethics has long existed it seems unlikely to me that it will be solved by looking for answers in the physical or biological sciences. The main value of looking at the dismal history of evolutionary ethics, then, is to direct our attention away from simple answers and blind alleys. We need to realize that values and their origins are embedded in a human cultural context. Biological evolution may be a precondition for culture, and it may even help us understand some of our deepest promptings. It is unable, however, to yield the answers we seek for ethical questions.

The history of evolutionary ethics also underscores the danger of accepting facile links between nature and society. Gleaning social lessons from nature should make anyone familiar with history uncomfortable. This, of course, does not mean that we can naively separate nature and society. Superficial judgements, however, about what is 'natural', or abstract intellectualizations of the 'natural state' of humans – or forests, for that matter – are not likely to be particularly productive. Such facile links, more likely, will distract us from exploring potentially fruitful avenues rather than providing keys for answers.

NOTES

1 For a more extensive discussion, see Paul Lawrence Farber, *The Temptations of Evolutionary Ethics* (Berkeley, 1994).

2 Charles Darwin, *The Descent of Man, and Selections in Relation to Sex* (London, 1871), p. 70.

3 *Ibid.*, pp. 71–2.

4 *Ibid.*, pp. 165–6.

5 For an interesting discussion of Spencer's social writings, see David Wiltshire, *The Social and Political Thought of Herbert Spencer* (Oxford, 1978). For a sympathetic account of Spencer's ethical writings and of evolutionary ethics, in general, see Robert Richards, *Darwin and the Emergence of Evolutionary Theories of Mind and Behavior* (Chicago, 1987).

6 Herbert Spencer, *The Principles of Sociology* (New York, 1898), III, p. 611.

7 See especially John Fiske, *Through Nature to God* (Boston, 1899).

8 See Leslie Stephen, *The Science of Ethics* (London, 1882). On Stephen's background and context, see Noel Annan, *Leslie Stephen. The Godless Victorian* (New York, 1984).

9 Thomas Henry Huxley, *Evolution and Ethics*, in Thomas Henry Huxley, *Collected Essays* (London, 1893–4), IX, p. 4. Huxley's *Evolution and Ethics* has been reprinted by Princeton University Press (1989) with a highly useful introduction by James Paradis. Also see James Paradis, *T.H. Huxley: Man's Place in Nature* (Lincoln, 1978).

10 See, for example, Michael Helfand, 'T. H. Huxley's "Evolution and Ethics":

'The Politics of Evolution and the Evolution of Politics', *Victorian Studies*, 20, 2 (1977), 159–77.

11 Huxley, *Collected Essays*, VI, p. 239. The position, to be sure, is a problematic one. For an interesting discussion of the difficulty Victorians like Huxley faced, see A. O. J. Cockshut, *The Unbelievers. English Agnostic Thought 1840–1890* (New York, 1966).

12 Spiritualism and its relationship to British science and philosophy has a complex history. For an excellent introduction, see Janet Oppenheim, *The Other World. Spiritualism and Psychical Research in England, 1850–1914* (Cambridge, 1985).

13 See A. J. Engel, *From Clergyman to Don: The Rise of the Academic Profession in Nineteenth-Century Oxford* (Oxford, 1983), and Sheldon Rothblatt, *The Revolution of the Dons: Cambridge and Society in Victorian England* (London, 1968). A similar revolution took place in the United States starting in the 1860s. See Laurence Veysey, *The Emergence of the American University* (Chicago, 1965).

14 Henry Sidgwick, *The Methods of Ethics*, 7th edn (London, 1907), pp. v–vi. For an excellent introduction to Sidgwick's thought, see J. B. Schneewind, *Sidgwick's Ethics and Victorian Moral Philosophy* (Oxford, 1977).

15 Henry Sidgwick, 'The Theory of Evolution in Its Application to Practice', *Mind*, 1, 1 (1876), 52. For Sidgwick's critique also see Henry Sidgwick, *Lectures on the Ethics of T.H. Green, Mr. Herbert Spencer, and J. Martineau* (London, 1902).

16 For Green's opinion, see Thomas Hill Green, *Prolegomena to Ethics* (Oxford, 1883). A good introduction to Hill's thought and its influence is Melvin Richter, *The Politics of Conscience: T.H. Green and His Age* (London, 1964).

17 See Benjamin Kidd, *Social Evolution* (London, 1894) and *The Science of Power* (New York, 1918). For a useful introduction to Kidd, see D. P. Crook, *Benjamin Kidd: Portrait of a Social Darwinist* (Cambridge, 1984). For Hutchinson, see Woods Hutchinson, *The Gospel According to Darwin* (Chicago, 1898). A good introduction to Hutchinson and his context is in James C. Whorton, *Crusaders for Fitness* (Princeton, 1982).

18 See George Edward Moore, *Principia Ethica* (Cambridge, 1903). For a discussion of Moore's critique of earlier ethical positions, see Thomas Baldwin, *G.E. Moore* (London, 1990), and for a discussion of his immediate impact, see Tom Regan, *Bloomsbury's Prophet: G.E. Moore and the Development of His Moral Philosophy* (Philadelphia, 1986).

19 See John Dewey and James H. Tufts, *Ethics* (New York, 1980). For a sympathetic discussion of Dewey's ethics, see H. S. Thayer, *Meaning and Action: A Critical History of Pragmatism* (Indianapolis, 1968).

20 Julian Huxley, *Evolutionary Ethics* (Oxford, 1943). For a discussion of Huxley's worldview, see John Greene, *Science, Ideology, and Worldview* (Berkeley, 1981), and his article 'The Interaction of Science and World View in Sir Julian Huxley's Evolutionary Biology', *Journal of the History of Biology*, 23, 1 (1990), 39–55.

21 See C. H. Waddington, *Science and Ethics* (London, 1942), and *The Ethical Animal* (London, 1960).

22 Edward O. Wilson, *Sociobiology: The New Synthesis* (Cambridge, MA, 1975), p. 564.

23 Edward O. Wilson, *On Human Nature* (Cambridge, MA, 1978), 2. Wilson's *On Human Nature* contains his most developed discussions on evolutionary ethics. A

strident critique of the general position can be found in Mary Midgley, *Evolution as a Religion. Strange Hopes and Stranger Fears* (London, 1985). Robert Richards has attempted to defend the overall position in his *Darwin and the Emergence of Evolutionary Theories of Mind and Behavior*, and in his article, 'A Defense of Evolutionary Ethics', *Biology and Philosophy*, 1, 3 (1986), 265–93.

24 Richard Alexander, *Darwinism and Human Affairs* (Seattle, 1979), p. 200. Also see Florian von Schilcher and Neil Tennant, *Philosophy, Evolution and Human Nature* (London, 1984).

25 *Ibid.*

26 Wilson, *On Human Nature*, p. 167.

27 *Ibid.*, p. 7.

28 *Ibid.*, p. 196.

29 *Ibid.*

30 Michael Ruse, *Taking Darwin Seriously. A Naturalistic Approach to Philosophy* (Oxford, 1986), p. 253.

EIGHTEEN

MAPPING THE HUMAN GENOME IN THE LIGHT OF HISTORY

MIKULÁŠ TEICH

THE aim of this essay is to contribute from a historical perspective to the debate about the Human Genome Project (HGP). The term covers several research programmes geared to the mapping and sequencing of total DNA (deoxyribonucleic acid) of the human cell that emerged in the mid-1980s in the USA. Coordinated by the Human Genome Organization (HUGO), they now operate throughout the world under the auspices of public and private organizations.[1] Broadly speaking, mapping is concerned with the allocation of genes to chromosomes and sequencing with the determination of the order of the nucleotide bases in the gene's DNA. About the gene, a crucial concept in the history of genetics, more will be said. As to the persistent debate, it ranges widely indeed over scientific, technical, medical, legal, commercial, ethical, philosophical and a host of other matters. They clearly indicate manifold threads that link the HGP both to nature and society. What follows is an attempt, giving consideration to this connection, to approach the HGP from a historical standpoint.

This is all the more necessary in view of unfading (but by no means negligible) inaccuracies and confusions to be found in accounts of the historical development of genetics and human genetics respectively of which the HGP is a part.

THE BEGINNINGS OF HUMAN GENETICS: ARCHIBALD EDWARD GARROD

This comment applies to much of what continues to be written about the beginnings of human genetics, commonly associated with the publication of Garrod's paper on alkaptonuria in 1902.[2] A. E. Garrod, who was a clinician interested in urinary pigments, studied alkaptonuria – a relatively rare and harmless condition – indicated by a dark urine. This is due to the presence of a chemical, homogentisic acid, normally not found there. Apparently, Garrod's first observation with genetic implications goes back to 1899 when he put forward the idea that alkaptonuria was not so much a disease as a peculiar variation from normal metabolism with a familial history.[3] Returning to this point in his 1902 paper, Garrod was struck by its prevalence in children of first cousins. Though Garrod provided the impetus for thinking about alkaptonuria in genetic terms, the claim that he 'was first to demonstrate Mendelian transmission of a character in man' cannot be sustained.[4] What can be stated is that he was influenced by William Bateson, the prominent English protagonist, with whom he corresponded. It was Bateson who, apparently, first suggested that alkaptonuria was an instance of a rare recessive condition in man, which could be explained along Mendelian lines.[5] According to Garrod, Bateson's use of 'the law of heredity discovered by Mendel offers a reasonable account'[6] of a condition such as alkaptonuria. Garrod remained sympathetic towards a Mendelian approach to hereditary metabolic disorders. He thought that they could be traced to interferences in the normal intermediate pathway and accumulation of abnormal metabolites due to the absence of appropriate enzymes. In the case of alkaptonuria, Garrod connected the appearance of homogentisic acid with the failure of the breakdown of the amino acid tyrosine present in dietary proteins. He set down this much in the two editions of *Inborn Errors of Metabolism.*[7] What he did not advance was that 'the blocks in metabolic pathways' were 'caused by abnormalities on particular genes'.[8]

BIOCHEMICAL INDIVIDUALITY AND VARIABILITY

Such a statement is ahistorical not only because Garrod appears not to have familiarized himself with the term 'gene', coined by the Danish scientist W. L. Johannsen in 1909 but, more significantly, because it neglects the historical context of Garrod's interpretation of alkaptonuria as a 'chemical individuality' or 'chemical sport' – that is, the contemporary discussions regarding the nature of inheritable variation, including the evolutionary role of natural selection. Thus in a letter to W. Bateson (14 January 1902) Garrod wrote:[9]

> I have for some time been collecting information as to specific and individual differences of metabolism, which seems to me to be a little explored but promising field in relation to natural selection, and I believe that no two individuals are exactly alike chemically any more than structurally. I fancy that monstrosities or rather malformations, vestigial remnants and individual differences all have their chemical analogues.

Indeed, it is apparent from Garrod's writing in this area that he was espousing the idea that, in order to understand species formation, chemical knowledge has to be called into play – not a run-of-the-mill view. This certainly emerges not only from his seminal article in *The Lancet*, but also from his later *Inborn Errors of Metabolism*. There consistent with his concerns with the chemical aspects of speciation and their relations to evolutionary processes in nature, Garrod argued:[10]

> Nor can it be supposed that the diversity of chemical structure and process stops at the boundary of the species, and that within that boundary, which has no real finality, rigid uniformity reigns. Such a conception is at variance with any evolutionary conception of the nature and origin of species. The existence of chemical individuality follows of necessity from that of chemical specificity, but we should expect the differences between individuals to be still more subtle and difficult of detection ... Upon chemical as upon structural variations the factors which make for evolution have worked and are working.

In this connection it is of more than passing interest to note the changes in the titles of chapters 1 and 2 in the two editions of *Inborn Errors of Metabolism*. In the first edition chapter 1 is simply called 'The inborn errors of metabolism'. In the second edition, chapter 1 subdivides, as it were, into two chapters. Chapter 1 is now called: 'The chemistry of the species and of the individual' and chapter 2: 'The incidence and heredity of inborn errors of metabolism'.

It is intriguing to trace Garrod's ideas regarding the use of chemistry as a means of deeper comprehension of the species concept. Here doubtless the major influence was K. H. Huppert, the Professor of Medical Chemistry at the German University of Prague, who also worked in the field of alkaptonuria. In *The Lancet* article Huppert (together with [Sir] William Osler, the Regius Professor of Physick at Oxford) is specifically thanked by Garrod 'for invaluable aid in collecting information' but the extent of Huppert's influence cannot be judged only by this acknowledgement. Indeed, it can be shown that Garrod's interpretation of alkaptonuria as an example of metabolic individuality or variation of chemical behaviour profited from Huppert's efforts to develop the subject. Huppert chose to discuss it in his Rectorial Address *Über die Erhaltung der Arteigenschaften*, given in 1895 and published a year later, but not easy to get hold of nowadays. The following quotation from *The Lancet* article testifies to the way in which Huppert's chemical approach to biological phenomena in general, and heredity in particular, appealed to Garrod:[11]

> If it be, indeed, the case that in alkaptonuria and the other conditions mentioned we are dealing with individualities of metabolism and not with

> the results of morbid processes the thought naturally presents itself that these are merely extreme examples of variations of chemical behaviour which are probably everywhere present in minor degrees and that just as no two individuals of a species are absolutely identical in bodily structure neither are their chemical processes carried out on exactly the same lines. Such minor chemical differences will obviously be far more subtle than those of form, for whereas the latter are evident to any careful observer the former will only be revealed by elaborate chemical methods, including painstaking comparisons of the intake and output of the organism. This view that there is no rigid uniformity of chemical processes in the individual members of a species, probably as it is *a priori*, may also be arrived at by a wholly different line of argument. There can be no question that between that the families, genera and species both of the animal and vegetable kingdoms, differences exist both of chemical composition and of metabolic processes. The evidences for this are admirably set forth in a most suggestive address delivered by Professor Huppert in 1895. In it he points out that we find evidence of chemical specificity of important constituents of the body, such as the haemoglobins of different animals, as well as in their secretory and excretory products such as the bile acids and the cynuric acid of the urine of dogs ... To the above examples may be added the results of F.G. Hopkins's well-known researches on the pigments of the pieridae and the recent observations of the precipitation of the blood proteids of one kind of animal by the serum of another.

Garrod's reference to investigations of Frederick Gowland Hopkins (Nobel Prize for work on vitamins, 1929) on the pigment of the wings of pierid butterflies relating it to uric acid[12] (erroneously, as it turned out) goes some way to illumine their collaborative enterprises and lifelong friendship.[13] That is, they shared a common position in attaching importance to the study of peculiarities of metabolism. With Hopkins it was the problem of end products of nitrogen metabolism: urea as the principal excretion product for terrestrial vertebrates, but uric acid for reptiles and birds. According to the distinguished biochemist N. W. Pirie, who was close to Hopkins, the latter 'was fascinated by the teleologically rational use of insoluble uric acid in place of soluble urea as the main vehicle for nitrogen excretion by those animals which have a manner of life that necessitates the economical use of water'.[14]

THE VIRTUAL NEGLECT OF GARROD'S WORK BY GENETICISTS AND BIOCHEMISTS

Any discussion of the starting point of the modern study of human genetics necessarily involves this question but to my knowledge no satisfactory answer has been given yet. Regrettably, this has a good deal to do with the recurrent ignorance of the historical record, already attested by the two quotations from contemporary writings above. But other examples, including from not so recent literature, abound. Thus in 1979 the editors of a volume, containing a selection of historically important papers for the development of human genetics, had this to say about Garrod's notions of inborn errors of metabolism:[15]

> These notions had a profound influence on subsequent work by George Beadle and Edward Tatum, out of which grew the hypothesis 'one gene – one enzyme', that is, genes effect their role in development through the control of the structure and rates of syntheses of enzymes. This hypothesis was subsequently broadened to recognize that genes might control the structures and rates of syntheses of nonenzymic proteins as well.

The geneticist George W. Beadle and the biochemist Edward L. Tatum were awarded the Nobel Prize 'for their discovery that genes act by regulating chemical events' in 1958. In the lecture delivered on receiving the award Beadle paid great tribute to Garrod's perspicacity. But regarding the background to the investigations on the genetic control of metabolic reactions (in the bread mould *Neurospora*), set out in the early 1940s, Beadle pointed out:[16]

> What was later called the one-gene-one-enzyme concept was clearly in our minds at this time, although, as I remember, we did not so designate it. Ours was a scheme closely similar to that proposed by Garrod for alcaptonuria, except that he did not have genes that blocked an adjacent reaction in the sequence. but at the time we were unaware of Garrod's work, partly because geneticists were not in the habit of referring to it and partly because we had failed to explore the literature. Garrod's book was available in many libraries.

If Beadle's recollection is correct, his first acquaintance with the work of Garrod dates to about 1942. He certainly did not refer to it in print before 1945.[17] This may serve to underline that, contrary to repeated statements one encounters in literature, the investigations of Beadle and Tatum were neither based nor inspired by the work of Garrod.

As to the reason for the neglect of Garrod's work, Beadle attempted to deal with this problem before and after 1958. In 1950, at a meeting commemorating the Golden Jubilee of Genetics Beadle proclaimed that 'most geneticists were not yet inclined to think of hereditary traits in chemical terms'.[18] Fifteen years later, participating in a Mendel Centennial Symposium, he expressed his opinion as follows:[19]

> Geneticists evidently regarded alkaptonuria as just another Mendelian trait and failed completely to see the biochemical implications. Bio-

> chemists made the complementary error; that is, they regarded it as interesting biochemistry but did not recognize its genetic significance.

Whatever the merit of these or other statements regarding the common attitude among geneticists such as that 'human heredity was refractory to analysis and that little basic insight could be gained from studies of hereditary abnormalities in an organism that could not be held at will',[20] there is a need to look more deeply into the historical reasons for the lack of contact between genetics and biochemistry during the first half of the twentieth century. The crucial dividing issue, I argue, was the different focus on 'life'. For geneticists, who largely accepted August Weismann's hereditary theory of the continuity of the germ plasm, it became the nucleus, the bearer of discrete units of inheritance. For biochemists it became the whole living cell. In the words of F. G. Hopkins: 'we cannot, without gross misuse of terms, speak of the cell life as being associated with any one particular type of molecule'.[21]

It is worth remembering that when Garrod was publishing his observations on inborn metabolic errors involving simple molecules in an ascertainable, albeit defective, chain of enzyme reactions, Hopkins was generalizing these aspects by promoting the 'dynamic side of biochemical phenomena' as the conceptual framework of biochemistry. This was the theme of his renowned Presidential Address to the Physiology Section of the British Association in 1913. There Hopkins also drew attention to the general significance of Garrod's study of the successive enzyme-linked stages in the intermediate processes of metabolism based on the interaction of small molecules:[22]

> Extraordinarily profitable have been observations upon individuals suffering from those errors of metabolism which Dr. Garrod calls 'metabolic sports, the chemical analogues of structural malformations'. In these individuals, Nature has taken the first essential step in an experiment by omitting from their chemical structure a special catalyst which at one point in the procession of metabolic chemical events is essential to its continuance. At this point there is arrest, and intermediate products come to light.

From the point of view of Garrod and Hopkins, metabolism encompassed the processes of heredity as manifestations of life. It is the inadequate appreciation of the metabolic approach by the geneticists that offers the clue to the neglect of Garrod's work. The implication of this is to put the onus on the geneticists for the lack of contact between the fields of genetics and biochemistry. In effect, there is another as it were, dialectical, side of the story to be told that biochemists, while elucidating the intermediate stages of many fundamental biochemical reactions underlying cellular life, virtually excluded consideration of heredity as part of these studies. In this respect their perception of the world of living things was less inclusive than that of Garrod and Hopkins. There were a very few exceptions, among them the versatile J. B. S. Haldane, who by 1920 comprehended the fruitfulness of inquiring into heredity at the chemical level. This was perhaps a factor which led to him being appointed in 1922 to the newly established Readership in the Department of Biochemistry under Hopkins at Cambridge.[23]

In 1937 to celebrate Hopkins's 75th birthday his students and colleagues produced a volume of thirty-one essays, headed by Haldane's contribution characteristically called 'The biochemistry of the individual.' The following passage provides succinct evidence that Haldane subscribed to the Garrod-Hopkins approach to human genetics:[24]

> The ultimate aim of biochemistry may be stated as a complete account of intermediary metabolism, that is to say, of the transformations undergone by matter in passing through organisms. As there are probably several million species, each with its own biochemistry, the opportunities for research are by no means negligible ... The history of biochemistry shows that the study of individual abnormalities has been of enormous importance. Indeed, one whole branch of biochemistry arose from the study of human beings whose abnormalities had attracted the attention of men who thought along chemical lines ... The most interesting of all these abnormalities are, I think, the disturbances of intermediary metabolism.

To conclude this section the following comment by L. S. Penrose, a prominent British figure in the field of human genetics, is of historical interest:[25]

> It had formerly been widely believed that man was an unfavorable subject for genetical study because of his long life cycle and the lack of facility for experimental breeding. In fact the reverse is true. The human species is particularly well suited for the study of genetics, especially in relation to inborn chemical differences, and Garrod's work on the genetics of metabolic errors in man anticipated the discovery of biochemical mutants in lower organisms by four decades. At first, few scientists were aware of this discovery. The outstanding exception was Haldane, who constantly emphasized, sometimes against ignorant opposition, the importance of biochemical effects of gene mutations both in plants and in animals. The current belief thirty years ago, that Garrod's inborn errors were rare and, consequently, unimportant diseases, actually encouraged those who came in contact with Haldane's outlook. He had derived this partly from Bateson, he said, whose watchword was 'treasure your exceptions'. In 1935 Haldane's influence was shown in the nomenclature of phenylketonuria and on the first attempts to understand and to treat the condition.

THE GENE

I begin this section with a quotation from an editorial in *Science* (7 March 1986), frequently cited in accounts of events believed to have fostered the genome mapping and sequencing programme.[26]

> We are at a turning point in the study of tumor virology and cancer in general. If we wish to learn more about cancer, we must now concentrate on the cellular genome. Knowledge of the genome and availability of probes[27] for any gene would also be crucial for progress in human physiology and pathology outside cancer. An effort of this kind could not be undertaken by any single group: it would have to be a national effort. Its significance would be comparable to that of the effort that led to the conquest of space, and it should be carried out with the same spirit. Even more appealing would be to make it an international undertaking, *because the sequence of the human DNA is the reality of our species, and everything that is happening in the world depends on those sequences.* (My emphasis)

As it happens the author Renato Dulbecco, a Nobel laureate and a leader in cancer research, refers to sequencing but not to mapping.[28] This is not accidental but intimately linked with the facile promotion of the idea that DNA sequences underlie everything that makes human beings human, including their history. What we have here is a manifestation of biological determinism in our time that goes back to the Weismannian notion (launched in the 1880s) about the substance of the cell nucleus being the sole bearer of the heredity process. After the rediscovery of Mendel's work (1900), this deterministic trend in genetical thinking became intertwined with the gene theory.[29]

As already mentioned, the term 'gene' is due to the Danish worker Wilhelm Johannsen, who introduced it into literature, together with the terms 'genotype' and 'phenotype', in 1909.[30] Without going into historical detail let it be noted that Johannsen's concept of the gene was at once complex, subtle and vague:[31]

> The word gene is completely free of any hypothesis; it expresses only the certain fact, that many characters of the organism are somehow or other stipulated by the special, separable and consequently independent *states* [Zustände], *rudiments* [Grundlagen], or *predispositions* [Anlagen] which are present in the gametes – in short, by that which we now wish to designate as genes.

As to the phenotype, Johannsen associated with it palpable attributes of an individual living being:[32]

> The phenotype of an individual is thus the embodiment of all his expressed characters. The single organism, the individual plant, an

animal, a man, – 'What it is and what it does' – has its phenotype, i.e., it appears as a sum of traits which are determined by the interplay between 'inherited predispositions' and elements of the environment.

For Johannsen the phenotype represented an entity that 'can be directly described, measured, weighed, chemically analyzed etc., and is therefore without doubt a tangible reality'.[33] In comparison he regarded the genotype as[34]

> something which we reach by inference, though we nevertheless dare to hold that it is a real entity. But the genotype as such we cannot measure, weigh etc., and the demonstrable *differences* between genotypes we can only know through such differences in phenotypes to which they give rise in the organism in question.

Though the Johannsenian terms are still in use, we know little about the historical side of their assimilations by genetics. Consider Thomas Hunt Morgan[35] whose contributions to the study of heredity (in conjunction with his younger co-workers Calvin Bridges, Hermann Joseph Muller and Alfred Henry Sturtevant) established it as a research discipline in its own right between 1910 and 1915. This was achieved by combining[36]

> two previously separate lines of thought: the chromosomal theory, which maintained that the cell structures known as chromosomes were directly involved in hereditary transmission, and the Mendelian theory, which postulated hereditary factors that segregate and assort themselves in the production of eggs and sperm. The chromosomal theory was based on extensive cytological analysis of plant and animal cells starting in the 1850. The Mendelian theory was based on analysis of breeding results and had grown out of a long tradition of plant and animal hybridization.

The co-authored publication which underpinned the role of Morgan and his group as pioneering figures in the field of genetics was *The Mechanism of Mendelian Heredity* (1915). In it, according to the historian of science Nils Roll-Hansen, 'the classical concept of the gene is fully developed'.[37] The problem with this statement is that in the book the authors refer to 'factors' – the word 'gene' does not occur. 'The reason they chose not to use this term, which has since become so common', writes Morgan's biographer Allen, 'reflects the group's commitment to the belief that the chromosome theory provides a material basis for Mendelian heredity'.[38] It is noteworthy that in the paper usually regarded as the beginning of gene mapping, the author is committed to 'factors' rather than to 'genes'.[39]

Factor or gene? Does it matter? If we wish to reach a deeper historical understanding of the theoretical framework of genetics at the time of its formation as an independent discipline, then it matters to pay attention to the historical relations between the two concepts. The issue comes to the fore with the development of genetic maps which, as cogently stated by Roll-Hansen,[40]

> giving each factor its particular locus on the chromosome, contributed greatly to an *intuitive* [my emphasis-MT] understanding of the factors as things which existed independently of any characters that they might produce.

Ostensibly Morgan and his collaborators relinquished factors for genes soon after the publication of *The Mechanism of Mendelian Heredity*. As discrete hereditary entities located linearly on chromosomes ('strings of beads'), genes appeared to account more directly and plausibly for hereditary traits (characters) than unspecific factors.

Inevitably questions were asked about the nature of the gene. Morgan, at any rate, was not particularly concerned with finding an answer and in this respect his empiricist approach resembled that of Johannsen. In a celebrated passage in his Nobel lecture (1934) he expressed his opinion as follows:[41]

> What are genes? Now that we locate them in the chromosomes are we justified in regarding them as material units; as chemical bodies of a higher order than molecules? Frankly, these are questions with which the working geneticist has not much concern himself, except now and then to speculate as to the nature of the postulated elements. There is no consensus of opinion among geneticists as to what the genes are – whether they are real or purely fictitious – because of the level at which genetic experiments lie, it does not make the slightest difference whether the gene is a hypothetical unit, or whether the gene is a material particle. In either case the unit is associated with a specific chromosome, and can be localized there by purely genetic analysis. Hence, if a gene is material unit, it is a piece of a chromosome; if it is a fictitious unit, it must be referred to a definite location in the chromosome – the same place as in the other hypothesis. Therefore, it makes no difference in the actual work in genetics which point of view is taken.

Probably already at the time of Morgan's speech in Stockholm, most working geneticists did not share his empiricist indifference regarding the materiality of genes. This certainly was true of Morgan's outstanding student Muller, who had no doubt that the gene constituted a real, discrete, material genetic unit. This conception of the gene underlay Muller's prolific experimental activity which gained him an international reputation. In particular it was his demonstration, in 1927, that mutation rate was hugely accelerated by X-rays. 'Perhaps the last great discovery in genetics' – this was the opinion offered by Haldane in 1936 when he reflected on forty years of development in genetics since 1896.[42] It was for this contribution, enhanced by concerns about the effects of radiation following the dropping of atomic bombs in Japan, that Muller was awarded a Nobel Prize nineteen years later (1946).

In hailing his achievements, this is how Carlson assesses Muller's contribution to the conceptualization of the gene:[43]

> To Muller we owe the transformation of the gene concept from an inchoate term to the physical model of a linear ribbon with dimensions, boundaries, properties, organization, and stability: each of these features being characterized by his experiments in the two decades between the World Wars.

By the late 1930s, in fact, the theory of the linear arrangement of the genes in chromosomes – although still espoused – began to look simplistic. The chromosomes appeared to be threads composed of nucleic acid and proteins but as the author of a renowned book on genetics, published in 1939, concluded that while[44]

> ... a series of facts emerge which are extremely suggestive of an essential connection between nucleic acid and proteins, but whose exact significance cannot yet be stated ... the exact knowledge at our disposal is so meagre that very many alternative hypotheses are still possible as to the nature of the chromosome, and the gene in its different senses.

Although, as the subsequent sentences show, the manifest uncertainties regarding the nature of the gene did not prevent the writer from speculatively replacing the cell by the gene as the basic unit associated with life and therefore the key to its understanding:

> However, the enormously important effects of the genes on development, their capacity for identical reproduction, and the fact that they, rather than the cells of an earlier time, seem to be the most ultimate units into which we can analyse living organisms, make the problem of their constitution one of the most fundamental questions of biochemistry, well worthy of discussion even long before it can be fully answered.

Until 1944 when O. T. Avery, in collaboration with C. M. Macleod and M. McCarty, published their findings on the transformation of pneumococcal types, virtually no attention was paid to the role of nucleic acids in the heredity process *per se*. The main object of the Avery group was to isolate and chemically to identify the transforming principle.[45] Their discovery that it was probably a nucleic acid of the deoxyribose type constitutes a landmark on the road to the double helical structure of the DNA, including its replication, proposed by J. D. Watson and F. H. C. Crick in 1953.[46]

At the time common wisdom subscribed to the existence of two kinds of nucleic acids named after the sugars (deoxyribose, ribose) they produced on decomposition: deoxyribonucleic acid and ribonucleic acid. Further, they were known to yield phosphoric acid and a mixture of nitrogenous bases, called purines and pyrimidines. 'Nucleotide' was the name given to the phosphoric-sugar-base complex. It was found that deoxyribonucleic acid contained the purines adenine and guanine, and the pyrimidines cytosine and thymine. In the ribonucleic acid the pyrimidine uracil replaced thymine.

How Watson and Crick came to work out the proposed structure of DNA, by combining molecular model-building on the basis of X-ray crystallographic data, caught the imagination not only of the scientific world. That is, that DNA is made up of two helically entwined phosphate-deoxyribose chains held together in such a way that the purines in one chain match the pyrimidines in the other chain. Adenine (A) always pairs with thymine (T) and guanine (G) with cytosine (C).

A most important consequence of the establishment of the link between DNA and genes, during the 1940s and 1950s, has been the reinforcement of the traditional distinction fostered by the geneticists, between the hereditary constitution (genotype) and the appearance of the organism (phenotype). For example, one of the stimulating contemporary writers on biological matters stated not long ago:[47]

> In classical genetics the 'phenotype' of an individual is its structure and behaviour, and its 'genotype' is its genetic constitution. The distinction reflects the more fundamental one between a mortal body and a potentially immortal genetic message ... The distinction between genotype and phenotype reflects a division of labour between nucleic acids and proteins.

The history of the gene, after 1953, has revolved around the gradual building-up of the concept that it constitutes a segment of DNA which specifies or codes for the production of proteins. That is, that the sequence of amino acids in proteins is prefigured by the sequence of nucleotide bases in DNA.

For one thing the Sequence Hypothesis (which is at the heart of the HGP) is in its unidirectional format not sustainable. Though DNA produces proteins, proteins (enzymes) produce DNA. There is not only a division of labour but co-operation between nucleic acid and proteins, as it were. As one writer points out 'This recalls the well-known dilemma: which came first, the chicken or the egg?'[48] For another thing, it is recognized that in addition to the coding part (exon), the gene contains a long non-coding part (intron) which apparently has a role in gene regulation. Not surprisingly, 'in our time the more we learn of the molecular basis over gene locus, the fuzzier the gene becomes'.[49] Therefore it is worrying when eminent workers, such as Dulbecco, perceive in the sequence of base pairs in human DNA the essence of man and the fundamental determining force of world events to boot.

BETWEEN FACT AND SCI-FICTION

'Astonishing' is probably the adjective most frequently applied to the HGP. 'Astonishingly sci-fictional' would be occasionally more to the point. Take the total number of human genes (100,000) and the total number of base pairs in the human DNA (3 billion) – they are guesses. Here I draw on two very prominent players in the project, Walter Gilbert (Nobel Prize in Chemistry, 1980) and Charles Cantor (Chief Scientist of the US Department of Energy genome project). According to Gilbert: 'Nobody knows how many genes are really involved, because we do not know the average size of a gene in the human body. Our estimate of 100,000 assumes that there are about 30,000 base pairs per gene, which is a reasonably good guess. But many genes are only 10,000 base pairs long, so perhaps there are as many as 300,000.'[50] In Cantor's view, however, the figure 100,000 'has been pulled from thin air'. Numbers matter if only for their bearing on the funding of the project. Referring to the conjectured 3 billion base pairs, Cantor points out: 'The cost of this project scales up roughly in proportion to the square of that number, so if it were 6 billion base pairs we would be in trouble; but 3 billion is probably right to within 5 or 10 per cent.'[51]

The expensiveness of the long-term research has continued to be a major issue between the opponents and proponents of the genome projects. The US Congress Office of Technology Assessment (OTA) has been at pains to stress that they do not belong in the category of the Manhattan Project (first atomic bomb), Apollo Project (Moon landing), the space station or the super conducting super collider.[52] Be that as it may, in 1991 when the HGP was launched formally as a federal programme it received about $135 million.[53] Not a mean allocation especially if a yearly appropriation at this level is to be sustained until 2005 when the goal of the HGP is supposed to be reached. That is, to establish the sequence of the conjectured 3 billion bases in the human DNA. As one reads the material about the scope and scale of the enterprise, one cannot help being struck by its sci-fictional features. For example, when Cantor discusses the eventuality of the project being only half-completed by 2005. Even so, the amount of data will be enormous with the consequence:[54]

> Laboratory notebooks will disappear because mapping and sequencing data cannot be conveniently stored in a hard-copy archive. Traditional data records will have to be replaced by something in electronic form, including images ... An analogy shows why genome data will be unmanageable manually. The complete human sequence, written out in type typically found in a telephone book would occupy 200 volumes of the thousand-page Manhattan directory. Clearly, no one could scan by hand a data base of three billion entries. The ultimate human data base, one that would incorporate all human diversity, would be at least four orders of magnitude (roughly ten thousand times) bigger. It should be obvious that our approach to dealing with biological data must change.
>
> Contrary to original expectations in the project, establishing a centralized genome data base will not be the optimal way to handle the new data. A data base is only as good as the people who maintain it. Sequencing is a tremendously error-prone technique; the accuracy of current sequencing may be no better than 99 per cent; the sequences are constantly updated, the data constantly changing. As scientists are learning about that data, they are constantly annotating the data base. And no one will care about keeping track of the day-to-day changes in a data base of 3 billion items. As a result, I expect a trend to constructive balkanization, the establishment of hundreds or thousands of data bases.

Not all protagonists of the HGP are worried about how to come to grips with the staggering mass of sequence data. Take the scenario advanced by Walter Bodmer (a former president of HUGO) and Robin McKie (scientific correspondent of the London *Observer*) in their widely acclaimed *The Book of Man* in which 'the quest that is leading to a new understanding of what it means to be a human being' (Preface) is addressed. Once the quest is completed and its results enshrined in the *Book of Man*, this is how Bodmer and McKie bring their euphoric vision to bear on how it will be read:[55]

> No longer will laboratories use personnel to carry out the laborious sequencing of a desired gene, as with cystic fibrosis and other diseases. Researchers will simply home in on a bit of chromosome, look up the pages of the Book of Man to find what genes lie in that region, and then select ones which might have a mutation that fits the symptoms of the ailment under study. Laboratories will not be filled with sequencers, but virologists, cell development specialists and all the other experts needed to exploit genes for their pharmaceutical potential.
>
> And we should be very clear on this point. The future of the development of new pharmaceuticals in the twenty-first century will rest squarely with the mapping and sequencing of all our genes. With the identification of the triggers of disturbed protein pathways, we should be able to develop drugs that will block them, so halting the pernicious progress of diseases, for instance in conditions such as Alzheimer's

disease. We should also be able to attack tumours with pinpoint precision, and correct the dreadful physical deterioration associated with immune disorders like rheumatoid arthritis.

As a historian, I cannot but recall the largely unheeded warning of F. G. Hopkins more than eighty years ago how absurd it is to trace the cell life to one specific molecular compound. The response has not been better when Pirie essentially reiterated his teacher's caveat some fifty years later:[56]

... when a biological activity is studied in a system that contains proteins, polysaccharides, nucleic acids, lipids and other substances less easily categorized, and when the activity has not been found unless all these are present, it is illogical to pick out arbitrarily the type of molecule that is currently fashionable and attribute it a key role ...

The molecule in question is DNA and to present it as a master molecule is to indulge in a fiction fuelled by reductionist and determinist thinking. The reality is described by the prominent evolutionary geneticists R. C. Lewontin, one in a minority of expert critics, as follows:[57]

First, DNA is not self-reproducing, second, it makes nothing, and third, organisms are not determined by it ... No living molecule is self-reproducing. Only whole cells may contain all the necessary machinery for 'self'-reproduction and even they, in the process of development, lose that capacity.

The adherents of the notion that DNA provides the complete blueprint for a human being tend to accept, despite disclaimers, the primacy of heredity (nature) over environment (nurture). Thus the editor of *Science*, D. E. Koshland, Jr., admits with respect to the question of how to make children behave, how to rehabilitate prisoners or to prevent suicides, that 'we are dealing with a very complex problem in which the structure of society and chemical therapy will play roles.' But then he argues that some persons are not redeemable because of their genetic endowment:[58]

Better schools, a better environment, better counseling, and better rehabilitation will help some individuals, but not all. Better drugs and genetic engineering will help others, but not all. It is not going to be easy for those without scientific training to cope with these complicated relationships even when all the factors are well understood.

Altogether the promotion of the HGP has been accompanied by an unmistakable transference of emphasis on the genetic origin of diseases. in the Foreword to a publication publicizing the HGP, the Secretary of the US Department of Health and Human Services C. W. Sullivan wrote:[59]

> Faulty genes have been directly implicated in more than 3000 human diseases and have been strongly linked to many major health problems, including cancer, heart disease, diabetes, mental illness and birth defects. Yet, despite our growing awareness of the role genes play in so many human diseases, our search to find them has been slow ... The goal of the Human Genome Project can be stated simply: to equip biomedical researchers with the tools they need to search for genes quickly and cheaply. Once genes have been pinpointed and isolated, researchers can then begin to understand the genetic errors that result in disease. *Only this information can pave the way for new treatments and perhaps even cures for the many disease sufferers who, without it, have little hope.* (My emphasis-MT)

The recognition of single gene defects underlying crippling disorders such as Huntington's disease or cystic fibrosis should not obscure the fact that most genetic disorders are polygenic, that is, they are the result of interaction of several genes, in conjunction with the person's environment. Furthermore, a genetic component does not necessarily mean that genetics is the determining cause of the disease.[60] As one student of the genetics-environmental issue, Robert N. Proctor, acutely observes:[61]

> In the rush to identify genetic components to cancer or heart disease or mental illness, the substantial environmental origins of those afflictions may be slighted ... One of the dangers of biological determinism, then, is that the root cause for the onset of disease is shifted from the environment (toxic exposures) to individual (genetic) defects.

We do not know well enough why ever since its discovery in the early 1830s, the cell nucleus was assigned a focal position in cell life. The similarity to Harvey giving the heart the pride of place in the body, akin to that of the sun in the universe, is unmistakable. Lewontin suggests that DNA's elevated status constitutes[62] 'the transfer onto biology of the belief in the superiority of mental labor over the merely physical, of the planner and designer over the unskilled operative in the assembly line'.

It is an unverified supposition pointing to the need to look more deeply into the sources of ideas that provide science with a theoretical framework within which it operates and develops. There can be little doubt that since Aristotle, at least, thinking about nature has been affected by concepts reflecting the hammer and anvil relationship, as it were, between rulers and ruled.[63] Thus in relation to the theme of this paper it is noteworthy that, by 1892 if not before, the historically influential Weismann was prone, as recently pointed out by the historian of science Jonathan Harwood, to speak of *Beherrschung* (domination) of the cell by the hereditary substance and to give the nucleus a military command connotation.[64]

A PERIL AND A HOPE

For better or for worse, the work on the human genome continues irrespective of dubious aspects of the theory underlying the HGP and the laboriousness of its practical execution. The knowledge arising from the access to the human genome may serve humane or base ends in the same way as the knowledge of the atomic nucleus has done. This has been recognized by J. B. S. Haldane almost fifty years ago when he proclaimed: 'A knowledge of the human nucleus may give us the same power for good or evil over ourselves as the knowledge of the atomic nucleus has given us over parts of the external world.[65]

There is already enough evidence that there is a real danger of misusing the new genetic knowledge. The following example, chosen at random, should illustrate in a small way the challenge of the HGP to all of us. In 1989 Victor A. McKusick, one of the most respected American human geneticists and member of the National Research Council of the National Academy of Sciences concerned with the HGP, wrote in the prestigious *The New England Journal of Medicine*:[66]

> In connection with funding, I believe that no member of the National Research Council committee saw the project as amenable to the commercial production of products that could be patented or copyrighted. Companies small and large may undertake contracts for research and development with respect to the technical aspects of the project, the manufacture, warehousing, and distribution of biomaterials, and perhaps the sequencing activity. Although the products of such companies will be necessary to the conduct and completion of the project, the end product itself – the complete map and sequence and the parts thereof – cannot be used for the profit of any single company.

But in 1991 the National Institutes of Health (NIH) applied for patents on hundreds of separate sequences even before their decipherment. This step was designed, apparently, to ensure free exchange of information and as a countermeasure against scientific secrecy practised by many a prominent American molecular biologist with corporate connections. It was no less a person than Walter Gilbert who launched the idea of copyrighting sections of DNA: 'I don't see any problem. It is just like writing a book. People can read the information but they will have to pay if they want to use it elsewhere.'[67]

More and more, copyrighting and patenting the human genome, on the one hand, and genetic screening and the use of genetic information, on the other hand, move into the centre of the debate about the HGP. It is not for nothing that its supporters with a social conscience do not like what they see:[68]

> ... the near-term ethical challenges of the human genome project lie ... in the grit of what the project will produce in abundance: genetic information. They center on the control, diffusion, and use of that information within the context of a arket economy, and they are deeply troubling.

It is in this connection that it is apposite to consider the recent comments on the HGP, written by Benno Müller-Hill and published in *Nature*. Müller-Hill, a distinguished German geneticist and author of a widely acclaimed book on the misuse of human genetics in Nazi Germany,[69] has never wavered in his support of the HGP. However, he fears that the discoveries emerging from the HGP will affect catastrophically the genetically disadvantaged, and therefore pleads for preventive action to be taken:[70]

> The knowledge will simply unveil reality, emphasizing the injustice of the world. It is certainly not enough to face reality bluntly if the future develops as I describe it. It is not enough simply that the right of privacy is acknowledged. If those who have this right have no education, health insurance or jobs, the right is not enough. Laws are necessary to protect the genetically disadvantaged. Social justice has to recompense genetic injustice. The details of such legislation can be spelled out only when the genetic facts are known. Deep changes in attitudes are also required. All we can do now is to be prepared. Progress may be painfully fast or slow, and will be full of contradictions. To master it demands firm values. At the extremes, people will have to chose between the values of the Nazis and those of Moses – that is, racism or an appreciation of equal human rights. The choice for politicians of the world's governments will be between international fascism or, if science and justice are combined, a fundamentally improved social structure throughout the world.

By and large exponents of the HGP do not show awareness, as Müller-Hill does, that social system has a critical bearing on how universally or restrictively the result of the expensive and extensive research effort will be applied to the benefit of all human beings. In fact, as to what constitutes the nature of human beings, their idea appears to be narrowly biological/genetical. Like Renato Dulbecco, there are other distinguished spokesmen for the HGP who go on to reduce the essence of human species to the sequences of bases in the DNA. This idea is reiterated in the euphoric anticipation of the future development outlined by Bodmer and McKie, in the concluding paragraph of the *Book of Man*:[71]

> It is a story of adventure and discovery, one that strikes at the essence of being a human. It is hard to see how one could get any closer to our own interests, for the question of our biological lineage touches, as we have seen, on understanding our role in evolution, and survival as a species. It also offers the prospect of creating new medicines, tracing our recent history and a host of other benefits. Far from worrying, we should relish the prospect before us. We are entering a golden era.

In an ahistorical starry-eyed vision of the HGP – in the absence of critical consideration of underlying theoretical and practical issues and examination of dominating political and economic forces at play, including full social implications and consequences – lies a peril.

The dream will have to be revised if the HGP is to have a prospect to come into its full human and humane heritage, then in the ambit of a social system very different from social organizations known so far – and therein lies the hope.[72]

NOTES

A good deal of material for this contribution was assembled during my stay in Corvallis as Fellow at the Center for the Humanities of Oregon State University (Jan.–June 1992). It was written in Uppsala when I was Fellow at SCASSS (Swedish Collegium for Advanced Study in the Social Sciences) (Jan.–June 1993). I would like to acknowledge most warmly the support and understanding I received from the directors and staff of these institutions. It would also like gratefully to acknowledge comments by Kurt Bayertz, Paul L. Farber, Silvia Frank-Elsner, Benno Müller-Hill, Roy Porter, Robert N. Proctor, Nils Roll-Hansen, who read the draft version. But, of course, they are not responsible for the printed text.

1 For a brief historical introduction, see D. J. Kevles, 'Out of Eugenics: The Historical Politics of the Human Genome', in D. J. Kevles and L. Hood (eds.), *The Code of Codes Scientific and Social Issues in the Human Genome Project* (Cambridge, MA, 1992), pp. 18f. This volume 'is probably the best available general introduction to the HGP', writes M. Susan Lindee, who also suggests 'that historians have so much to contribute to the ongoing debate'. See her 'The ELSI hypothesis', *Isis*, 85 (1994), 293–6. (ELSI stands for ethical, legal and social implications).

2 A. E. Garrod, 'The Incidence of Alkaptonuria: A Study in Chemical Individuality', *The Lancet*, 2 (1902), 1,616–20. See also chapter 2 in J. Sapp, *Where the Truth Lies. Franz Moewus and the Origins of Molecular Biology* (Cambridge, 1990).

3 A. E. Garrod, 'A Contribution to the Study of Alkaptonuria', *Medico-Chirurgical Transactions of the Royal Medical and Chirurgical Society of London*, 82 (1899), 369–94.

4 H. F. Judson, 'A History of the Science and Technology behind Gene Mapping and Sequencing', in Kevles and Hood, *Code of Codes*, p. 42.

5 W. Bateson and E. R. Saunders, 'Experimental Studies in the Physiology of Heredity', Report I (1902) in *Reports to the Evolution Committee of the Royal Society* (London, 1910), 133–4. It is worth recalling that Mendel himself was concerned

with plant hybridization which he investigated by crossing pure strains of *Pisum*, the edible pea. Peas were distinguished by a contrasting pair of traits (characters) of which one was clearly dominant (e.g. round seed shape, yellow seed colour) and the other recessive (e.g. angular seed shape, green seed colour). Mendel's experimental work included studies of two- and three-trait differences. Analysing the inheritance pattern of the parental traits in statistical terms and finding that they retained their identity in successive generations, Mendel formulated the principles of heredity which bear his name: 'Mendel's rules (laws) of the segregation and of the independent assortment of characters.' Regarding the proportion of dominance to recessives in the first and subsequent hybrid generations, Mendel established the historically influential numerical relation of 3:1 and 1:2:1 respectively (the 'Mendelian ratio').

6 Garrod, 'Incidence', pp. 1,116–18.

7 Cf. A. E. Garrod, *Inborn Errors of Metabolism. The Croonian Lectures Delivered Before The Royal College of Physicians of London in June 1908* (London, 1909), pp. 26–31; 2nd edn (1923), pp. 21–4.

8 See *Our Genetic Future The Science and Ethics of Genetic Technology. British Medical Association* (Oxford, New York, 1992).

9 Quoted by A. G. Bearn and E. D. Miller, 'Archibald Garrod and the Development of the Concept of Inborn Errors of Metabolism', *Bulletin of the History of Medicine*, 53 (1979), 315–28 (323). See also A. G. Bearn, *Archibald Garrod and the Individuality of Man* (Oxford, 1993), p. 61.

10 Garrod, *Inborn Errors* (1909), p. 3; (1923), pp. 2–3.

11 Garrod, 'Incidence', pp. 1,620.

12 F. G. Hopkins, 'The Pigments of the Pieridae; A Contribution to the Study of Excretory Substances which Function in Ornament', *Philosophical Transactions of the Royal Society* (B), 186 (1895), 661–82.

13 The second edition of Garrod's classical book (1923) was dedicated to Hopkins, the 'friend of many years' and Hopkins wrote for the Royal Society an affectionate appreciation of Garrod's life and work: F. G. Hopkins, 'Archibald Edward Garrod 1857–1936', *Obituary Notices of The Royal Society*, 2 (1938), 225–8.

14 N. W. Pirie, 'Sir Frederick Gowland Hopkins (1861–1947); in G. Semenza (ed.), *A History of Biochemistry. Selected Topics in the History of Biochemistry Personal Recollections I* (Amsterdam, 1983), p. 114.

15 W. J. Schuhl and R. Chakraborty (eds.), *Human Genetics. A Selection of Insights. Benchmark Papers in Genetics*, vol. 10 (Stroudsburg, PA, 1979), 152.

16 G. W. Beadle, 'Genes and Chemical Reactions in Neurospora. The Concepts of Biochemical Genetics began with Garrod's "inborn errors" and have evolved gradually' (Nobel Lecture, 11 Dec. 1958), *Science*, 129 (1959), pp. 1715–19 (1717).

17 Cf. Bearn and Miller, 'Archibald Garrod', p. 315. See also Bearn, *Garrod*, p. 151.

18 G. W. Beadle, 'Chemical Genetics', in L. C. Dunn (ed.), *Genetics in the 20th Century* (New York, 1951), p. 223.

19 G. W. Beadle, 'Mendelism, 1965', in R. A. Brink (ed.), with the assistance of E. D. Styles, *Heritage From Mendel* (Madison, Milwaukee and London, 1967), p. 340.

20 B. Glass, 'A Century of Biochemical Genetics', *Proceedings of the American Philosophical Society*, 109 (1965), 227–36.

21 F. G. Hopkins, 'The Dynamic Side of Biochemistry', *Report of the British Association for the Advancement of Science* (1913), 652–68 (663).

22 *Ibid.*, p. 659.

23 J. B. S. Haldane, 'Some Recent Work on Heredity', *Transactions of the Oxford University Junior Scientific Club*, 3, 1 (1920), 3–11. See also S. Sarkar, 'Haldane as a Biochemist: The Cambridge Decade, 1923–1932', in S. Sarkar (ed.), *The Foundations of Evolutionary Genetics. A Centenary Reappraisal* (Dordrecht, Boston, London, 1992), pp. 53–81. For a brief insightful introduction to Haldane's life and work, see N. W. Pirie (with S. Wright, M. Kimura, L. S. Penrose, M. S. Bartlett and F. N. David), 'John Burdon Sanderson Haldane 1982–1965 Elected F.R.S. 1932', *Biographical Memoirs of Fellows of The Royal Society*, 12 (1966), 219–49.

24 J. B. S. Haldane, 'The Biochemistry of the Individual', in J. Needham and D. E. Green (eds.), *Perspectives in Biochemistry* (Cambridge, 1937), pp. 1–10 (p. 1).

25 L. S. Penrose, 'Presidential Address – The influence of the English tradition in human genetics', in J. F. Crow and J. V. Neel (eds.), *Proceedings of the Third International Congress of Human Genetics, September 5–20, 1966 Chicago* (Baltimore, MD, 1967), pp. 13–25 (p. 18).

26 R. Dulbecco, 'A Turning Point in Cancer Research: Sequencing the Human Genome', *Science*, 241 (1986), 1,055–6 (1056).

27 This refers to a labelled portion of DNA (radioactively, immunologically, with a fluorescent dye). It is used to identify complementary sequences in DNA fragments.

28 Also noticed by V. A. McKusick, 'Mapping and Sequencing the Human Genome', *The New England Journal of Medicine*, 320 (1989), 910–15 (910).

29 Our historical understanding of the gene concept is patchy, which is remarkable, in view of the major role it played in the making of genetics. To my knowledge E. A. Carlson, *The Gene. A Critical History* (Philadelphia and London, 1966) remains the one comprehensive book-length attempt to deal with the topic. Among articles, I find stimulating R. Falk, 'The Gene in Search of an Identity', *Human Genetics*, 68 (1984), 195–204.

30 For brief but invaluable accounts of Johannsen's work, see F. B. Churchill, 'William Johannsen and the Genotype Concept', *Journal of the History of Biology*, 7 (1974), 5–30; N. Roll-Hansen, 'The Genotype Theory of William Johannsen and its Relation to Plant Breeding and the Study of Evolution', *Centaurus*, 22 (1970/9), 201–35. Cf. also N. Roll-Hansen, 'The death of spontaneous generation and the birth of the gene: two case studies of relativism', *Social Studies of Science*, 13 (1983), 481–519.

31 W. Johannsen, *Elemente der exakten Erblichkeitslehre* (Jena, 1909), p. 124.

32 *Ibid.*, p. 163.

33 Quoted by Roll-Hansen, 'Genotype Theory', p. 224.

34 *Ibid.*

35 For an authoritative account of Morgan's life and work, see G. E. Allen, *Thomas Hunt Morgan. The Man and his Science* (Princeton, 1978).

36 *Ibid.*, p. 125.

37 N. Roll-Hansen, 'Drosophila Genetics: A Reductionist Research Program', *Journal of the History of Biology*, 11 (1978), 159–210 (190).

38 Allen, *Morgan*, p. 209.

39 A. H. Sturtevant, 'The Linear Arrangement of Six Sex-Linked Factors in *Drosophila*, as shown by their Mode of Association', *Journal of Experimental Zoology*, 14 (1913), 43–59.

40 Roll-Hansen, 'Drosophila Genetics', p. 189.

41 T. H. Morgan, 'The Relation of Genetics to Physiology and Medicine', *Scientific Monthly*, 41 (1935), 5–18 (7–8).

42 J. H. Muller, 'Artificial Transmutation of the Gene', *Science*, 66 (1927), 84–7. Cf. J. B. S. Haldane, 'Forty Years of Genetics', in J. Needham and W. Pagel (eds.), *Background to Modern Science* (Cambridge, 1940), pp. 225–43 (p. 236).

43 Carlson, *The Gene*, p. 253.

44 C. H. Waddington, *An Introduction to Modern Genetics* (London, 1939), pp. 394, 401.

45 O. T. Avery, C. M. Macleod and M. McCarty, 'Studies on the Nature of the Substance Inducing Transformation of Pneumococcal Types', *Journal of Experimental Medicine*, 79 (1944), 137–58.

46 J. D. Watson and F. H. C. Crick, 'Molecular Structure of Nucleic Acid', *Nature*, 171 (1953), 737–8; 'Genetical Implications of the Structure of Deoxyribonucleic Acid', *Nature*, 171 (1953), 964–7.

47 J. M. Smith, *The Problems of Biology* (Oxford, 1986), pp. 62–3.

48 Cf. T. Hunt, 'Introduction: The General Idea', in T. Hunt, S. Prentis and J. Tooze (eds.), *DNA makes RNA makes Protein* (Amsterdam, New York and Oxford, 1983), pp. vii–xiv. See also J. Étienne-Decant, *Genetic Biochemistry: From Gene to Protein* (New York, Chichester, Brisbane, Toronto, 1988), p. 130; T. J. Horder, 'The Chicken and the Egg', in H. G. Othmer, Ph. K. Maini and J. D. Murray (eds.), *Experimental and Theoretical Advances in Biological Pattern Formation* (New York and London, 1993), pp. 121–48.

49 J. A. Moore, 'Science as a Way of Knowing-Genetics', *American Zoologist*, 26 (1986), 583–747 (665).

50 W. Gilbert, 'A Vision of the Grail', in Kevles and Hood (eds.), *Code of Codes*, pp. 833–97 (p. 83).

51 See Cantor, 'The Challenges to Technology and Informatics', *Ibid.*, pp. 98–111 (p. 98).

52 *Mapping Our Genes Genome Projects: How Big, How Fast? Congress of the United States Office of Technology Assessment* (Baltimore and London, 1988), ch. 1, summary, 10.

53 Kevles, 'Out of Eugenics', p. 36. A year later the funding was close to $200 million. See W. Bodner and R. McKie, *The Book of Man. The Quest to Discover our Genetic Heritage* (London, 1995), p. 322.

54 Cf. Cantor, 'Challenges', pp. 109–10.

55 Bodmer and McKie, *Book of Man*, p. 344.

56 N. W. Pirie, 'Patterns of Assumption about Large Molecules', *Archives of Biochemistry and Biophysics*, Suppl. 1 (1962), 21–9 (23).

57 R. C. Lewontin, 'The Dream of the Human Genome', *The New York Review of Books*, 39 (1992), 31–40 (33). Partially reprinted in R. C. Lewontin, *Biology as Ideology. The Doctrine of DNA*, 1st US edn (New York, 1992), pp. 59–83.

58 D. E. Koshland Jr., in 'Nature, Nurture, and Behavior', *Science*, 235 (1987), 1,445.

59 *The Human Genome Project New Tools for Tomorrow's Health Research*, prepared by the *Office of Communications, National Center for Human Genome Research* (Bethesda, MD, 1991), 1.

60 Cf. D. Nelkin and L. Tancredi, *Dangerous Diagnostics. The Social Power of Biological Information* (1989), p. 41.

61 R. N. Proctor, 'Genomics and Eugenics: How Fair is the Comparison?', in G. J. Annas and S. Elias (eds.), *Gene Mapping: Using Law and Ethics as Guides* (Oxford, 1992).

62 Lewontin, 'Dream', p. 33.

63 Aristotle, *Politics*, 1254b. See also Janko, 'Two Concepts', note 16 (this volume, p. 35).

64 J. Harwood, *Styles of Scientific Thought The German Genetics Community 1900–1933* (Chicago and London, 1993), p. 331. As a work of historical scholarship, Harwood's contribution is pioneering. For one thing, he took up the virtually neglected question of cytoplasmatic inheritance, seriously pursued in Germany during the first four decades of this century but not much so elsewhere. For another thing, Harwood attempted to link this interest of German geneticists with social change in Germany. See also J. Sapp, *Beyond the Gene: Cytoplasmatic Inheritance and the Struggle for Authority in Genetics* (Oxford, New York, 1987). Robert Olby points out that by the 1860s Ernst Haeckel viewed the nucleus as a central governor of the cell. 'The latter decision rested not on any knowledge about the role of the nucleus in fertilization but on the observation that the cells are organized around nuclei and that nuclear division precedes cell division. The role of the nucleus in heredity was still in doubt ...' Cf. R. Olby, 'Miescher's study of the nucleus. A reassessment', *XIIe Congrès International d'Histoire des Sciences Actes*, vol. VIII (Paris, 1971), pp. 135–7.

65 J. B. S. Haldane, 'The Formal Genetics of Man', *Proceedings of the Royal Society of London (B)*, 153 (1948), 147–70 (149). [Croonian Lecture].

66 McKusick, 'Mapping', p. 912.

67 *Observer*, 11 Oct. 1987. Keen as he was on profiting financially from his discoveries, Walter Gilbert cofounded Biogen, one of the first biotechnological companies (1981).

68 D. J. Kevles and L. Hood, 'Reflections', in Kevles and Hood (eds.), *Code of Codes*, pp. 300–28 (p. 320).

69 B. Müller-Hill, *Murderous Science Elimination by Scientific Selection of Jews, Gypsies, and Others, Germany 1933–1944* (Oxford, 1988).

70 B. Müller-Hill, 'The Shadow of Genetic Injustice', *Nature*, 362 (1993), 491–2 (492).

71 Bodmer and McKie, *Book of Man*, p. 353.

72 It is apparent, against the background of history, the HGP constitutes a part of the chain of scientific-technical developments set in motion, since the turn of the century, with the discovery of the nuclear atom and rediscovery of Mendel's work on inheritance in plants. To the chain's perturbing influence on individual and social life worldwide there is no obvious historical parallel and therefore it seems apt to speak of a Scientific-Technical Revolution. It is a historical product of and a factor in the social transformations of the world since the beginning of the twentieth century. I plan to return in a separate work to this question which I have had occasion to raise before. Cf. M. Teich, 'The Scientific-Technical Revolution: An Historical Event in the Twentieth Century?' in R. Porter and M. Teich (eds.), *Revolution in History* (Cambridge, 1986), pp. 317–30; and 'Re-

flecting on the Golden Jubilee of Bernal's *The Social Function of Science*', *History of Science*, 28 (1990), 411–18; and 'The Twentieth-Century Scientific-Technical Revolution in Historical Context', *18th International Congress of Historical Sciences, 27 August–3 September Proceedings* (Montréal, 1995), 235.

NINETEEN

THE WAY THE WORLD IS GOING: THE SOCIETY–NATURE DICHOTOMY IN DEVELOPMENT RHETORICS

BENGT-ERIK BORGSTRÖM

THE argument in this essay is that development issues are no longer seen, as they have been for the past half-century, solely in terms of some variant of modernization theory where the aim of development is industrialization and a welfare society of a capitalist or a socialist kind. Modernization theories are no doubt still very much alive in the ongoing debate over development, but increasingly they are being supplemented with arguments that are reminiscent of earlier periods in the history of Western constructions of the societies of the former colonies, periods that saw the relationship between colonizer and colonized in terms of society versus nature. Perhaps the post-war era of picturing the First versus the Third World in terms of a difference of degree rather than a difference in kind, in itself a fairly democratic appreciation of the relationship, will turn out to be a brief moment in a longer, and more problematic, history of Western constructions of 'the Other' as different.[1]

One could list several reasons for this, some of which are political while others have to do with changes of the economy and the environment. As a consequence of the ending of the Cold War and the demise of the Communist power sphere, the salient and attention-catching contrast on the global scene is that between the capitalist industrialized world, the North in development parlance, and the developing countries, the South. To say this is not to deny that there are differences within each category. The North is divided both by economic and political rivalry, the South comprises countries with very different economic potential and differing political systems.

In addition to these political factors there is also a growing awareness of a looming ecological crisis on a global scale. This perceived crisis of the environment has in turn been linked to some of the issues in the Global Agreement on Trade and Tariffs (GATT), where the opposition between the South and the North was one of the main bones of contention, although far from the only one. All these dividing issues and disagreements between the North and the South were also clearly to be seen in the 1992 UN Conference in Rio on the Environment and Development (UNCED).

In the pages that follow I shall discuss some of the issues that seem to indicate that a definition of North–South relations in terms of nature versus society is complicating the picture of a process of development that leads from a state of 'underdevelopment' to a position as a 'developed' nation. I shall do this by pointing to a number of areas ranging from the ideologies and 'schools' surrounding development and the environment to strategies in the fields of politics and trade.

THE LEGACY OF HISTORY

As noted already, the dichotomy society – nature has very old antecedents. It is the view of the world where the West, Europe and North America, are identified with society, and what we term the Third World is equated with nature.

In this definition of the world, the West is part of history, while the Third World is outside history. In the latter, notably Africa, Australia and the Americas, history was, one could say, introduced, or even invented by the Europeans.[2] The Europeans' gaze classified the nature and peoples of the discovered and explored continents and gave them a place in world history.[3] And Wallerstein argues that an economic world system has existed since the sixteenth century with Europe as the engine and centre. One could also note in this context Lévi-Strauss' famous distinction between 'hot' and 'cold' societies, the former being the industrialized ones and the latter those that were colonized by the West.[4] Lévi-Strauss discusses this Western domination of the rest of the world in terms of the second law of thermo-dynamics that states that heat moves from the object that is warmer to that which is colder. In other words, societies with history transform those without history into becoming societies with history (in the process extinguishing them). And Karl Marx saw the British Empire as a vitalizing force in India, setting in motion the forces that would transform that society and give it a history in the Western sense.

Another important dichotomy between the West and the Third World, is found in the ways in which Europeans have, throughout the history of colonization, classified subject peoples. Two extremes are well-known: the noble savage, Rousseauean idealization of life in 'the natural state', on the one hand; and the cruel savage, the Hobbesian version, on the other. Poised between these extremes we find the cultivated European, who never goes to extremes. His is a rational and measured way of going about things.[5]

The argument is, then, that the rich world versus the poor countries also translates as society with a history, i.e. evolution, in opposition to nature without known history, i.e., societies engaged in a circular process of existence. A corollary to this is a view of the West as existing in time, changing from one state to another, and of societies of the Third World as existing outside time, duration rather than change.

In all this it is possible to discern a typology at work that equates the North with heat, i.e., energy, activity, history (existence in time), change; and the South with lack of excess energy, repetitive existence, absence of history (existence outside time), non-change. These lists also betray a certain interesting contradiction in the development–ecology debate. It is obvious that it is the North that transforms the world, both through the capacities inherent in that form of society and through its people's superior use of a rational and emotion-free way of thinking and behaving.

And this transformative capacity that is seen to be inherent in the Northern civilization puts (Northern) Man in the centre as the mover of things, or perhaps more accurate, as the creator of things. Man formulates the future and invents/creates the (artificial) means with which to reach that future. In this overall plan of change, progress, nature is but one component among many in Man's transformational activities. The unforseen consequences, for instance environmental pollution or other forms of degradation of the environment can be rectified by further technological development. The South is, by contrast, characterized precisely by its lack of artificiality and ability to transform itself and its environment. This is, in accordance with the two extreme images of the 'savage' that exist in the West, sometimes seen as something negative, they have to be developed; and sometime as something positive, they live in harmony with nature.

It is, then, this view of the world, of the North and the South, a view that is the legacy of European colonialization and dominance of the globe, that forms the background to the debates of development and environment. It exists as a landscape where each protagonist recognizes the different features, and all agree that they are there, but there is no agreement as to whether they point in the desired direction or not.

SOCIETY AND NATURE AS DEVELOPMENT AND ECOLOGY

Development in the modern sense of the word, i.e., planned action for the alleviation of poverty and disease through the planned uplift of 'backward' or 'underdeveloped' societies gained momentum after the Second World War. Its motive force was as much practical political as it was humanitarian, and for this reason its concern became global, mirroring the global political struggle between the two rival super powers of the post-war era.

The goals of development activities were straightforward and so were the methods. Industrialized society, notably in its North American version, was seen as the epitome of development, and the road to be travelled was through economic efficiency and a rational means–ends outlook on the world, an outlook freed from 'superstition' and 'irrational' beliefs and customs. 'Take off'[6] became the magical spell for this kind of thinking about development.

If modernization paradigm this of development thinking saw globalization in the form of trade and aid as the solution to underdevelopment, its critics, coming mainly from Latin America, saw this interdependence as the root cause of underdevelopment. Frank became perhaps the most influential expounder of this alternative view, according to which the Third World can better its situation only if it breaks free from the dependency on the rich world, which extracts its resources by economic and political means.[7] This school of thought acknowledged that there was a global system, but in their view it was a system that created and perpetuated poverty. As we shall see, there is more than a shade of this view of the causes of underdevelopment in the current critique of mainstream development–environmentalism.

With the progressive coming together of development thinking and ecology, the former has taken a turn towards a more normative and utopian character, stressing the content of development rather than the form, as Hettne puts it.[8] It is Man and his or her needs that forms the basis of this version of development, not abstract political and economic structures of power and influence. This approach is a direct counterpoint to mainstream development theory in the sense that it does not accept the need for economic growth. This is also a point on which it differs from dependency theory. However, it agrees with the latter on the need to break free from the rich nations' economic and political stranglehold.

If it can be argued that development thinking has, over the past fifty years or so, moved from being more or less exclusively a concern with society, to a position where nature is very much in the picture, ecology has gone in the other direction, moving from a more or less exclusive concern with nature to a situation where nature and society are seen to be tightly interwoven. The traditional form of managing nature was through activities designed towards conservation, epitomized above all through the establishment of national parks. This was a form of thinking that firmly set nature in opposition to society. Nature is where Man is not (except where they are defined as 'tribes' and presumed to live in close harmony with nature; and then there are the tourists of course, who are allowed in to marvel at nature). This approach is still very much alive, but over the past few decades it has been complemented, and overshadowed, by a process stemming from a growing realization that the idea of continuous economic growth has had unwanted effects on nature, effects that might, if they are to continue, strike back at society. The first loud and clear warning is credited to Rachel Carson and her book *Silent Spring* (1962), but others were to follow. Paul Ehrlich's *The Population Bomb* (1972) was another book that pointed to another man-made (in the literal sense of the word) device for destruction. Ehrlich squarely put man within the ambit of nature treating him as a creature who, through his biologically grounded drives, was heading for disaster.

Alarmist reports on the deteriorating state of nature became legion during the 1960s and 1970s, leading to a new kind of environmental consciousness where the borderlines between nature and society became increasingly problematic. The remedies were sought in administrative and technological development. Systems ecology furnished the model for the more ambitious efforts at drawing up blueprints for future nature–society interaction. The adverse effects of the technological systems that existed could be planned away, and new technology developed that would have less harmful effects. The catchword became sustainable development; that is to say, economic growth without depletion of resources, or the art of living off the interest rather than the capital.

But there was also another form of reaction to what was happening, an anti-establishment movement that rejected technological and large-scale solutions, and instead advocated that man live in close harmony with nature, a version of ecology and society–nature interaction that obliterates the distinction between the two.

This is, of course, a version of nature–society relationships that is identical to ecodevelopment. The significance of this convergence is that it has led to an alternative to more traditional ways of looking at development and the environment. Modernization theories, as well as dependency arguments in development, and the conservation movement and environmentalism that saw technological reform as the solution to ecological problems, were on the whole compatible in that they did not explicitly deny the possibility and desirability of continued economic growth.

There are, then, both in the field of development and that of ecology, a number of theories and outlooks that both mirror and stand in opposition to one another. On the one hand, there is development as a planned and rational large-scale activity, with its point of gravity in technology, and complemented by a conservationist attitude to nature. On the other hand, there is ecodevelopment, rejecting technology and large-scale solutions, and pointing to small-scale societies in the South as the best examples of successful adaptations to nature.

MARKET RATIONALITY AS SOCIETY AND NATURE

Since a good deal of the debate between mainstream development and ecodevelopment, and by extension between spokesmen for the North and the South, revolve around the ties that unite the latter two, it is necessary to briefly look at the place of economics, or the market, in the controversy.

Viewed from the vantage point of Western society, economic behaviour, expressed through the market principle is ultimately grounded in human nature. Furthermore, it obeys its own laws, as immutable as those of nature. By manipulating these laws in certain ways the economy may be steered in the desired direction, and the desired form of development will be brought about. Evolution is, as in biology, the figure of thought that guides economic thinking: growth, progress, increased differentiation.

The ecodevelopment perspective is different. To it the market is solidly a social phenomenon. It is brute force, exploitation and power politics dressed up in ideological terms. There is nothing 'natural' about the market and its supposed ways of functioning. On the contrary, it is a ruse and an excuse for the rich to go on enriching themselves.

Thus, the controversy is, at the level of symbolism, one revolving round the question where society ends and nature begins. To the North economics and the function of the market are natural phenomena, to its opponents they are part of society. Consequently, it is in line with such a perception that the protagonists of main-stream development make references to one form of nature, the market, in order to justify modification of another form of nature (the opposite of society). That is, they argue in favour of saving the environment by the informed application of the laws of the market, laws that are outside society and grounded in human nature. The ecodevelopment point of view is to resist such intrusion, and to argue that market rationality is a social construction, the application of which will only further damage the tender fabrics of the environment.

POLES APART: THE EXAMPLE OF SUSTAINABLE DEVELOPMENT

The polar rationalities outlined above, main-stream development and ecodevelopment, have to an increasing degree come to colour the development debate on a global scale. A good example of this is their controversy over the concept 'sustainable development'.

The term sustainable development was used at the UN Conference on the Human Environment in Stockholm in 1972, and it has gained even stronger currency since, notably as the main theme of the 1987 report of the World Commission on Environment and Development, Our Common Future, known as the Brundtland report, after the Commission's chairperson, the Norwegian Prime Minister Gro Harlem Brundtland. In that report sustainable development is given a reformist interpretation in the sense that it argues for continued growth as the only solution to the poverty and the continuing degradation of the environment in the Third World. This is, one could say, the development part of the argument. The ecological component is the plea for a growth that takes into consideration the limits that the environment sets to any kind of human activity. That is to say, the point of departure is socio-economic needs that are then allowed to define attitudes and activities with regard to ecology. The limits set by nature are no absolute limits, they vary with the goals that development sets. The ultimate aim is to proceed with development in such a way that the resources used are not depleted beyond recovery. As will be discussed later, this also points to the possibility of development, understood as economic growth, to make itself independent of nature through technological innovation that allows for artificial substitutes.

Sustainable development means something quite different when approached from the political culture of ecodevelopment. Here it stands for a fusion between nature and society in a manner that naturalizes society, i.e., in the sense that natural groupings of people that live in a natural and harmonious, homeostatic, relationship with their surroundings are to form the units for development. The goal is not economic growth but self-sufficiency without disturbing the balance of the socio-ecological whole. The concept of 'bio-region' expresses this view quite well.

So what we have here are two contrasting ways of defining and understanding 'sustainable development'; one which stresses development at the expense of ecology and sees growth as the only solution to problems of poverty and ecological degradation; and another that is in search of harmony and balance and views economic growth as the very cause of these same conditions[9] – ecology defines development, and society is included in this cybernetic system.

As for the origin of development problems, there is a similar lack of congruence between the two sides. The argument from ecodevelopment is that Western style development, which mirrors uneven trade and power relations, has created the problems in the first place, and giving full reign to the very same forces through free trade is not going to improve the situation. European dominance has destroyed the fabrics of sustenance that once existed in the Third World countries. The North has exploited the South (the debt crisis being only the most recent example), creating poverty while enriching itself. Now, it has the arrogance of declaring that the environmental crisis in the South can only be solved by resources and technology from the North.[10]

In this Northern view resources in the form of money, technology and agreements on free trade, flow from the North to the South, creating life and prosperity. The counter argument from ecodevelopment is that it is necessary to get out of the vicious circle of unequal exchange that only further devastates the poor countries, and embark on a new road to development, a road that is in fact a rediscovery of the balance between nature and society, epitomized above all by homogeneous small-scale societies that are threatened by the present mode of development. They form part of a homology where man cannot be separated from nature and where both draw sustenance from one another.

While the solution of main-stream development approaches to environmental problems is conservation, i.e., nature as distinct from man – nature without people, the ecodevelopmental concept is people as part of nature. With this goes also a civilizational critique of another kind. The dominance of the world by the affluent West has made humans less than what they could be, it has suppressed their potentialities, potentialities that will only be realized when the poor are able to break free from their dependency on the rich. It is interesting to note that, in this view, man will develop only when development as we know it ceases, and man becomes more fully part of nature. In other words, current development, which is artificial in the sense of relying on the transformation of nature, is unnatural (against man's true nature), while ecodevelopment, which is achieved by natural means is liberating and hence reveals itself as true development.

A consequence of this is that for main-stream developers in the North, the solution to perceived developmental and environmental problems, whether they occur in the North or in the South, are technical problems. By changing people's living conditions their lives are changed (for the better). For someone who holds the opposite view, the problem is not to interfere, but to refrain from interference, and to restore a state that has been lost by previous interference (from the North). And this restoration does not only restrict itself to the environment, it is also a restoration of human dignity, of aspects of the human being that have been suppressed as a result of development of the wrong kind. The goal is not to improve conditions by artificial means in order to allow man to enjoy the fruits of development at the cost of a separation from nature; the goal is instead to integrate man and nature, man as part of nature.

It may be noted that both versions of sustainable development seem to suffer from a lack of realism. Neither is able to spell out how the leap from today's condition to that of the ideal spelled out in the respective view of sustainable development is to be realized. In the main-stream argument, there is no suggestion as to how the necessary changes in global politico-economic structures are to be achieved; as for the ecodevelopment version, the transition towards self-supporting regions is not discussed.[11] Thus, the two images of the future stand separated from the present. In this sense they are both utopian.

PROBLEMS OF THE ENVIRONMENT: SOCIETY AND NATURE IN ACTION

A similar equation of the North with society and the South with nature can also be seen in the way that development problems are phrased. The problems that plague the North (and also the South by extension) are related to technology; they include pollution of the atmosphere, the thinning ozone layer, acid rain. The problems identified in the South are more directly related to the (careless and shortsighted) activities of common people, such as the cutting down of forests (especially the rain forest), desertification, shortage of food and water. Thus, Northern problems are more 'refined' or 'advanced' in that they relate to technology and science, privileged areas of human activity. In the South, by contrast, environmental problems are transparent in the sense that they can be related to people's daily activities, without any form of 'mediation' by high technology.

An even starker indication of this is the role that is being played by the South's 'teeming masses' which are seen as an environmental hazard of the first magnitude. Simply by being there and harbouring aspirations to emulate the North they pose a problem and a potential threat to rich countries. The South is, in this Northern discourse, helpless at best, a threat at worst. And it is the people themselves who pose the threat. By multiplying indiscriminately they become a natural hazard in the way that does any biological population that multiplies beyond the carrying capacity of the environment. Similar views of the South are found not only in the fields of ecology and development. The discussions about an emerging 'Festung Europa' follow similar lines of argument. Here, too, the millions of the poor are seen as a threat to the wellbeing of Europe, simply by being so many. Society has to demarcate a space for itself and hold Nature at bay, lest it be conquered by it as the forest takes possession of abandoned fields or weeds of a badly tended garden.

An important consequence of the definition of the Third World as part of nature is that the responsibility for saving the world for the future is laid on them; they must not rock the boat and they must lower their aspirations, since the world's resources will be depleted, and its inhabitants will have suffocated in the waste long before the masses of the South have reached the living standard of the North. Another implication is the continued dependence of the South on the North, given the belief that only technological and economic resources from the latter can really save the former. The 'hot' societies keep on blowing life into the lethargic, 'cold', ones.

In this battle of problem formulation, the argument from the ecodevelopment side, implicitly accepting the society – nature equation, is that it is the overconsumption of the North that is the main problem, an overconsumption of resources that starves the South. The solution is a way of life modelled on a non-exploitative relationship to nature that existed in the South prior to colonialization, and which has survived in isolated pockets into the present. In opposition to the image of the irresponsible 'savage', destroying its habitat that lurks behind Western definitions of the South's environment problems, they draw a picture of the 'noble savage', who, left to himself, will be able to lead a happy life in harmony with nature.

It is interesting to note that the North–South dichotomy is sometimes actively upheld, by both sides, as was the case when Malaysia, arguing against the Forest Treaty to be signed in Rio, said it would decline to halt logging of its rain forest, and opined that the North should take its responsibility and plant forest over 40 per cent of its territory (40 per cent being at present the average of forest cover in the South). For this the Malaysian Minister was censored by both Northern and Southern spokesmen. The lessons were clear: (1) Nature is for the South and should not be forced on the North; (2) Nature (including tribals) in the South must be protected and left intact.

WHERE IS THE PROBLEM? THE STRUGGLE OVER COMMONS

The confrontation between Southern and Northern versions of the world is not only a matter of using words. This becomes obvious when we look at some issues that have been up for discussion during the past few years. The Rio Conference highlighted some of them, in the process bringing out both the uneven power structures and the society–nature polarity.

One key question in this whole discussion is to do with how problems are formulated. We have already seen that to the North, it is mainly a problem of technology and monetary resources, where trade will contribute the resources to the South that the North feels unable to provide via grants and favourable loans. At the same time North defines the environmental problems as problems that involve the whole of the globe, i.e., as giving everyone, in North and South, the responsibility of contributing to a solution. That is to say, the North defines such issues in general terms. The solution proposed is two-fold: (1) to develop new, and less damaging, forms of technology, which will be done in the North; (2) to urge restraint on the South, since mass use of cars, refrigerators and other gadgets of the affluent society are wont to deplete the stock of non-renewable resources and to pollute the atmosphere, in the long run maybe even contribute to violent changes in the climate.

To say that the North has been able to define ecological problems mainly of its own making into general ones, is also to argue that part of the battle on the development/ecology front is being fought in terms of defining (or resisting definitions) of what should be regarded as commons to be used by whoever has the need and the resources to exploit them.[12] Thus, Northern suggestions that the forests of the South can be used as sinks for carbon dioxide released by human activity is one such attempt to see the South's natural resources as a common to be used, perhaps with some compensation, by the North which, lacking abundant natural resources, needs space to dispose of the waste resulting from its 'production of society'. A more straightforward approach to this very same problem, and rather more perverted, is to ship waste and garbage from the North to the South. Here the image of the South as something outside society becomes absurdly clear.

An even clearer example of the role-taking, society versus nature, can be seen in the field of the struggle over ownership of genetic, animal and plant, resources. This was a bone of contention at the Rio Conference under the name of the Convention on Biological Diversity. The name is slightly misleading. It was not so much an issue of preserving natural species, as an attempt at threshing out problems relating to the patenting of products of genetic engineering. The argument from the North was that such breeds were to be covered by patent laws and other laws pertaining to intellectual property, thus giving the scientists or the laboratory that had produced them exclusive rights over their use. This would mean that modified plants originally taken from the South could be sold or hired out to the Southern farmer who had cultivated them in the first place. This has been seen by ecologists in the South as a clear example of a society–nature scheme, where the North gives value only to work which is carried out in accordance with the (socially constructed) tenets of science, while devaluing the traditions of Southern practical knowledge.

The North's definition of genetic resources in the South as a commons has met with resistance, and in the charter to be signed at the Rio Conference there was a stipulation that such resources were to be the property of the country of origin. This was met by the argument that such resources rightly belong to the minorities who had cultivated them over thousands of years, and who were now being deprived of their ownership.

At the Rio Conference President Bush refused to sign the convention because he felt that it did not go far enough in terms of rights to patent and intellectual property, while representatives of the South felt that it defined 'country of origin' in such a way that it would give the same status in this regard to Northern gene banks as to the 'true' countries of origin in the South where it is part of the natural flora. (President Clinton has since agreed to sign it.)

Without pushing the issue too far, and without in any way belittling the economic importance of this controversy – that is obviously enormous – it may still be worthwhile to discuss it in terms of the society–nature divide. It is quite clear that the Northern strategy perpetuates the definition of the South as nature, i.e., the essentially colonialist view of the Third World as producer and exporter of raw materials, that are then refined and transformed in the North and then sold back to the South. The South resists this, overtly because such a strategy deprives it of resources to which it feels it has the sole right. But behind the economic argument is also the society–nature map of the world. In the South is found the main part of the species that exist on earth in a natural state. Duplication and mutations of these in laboratories in the North threaten this state of affairs. As noted, it deprives the South of a source of income, but it also threatens to undermine its role in the world as the provider of nature. If even nature becomes a product of society, there is not much left for the South.

The fact that part of the struggle is fought out through the definition and redefinition of commons should come as no surprise. The understanding of a commons is that it is empty of people and is to be used by anyone who has a defined right of access. A generous definition of the concept is clearly in the interest of the North which has the technology and financial resources to exploit such areas or use them in other ways, while the South is mainly in a position of disadvantage. The fact that ecology and development are linked becomes of crucial importance in the politics of the commons for two reasons. Firstly, through this linkage ecology and the solutions to environmental problems are seen as part of development, which is, in turn, defined as a form of evolution, most often as economic growth. Secondly, the presence of the term 'development' puts the focus on the Third World. Thus, a successful definition of a problem as a common problem leads to more areas being treated as commons. Through this allotment of roles in the global drama the South is seen as the passive part, nature to be acted on, and the North as the active agent, society imbued with will and power.

THE FUTURE: TOWARDS SELF-SUFFICIENCY?

As we have seen the Northern approach to future relationships with the South follows the logic of seeing the world as one. In accordance with this line of reasoning Northern resources shall be put in the service of the South to solve the latter's developmental and environmental problems. (Superior) society transforming (inferior) nature is the thought figure that dictates this strategy.

The opposite view is, not surprisingly, taken by ecodevelopment activists and many Southern governments. Their argument is that resources for development should be transferred as aid without any strings attached. That is to say, it should be aid in a form that is not coloured by the cultural and politico-economic designs of the donor. Put in symbolic terms, this is the statement of separation rather than unity; the logic of development in the South is different from that in the North, and any form of acceptance of the terms set forth by the latter are (quite rightly) construed as attempts at domination and symbolic incorporation.

But there are also two other, complementary, processes going on that work in the direction of separating North and South, processes that will deepen the dichotomy society–nature. It is in this context one must see the Northern hopes that are attached to genetic modification, and the sometimes gleeful prognostications by various experts that science in alliance with the prudence that sustainable development instructs, will make possible the future artificial production of non-renewable resources. Such a turn of events would make eternal economic growth come within reach. It would also make the North more or less independent of the South.

The contribution by ecodevelopment to future strategies for sustainable development does not go via technology and the artificial production of natural resources. It is rather a shift back to sustainable forms of using the environment that still exist in the South. This is, in view of the high hopes that development has held out for the Third World, a considerable lowering of aspirations, but one which, at least on the level of rhetoric, is put forth as the only form of genuine sustainable development that is realistic and ethically defensible.

Thus, if the future for the development optimists in the North will make the resources of the South superfluous, the ecodevelopment answer is to cut the ties to the North and have the South develop on its own, relying on its own resources. In other words, society and nature finally separated from one another.

SUMMARY REMARKS

The representation of the future of the world is still very much in terms of development and the progressive change by 'developing' countries in the image of the 'developed' ones. However, there are also a number of oppositions to this, some of which are part of the history of development thought. There is also a growing awareness that uninhibited 'development' in the South will bring problems on a global level, hence new forms of development will be necessary. In this debate there seems to be a rhetorical conjunction between, on the one hand, activists who see the future in terms of society coming to terms with nature in ways that are opposed to the Northern road to development, and, on the other, Northern interests who see a need for a continued dominance by the North of the South for environmental, political and economic reasons. Despite their diametrically opposed interests these two sides fall back on a nature–society distinction, sometimes explicitly sometimes implicitly in ways that build on age-old Western views of the 'Other'. 'Development' rhetoric, that takes its point of departure in the postulation that the difference between North and South is one of degree, is thereby combined with a rhetoric of difference in kind. Whether this is something that heralds a desire on the part of the North to 'dump' the South (a strategy that the ecodevelopmentalists and their sympathizers unwittingly facilitate), or if it is simply a mode of rhetorically coming to terms with a new and unfamiliar situation of global threats to the environment coupled to a new geo-political era, is too early to say. The debate is going on, however, and it is certain to have an impact on the way the world is going.

NOTES

I am indebted to the Swedish Council for Planning and Coordination of Research (FRN) for a grant that made the writing of this essay possible. I am also indebted to Bo Gustafsson and Ulf Hannerz for their comments on an earlier version of it. Any remaining mistakes or shortcomings are of course entirely my own responsibility.

1 J. Fabian, *Time and the Other* (New York, 1983); G. E. Marcus and M. M. J. Fischer, *Anthropology as Cultural Critique* (Chicago, 1986).

2 E. Wolf, *Europe and the People without History* (Berkeley, 1982).

3 M. L. Pratt, *Imperial Eyes* (London, 1992).

4 C. Lévi-Strauss, *The Savage Mind* (Chicago, 1966).

5 Cf. R. Inden, *Imagining India* (Cambridge, MA, 1992).

6 W. W. Rostow, *The Stages of Economic Growth* (Cambridge, 1960).

7 A. G. Frank, *Latin America: Underdevelopment or Revolution* (New York, 1969); and *Lumpenbourgeoisie, Lumpendevelopment: Dependence, Class and Politics in Latin America* (New York, 1973).

8 B. Hettne, 'Development Theory and the Third World', *SAREC Report* no. 2, Stockholm, 1982. See also W. M. Adams, *Green Development* (London, 1990), ch. 4, and I. Sachs, 'Developing in Harmony with Nature', in B. Glaeser (ed.), *Ecodevelopment* (Oxford, 1984).

9 V. Shiva, *Recovering the Real Meaning of Sustainability* (Dehra Dun, n.d.).

10 V. Shiva, 'The "Global" Environment: A Green Imperialism', *East Newsletter*, 11, 3 (1992).

11 For instance, Adams, *Green Development*; see also M. Redclift, *Development and the Environmental Crisis* (London, 1984), for a related argument.

12 G. Hardin, 'The Tragedy of the Commons', *Science*, 162 (1968), 1, 243–8; J. M. Acheson, 'Management of Common-Property Resources', in S. Plattner (ed.), *Economic Anthropology* (Stanford, 1989).

TWENTY

NATURE AND ECONOMY

BO GUSTAFSSON

Man spricht, wie man mir Nachricht gab,
Von keinem Graben, doch vom – Grab.

(They talk – such news to me they gave –
Not of a groove, but of a grave.)

J. W. Goethe, Faust, part 2, Act 5.

[Mephisto's comment to the blind Faust believing that he is hearing the noise of the labourers when reclaiming new land at the coast, a noise firing his great vision and therefore making him completely satisfied.]

The market mechanism is reasonably acceptable except for important goods.

H. D. Dickinson, quoted in D. Collard, *Altruism and Economy. A Study in Non-selfish Economics* (Oxford, 1981), p. 149

DARWIN taught us that human beings are a part of nature. But human beings are a very special species. While living organisms usually adapt to nature, human beings transform nature by engaging in economic activity. All living creatures are equipped with instruments that are part of the organism, such as fins, limbs, claws or hands. Alfred Lotka called these instruments *endosomatic* instruments. But human beings early developed what Lotka called *exosomatic* instruments, like knives, hammers, boats, engines, nuclear reactors and space ships and these exosomatic instruments have become more and more powerful over time due to technological progress.[1] While the economic activity of man is conditioned on the life-supporting functions of the biophysical environment, the growth of technology gives rise to a conflict between society and nature. The reason is that the economic activity has freed human beings from their immediate dependence on nature and made their transformational activity seemingly limitless, while the biophysical environment is finite. But since human beings are a part of nature and nature is finite, economic activity cannot be unlimited. Sooner or later this conflict must become manifest. During the twentieth century the conflict became manifest in the form of the environmental problem.

The relationships between nature and economic activity are exceedingly complex and not only contradictory but also complementary. Take, for example, technological change, which we will regard as induced by economic incentives rather as an autonomous factor. Scientific progress and technological change admittedly increase the known available stocks of resources and also increase usable stocks; they may 'improve' nature, as when they make it possible to transform deserts to cultivated land and to plant forests on barren steppes; new technologies may increase the durability of products, design products and processes that facilitate recycling, lower resource use per unit of final output and introduce products and processes that have less harmful effects on nature than old ones.

Hence, technological change removes old limits set by nature. But the progress of science and technology also introduce new limits and it is not at all certain that new knowledge abolishes limits faster than it imposes new ones. The discovery of uranium and asbestos to begin with increased the resource base of human beings but new knowledge led to a contraction of their use. When in the early twentieth century compressed ammonia gas replaced ice for refrigeration, deaths from food poisoning decreased markedly. But the toxicity and explosive properties of ammonia gas favoured the invention in the early 1930s of chlorinated fluorcarbon gas (Freon 12), which is non-flammable, non-toxic and non-explosive. The new stuff had these beneficial effects because it was stable. But it was precisely this stability that proved to be its greatest hazard. Once released into nature freon began to permeate the atmosphere, eventually reaching the ozone layer. In the presence of sunlight freon molecules started to destroy many times their number of the ozone molecules which filter out much of the sun's ultraviolet radiation and protect living organisms on the surface of our planet from the effects of radiation. The problem of the 'ozone hole' appeared.[2]

Secondly, and probably more importantly, economic and technological change proceed exponentially, while the bio-physical natural environment is limited. The power of exponential growth is well known. Still, it seems as if we prefer to believe that a long successful history of exponential growth also implies that we can accommodate a long future of exponential growth. But this is not true. As a consequence, growth may give rise to big surprises. The classical example is of course the pond of weed that every day doubles the surface. In thirty days the whole surface will be covered. When will half of the surface be covered? The answer is: in twenty-nine days and the last day the entire surface will be covered. This bio-physical constraint can be eased but not eliminated by diminishing resource input and diminishing waste output per unit of final output as well as by substitution with respect to specific activities. But since natural resources and the surface of the earth are finite, there is an ultimate limit.

This can be shown by an elementary accountant identity (where output is Y, resource use R and thus resource use per unit of output is R/Y:

$$R=R/Y\times Y$$

If Y is growing infinitely, R must also grow infinitely, even if R/Y declines, since R/Y cannot decline to zero (because there must be *some* positive resource use per unit of output). The same reasoning can be applied to output of waste ($W=W/Y\times Y$). The implication of this is that the problem of *scale* of economic activity is important in relationship to nature. If the scale of economic activity (production, consumption and capital accumulation) is continuously enlarged, this enlarged scale must sooner or later come into conflict with the limits of the bio-physical environment.

This conflict can be laid bare also in another way. In the process of production labour (L), man-made capital (C) and natural capital (R) is put in and transformed and out come final output (Y) and waste (W). Thus:

$$(Y, W)=f(L, C, R)$$

Thereby it should be noted that the scope of substitutability is limited between natural and man-made capital. Thinner and sharper saws generate less saw-dust and thus save some timber, when lumber is transformed into furniture. But if the number of saws is doubled, this does not imply that the input of timber into the process of sawing is halved. Neither do additions of saw-mills substitute for diminishing forests, more refineries for depleted oil wells or larger fishing nets for declining fish populations. On the contrary, the more man-made capital increases, the more natural capital is needed. The lesson is that natural capital as a provider of raw materials and energy to the process of production is not a substitute but essentially a complement to man-made capital.

While economic activity represents an act of transformation and of addition of utilities (economic values) over time, it represents from a physical point of view *a process of destruction and depletion.*

In the process of production it takes an *increase* of values; if not the transformation would not be undertaken. In a market economy this value-adding process is measured by prices, whereby output in value terms (Y) is balanced against inputs of labour (L) and capital (C). Since the physical form of capital is uninteresting from the point of view of value creation, capital (C) includes both man-made capital and natural capital (R), i.e. raw-materials and energy. In the process of economic growth the transformation is successful, if $(Y) > (L+C)$. But, from the point of the bio-physics of the transformation, production, first, does not only generate (Y) but also (W) and, secondly, it cannot be literally true that $Y > (L+C)$, since this violates the first law of thermodynamics, according to which matter-energy can be neither created nor destroyed but only change form. From the bio-physical point of view the process of production implies:

$$(Y) + (W) = (R) + (C) + (R) \quad \text{or rearranged:}$$

$$(R) - (W) = (Y) - (L + C)$$

The meaning of this fundamental equation is that human beings live on the difference between the flow of natural resources and the flow of waste.

This is precisely what we should expect granted the validity of the second law of thermodynamics, according to which available energy (low entropy) is transformed into unavailable energy (high entropy), as when coal is burned and transformed into heat and ashes and some amount of available energy is lost forever. This law is valid for a closed system, where there can be only a finite amount of low entropy and low entropy continuously and irrevocably dwindles away. If mankind in the future succeeds in utilizing solar energy on a large scale for industrial purposes, we do not need to bother much about the energy supply, since the world's total energy consumption at present may be only 0.005 per cent of total solar inflow. The time perspective is more limited with respect to estimated stocks of natural resources, although they vary in amounts. According to one estimate the stocks of coal, oil and gas would last for 2,500 years at the 1968 rate of world use.[3]

From a historical point of view mankind, since the start of the industrial revolution, has lived in a very special relationship to nature. Before the industrial revolution, when agriculture and cattle-raising were the main economic activities, mankind lived mainly on the solar source of low entropy. This source, which breeds the photosynthesis and plant growth, is very large in its stock dimension but limited in its flow dimension when arriving to our planet. The low intensity of solar energy, which is a blessing for agriculture, since it supplies the soil of the planet with energy necessary for plant growth, cannot (at least yet) be used for industrial purposes. The solar energy however once created the terrestrial dowry of fossil fuels. It was precisely this dowry that made possible the rise of industrial society and the introduction of the regime of high economic growth of modern history. Mankind cut loose from the solar source of energy and instead started to utilize the terrestrial source of low entropy: the stocks of coal and oil created by solar energy and past geological change. This source of low entropy energy has been large in its flow-dimension making industrialization and rapid growth possible. But in contradistinction to solar energy it is limited in its stock dimension and this has created the problem of scale in the relationship between nature and economic activity.[4]

The preceding observations on the (potential) conflict between nature and economic activity provide a starting point for the specification of rules for a potentially harmonious relationship between the two. Which are those rules that may provide our descendants with at least as good a life as the present generation? Nature provides resources that become material and energy inputs into the economic process; it assimilates wastes from the economic processes; and it provides a flow of 'natural' services to individuals and to society. The first of these three functions includes the provision of economically valuable non-renewable resource stocks like fossil fuels and mineral resources but also renewable resources like forests, fisheries and water supplies. The second function refers to the absorption by nature of waste residuals through its biological chains and material cycles. The third function refers to the preservation of nature and the maintenance of certain natural resources and ecological relationships (recreational benefits, health and life-support amenities, ecological mechanisms, climate, materials cycling, genetic diversity, plants useful for the development of medical drugs etc.).

Not any infringement on *in situ* natural resources or ecological relationships is negative. This is obviously true with respect to historically speaking such important activities as forestation of deserts, improvements of soil quality or certain kinds of land reclamation. Deforestation and transformation of forest land and wetlands into cultivated land have often had ambiguous effects. On the one hand they have contributed to the increase of economic values and on the other hand ecological mechanisms have sometimes been impaired and scenic views of high aesthetic value may have disappeared.

With respect to the first function of nature – resource and energy use – two sets of equilibrium conditions should be fulfilled. For renewable resources harvest rates should equal regeneration rates (sustainable yields) and for non-renewable resources the rate of depletion should ideally equal the rate of creation of new substitutes. With respect to the second function – waste emissions – waste emissions rates should equal the natural assimilative capacities of those ecosystems into which wastes are emitted. When it, lastly, comes to the third function of nature – the preservation of nature and the maintenance of life-supporting ecological relationships – it is difficult or even impossible to define a suitable equilibrium condition, because of the heterogeneity of the services involved as well as the associated genuine uncertainty as to consequences of human interference. The prevalence of uncertainty suggests some kind of cautionary principle, since the value of expected benefits under uncertainty is less than the value of expected benefits under certainty. Since the two preceding equilibrium conditions seem to imply that the stock of natural capital should be held constant over time, this objective may serve as a rough rule of the thumb for the third function.

II

We have so far assumed that economic activity is taking place in the abstract so to speak. But economic activity has always historical and institutional dimensions and it includes a wide variety of properties relevant for the interrelationship between nature and economy. There are many types of economic systems and any economic system is made up of various organizational structures and activities. An economic organization possesses a specific system of property rights, is guided by an objective function, is propelled by specific incentives and allocates resources accordingly. The activities consist in production, consumption and exchange. The scale of activities is determined by the state of technology and the resource endowments. Moreover, various properties of economic systems can be variously combined. So, for example, can the members of an economy of small producers be self-sufficient or market oriented and a collectivist economy can allocate resources by fiat or by the market mechanism. In one economic organization resources may lack specific owners (free access economy), in another they may be owned in common or be privately owned. Different economic organizations may adhere to different objective functions, like profit, average income or output maximization or just aiming at some target of satisfying returns. These variations of systems, organizations and properties may have considerable importance for the interaction between economy and nature. If property rights are lacking (*res nullius*) economic activity, *ceteris paribus*, usually affects nature more adversely than if property rights exist and are enforced, since no one has an interest in the long-run preservation of the resource exploited. An economic organization that aims at maximizing output uses more resources per unit of output than an economic organization that aims at maximizing rents, while collective (common) ownership in small groups aiming at maximizing average revenue per member may be superior to them both. On the basis of such observations it has been conjectured that the tremendous environmental destruction that took place in the former Soviet Union was conditioned by a combination of output maximizing of production and badly enforced (and enforceable) collective property rights, because centralized ownership of resources in effect functioned like an open access régime (*res nullius*).[5]

Investigating the relationship between nature and economy it is, hence, important to specify the nature of economic régime considered. Within environmental economics much interest has focused on the effects of various property rights arrangements and on the role of the market as a mechanism for allocating resources and even for managing the use of nature. Even if the market as a mechanism for allocating resources between property owners is compatible with various decentralized property rights régimes (independent property owners, capitalist property, cooperative (common) property), the standard case considered is an economic system made up of private capitalist property owners maximizing profits in competition with other capitalist property owners. It is this standard case we shall consider with respect to the interaction between nature and economic activity.

When the environmental problem became a public concern in the West from the 1960s, many took for granted that the destruction of nature was caused by an economic system based on private property and market exchange and that the harmful effects should be counteracted by administrative regulation setting standards, allowing targets and granting permissions for products and processes that might harm nature. The tide turned with two important events. One was the victorious return of the ideology and politics of the market – and the corresponding exit of planning and regulation – on a world scale since the 1980s.[6] The other was the success of the US tradeable permit approach to air pollution control.[7] In a recent book on environmental economics, *Green Markets. The Economics of Sustainable Development*, the author confidently declares: 'Ultimately, excessive environmental damage can be traced to "bad" economics stemming from misguided governmental policies and distorted markets that set appropriate prices for natural resources.'[8] The implication is that the general application of the market mechanism (as well as enlightened government policies), safeguarding undistorted markets and correct prices for natural resources, would be a necessary and sufficient condition for sustainable development. There would be no problems of scale of economic activity, all aspects of the world of nature would be accessible to the workings of the market mechanism and the laws of nature would be completely and harmoniously subsumed under the laws of perfectly competitive markets.

In order to be able to define the scope and limits of the market mechanism in the interaction between nature and economy, we should, first, consider what nature provides us and, secondly, investigate the conditions, properties and workings of the market mechanism. Only then will we be able to judge if and to what extent they may be compatible.

Nature provides four types of functions making existence of the human species possible: (1) regulation functions, (2) carrier functions, (3) production functions and (4) information functions. Most functions of nature are regulation functions, like the regulation of energy balances, the chemical composition of the atmosphere, the composition of the oceans and the climate but also storage and recycling of organic matter, nutrients and human waste as well as regulation of biological control mechanisms and maintenance of biological and genetical diversity. Examples of important carrier functions are cultivation and energy conversion. Production functions include production of oxygen, water, food, raw materials, fuel and genetic and medical resources, while the information functions include aesthetic, spiritual and historical information as well as cultural and artistic inspiration.

These functions are conditioned by a series of complex characteristics, processes and components, like geological, atmospheric, geomorphological and hydrological properties and processes, vegetation and habitat characteristics, species properties and population dynamics, food chain interactions and integrated ecosystem characteristics. Examples are precipitation, sedimentation, water runoffs, evaporation, nutrient uptake, species composition and diversity, photosynthesis, food chain interactions, critical ecosystem sizes and carrying capacities.

The functions of nature provide certain services to which we may attach values of various types. Environmental economists, reflecting the strongly reductionist bent of neoclassical economics, often prefer to see all types of nature's values as economic values and suggest that they consist of use values and non-use values. Use values are (1) direct values, (2) indirect values and (3) option values, while non-use values are (4) existence values. Thus TOTAL ECONOMIC VALUES = USE VALUES (direct values + indirect values + option values) + NON-USE VALUES (existence values). As an example of this reasoning, the total economic value of a forest would consist of timber products + nutrient recycling +

future use of products and nutrient recycling + the value of forest existence for its own sake. This taxonomy would be useful, if it were possible to assign meaningful economic indices to this mixture of qualitatively different kinds of values. But it is not. Direct use values of timber are easily inferred from sales on the market. But already the assignment of monetary values to indirect use values like nutrient recycling or watershed protection of a forest meets with difficulties. The difficulties increase, when we try to measure option values of a forest, i.e. the importance people would assign to its future potential benefits for harvesting, undiscovered species, maintenance of microclimate or whatever. The simple reason is that any assignment of quantitative values – not to speak of monetary values – would be completely arbitrary due to lack of information. Existence values like intangible ethical or aesthetical values are still more elusive and such values are by definition and function non-economic.

Let us take two concrete examples of the difficulties of assigning economic values to important values of nature. For many people the conservation of elephants may be a direct use value. They are prepared to pay for looking at them in a national park. But their willingness to pay differs for those people who are only interested in the products of elephants' tusks. While the former pay for seeing living elephants, the latter pay for (a part of) dead elephants. For those people, moreover, who are only interested in the existence of elephants for their own sake, the willingness to pay may vary from zero to very high prices. Or take an indirect use value like the global photosynthesis the process in which carbon dioxide plus water plus light energy, in the presence of enzyme systems associated with chlorophyll, results in glucose plus oxygen. During photosynthesis part of the sunlight energy is stored as potential or 'bound' energy. It is absolutely essential for life processes. It is thus a carrier of a tremendous indirect use (and economic) value in the jargon of the economists. Now according to some estimates about 40 per cent of the global photosynthesis is carried by algae and cyanobacteria (blue-green algae). It would be a daunting exercise for anybody – economist or not – to assign economic values to the estimated 0.2–1.0 million species of algae.[9]

It would be much more meaningful to acknowledge the inherently incommensurable nature of the values of nature. Following de Groot we may rather group these values into three sets: ecological values, social values and economic values. Ecological values are associated mainly – but not exclusively – with the regulation and information functions of nature as in the case of biophysical mechanisms (energy balances, hydrological cycles, storage and recycling of nutrients) or genetic information for scientific purposes. We may discern two subsets of ecological values: conservation and existence values respectively. Like all entities, ecological values also possess quantitative aspects. But usually these aspects are so difficult to define in a meaningful way so that we for practical purposes regard ecological values as qualitative entities as when we say about a human being that she or he is 'good', 'OK' or 'bad'. Sometimes it is possible to set standards or limits for an ecological function, e.g. for waste absorption, but this still does not take us into the domain of economic values. Sometimes there is no correspondence between the importance of a natural entity to human beings and its importance to an ecological mechanism. Some species who are very rare or narrowly distributed and therefore most likely to become extinct are the ones least likely to be 'missed' by the biosphere. But they may be greatly missed by human beings like the wild rice *Oryza nivara* that is the only source of resistance to grass stunt virus. Ecological values are, moreover, difficult to observe, because they are often unlikely to be recognized until some disastrous event has happened: erosion of soils after over-grazing, landslides after deforestation etc.

While ecological values are strongly nature oriented, the social values of nature are a category in between nature oriented and individual oriented values like use values. While they are rooted in and expressed by individuals they become meaningful only in so far as they are community oriented. Option values belong here, since an individual that favours future choices may not herself benefit from them. Generally speaking the social values of nature refer to the importance people assign to safety or health – including a safe future and a future health – and to potential benefits of natural processes or species, including those not yet discovered. My valuation of the continued existence of humankind would thus qualify as a social value of nature. Likewise, if I value the preservation of natural parks or species, even if I myself never would be able to enjoy or see them (except on a TV screen or by reading about them).

Economic values of nature are values that to a greater or smaller extent can be expressed in prices, i.e. measured by some monetary standard. As a category they are the most individual-oriented of the values of nature. Still economic values are also of various kinds, from regulated values that are assigned in a political-administrative process like taxes or charges, primarily reflecting the preferences of the regulators on their perceptions of the preferences of experts, political parties and voters as well as strategic considerations about what is possible or suitable; imputed prices, like shadow prices, that represent more or less imperfect attempts to interpret and translate opportunity costs and consumers' preferences; and lastly market prices, that ideally have originated in a spontaneous allocation process, where free choice and extensive information of the consumers, extensive competition among producers and absence of pervasive externalities, of public goods and of increasing returns, give rise to a unique set of equilibrium values. *What is important to observe here is that market values are a subset of economic values, that in their turn are a subset of the values of nature.*

If we now try to correlate the four functions of nature – regulation, carrier, production and information – with the values of nature, we may make the following observations. In the first place, ecological values are mainly associated with regulation and information functions, that represent the most important functions of nature. Social values are, secondly, associated with all four functions of nature. Thirdly, economic values are mainly associated with the carrier and production functions. The conclusion is that economic values are relevant only for a limited part of the functions and values of nature and among economic values market values represent only a subset.

III

These observations lead us to take a closer look at the role of the market mechanism in the relationship between nature and economy. The market is a mechanism for allocating resources between economic agents by free exchange. The existence and usefulness of markets are conditioned by a series of conditions: (1) Self-interested utility maximizing traders. (2) Institutions, i.e. formal and informal rules specifying permissible choices; among these decentralized and well-defined property rights with accompanying enforcement mechanisms are the most important ones. (3) Excludibility in supply and rivalry in demand, which technically defines private in contradistinction to public goods and which also excludes pervasive external (non-intended and non-demanded) effects. (4) Comparative advantage in the conditions of production and hence division of labour between producers. (5) Differences in preference scales of consumers. (6) Free entry and exit to exchange between traders. (7) The number of traders must be 'large' to ensure competition and in order to make traders 'price takers', i.e. not being able to manipulate prices. (8) 'Sufficient' and symmetrically distributed information between traders about goods, terms of trade and opportunities to trade. (9) Lastly, transactions costs (search costs, bargaining costs and enforcement costs) must not be 'too high'.

In actually existing market economies these conditions are only imperfectly fulfilled and therefore also actually existing markets are only imperfect. If the imperfections become too large and too many, markets fail and may disappear (or fail to arise). If this is the case other mechanisms of allocation replace the market mechanism, e.g. by command (as in a patriarchal family, a capitalist firm, a government agency or in a centrally planned collectivist economy), by majority vote (as in a parliament or in a democratic organization, e.g. a cooperative) or by collective consensual decision making (as e.g. an ideal family).

Even under the most favourable conditions market mechanisms are not only imperfect but are responsible for only a minor share of all allocation decisions taking place, e.g. by central and local governments, by organizations, within firms, in families or between neighbours or friends or in isolated exchange acts between individuals or big organizations. Nature allows for a still more restricted scope for the market mechanism. (1) Self-interested utility maximization of individuals conflicts with the existence of non-renewable resources as well as with the interests of future generations, since not even the bequest motive and overlapping generations could prevent gradual physical exhaustion. (2) Property rights to regulation functions, air or pelagic resources cannot be established and if they were established they could not be enforced because of forbiddingly high transaction costs. (3) This is so because natural goods are often public goods and hence not accessible to excludibility in supply and rivalry in demand. (4) Division of labour implies specialization and the market mechanism thrives on specialization, because it brings lower costs and increased rewards. But specialization on the one hand diminishes bio-diversity and on the other hand makes the links between decisions of production and decisions of consumption more and more complex and anonymous. Nature thrives on diversity, because diversity facilitates resilience. But since the introduction of agriculture and, at an accelerated rate, since the introduction of the market mechanism the last two centuries, a large-scale extinction of species has been going on. While there are thousands of edible plant species, the vast majority of the world's food is produced by only twenty species. The genetic uniformity of food crops has advanced so far, so that 50 to 75 per cent of varieties may descend from one maternal parent plant and 50 per cent or more of crops are supplied by 3–10 varieties. While the number of domesticated cattle on the globe increases all the time, the number of almost all other species declines continuously. This process is propelled by the market induced specialization, which brings higher productivity. But at the same time this depletion of bio-diversity is spoiling 'a uniquely formulated insurance policy against shocks to the life system itself ... because existing life forms encapsulate a history of successful adaption within a changing physical environment'.[10] The current drive toward uniformity, propelled by the market mechanism, reduces evolutionary fitness that is conditioned by diversity.

The increasingly complex and anonymous links between decisions of production and decisions of consumption, as a consequence of increasing specialization, make it more and more difficult for consumers on the market to signal adequate environmental preferences to producers in various parts of the world. They may not even be aware of their existence especially if many different producers have contributed to the production of a specific good. Swedish consumers of Swedish pork have a fair chance to influence Swedish pig farmers not to use too much chemicals. But Swedish consumers of Dutch pork are hardly influenced in their consumption decision by the fact that chemical intensive Dutch pig farming threatens Dutch soil with destruction. The smaller the share of a good in the expenditure of any single consumer's budget, the less the incentive to bother, while the added expenditure of millions of consumers may have catastrophic consequences for nature.

(5) The stocks and flows of information about ecological mechanisms are notoriously deficient. This is because the functions of nature are interrelated and systemic and maintain themselves by diversity. They are fundamentally non-linear in causation and demonstrate multi-stable states and discontinuous behaviour in time and space. There are limits to their capability for resilience and when these limits are transgressed, due to the accumulation of human impacts, sudden changes occur. Their spans of connections are also often overlapping in space and time and are becoming more so due to the transformation of earth by human economic activity.[11] There does not exist any mechanism that can guarantee that the behaviour of nature and the behaviour of the market are adjusted to each other except by pure chance. If the market emits a signal to farmers to grow broccoli, they write contracts with buyers specifying quantities, prices, qualities etc. and the farmers buy seeds, allocate land, plant, harvest and sell outputs more or less according to plans, because they are able to entice and use sufficient information. But if the market emits a signal to fishermen to catch cod, they are largely dependent upon chance due to the lack of information about fish stocks and the biological structure of the fish population. They may be lucky and catch big, old fish of high economic value. But even if they happen to optimize harvest rate, they may affect age of capture negatively. As a consequence they may bring mainly herring in the future, since the diminished stock of cods would favour the growth of herrings (a favourite food of cods). Alternatively catches would deplete vulnerable sub-species of cod or bring species or sizes of fish that are low-priced and less desired by the market.

(6) Due to the fact that the goods of nature are often public in nature, escape attempts to appropriate them by private property rights and, when exploited, give rise to external effects, efforts to market them meet usually with high transaction costs and the higher the transaction costs, the more imperfect the markets.

But if the market does not provide a useful and reliable mechanism for handling the interaction between nature and economy, we cannot rely on it for the valuation of the goods of nature. Imputation of values and assignment of implicit prices may solve certain problems and in specific areas extend the domain of the market mechanism. But from the theory of the second best we know that such partial corrections may bring outcomes that harm more than they help. Summing this up we may say that, *within a very limited range*, the extended use of the market mechanism would bring a more efficient utilization of the goods of nature. But outside this range there are spheres of nature that are inaccessible to this mechanism and these spheres are the most important for the continued existence of mankind.

IV

If this conclusion is sound, we should not expect too much from the use of the market mechanism in environmental management now much in vogue. In many texts on environmental policy terminology is sometimes confusing and 'market mechanisms' are often contrasted with 'regulation'. But in fact environmental policy always implies regulation of one kind or another. There are two subsets of regulation: administrative mechanisms, when standards and targets are set and permissions issued; and incentive mechanisms, when the regulation is designed in such a way that the incentives of the economic agents to comply with the regulation are involved. These incentive mechanisms consist in their turn of two subsets: price mechanisms, when government uses taxes, charges or subsidies to affect behaviour toward nature; and market or quantity mechanisms, when government creates a market for resource exploitation (tradeable quotas) or for pollution (tradeable permits) and lets traders find prices. Only this last mentioned policy option, i.e. quantity mechanisms, can be regarded as market mechanisms. But it is important to observe that these market mechanisms are created and changed by policy decisions and enforced and monitored by administrative structures. They have family resemblance with proper market mechanisms in so far as there are traders, contracts, prices, incentive mechanisms and cost minimization behaviour involved. But in contradistinction to proper market mechanisms, more or less representing a 'spontaneous order' in

Hayek's sense, the market mechanisms of environmental management should be compared rather with markets in socialist economies: government creates them; market agents would, if offered the option to choose, rather do without them, since they represent a costly constraint; there are no inbuilt mechanisms in exchange for control of quality of traded goods; and they presuppose a substantial amount of metering and monitoring by environmental administration.

The over-enthusiasm for the use of market mechanisms in environmental management is explained largely by their successful career in US air pollution control. But even in this 'niche' of environmental policy their success is mainly limited to stationary-source local air pollution. They have not been applied to regional or global air pollution, mobile-source air pollution (like cars), water pollution or the use of toxic substances. In these areas administrative as well as price mechanisms can be used and are, indeed, used. The last-mentioned mechanisms should be used whenever market failures, as in the case of the goods of nature (see above), are prevalent and, especially, when (1) uncertainty prevails and precautionary action is suggested; when (2) the interests of future generations are involved; when (3) swift action is necessary; and when (4) ecological limits evidently have been reached.

The advocates of market mechanisms in environmental management quite correctly point out that, on the one hand, administrative mechanisms have limited flexibility, meet problems in enticing information from agents and do not make use of the incentives of agents to participate in environmental management; on the other hand, that market mechanisms should bring about cost efficiency and, first and foremost, that they let the market agents themselves work for the interests of nature. This is so because environmental administrations set quantities (of pollution or resource use) and let the market agents themselves find out, by trading pollution permits or resource use quotas, the proper prices/costs for these so that the marginal costs for pollution or resource control should be equal to the price of permits or quotas in the market. From the point of view of cost-efficient environmental management, the market mechanism thus is an ideal policy instrument, since it permits authorities to have the polluters/resource users themselves to control, on efficiency grounds, what authorities first and foremost want to control: physical exploitation of nature.[12]

But, as we already have seen, it is quite unlikely that nature permits this possible world to be extensively realized. Empirical studies of the use of market mechanisms in environmental management tend to confirm this intuition. The goods traded (pollution permits and resource quotas) are heterogenous and difficult to define; property rights are fuzzy; prices are sticky; uncertainty about future markets and prices is widespread, partly because future policy changes cannot be predicted; and transaction costs – search costs as well as bargaining costs and enforcement costs – are often staggering.[13] The underlying causes are, firstly, the fact that environmental regulation is essentially a political-administrative process that creates changing frameworks and constraints for environmental markets; secondly, that this gives rise to uncertainty and limitations on property rights; thirdly, that efficient environmental management has to be monitored and implemented and this in its turn necessitates segmentation of markets and, consequently, also 'thin' and therefore imperfect markets. A successful coping with the relationship between an expanding social and a limited natural system has, for the foreseeable future, to rely, not on less but on more extensive use of political-administrative mechanisms, legal enactments and, ultimately, on a new ethics towards nature. Markets can help mankind *sticking to* a cost-efficient development trajectory. But they are of little help, if any, in *finding* the trajectory that safeguards sustainability.[14]

NOTES

1 The reference to Lotka is found in Nicholas Georgescu-Roegen, *The Entropy Law and the Economic Process* (Cambridge, MA, 1971), p. 11.

2 Paul C. Stern, Oran R. Young and Daniel Druckman (eds.), *Global Environmental Change. Understanding the Human Dimensions* (Washington, D.C., 1992), pp. 54–60.

3 Partha Dasgupta, 'Exhaustible Resources', in Laurie Friday and Ronald Laskey (eds.), *The Fragile Environment. The Darwin College Lectures* (Cambridge, 1988), pp. 107–26.

4 Nicholas Georgescu-Roegen, *Energy and Economic Myths. Institutional and Analytical Economic Essays* (New York, 1976), pp. 3–36.

5 Bo Gustafsson, 'Economic Organization and Environment', discussion paper, Swedish Collegium for Advanced Study in Social Sciences, September 1993, Uppsala.

6 John Donahue, *The Privatization Decision. Public Ends, Private Means* (New York, 1989).

7 Tom Tietenberg, 'Economic Instruments for Environmental Regulation', in Dieter Helm (ed.), *Economic Policy Towards the Environment* (Oxford, 1991).

8 Theodore Panayotou, *Green Markets. The Economics of Sustainable Development* (San Francisco, 1993).

9 Per Molander, *Miljön som långsiktig restriktion. Långtidsutredningen 1995*, bilaga 2. Finansdepartementet. Stockholm (The Environment as a long-term Constraint. The Long-term Report 1995, Supplement 2. Minister of Finance. Stockholm).

10 Timothy M. Swanson, *The International Regulation of Extinction* (London, 1994), ch. 2.

11 C. S. Holling, 'New Science and New Investment for a Sustainable Biosphere', in A. M. Jansson, M. Hammer, C. Folke and R. Costanza (eds.), *Investing in Natural Capital* (Washington, 1994).

12 Tietenberg, 'Economic Instruments' (see note 7).

13 See e.g. Vivien Foster and Robert W. Hahn, 'Designing more Efficient Markets: Lessons from Los Angeles Smog Control', *Journal of Law and Economics*, 38 (April 1995), 9–47. For a fuller treatment of the role of the market mechanism in environmental management, see the author's forthcoming 'Scope and Limits of the Market Mechanism in Environmental Management' in the journal *Ecological Economics* (1997).

14 Suppose all goods consist of nature's goods (NG) and other goods (OG) and that we can produce and consume one subset of goods at the expense of the other subset. Then the total space of goods would be like the production (and consumption) possibility curves AB and CD in the following diagram. CD represents an increase of available goods compared to AB. There are two development trajectories. I represents a cost-efficient but not desirable trajectory. It is efficient because the points a and b represent optimal (largest possible) combinations of NG and OG, since they are located on (and not inside or – which would be a non-feasible combination – outside) the possibility frontier. I is assumed to be the result of the working of a perfect market. It is a non-desirable trajectory, because it leads to increasing relative production and consumption of nature's goods. II, on the other hand, consequently represents a trajectory that is desirable but not cost-efficient (a′ and b′ signify that resources are not used optimally). The market mechanism can only safeguard the efficiency of trajectory I, not that that it is desirable. Since there are physical limits to growth and I heads towards catastrophical outcomes, we should prefer II to I, even if II is not cost-efficient. If II could be obtained cost-efficiently, we would be grateful. But if the argument of this paper is correct, the market mechanism, to be (close to) perfect, requires conditions that prevent the realization of the efficiency of II.

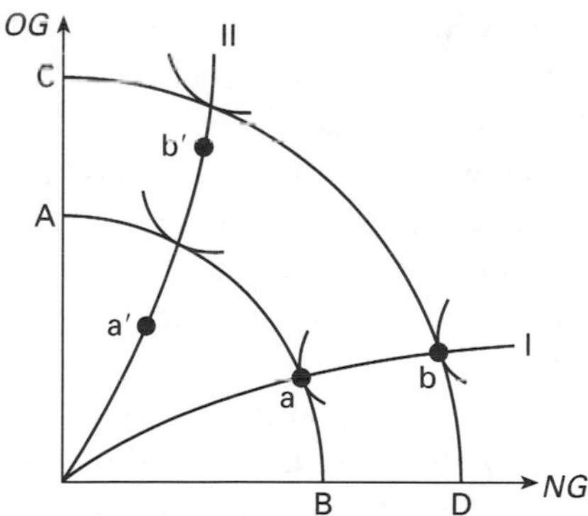

100%

TWENTY-ONE

THE NATURE OF MORALITY AND THE MORALITY OF NATURE: PROBLEMS AND PARADOXES OF A NORMATIVE NATURAL PHILOSOPHY

KURT BAYERTZ

THE IDEA OF A PRACTICAL PHILOSOPHY OF NATURE

AT the end of the twentieth century, the problem of nature has assumed a position within philosophical thinking which would have been scarcely imaginable a few decades ago. Of course, the concept of nature has had a dominant position within eighteenth century philosophy; yet the following century was to be witness to a process that could be termed a gradual – albeit never totally successful – exclusion of nature from the realms of philosophy. The successes of scientific research had been so impressive that any genuine philosophical reflection about nature appeared superfluous and senseless. Stemming from a conviction that any true and real knowledge to be gained from nature can only take place within the sciences, Ludwig Wittgenstein came to a conclusion within his *Tractatus* which was to retain its authority for decades to come: Assuming that science is identical to the 'totality of true propositions', philosophy no longer has a place 'beside the natural sciences', but stands 'above or below' them.[1] To put it another way: philosophy does not possess any lessons of its own, instead making do with the explanation and clarification of scientific statements. Subsequent to the 'linguistic turn', philosophy was therefore denied direct access to nature. It could only turn to her indirectly, as a metatheory of the natural sciences. A philosophy of nature was replaced by a philosophy of natural science.

Over the last two decades, this situation has changed drastically. Whilst analytical philosophy has become less influential, approaches towards a 'material' philosophy of nature – Whitehead's philosophy, for example – have gained considerably in esteem. At the same time, a change in perspectives has occurred. Nature is no longer perceived merely as the correlate of theoretical knowledge but increasingly as the object of human practice and, above all, of modern technology. This change in perspective has consequences which amount to a paradigm shift within the philosophy of nature. As soon as the attempt to comprehend not only nature *per se* but nature in its relationship to the human race, i.e. as soon as human action becomes part of the object of a philosophy of nature, normative issues can no longer be excluded. Natural philosophy begins to be concerned with the 'ought' of nature (insofar as the latter is exposed to the powers of human action), instead of being restricted to her 'is'. According to Aristotle's distinction between theoretical and practical philosophy,[2] one may say that classical, i.e. theoretical, philosophy of nature has been supplemented with practical philosophy of nature, examining the theme 'nature' from a normative point of view.

This idea of a practical philosophy of nature did not arise for internal philosophical reasons. The current global, ecological crisis is behind it. Over the last few decades it has become clear that further treatment of our natural resources in the manner to which developed industrial nations are presently accustomed – not to mention the extension of such treatment to the developing countries – may, in the not too distant future, lead to a collapsing of the terrestrial ecosystem. Such a collapse would pose a serious threat to the living conditions of the human race. It should be emphasized that this insight is unprecedented within human history. The past has, admittedly, seen many prophecies regarding the end of the world, two (very different) examples being Christian eschatology and a theory, popular in the nineteenth century, that the universe will die from the increase of entropy ('Wärmetod'). Yet these and other examples represent visions of a downfall overpowering the human race 'from beyond'. In contrast, a collapse of the terrestrial ecosystem which would rob the human race – and possibly all higher forms of life – of their natural and existential basics would be a downfall caused by the human race itself: a downfall for which it would therefore also have to assume moral responsibility. The idea of such self-destruction blows up all previous philosophical conceptions of the human race. Former philosophies, prevalent in ancient times or within civilizations outside of Europe, could never have conceived of the human race possessing so much power, and modern views simply do not allow for nature 'reacting' in this way. Nature now appears as the more or less passive object of human action – unruly from time to time, but manageable after all. When Hume maintained in the mid eighteenth century that ''Tis not contrary to reason to prefer the destruction of the whole world to the scratching of my finger',[3] this theory was not only totally hypothetical, but particularly far removed from the notion of a complete world destruction *by the human race.* At about the same time in France,

Buffon had attributed to the human race the power to change, reform and develop nature. The human race is denied but two things: the ability permanently to destroy nature, and the ability to create something totally new. According to Buffon, God had reserved these two capabilities for Himself.[4] Today we can no longer be discharged of the potentially catastrophic consequences of human action. The human race has burdened itself with the responsibility for the continuation of nature, maybe not in her entirety, but certainly of the terrestrial biosphere in its current form.

The idea of a practical philosophy of nature is a reaction to this not only ethically, but also (to put it somewhat dramatically) metaphysically new situation. This philosophy of nature is 'practical', not least because it has a practical goal: 'not knowledge but action'.[5] It aims to work out the normative principles behind a new relationship between the human race and Nature, and in this way to contribute to preventing an ecological catastrophe. Its central theory is that this aim can only succeed if the human race recognizes a *value inherent to nature*. Accordingly, its entire efforts are channelled towards confirming such an inherent value. This theory also distinguishes a practical philosophy of nature from other philosophical reactions to the ecological crisis. These rather more pragmatically orientated approaches also aim at a more careful treatment of nature, but they do so without relying on the idea of confirming a value inherent to nature. They prove, for example, that careful treatment is *prudent* with regard to ensuring human interests in the long term. This second trend within environmental ethics may be termed the 'weak programme', whereas the first trend may be termed the 'strong programme'. The crucial difference between the two within our context here is that the 'strong programme' would like to attribute its formulated norms to *a normatively contentful concept of nature* – an idea which would put paid to the entire paradigm of modern philosophy.

Unable to present even an attempt at a thorough analysis of this strong programme, in the following paragraphs I would like at least to examine some of the basic ideas behind it. They primarily involve three different, but not totally independent, attempts at establishing the normative content of the concept of nature. They are the idea of a *sacredness* within nature, the idea of a return to *teleology* and the call to overcome *anthropocentrism.*

RESTORING THE CATEGORY OF SACREDNESS

All the philosophical efforts contained within a practical philosophy of nature may be interpreted as attempts to raise nature above the status of a value-for-us to that of a value-as-such. In other words: ascribe to her inherent moral values. In its strictest version such a remoralization of nature would postulate that nature be sacred. For if individual natural phenomena, or even nature in her entirety, possess inherent moral qualities, only a minor change of accent towards the religious is needed in order to come to a sacredness of nature. The practical goal behind such a reformation of ethics is obvious: with the advancing destruction of our natural environment in mind, inconsiderate treatment of nature is to be stopped by a morality which demands that nature be respected as a moral obligation. Hans Jonas, therefore, has raised the question:

> It is moot whether, without restoring the category of the sacred, the category most thoroughly destroyed by the scientific enlightenment, we can have an ethics able to cope with the extreme powers which we possess today and constantly increase and are almost compelled to wield. Regarding those consequences that are imminent enough still to hit ourselves, fear can do the job – fear which is so often the best substitute for genuine virtue or wisdom. But this means fails us toward the more distant prospects, which here matter the most, especially as the beginnings seem mostly innocent in their smallness. Only awe of the sacred which its unqualified veto is independent of the computations of mundane fear and the solace of uncertainty about distant prospects.[6]

Assuming that Jonas is right in suggesting that we have to restore the category of the sacred, this immediately gives rise to further questions. One of them is: how far should we expand this idea of 'sacredness' over the different parts of nature? One possibility would be to view all *living* nature as sacred. Albert Schweitzer has philosophized along these lines:

> Human beings are only truly ethical when they obey the compulsion to help everything alive which they are able to help, and when they shrink back from inflicting harm upon the same. They do not question the extent to which this life or that is worthy, nor the extent to which it is able to feel. They perceive life itself as holy. They do not tear leaves from trees, nor do they pick flowers, and they are careful not to tread upon any insects. At work by lamplight on a Summer's night, they prefer to keep the windows closed and to breathe stale air, than to watch the insects fall one by one onto the table with their wings singed.[7]

Whereas Albert Schweitzer limits sacredness to living nature, other authors would like to see it extended to the whole of nature, to non-living matter, including landscapes, rivers, mountains or stones. They like to formulate this idea of an all-encompassing sacredness in a more modern language, using 'reverence' instead of 'sacredness' and 'eco-system' instead of 'creation'. Especially the language of systems theory seems to be well suited for the purposes of such 'holistic'[8] conceptions of environmental ethics:

> Albert Schweitzer called for reverence for life. On this basis we must call for reverence for the level-structure of the microhierarchy, including all systems on all its levels, from atoms to an emerging planetary culture, economy, and ecology. We must envision the biosphere as a whole – the earth as a 'spaceship', with mutually destructive interdependencies. The emergence of a planet-wide interdependent ecology is an imminent reality, and it needs to be dealt with. We must regain our implicit natural values: our instinctual and long-buried adaption to the order of nature in the microhierarchy. I believe that we can express the recovery of our intrinsic natural values in requesting a *reverence for natural systems*.[9]

Yet it is obvious that this position – carried to its radical conclusion – would make human life impossible. As a natural being, the human being depends upon a metabolism with its natural surroundings. It has to kill animals and plants in order to feed and clothe itself. If it refrained from killing them out of respect for their 'sacredness', it would kill itself – thus killing a being which is no less sacred than the animals and plants it is called to protect. We are thus faced with a choice which can be formulated as a classical dilemma: *either* we gear our actions affecting nature towards ensuring our own survival, *then* we are forced to dismiss the sacredness of many natural objects. We have to breed and slaughter animals, fight pathogens, dam rivers or force them to flow through power plants, etc. *Or* we respect the sacredness of nature as an absolute limit for our actions, *then*, however, we bring about the sure death of the human race, thus violating its sacredness. For human beings are no less sacred than any other natural objects. This dilemma has not escaped the advocates of nature's sacredness. The practical unavoidability of control over and exploitation of nature is too obvious to be ignored. Albert Schweitzer states:

> There are thousands of ways in which my existence comes into conflict with the existence of others. The necessity of destroying and harming the lives of others has been forced upon me. Whenever I wander along a lonely path, my feet inflict destruction and pain on all the tiny creatures living there. In order to preserve my existence, I have to fend off the existences which harm it. I become the persecutor of the little mouse which lives in my house, the murderer of the insect which chooses to nest there, the mass murderer of the bacteria which could endanger my life. I destroy plants and animals in order to feed myself.[10]

Some Asian religions have attempted to avoid this dilemma by retreating from the world, practising quietism and asceticism. Schweitzer is not in favour of this course, for not even the strictest limitation of one's needs or the most consistent passivity are able to put a complete end to the dilemma. What he does not want, however, is to take comfort in the unavoidability of this conflict. He wants to make the point that in killing the living – however unavoidable this may be – we are morally guilty, and that we have to be aware of this guilt. 'We must never become blunted. The more intensely we experience conflict, the more we remain truthful. The good conscience is an invention of the Devil.'[11] The problem with this viewpoint is that, although it may concede the unavoidability of destroying life, it regards this as a guilty act. This abandons the traditional concept of guilt – which presupposes an intention to act, as well as the avoidability of its consequences – and dissolves the specifically *moral* dimension of the concept. Morally attributable guilt and casual 'authorship' become identical. The consequence of such an extension to the concept of guilt is the exact opposite of that intended: the concept of 'guilt' loses its moral meaning. The difference between moral and immoral behaviour vanishes. For if the human being is constantly, unavoidably and necessarily guilty, then all actions may ultimately be attributed with the same – immoral – value, and there is no longer any reason to behave morally. Protagonists of the practical philosophy of nature have attempted to avoid this consequence and to relativize the principle of sacredness in such a way that it is compatible with the human interest in self-preservation. They concede

> that we need plants, or at least their fruit, in order to live, and that we have to protect ourselves against diseases, whether we do so by strengthening the human body's powers of resistance, or by combatting pathogens. Living in peace with Nature may therefore not exclude combatting the smallpox pathogen, for example. I even believe, to take a very extreme example, that not even animal experiments should be fundamentally excluded, provided that they are for medical and veterinary purposes, that there are no other methods available, and that they are not linked with terrible suffering.[12]

The problem with this reasonable line of argument is that it weakens the idea of the sacredness of nature to a considerable extent. The original intention of justifying moral limitations to human actions with the concept of nature's sacredness has proved to be illusory. 'Sacredness' implies no more any absolute limit to human actions. A plea is made that nature be respected and that human interests by *principally* more important than the 'interests' of nature. This would mean that in a particular case, the human interests and those of nature would have to be weighed up against each other carefully. We are, therefore, referred back to the necessity of conducting a calculation of interests, in which no parameter is in principle untouchable.

Another problem posed by sacredness is that the religious implications behind this term make it difficult to take it as the basis for an ecological ethics within a pluralistic society. Jonas recognized this difficulty, writing that the basis for a practical philosophy of nature cannot be found in religious faith. He believes *metaphysics* to be the only possible foundation for the ethics both necessary and sought after:

> Faith in revealed truth thus can very well supply the foundations for ethics, but it is not there on command, and not even the strongest argument of need permits restoration to a faith that is absent or discredited. Metaphysics on the other hand has always been a business of reason, and reason can be set to work upon demand.[13]

RENEWING TELEOLOGY

According to Jonas, this metaphysic is centered around a renewal of teleological thinking. Modern destruction of the idea of nature having a destination is closely connected with a multitude of problems further complicating the strong programme of an ecological ethics. One of these is the strict division between nature and the human race on the one hand, and between 'is' and 'ought' on the other. Jonas sees it as his main task to construct a metaphysic which can overcome the *scandalon* throughout the field of modern ethics: the gulf between 'is' and 'ought'. His aim is to make plausible the futility of this gulf, by proving the existence of purposes within nature. He attempts to achieve his aim with the argument that the fact that human individuals define their purposes *subjectively* has to be taken as an indication of the existence of purposes throughout nature. Since, (a) subjectivity has emerged from organic and inorganic nature as a product of evolution and (b) evolution is a gradual, developmental process, not party to sudden leaps or the surprising emergence of new characteristics, then (c) subjective definitions of purpose must have their roots in pre-subjective nature: purposes must be prevalent throughout the *whole* of nature.

I cannot go into the details of this argument. But Jonas is not alone in his efforts. There have been various approaches towards a revision of modern metaphysics, some of them as early as in the first half of the 1970s: 'I suspect that we may be forced to a much older classical medieval notion that there is, indeed, a nature, man is part of that nature, and that nature is teleological in some very fundamental sense.'[14] Behind these efforts to revitalize teleology is the conviction that the problems facing us today are a consequence of the modern view of the world, according to which the human being no longer sees itself as a member of a purposeful ordering within nature, but as a subject, confronted with a morally neutral world. 'The ecological crisis stems from the explosive expansion in human control over Nature ideologically embedded in the anti-teleological philosophy prevalent since the early Modern Ages.'[15] A universe which is governed by 'blind' natural laws and mere chance does not offer the human being any ontologically predefined, behavioural guidelines, instead burdening it with the construction of such guidelines itself.

Returning to a teleological world-view would mean ontological support for the field of ethics. Reality would acquire an inherent meaning, which would have to be the orientation for human action if the latter is to qualify as morally legitimate. In a teleologically ordered cosmos certain circumstances and processes are to be assigned inherent moral qualities, justifying rights and claims towards acting human beings. Nature is no longer to be considered as a mere means, as a neutral object, at the mercy of all and sundry, but must be respected as inherently valuable. Efforts to reintroduce teleological thinking are nothing else than attempts to *remoralize* nature. Their aim is to bridge the gulf between 'is' and 'ought', clearing the way for an ontological anchoring of moral values and norms, as was the case in former times with the teleological world view.

I have two objections to such attempts to resuscitate teleology. Firstly: what guarantee can a teleological world-view offer with regard to a better and more careful treatment of the environment? The advocates of a teleological understanding of nature seem to ignore the fact that an instrumental relationship to nature, primarily or even exclusively restricted to human treatment, can also be supported by teleological argumentation – and that this has, in fact, already been done. In his *Politics*, Aristotle wrote, for example:

> In like manner we may infer that, after the birth of animals, plants exist for their sake, and that the other animals exist for the sake of man, the tame for use and food, the wild, if not all, at least the greater part of them, for food and for the provision of clothing and various instruments. Now if nature makes nothing incomplete, and nothing in vain, the inference must be that she has made animals for the sake of man. And so, in one point of view, the art of war is a natural art of acquisition, for the art of acquisition includes hunting, an art which we ought to practise against wild beasts, and against men who, though intended by nature to be governed, will not submit; for war of such a kind is naturally just.[16]

The fact that some interpret this passage as being far from typical for Aristotle, as a vulgar insertion by a third party, bears no relevance to my argument. Important here is the fact that a teleological world-view offers no guarantee for an understanding of nature which would respect nature's own value (assuming she has one at all) or restrict human egotism as far as nature is concerned. In later times, too, teleological arguments often were used not to increase the respect for nature but to glorify the human being. The eighteenth century *physico-theology* provides illuminating examples for this kind of *anthropocentric teleology*, as Arthur O. Lovejoy has shown:

> For it rested in great part upon the supposition that all other created beings exist for man's sake. *Tout est créé pour l'homme* is at once the tacit premise and the triumphant conclusion of that long series of teleological arguments which constitute so large a fraction of the 'philosophical' output of the eighteenth century – and is one of the most curious monuments of human imbecility.[17]

The fact that teleological thinking does not necessarily imply respect for nature is emphatically emphasized if one looks at the *actual* treatment of nature prevalent in pre-modern societies. It is an historical fact that, in practice, these societies were on no account more considerate of, nor more careful with nature than their modern counterparts. In Antiquity, as in the Middle Ages – that is in historical eras which were characterized by a teleological world-view – the vegetation originally to be found around the Mediterranean was extensively destroyed by human hand.[18] This was all possible due to the fact that, in certain circumstances, even primitive technologies and (seemingly) small interventions in nature are enough to cause such extensive alterations as the destruction of large forest areas or changes in climate.

This brings me to my second objection to the project concerned with resuscitating teleology. It is based on the view that nature is stable and harmonious, and that abrupt changes or disharmonies are introduced by the human race alone. Nature is identified as a global idyll, the different parts of which are in a finely-tuned and unchangeable balance. So Ervin Laszlo pleads for a world-view which

> is wide enough to see ourselves not only in our children, family and compatriots, and not even in all human beings and all living things, but in all self-maintaining and self-evolving organizations brought forth on this good earth and, if not perturbated by man, existing here in complex but supremely balanced hierarchical interdependencies.[19]

It is a view of nature which can be described as secularized physico-theology: what was previously the wisdom of the Creator has been replaced by the wisdom of evolution. It is not by accident, therefore, that extensive use is made of a moralizing vocabulary when describing nature: 'Have we the right to counteract, irreversibly, the evolutionary wisdom of millions of years, in order to satisfy the ambition and curiosity of a few scientists?[20] The problem is that this harmonious picture of nature contradicts much of what we know about her. The impression that nature is constant and balanced disappears as soon as we observe periods of time which are large enough to include evolutionary processes. The idea of a universal homoeostasis of nature is then relativized by numerous examples of the destruction of such homoeostases by vegetable or animal organisms.[21] This is not only true of local systems of stability, but also of life in general. During the history of the earth so far, the palaeontologists are aware of five faunal ages, i.e. large-scale periods of extinction of biological species. It should be assumed, despite the impression that our global ecosystem is naturally stable,

> that, even without human intervention, Nature is in no way stable or self-regenerating. Life is always being threatened and endangered, most of all by itself. The 'consistency' of Nature is largely an illusion, arising from a perspective which is temporally too short. Natural catastrophes mark the various epochs of the history of the Earth. What geologists describe as different ages of the Earth are characterised by the fossilised leftovers of different life forms in successively deposited layers of rock. During the transition from one age to the next, a whole range of previously dominant animal and plant life disappears and is replaced by a host of new life forms.[22]

Considering the fact that, periodically, life forms are destroyed *en masse*, talk of an 'evolutionary wisdom' is even less plausible than of God's wisdom before it. Evolution – if one may personify it – is not aware of a planned strategy for achieving particular purposes. All of our empirical knowledge about evolution shows that its method of procedure involves opportunist advancement, in the circumstances given at a particular time, with the chances available at that time. Accordingly, nature has no respect for the things she creates. She does not care if an organism or an entire species dies, if an entire group of species is extinguished, or even if the complete biosphere of our planet is destroyed. A collapse of this kind would merely signify the starting-point of a new phase of evolutionary development, in which new species emerge and a new biosphere is constructed. The extent of this 'natural' destruction of nature becomes clearer when we consider the fact that more than 99 per cent of all the biological species which have ever lived on the earth are now extinct.

The destruction of existing ecological balances and the extermination of numerous biological species is not at all foreign to nature, and is not inflicted upon nature 'from without' by human activity. It would *not* be 'unnatural' behaviour if the human being were one day to destroy its environment or even (for example, in a nuclear war) the entire terrestrial ecosystem. That is just what happened in the early stages of life on our planet, when green plants set free huge quantities of oxygen (which gave rise to the atmosphere we know today) with their photosynthetic metabolism, causing environmental poisoning of global proportions and killing the anaerobic organisms which, until then, had dominated.[23] This means: *if* nature has a destination, then such events can far more readily be interpreted as means used by nature in order to reach her *telos*. And since the human race is a part of nature, we even have to conclude that the human race itself plays a role as a means of furthering nature's purposes, even if this includes the destruction of thousands of species and flourishing ecosystems. In short: it then would be *against* nature, against her *telos*, and thus *immoral*, if the human race were to put an end to the common practice of exploiting nature, extinguishing species, and destroying ecosystems.

THE OVERCOMING OF ANTHROPOCENTRISM

The core or the strong programme within a practical philosophy of nature is the refutation of ethical anthropocentrism. The human being should not see itself as beyond or even above nature, but as part of nature: as a being which has emerged with evolution, which is related by natural history to the other living organisms, and which remains dependent upon its metabolism with nature, even within the most highly developed societies. Taking this seriously would imply revising some of the most fundamental assumptions of modern philosophy. Among them, especially, the dogma that morality has to do with regulating the interaction only between human beings. According to this dogma of modern ethics, we only have moral obligations towards our fellow human beings, because only human beings possess moral rights. Insofar as traditional ethics takes into consideration an obligation towards objects, this indirectly involves an obligation towards a human being. We are obliged to treat an object with care when it belongs to somebody else, and when damaging it would infringe the owner's rights. This restriction to human relationships is usually justified with the argument that moral rights may only be claimed by those subjected to moral obligations themselves. Yet since only a human being may be the subject of moral behaviour – only the human being possesses the characteristics which render behaviour possible, such as reason, autonomy, freedom – we may also conclude from the postulate of reciprocity that only a human being may be the object of morality. In this sense, modern ethics is 'anthropocentric': it refers to the human being as the only source of values and norms.

A practical philosophy of nature aims to curb this restriction to inter-human relationships. Just as ethics was previously aimed at regulating the behaviour of the individual towards his/her fellow human beings, and at preventing inconsiderate assertion of selfish interests, it is now aimed – analogously – at regulating human behaviour towards nature. Despite their remaining differences, many writers agree that such ethics is only feasible if the anthropocentric point of view be abandoned. The failure of ethics to date to norm human behaviour with regard to nature, as is coming to light in the present ecological crisis, is attributed to the underlying fact that this ethics has concentrated solely on preserving *human* interests. Limiting the domain of validity of moral norms and values to human interaction has created enormous scope for human action beyond moral restrictions, and with it – albeit unintentionally – the legitimate destruction of nature. Thus a moral sanctioning of inconsiderate and selfish behaviour towards nature only seems to be possible if we recognize the intrinsic value of nature.

> Our ethical heritage largely attaches values and rights to persons, and if nonpersonal realms enter, they enter only as tributary to the personal. What is proposed here is a broadening of value, so that nature will cease to be merely 'property' and become a commonwealth. The logic by which goodness is discovered or appreciated is notoriously evasive, and we can only reach it suggestively ... We have a parallel, retrospectively, in the checkered advance of the ethical frontier recognising intrinsic goodness, and accompanying rights, outside the self. If we now universalize 'person', consider how slowly the circle has been enlarged fully to include aliens, strangers, infants, children. Negroes, Jews, slaves, women, Indians, prisoners, the elderly, the insane, the deformed, and even now we ponder the status of foetuses. Ecological ethics queries whether we ought again to universalize, recognizing the intrinsic value of every ecobiotic component.[24]

The strong programme aims at a principal alteration of the structure of morality, especially of the foundations of ethical norms and rules. Giving up the anthropocentric point of view would cast doubt on the legitimizing strength of human interests and needs over our behaviour towards nature, and thus for the justificatory basis of this behaviour.

And even more: it would not only rob these interests and needs of their legitimizing strength, but would allow them to appear *in need* of legitimization. Presuming that nature has rights, the question of the legitimacy of human interests in nature and of human needs regarding nature has become unavoidable, because these interests and a satisfaction of these needs may result in a conflict with precisely these rights of nature. A practical philosophy of nature thus expects a lot of us: it challenges us on a *practical* level to relativize our interests and needs with regard to nature's rights, and on a *theoretical* level to turn away from a philosophical tradition of moral justification which has existed for hundreds of years.

Yet within this context, two different meanings of 'anthropocentrism', which should analytically be kept separate, are constantly being confused with each other. The term 'anthropocentrism' can mean (1) concentrating on the human being as the *subject* of morality and (2) concentrating on the human being as the *object* of morality. In the first case we are interested in the instance constituting the moral norms and values, in the second in who or what may possess moral rights, and of what these rights may consist. A look at the first interpretation shows that the call for a refrain from the anthropocentric perspective leads to a contradiction. This call is based, *on the one hand*, on expressed insistence upon human naturalness: the human being is part of nature and should regard itself this way. This reflection of one's own naturalness aims at a world-view ensuring reverence for, and a caring treatment of nature. Yet we have seen that this kind of behaviour is not necessarily natural: organisms are programmed by nature to maximize their own individual offspring, and not to preserve their species, let alone to treat the environment with consideration. Even if one has no desire to follow a vulgar Darwinist 'struggle for existence', it is nevertheless impossible to overlook the fact that the ecological ethicists' view of nature is extremely harmonistic. No fox pays attention to the 'rights' of the rabbit, no rabbit has respect for the desire to live of grasses and herbs, and even the grasses and herbs treat the ground in which they grow solely as a resource. Organisms treat their environment exclusively from the point of view of their own survival and reproduction interests, whereby interest in the species itself is followed – just as it is by the human being – short-sightedly and opportunistically, sometimes resulting in long-term self-damage, even self-destruction. Examples of natural destruction in gigantic proportion by nature herself have already been mentioned. Thus, however much a practical philosophy of nature emphasizes the naturalness of the human being on the one hand, realization of this postulate assumes, *on the other hand*, that the human being is *not* what it is supposed to be regarding itself as being: one natural creature amongst many. If the human being really were merely a natural being, no other behaviour could be expected of it than an exponential reproduction of its species and an exploitation of its natural resources to the point of a global catastrophe. The challenge to refrain from an anthropocentric point of view and to recognize equal rights for all forms of life, making them the criterion by which to measure one's own actions, only makes sense as an appeal to human reason and/or morality, thereby assuming just that special position of the human race within Nature against which it inveighs.

Critics of anthropocentrism may respond that this objection totally misses their key intention. It is not a case of reducing the human being to just any natural creature amongst many and of casting doubt on the human capacity for reason and morality. Neither should it be doubted that the challenge to refrain from anthropocentrism presumes a certain special position of the human race within nature. Something quite different is meant: precisely because the human being has a special position within nature it must be able to see that such a catastrophe can only be avoided if it decides – on the strength of its reason and morality – not merely to regard nature as a resource, but to respect her as a partner with equal rights. Consequently, it is not a case of questioning the central position of the human race as the subject of its own morality, but of changing the *content* of this morality in such a way that nature may – and must – also be respected as possessing certain rights. The ecological ethicist subtly switches at this point to the *second* interpretation of anthropocentrism: it is no longer the fact that the human being has a special position within nature, and that this is necessary as a moral subject which is criticized, but rather the inconsiderate exploitation by the human being of this special position for its own interests.

The question is now: is it possible to have a morality in which nature has the same rights as human beings? Whether two parties actually do have the same rights may only be established when they come into conflict with each other. We have already seen that extending morality to the realm of nature meets with difficulties where human interests and those of nature collide. Human interest in survival, for example, makes it necessary to kill countless plants and animals for food. These organisms (at least some of them) are interested, however, in their own survival. How is the principle of equal rights to be made valid in this everyday case? If the advocates of non-anthropocentric ethics make provision for the various rights to be weighed up against each other in such cases, allowing human interests to be put before those of micro-organisms, plants and animals, then this is a sensible, pragmatic guideline. Accordingly, refraining from the anthropocentric point of view would mean not putting human interests, whatever they may be, automatically before the interests of natural objects in every case. If, at one end of the spectrum, it is legitimate in a case of smallpox to kill the viruses in order to save the human being, it must also be possible, at the other end of the spectrum, to do without fur coats in order to prevent a species of animal from becoming extinct. Yet both examples are extreme cases: in the first, the human right to life is so significant and the 'rights' of the smallpox viruses so insignificant that it is only possible to come down in favour of the former. In the second case, the interest in fur coats is so insignificant – at least for ethicists – and the right to life of an entire species so significant that it is only plausible to decide in favour of the latter. Yet hidden behind examples such as these are not only the pragmatic difficulties forming part of all those cases in the middle, where the situation is not as clear, but also the principal problem of how to *justify* such decisions. For if we decide to abandon the anthropocentric point of view, it is not *a priori* obvious that – and, more than anything, *why* – one human being should be 'worth' more than millions of viruses. From the point of view of nature as a whole, there can hardly be a grading of life according to its value and it is precisely a division of nature into an inherently worthy part (the human being) and an inherently worthless part (the rest) which the critics of anthropocentrism are against, believing that the *whole* of nature must be respected as worthy.

The conclusion to be drawn from these considerations is that criticism of the anthropocentric point of view is aiming in the right direction, insofar as it is aimed at a *pragmatic* relativization of human interests. This means an obligation upon the human being to consider carefully, in every situation calling for a decision, whether the interests which it follows in its treatment of nature justify the damage to nature which this treatment possibly or surely will inflict. However, this pragmatic relativization cannot ultimately be a *principal* one, since this would be incompatible with the human interest in self-preservation. To put it pointedly: we can only afford to respect the rights of nature where the interests affected are relatively insignificant – as in the case of the fur coat – but not where our vital interests are touched upon – as in the example of the smallpox viruses. We can therefore only decide according to *our own* interests where and when we are to respect the interests of nature as having equal rights to our own.

CONCLUSION

At this point I shall interrupt my thoughts in order to draw a preliminary conclusion. I interpret the strong programme of environmental ethics as a remarkable attempt to react philosophically to the ecological challenge – a challenge which will be very significant with regard to the Fate of the human race in future. Although this programme provides vital food for thought, I nevertheless regard it as non-viable due to the problems put forward in this paper. I would like to conclude by making it plausible that this programme is, additionally, in (at least) two respects self-contradictory.

Firstly, if the strong programme demands of us that we relativize our self-interest for reasons of self-interest, then, from a pragmatic point of view, this is certainly a sensible recommendation. Yet the strong programme is not content with mere prudence. It demands of us that we accept the inherent value of nature as a metaphysical fact *because* this is the condition necessary for the human race to survive. Spaemann and Löw write: 'There is a practical imperative which, as far as life within the Natural world is concerned, commands us not to relinquish our natural, teleological way of viewing things.' Otherwise we will be faced with the following alternative:

> Either we manage to integrate our domination over Nature into a new, at first somewhat vague, relationship between us and Nature, or we ourselves will become the victims of our domination over Nature. Either we have to decide to interpret the living world anthropomorphologically, or we ourselves will become an anthropomorphism, worldless subjects cutting the ground from under our own feet.[25]

This line of argumentation is an obviously problematic one, however. If, for the reasons mentioned, teleology is called for, then the ontological structures of reality are deduced from human interests. To put it another way: the strong programme draws the naturalistic fallacy backwards: it concludes from the 'ought' of survival of the human species, the 'is' of a teleologically structured nature.

Secondly, the idea of a practical philosophy of nature is based on an extremely critical perception of the Modern Age, its philosophy and, altogether, its world views. This philosophy regards all of these, and especially modern rationality, as the deepest causes of the ecological catastrophe threatening us today. After all, it was this rationality and its particular predominance within science which destroyed the ideas of a sacredness of nature and teleology, and which have enthroned human interests as the sole source of values and norms. The postulate of resuscitating sacredness and teleology may be interpreted as an attempt to limit not only human self-interest, but also human rationality. Yet, firstly, there must be doubt as to whether such a resuscitation is at all possible: whether belief in the holy and the convincingness of teleology may be reinstated as solutions to our ecological problems. It is obvious that the categories sacredness and teleology are being used here *strategically*, i.e. as the means to solving a problem. This strategic use reduces the concepts of sacredness and teleology to a metaphysically subordinate sociotechnology and encourages the human race to make the decision to believe in it. This project is self-contradictory because it believes rationality to be capable of nothing and everything at the same time. On the one hand, the strong programme mistrusts the expectation that the human race could begin to treat its natural surroundings with more care for reasons of rational self-interest. This programme is aimed after all at formulating norms and rules for the treatment of nature which are based not on human self-interest, but on the *inherent* value of a nature full of values. On the other hand, the strong programme demands that we recognize and accept nature's inherent value, not because nature *is* valuable in itself, but because the human race would otherwise continue to destroy nature, and thus destroy its own necessities of life. Thus not 'facts' are to move us to this recognition, but rather a rational calculation regarding our interest in surviving. To put it briefly: the same rationality which is mistrusted on the level of our practical treatment of nature is honourably reinstated on the moral meta-level, the level concerned with justifying ecological norms.

NOTES

In some parts of this paper I draw on arguments and formulations of chapter 8 of my book *GenEthics. Technological Intervention in Human Reproduction as a Philosophical Problem* (Cambridge, 1994).

1 Ludwig Wittgenstein, *Tractatus logico-philosophicus*, intro. Bertrand Russell (London, 1922), 4.11 and 4.111.

2 Aristotle, *Ethica Nicomachea, The Works of Aristotle*, trans. W. D. Ross, vol. 9 (Oxford, 1931), 1095a 5–6, 1103b 26–9.

3 David Hume, *A Treatise of Human Nature*, ed P. H. Niddich (Oxford, 1992), p. 416.

4 Georges-Louis Leclerc Comte de Buffon, *Histoire Naturelle*. Here quoted from Wolf Lepenies, 'Historisierung der Natur und Entmoralisierung der Wissenschaften', in Hubert Markl (ed.), *Natur und Geschichte* (Munich, Vienna, 1983), p. 273.

5 Aristotle, *Ethica Nicomachea*, 1095a 6.

6 Hans Jonas, *The Imperative of Responsibility. In Search of an Ethics for the Technological Age* (Chicago, London, 1984), p. 23.

7 Albert Schweitzer, 'Kultur und Ethik', in *Gesammelte Werke in 5 Bänden*, Bd. 2. (Munich), pp. 378–9.

8 Cf. William K. Frankena, 'Ethics and the Environment', in K. E. Goodpaster and K. M. Sayre (eds.), *Ethics and the Problems of the 21st Century* (Notre Dame and London, 1979), p. 12.

9 Ervin Laszlo, *Introduction to Systems Philosophy: Towards a New Paradigm of Contemporary Thought* (New York, 1972), p. 287.

10 Schweitzer, 'Kultur und Ethik', p. 387.

11 Schweitzer, 'Kultur und Ethik', p. 388.
12 Klaus Michael Meyer-Abich, *Wege zum Frieden mit der Natur. Praktische Naturphilosophie für die Umweltpolitik* (Munich, Vienna, 1984), p. 146.
13 Jonas, *The Imperative of Responsibility*, p. 45.
14 Daniel Callahan, 'Discussion', in Owen Gingerich (ed.), *The Nature of Scientific Discovery. A Symposium Commemorating the 500th Anniversary of the Birth of Nicolaus Copernicus* (Washington, 1975), p. 589.
15 Robert Spaemann and Reinhard Löw, *Die Frage Wozu? Geschichte und Wiederentdeckung des teleologischen Denkens* (Munich and Zurich, 1981), p. 287.
16 Aristotle, *Politica. The Works of Aristotle*, trans. the editorship of W. D. Ross by Benjamin Jowett, 10 (Oxford, 1921), 1256 b16–26.
17 Arthur O. Lovejoy, *The Great Chain of Being. A Study in the History of an Idea* (Cambridge, MA, and London, 1982), p. 186.
18 Cf. Horst Mensching, 'Die Verwüstung der Natur durch den Menschen in historischer Zeit: Das Problem der Desertifikation', in Markl (ed.), *Natur und Geschichte.*
19 Laszlo, *Introduction to Systems Philosophy*, p. 288.
20 Erwin Chargaff, 'On the Dangers of Genetic Meddling', *Science*, 192 (4 June 1976), 940.
21 Hermann Remmert, *Ökologie. Ein Lehrbuch* (Berlin, Heidelberg, New York, 1989), pp. 243–4.
22 Hubert Markl, 'Untergang oder Übergang – Natur als Kulturaufgabe'. in *Mannheimer formum 82/83* (Mannheim, 1982), p. 64.
23 Remmert, *Ökologie*, p. 1.
24 Homes Rolston III, 'Is there an Ecological Ethic?', *Ethics*, 85 (1975), 101.
25 Spaemann and Löw, *Die Frage Wozu?*, pp. 287–8.

INDEX